HARDPRESS.NET
HOME OF HARD-TO-FIND BOOKS

General Laws of the State of Texas
by Texas

GENERAL LAWS

OF THE

STATE OF TEXAS,

PASSED AT THE

SESSION OF THE FIFTEENTH LEGISLATURE

BEGUN AND HELD

AT THE CITY OF AUSTIN,

APRIL 18th, 1876.

BY AUTHORITY.

GALVESTON :

SHAW & BLAYLOCK, STATE PRINTERS.

1876.

CONTENTS.

CHAPTER XVIII.

CHAPTER XIX.

CHAPTER XX.

CHAPTER XXI.

CHAPTER XXII.

CHAPTER XXIII.

CHAPTER XXIV.

CHAPTER XXV.

CHAPTER XXVI.

CHAPTER XXVII.

CHAPTER XXVIII.

CHAPTER XXIX.

CHAPTER XXX.

CHAPTER XXXI.

CHAPTER XXXII.

CHAPTER XXXIII.

CHAPTER XXXIV.

CHAPTER XXXV.

CHAPTER XXXVI.

CHAPTER XLV.

CHAPTER XLVI.

CHAPTER XLVII.

CHAPTER XLVIII.

CHAPTER XLIX.

CHAPTER L.

CHAPTER LI.

CHAPTER LII.

CHAPTER LIII.

CONTENTS.

CONTENTS.

CHAPTER LXXXII.

CHAPTER LXXXIII.

CHAPTER LXXXIV.

CHAPTER LXXXV.

CHAPTER LXXXVI.

CHAPTER LXXXVII.

CHAPTER LXXXVIII.

CHAPTER LXXXIX.

CHAPTER XC.

CHAPTER XCI.

CHAPTER C.

CHAPTER CX.

CHAPTER CXI.

CHAPTER CXII.

CHAPTER CXIII.

CHAPTER CXIV.

CHAPTER CXV.

CHAPTER CXVI.

CHAPTER CXVII.

CHAPTER CXXVII.

2 c

CHAPTER CXLVII.

CHAPTER CXLVIII,

CHAPTER CXLIX.

CHAPTER CL.

CHAPTER CLI.

CHAPTER CLII.

CHAPTER CLIII.

CHAPTER CLIV.

CHAPTER CLV.

GENERAL LAWS OF TEXAS.

CHAPTER I.—*An Act making an appropriation to defray the contingent expenses of the first session of the Fifteenth Legislature.*

WHEREAS, It is of sufficient public importance that the contingent expenses of this Legislature be promptly paid, in order that the material furnished and labor performed may be procured at cash prices; therefore,

SECTION 1. *Be it enacted by the Legislature of the State of Texas,* That the sum of twenty-five thousand dollars, or so much thereof as may be necessary, is hereby appropriated out of any moneys in the Treasury, not otherwise appropriated, to pay the contingent expenses of the Fifteenth Legislature; and that the approval by the Chairman of the Committee on Contingent Expenses, of either House, countersigned by the President of the Senate or Speaker of the House, shall be sufficient authority to authorize the Comptroller to issue his warrant on the State Treasurer for the payment of any account against said fund.

SEC. 2. That the balance of moneys remaining in the Treasury, heretofore appropriated for the contingent expenses of any preceding session of the Legislature of the State of Texas, be and the same is hereby re-appropriated for the purposes specified in this act. That this act take effect from and after its passage.

Approved May 1st, 1876.

Takes effect from and after its passage.

CHAPTER II.—*An Act fixing the per diem pay and mileage of the members of the Legislature.*

SECTION 1. *Be it enacted by the Legislature of the State of Texas,* That hereafter, until otherwise provided by law, the pay of members of the Legislature is hereby fixed at five dollars per diem for the first sixty days of each session, and after that time, the sum of two dollars per diem for the remainder of the session; except the first session under this act, during which session the pay of members is hereby fixed at five dollars per diem for the first ninety days, and after that time, at two dollars per day for the remainder of the session.

SEC. 2.   That hereafter, until otherwise provided by law, the mileage of members of the Legislature is hereby fixed at five dollars for every twenty-five miles in going to and returning from the seat of government, to be computed by the nearest and most direct route of travel by land, regardless of railways or water routes ; and the Comptroller of the State shall prepare and preserve a table of distances to each county seat now or hereafter to be established, and by such table the mileage of each member shall be paid : *provided*, that no member shall be entitled to mileage for any extra session that may be called within one day after the adjournment of a regular or a called session.

SEC. 3.   That this being the first session of the Legislature held under this act, and it being necessary that members of the Legislature should receive their per diem pay and mileage immediately for their services, therefore, this act take effect, and be in force from and after its passage.

Approved May 1st, 1876.

Takes effect from and after its passage.

CHAPTER III.—*An Act making an appropriation for mileage and per diem pay of members, and per diem pay of officers and employees of the Fifteenth Legislature.*

SECTION 1.   *Be it enacted by the Legislature of the State of Texas*, That the sum of eighty thousand dollars, or so much thereof as may be necessary, be and the same is hereby appropriated out of any moneys in the Treasury not otherwise appropriated, for the payment of mileage and per diem pay of the members, and the payment of the per diem of the officers and employees of the Fifteenth Legislature of the State of Texas.

SEC. 2.   That the certificate of the Secretary of the Senate, approved by the President thereof, or the certificate of the Chief Clerk of the House, approved by the Speaker thereof, shall be sufficient evidence to the Comptroller, upon which he shall audit the claims and issue his warrants upon the Treasurer for the respective amounts.

SEC. 3.   That the balance of moneys remaining in the Treasury heretofore appropriated for the per diem pay and mileage of the members and the per diem pay of the officers and employees of any preceding session of the Legislature of the State of Texas be and the same is hereby re-appropriated for the purposes specified in this act.

SEC. 4.   And, whereas, the Fifteenth Legislature, for the payment of the members and officers, of which this law is enacted, is now in session, and public policy requires their payment; therefore, that this law be in force from and after its passage.

Approved May 1st, 1876.

Takes effect from and after its passage.

CHAPTER IV.—*An Act to fix the first terms of the District Courts under the present Constitution.*

SECTION 1.   *Be it enacted by the Legislature of the State of Texas*, That when a term of a District Court by the ordinance entitled, "An Ordi-

nance fixing the terms of the District Courts of the State of Texas,"
which is part of the Constitution, is therein specified to commence at a
day prior to the eighteenth of April, and can continue to a day later than
the eighteenth of April, all District Courts that have been held, and
are now being held for the part of such term, on, and subsequent to,
the eighteenth of April, 1876, have been, and shall be, valid terms of
court, and the same are fully legalized and validated.

SEC. 2.   As an emergency exists, a number of the courts of the State are
now being held and can continue to be held for parts of their term on,
and subsequent to, the eighteenth of April, and their validity shall be
immediately made free from all doubt. This act shall take effect and be
in force from and after its passage.

Approved May 3, 1876.

Takes effect from and after its passage.

CHAPTER V.—*An Act organizing a Court of Appeals.*

WHEREAS, An imperative public necessity and emergency exist for
immediate legislation to organize the Court of Appeals that it may at
once hear and determine criminal and other.causes exclusively cognizable on appeal in said court; therefore,

SECTION 1.   *Be it enacted by the Legislature of the State of Texas,* That
the Court of Appeals shall hold its sessions at the city of Austin during
the same time the Supreme Court shall be in session at said place, and
at such other times and places as the Supreme Court is now or may be
hereafter required to hold its sessions.   The clerk of the Court of Appeals shall, before entering on the duties of his office, take the oath of
office prescribed by the Constitution.   He shall give the same bond, to
be approved by the Court of Appeals or the Judges thereof, required to
be given by the Clerk of the Supreme Court; be subject to the same liabilities; entitled to the same fees of office, and shall perform, as Clerk
of the Appellate Court, the duties now imposed by law on the Clerk of
the Supreme Court.

SEC. 2.   It shall be the duty of the Clerk of the Court of Appeals at Austin to procure a seal for said court, and a copy thereof shall be made
for each place where its sessions may now or may hereafter be required
by law to be held; it shall have a star with five points, with the words
"Court of Appeals of Texas," engraved thereon.

SEC. 3.   The Clerk of the Court of Appeals shall receive from the
Clerk of the Supreme Court, and receipt for, all records which have been,
or which may be hereafter, received in his office, of cases of which the
Court of Appeals has, under the Constitution, exclusive appellate jurisdiction, and file the same in his office; which causes shall be considered
and disposed of by the Court of Appeals as though they had been appealed to said court.

SEC. 4.   The laws regulating practice and proceedings in the Supreme
Court, and regulating appeals and writs of error thereto, shall apply to
the Court of Appeals, but when the District Court from which an appeal has been or may be taken, is by the Constitution deprived of jurisdiction over the subject matter in controversy, in such case the mandate
issuing from the Court of Appeals, on the disposition of a cause transferred to it under the third section of this act, shall be directed to the

highest court of the county from which the appeal was taken, having original jurisdiction over the subject matter in controversy; and in such case the Clerk of the court to which the mandate is directed, shall demand and receive from the Clerk of the court from which the appeal was taken, the original papers in said cause, and the court to which the mandate is directed shall then exercise jurisdiction over the case.

Sec. 5.   The Attorney General shall represent the State in all cases to which the State is a party before the Court of Appeals.

Sec. 6.   The Sheriff of Travis county shall furnish one of his deputies to attend before the Court of Appeals during its sessions at Austin, and to execute its orders; he shall receive such compensation as may be allowed by said court, not to exceed three (3) dollars per day, to be paid by the State Treasurer.

Sec. 7.   Appeals and writs of error may be taken to the Court of Appeals, in cases over which said court may have appellate jurisdiction, in the same manner that appeals are allowed to the Supreme Court.

Sec. 8.   The Judges of the Court of Appeals shall choose a presiding Judge for said court, from their number, at such times as they think proper, and all writs and process issuing from said court shall bear test in the name of said presiding Judge and the seal of the court.

Sec. 9.   The Court of Appeals shall hold its sessions at Austin in the room now occupied as an office by the Attorney General, in the Supreme Court building, which shall be fitted up and supplied with proper furniture, books of record and stationery, to be contracted for by the Clerk of said court, subject to the approval of the court.

Sec. 10.   That there being no law in force to enable said court, or the Judges thereof, to proceed with their labors and duties, as prescribed in the Constitution, an emergency exists that this bill shall, and it is hereby declared that it shall take effect from and after its passage.

Approved May 6, 1876.

Takes effect from and after its passage.

CHAPTER VI.—*An Act to transfer all cases, civil and criminal, now pending in courts of Justices of the Peace whose jurisdiction has been heretofore increased by special law, to the courts having jurisdiction thereof under the Constitution.*

Section 1.   *Be it enacted by the Legislature of the State of Texas,* That all cases, civil and criminal, now pending in courts of Justices of the Peace, whose jurisdiction has been heretofore increased by special law, be and are hereby transferred to the courts having jurisdiction of the same under the Constitution.

Sec. 2.   Whereas, the new Constitution having changed the original jurisdiction of the several courts of this State, and abolished other courts, and as business yet remains undisposed of in some of the courts not now having jurisdiction to try the same, and it being necessary to the ends of justice that such business should immediately be transferred to the proper tribunal for trial and disposal, it is therefore declared that this act shall take effect and be in force from and after its passage.

Approved May 9, 1876.

Takes effect from and after its passage.

CHAPTER VII.—*An Act to provide for the current printing of the Fifteenth Legislature.*

SECTION 1. *Be it enacted by the Legislature of the State of Texas*, That the State Treasurer be and is hereby authorized and required to contract with a suitable person or persons, firm or firms, for the printing of all bills, memorials, messages, and all other current printing of both Houses of the Fifteenth Legislature.

SEC. 2. That the State Treasurer is authorized and required to advertise in the *Daily Democratic Statesman* and *Daily State Gazette*, newspapers published in the city of Austin, for two days, for sealed proposals for doing said current printing, and shall in said advertisement state the time and place, when and where said proposals shall be received and opened, and the contract awarded, and shall fix the time for awarding said contract at not exceeding three days from the date of the first insertion of said advertisement. And all said current printing shall be awarded to the lowest responsible bidder, who shall agree and contract to do said printing at the city of Austin, below the maximum rates herein prescribed.

SEC. 3. All proposals for executing said printing shall be sealed and addressed to the Treasurer, and shall be endorsed with the statement that they are proposals for the current printing for the Fifteenth Legislature, and shall be filed in the office of the Secretary of the State, and the seals of such proposals shall not be broken until the day named in the advertisement for awarding the contract, and said proposals shall be opened in the presence of the Governor, Secretary of the State and Comptroller of Public Accounts, and a committee of three members of each House, and such bidders as may desire to be present.

SEC. 4. That the rates allowed by said contract for said current printing shall be below the following maximum rates, to-wit: for printing the Governor's messages, reports, or other documents provided by law, or ordered by the Legislature, or either branch thereof, one-fourth of one cent per page for five hundred copies of each, and for any number of additional copies of the same, one-fifth of one cent per page, and printed on small pica type, forty-four lines long, exclusive of the folio, and twenty-seven ems wide, without side notes. The paper shall be white, of uniform color, and of a quality weighing not less than forty pounds to the ream, and shall be neatly stitched and trimmed. For printing two hundred copies of bills, memorials or resolutions, or any number of copies less than two hundred, ordered by either house of the Legislature, printed on pica type, lines numbered on the margin, with space between the lines of the size of pica, on sixteen pound flat cap paper, to be twenty ems wide and sixty-five ems in length, with four pages to the sheet, the sum of two dollars and sixty-five cents per page.

SEC. 5. That said contract shall be approved by the Governor, Secretary of the State, and Comptroller of Public Accounts, and no member or officer of any department of the government shall be in any way interested in said contract.

SEC. 6. That the parties to whom said contract may be awarded shall immediately enter into a bond, with two good and sufficient sureties, in the sum of five thousand dollars, payable to the State of Texas; conditioned that he will faithfully comply with and carry out the conditions of said contract, which bond shall be approved by the Governor, Secretary of the State and Comptroller, and filed in the office of the Secretary of State.

SEC. 7. The Printing Committee of each House of the Legislature shall certify to the Comptroller of Public Accounts the quantity of each item of printing ordered by such House, and also the number of copies of the same so ordered, and also the number of copies of the same they may have received, and the Comptroller shall thereupon authorize the payment of the accounts for said printing in accordance with the provisions of the contract: *provided*, that said contract shall terminate when other provisions for the public printing shall have been made by the Legislature of Texas.

SEC. 8. That as the contract for State printing under which the current printing of the Fifteenth Legislature has been done will expire on the first day of May, 1876, leaving no law in force authorizing the making of a contract for the current printing of this Legislature, an imperative public necessity and emergency exist, and that this act shall take effect and be in force from and after its passage.

Approved May 11, 1876.

Takes effect from and after its passage.

CHAPTER VIII.—*An act supplemental to "An act to provide for current printing of the Fifteenth Legislature of the State of Texas," passed April 28, 1876.*

SECTION 1. *Be it enacted by the Legislature of the State of Texas,* That the Governor of the State is hereby authorized and required to employ a practical printer, whose duty it shall be to measure all the work done for the State, whenever required to do so by the Governor or Chairman of the Printing Committee of either House of the Legislature: *provided*, he shall not receive more than seventy dollars per month for his services.

SEC. 2. That the Chairman of the Printing Committee of each House of the Legislature shall preserve a sample of each and every piece of work done under the act to which this is a supplement, and shall present the same to the expert printer provided for in section one, hereof in order that he may measure the same. All accounts due the Public Printer for work done under the act to which this is a supplement, shall, after being pronounced correct, and approved by said expert printer, be approved by the Committee on Public Printing, of the House ordering the work, and shall be examined and approved by the Governor, Secretary of State and Comptroller, and upon the presentation of any claim thus examined and approved, it shall be the duty of the Comptroller to draw his warrant in favor of the Public Printer for the amount of said account, to be paid out of the contingent fund set apart for the use of the House ordering the work: *provided*, that the maximum rate to be paid for printing bills ordered to be printed by either House of the Legislature, as provided for in the act to which this is a supplement, shall not exceed two dollars and sixty-five cents per page for the number of pages in each copy thereof.

SEC. 3. That there being no law in force under which the Legislature can get its current printing done, a public necessity exists for the immediate passage of this act, and it is hereby declared that the same shall take effect from and after its passage.

Approved May 11, 1876.

Takes effect from and after its passage.

CHAPTER IX.—*An Act to provide for and regulate the safe keeping of trust funds by officers of courts.*

SECTION 1. *Be it enacted by the Legislature of the State of Texas,* That whenever, for any legal cause, any money, evidence of debt, scrip, instrument of writing, or other article, shall be paid, or deposited into court, there to remain to abide the result of any legal proceedings, the officer having the custody of the same shall seal up the identical money or other article received by him in a secure package, and deposit it in some safe or bank vault, keeping it always accessible, and subject to the control of the proper court; and he shall also keep in a well bound book a correct statement showing each and every item of money so received, on what account received, and what disposition has been made of the same.

SEC. 2. On the expiration of his term of office, such officer shall turn over to his successor such record of trust funds and the packages of money remaining on hand, and take his receipt therefor.

SEC. 3. If any officer of any court, having such funds on hand, shall appropriate the same to his own use, he shall be deemed guilty of embezzlement, and, on conviction, punished as is provided for that offense by law.

SEC. 4. If any officer shall fail, or refuse to comply with the provisions of this act, he shall be deemed guilty of a misdemeanor, and, on conviction, be punished by fine of not less than ten nor more than two hundred dollars, or by imprisonment in the county jail for not more than three months, and may, in addition thereto, be punished by the proper court for contempt.

SEC. 5. This act shall not be construed to exempt any officer from liability on his official bond for any default, or neglect, in regard to the funds herein mentioned.

Approved May •19th, 1876.

Takes effect ninety days after adjournment.

CHAPTER X.—*An Act to provide for the manner in which publication of notice of intention to apply for the passage of a local or special law, and proof of such publication, shall be made.*

SECTION 1. *Be it enacted by the Legislature of the State of Texas,* That any person or persons intending to apply for the passage of any local or special law, shall give notice of such intention by having a statement of the substance of such law published in some newspaper published in the county embracing the locality to be affected by said law, at least once a week for the period of thirty days prior to the introduction into the Legislature of such contemplated law : *provided,* where there is no newspaper published in said county, a written copy of such statement shall be posted on the court-house door and in five other public places in the immediate locality to be affected thereby, in said county, for said thirty days, and such notice shall accurately define the locality to be affected by said law : *provided, further*, that where the locality to be affected by said law shall extend beyond the limits of any one county, such notice shall be given for each county to be affected.

SEC. 2.   Whenever any person or persons intend applying for the passage of a special law, which shall affect persons chiefly, and not directly affect any particular locality more than others, such person or persons if residing within this State, shall make publication of notice of such intention in the county or counties of the residence of such person or persons, in the same manner as if the said law was to affect those localities, and if residing without the limits of this State, said publication need only be made in a newspaper published at the Capital, in like manner as if such person or persons resided at the seat of government.

SEC. 3.   It shall not be necessary to embrace, in said notice, the particular form and terms of such contemplated law, but a statement only of the general purpose and nature of the same shall be sufficient.

SEC. 4.   The publication in a newspaper at the county of the locality, or at the residence, or at the State Capital, as the case may be provided for in this act, may be shown by the affidavit of the publisher, or of one of several publishers of such newspaper, accompanied with the printed copy of the notice as published; and the posting on the court-house door and at five other public places of the county provided for in this act, may be shown by the return of the Sheriff or other officer of the county authorized to execute process from courts of general jurisdiction, or by the affidavit of any credible person made on a written copy of the notice so posted, showing the fact of such posting, and such proof, or other competent proof of the giving of said notice, shall accompany the introduction of every local or special law.

SEC. 5.   In all cases where notice of an intention to apply to the Legislature for the passage of a local or special law has already been given, or is now in process of being given, in the manner provided for in this act, the same shall be as effectual as if given after the taking effect of this act.

SEC. 6.   To enable the present Legislature to act upon matters proper to be embraced in local or special laws, it is necessary, and is so enacted, that this act take effect and be in force from and after its passage.

Approved May 23, 1876.

Takes effect from and after its passage.

CHAPTER XI.—*An Act to amend Article 389 of an act entitled " An Act to establish a code of criminal procedure for the State of Texas."*

SECTION 1.   *Be it enacted by the Legislature of the State of Texas*, That Article 389 of an act entitled "An act to establish a code of criminal procedure for the State of Texas," be amended so that the same shall hereafter read as follows, viz :

ARTICLE 389.   The fact of the presentment of the indictment in open court by a grand jury shall be entered upon the minutes of the proceedings of the court, noting briefly the style of the criminal action and the file number of the indictment, but omitting the name of the defendant, unless in custody or under bond.

Approved May 25th, 1876.

Takes effect ninety days after adjournment.

CHAPTER XII.—*An Act to repeal Article 76 of an act entitled " An Act to adopt and establish a Penal Code for the State of Texas."*

SECTION 1. *Be it enacted by the Legislature of the State of Texas,* That Article 76 of an act entitled " An act to establish a Penal Code for the State of Texas," be and the same is hereby repealed.

Approved May 25th, 1876.

Takes effect ninety days after adjournment.

CHAPTER XIII.—*An Act to amend Article 771 of " An Act to adopt and establish a Penal Code for the State of Texas," approved August 28, 1856.*

SECTION 1. *Be it enacted by the Legislature of the State of Texas,* That Article 771 of " An Act to adopt and establish a Penal Code for the State of Texas," approved, August, 28, 1856, be so amended as to read as follows, to-wit:

ARTICLE 771. If any officer, agent, clerk or attorney at law of any incorporated company, or institution, or of any city, town or county; or if any clerk, or agent, or attorney at law of any private person or copartnership; or if any consignee or bailee of money or property, or town, city or county scrip, or of any draft, promissory note, bank bill, national bank note, treasury note of the United States of America, or of any article of value, shall embezzle or fraudulently misapply, or convert to his own use, without the consent of his principal, employer or client, any money, property, town, city or county scrip, or any draft, promissory note, bank bill, national bank note, Treasury note of the United States of America, or any article of value belonging to such principal, employer, or client, or the proceeds of such property, after the sale thereof, which shall have come into his possession, or shall be under his care, by virtue of such office, agency or employment; and if the value of the property or money or other article so embezzled shall be twenty dollars or over, he shall be punished by imprisonment in the Penitentiary not less than two nor more than ten years. If the value of such property, money or other article, shall be less than twenty dollars, he shall be punished as for theft of property under the value of twenty dollars. Within the meaning of money as used in this article, is included any circulating medium current as money.

Approved May 25th 1876.

Takes effect ninety days after adjournment.

CHAPTER XIV.—*An Act to repeal the Act regulating the removal of the disabilities of minors.*

SECTION 1. *Be it enacted by the Legislature of the State of Texas,* That the act regulating the removal of the disabilities of minors, approved October 24, 1871, be, and the same is hereby repealed.

Approved May 25, 1876.

Takes effect ninety days after adjournment.

CHAPTER XV.—*An Act to define and regulate the duties of County Clerks throughout the State.*

SECTION 1. *Be it enacted by the Legislature of the State of Texas,* That the County Clerks of the several counties in this State shall have the custody of all the minutes, records, books, and papers, including probate records and all records of deeds and mortgages, and other instruments of writing required or permitted by law to be recorded, and of the records of the County Commissioners' Courts of their respective counties; and it shall be their duty to attend to the arrangement and preservation of the same.

SEC. 2. Every person elected County Clerk shall, before entering upon the duties of his office, enter into bond, with two or more good and solvent sureties, to be approved by the County Commissioners' Court in such sum as said court may determine, not less than two thousand dollars, nor more than ten thousand dollars, payable to the Governor of the State and his successors in office, conditioned for the faithful performance of all the duties of his office, as are prescribed by the Constitution and laws of this State; and he shall also take and subscribe the oath of office prescribed by the Constitution, before some officer authorized to administer oaths of office, which oath shall be endorsed on or attached to said bond, together with the officer's certificate before whom the oath is taken that such oath was taken, which bond and oath shall be recorded in the County Clerk's office, and shall be deposited in the office of the District Clerk of the county. Such bond may be sued upon by any person injured by the breach thereof until the full amount is recovered: *provided,* that in all cases the officers herein enumerated, who have been elected under the present Constitution of the State of Texas, and who have already given bonds, as required by law, before the passage of this act, shall not be required to give any new or additional bond.

SEC. 3. The County Clerks shall have power to appoint in writing, under their hand and seal, a competent deputy or deputies, for whose official acts they shall be responsible, and such deputy shall take and subscribe the oath of office prescribed by the Constitution for all officers, before some officer authorized to administer oaths, which shall be endorsed on or attached to said appointment, together with the certificate of the officer administering the oath that such oath has been taken. The appointment and oath shall be recorded in the County Clerk's office, with the records thereof, and deposited in the office of the District Clerk.

SEC. 4. That the County Clerks are hereby required to keep their offices at the county seats of their respective counties, and give their personal labor, attendance and supervision to the duties of said office, and in all cases where the said Clerks do not reside at the county seats of their respective counties, they are hereby required to have one or more of their deputies residing at said county seats, and all deputies appointed in accordance with this act, shall have power to do and perform all other acts that may be lawfully performed by the County Clerks.

SEC. 5. That the County Clerks of the several counties of this State, or their deputy or deputies, shall have power, and it shall be their duty, when applied to for that purpose, to take the separate acknowledgment of married women, in all cases where such acknowledgment is required by law to be taken, to the execution of any deed or other instrument in writing, or conveyance executed by them, and to take the acknowledgment of all other persons to deeds or other written instruments or conveyances, and to take proof by witnesses of all such deeds, written instruments or conveyances, which are required or permitted by law to be so acknowledged or proven for record ; and it shall also be their duty to record, in accordance with the registration laws now or hereafter in force, all such deeds, mortgages, deeds of trust or any other instruments in writing, or judgments, which may be permitted or required by law to be recorded.

SEC. 6. The County Clerks shall be authorized to issue all marriage licenses, take depositions of witnesses in all cases where the same are permitted by law, and to administer oaths, and take affidavits in all judicial proceedings to be used in any of the courts of the State.

SEC. 7. Any and all acts heretofore done by County Clerks on and since the 18th day of April, 1876, which are authorized under this act, or any pre-existing law, are hereby legalized, and shall be as valid as though this law was in effect on the said day and date.

SEC. 8. That all laws in conflict with this act be and the same are hereby repealed.

SEC. 9. That in view of the fact that no laws are now in force regulating the duties of County Clerks, an emergency exists which requires that this act take effect and be in force from and after its passage, and it is therefore enacted that this act take effect and be in force from and after its passage.

Approved May 25, 1876.

Takes effect from and after its passage.

CHAPTER XVI.—*An Act prescribing the times of holding the District Courts in the Twenty-Second Judicial District.*

SECTION 1. *Be it enacted by the Legislature of the State of Texas,* That the District Courts of the Twenty-Second Judicial District shall be held at the times hereinafter specified in each year, to-wit: In the county of Atascosa, on the first Mondays in January and September, and may continue in session two weeks. In the county of Comal, on the third Mondays in January and September, and may continue in session two weeks. In the county of Bexar, on the first Monday in February, and may continue in session until the business is disposed of; on the first Monday in April, and may continue in session until the business is disposed of; on the first Monday in June, and may continue in session four weeks; on the first Monday in October, and may continue in session until the business is disposed of; on the first Monday in December, and may continue in session four weeks.

SEC. 2. All writs and process returnable to the said district courts as heretofore fixed, shall be returnable to the first terms of said courts held under the provisions of this act, and shall be as valid as if no change in the time of holding said courts had been made.

SEC. 3.   All laws and parts of laws in conflict with the provisions of this act are hereby repealed.

SEC. 4.   And, whereas, by the changes herein made of the times of holding the district courts of said district, a conflict would arise between the present law and this act, if this act did not go into effect until ninety days after the adjournment of this legislature; and, whereas, this creates such an emergency as is contemplated by the Constitution, therefore, it is further enacted, that this act shall take effect and be in force from and after its passage.

Approved May 30, 1876.

Takes effect from and after its passage.

CHAPTER XVII.—*An Act to provide for the transfer of the cases in the late Criminal Courts of the State to the District Courts, and to legalize the proceedings of the District Courts in certain cases.*

WHEREAS, Doubts have arisen as to the power of the District Courts of those counties wherein Criminal Courts have hitherto been established under section one, article five of the Constitution of 1869, and wherein Criminal Courts no longer exist, to exercise jurisdiction over causes pending in said Criminal Courts at the time said courts were abolished, without legislation; and

WHEREAS, An emergency exists for the removal of such doubts by the passage of a law to go into immediate force and effect, therefore,

SECTION 1.   *Be it enacted by the Legislature of the State of Texas,* That the District Courts of the several counties in this State, wherein Criminal Courts have been heretofore established under section one, article five of the Constitution of 1869, and wherein such Criminal Courts have been abolished by the adoption of the present Constitution, shall take control of, hear and determine all causes in said Criminal Courts in their respective counties over which said District Courts have jurisdiction; and all parties now under bond or recognizance to appear before said Criminal Courts to answer charges of felony shall appear and answer before the respective District Courts having jurisdiction of their respective causes.

SEC. 2.   That all process heretofore issued from such Criminal Courts shall be returnable to the District Courts of the respective counties in which said Criminal Courts were established.

SEC. 3.   That all proceedings heretofore had in said District Courts on and after the eighteenth day of April, 1876, in causes pending in said Criminal Courts at the time the present Constitution went into effect, are hereby legalized and made valid.

SEC. 4.   That this act take effect from and after its passage.

Approved May 30, 1876.

Takes effect from and after its passage.

CHAPTER XVIII.—*An Act to authorize the Secretary of State to employ extra clerks in his office, and to make an appropriation to pay the same.*

SECTION 1. *Be it enacted by the Legislature of the State of Texas,* That the Secretary of State be, and he is hereby authorized to employ such extra clerks in his office as may be necessary to enable him to do the business of his office promptly and without delay : *provided,* that said clerks shall be employed at such times as he may deem proper after the passage of this act and before the first day of September, A. D., 1876 : *and provided further,* that the aggregate amount of the pay of said extra clerks employed under this act shall not exceed five hundred dollars.

SEC. 2. That the sum of five hundred dollars, or so much thereof as may be needed, be, and the same is hereby appropriated, out of any money in the Treasury not otherwise appropriated, to pay said extra clerks, and the certificate of the Secretary of State that such clerk or clerks have been employed by him, stating the time they have been so employed, and the amount due them, shall be sufficient authority for the Comptroller to draw his warrant on the Treasurer for the payment of the same.

SEC. 3. Whereas, the business of the office of the Secretary of State cannot be done with the present clerical force in the office, without great delay, there being several thousand officers to be commissioned, besides the other current business of the office, therefore it is declared that an emergency exists that this act should take effect immediately ; therefore it is enacted that this act take effect and be in force from and after its passage,

Approved May 30, 1876.

Takes effect from and after its passage.

CHAPTER XIX.—*An Act to authorize the Commissioner of the General Land Office to appoint one draftsman, two corresponding clerks, and special clerks in certain cases.*

SECTION 1. *Be it enacted by the Legislature of the State of Texas,* That the Commissioner of the General Land Office be and is hereby authorized and empowered to appoint a draftsman under an act to provide for the re-compilation of an abstract of the located, titled and patented lands in Texas, and two corresponding clerks, and that the payment of the salaries of the above draftsman and corresponding clerks shall be provided for in the deficiency appropriation for the General Land Office.

SEC. 2. That when the force in the General Land Office shall not be sufficient, owing to the pressure of other duties, to furnish, within a reasonable time, the copies of field notes and surveys provided for under an act to require the Commissioner of the General Land Office to furnish copies of surveys and field notes to the counties of the State, approved April the twenty-ninth, one thousand eight hundred and seventy-four, then the Commissioner of the General Land Office is hereby authorized and empowered to employ special clerks to make said copies, who shall be allowed at the rate of eight cents for every one hundred words so copied ; to be paid by the county applying for the same, upon the certificate of the Commissioner of the performance of the service.

Sec. 3. That, whereas, the exigencies of the service require the appointment of the draftsman and clerks provided for in section one of this act; and, whereas, the appropriation for their services was through a clerical error, which the records show, omitted in the General appropriations for eighteen hundred and seventy-five and eighteen hundred and seventy-six; this act shall take effect and be in force from and after its passage.

Approved June 1st, 1876.

Takes effect from and after its passage.

CHAPTER XX.—*An Act to make an appropriation to pay the salaries of the Judges, and other expenses connected with the Court of Appeals, for the fiscal year ending August* 31, 1876.

Section 1. *Be it enacted by the Legislature of the State of Texas,* That the following sums of money, or so much thereof as may be necessary, be and the same are hereby appropriated out of any moneys in the Treasury not otherwise appropriated to pay the salaries of the Judges of the Court of Appeals, and for other expenses connected with said court, for the fiscal year ending August 31, 1876, viz: For three Judges, $3,993.75; for books and stationery, $400; for postage and other contingent expenses, $606.25.

Sec. 2. That the certificate of the Clerk of the Court of Appeals, approved by the presiding Judge thereof, shall be sufficient evidence to authorize the Comptroller to draw his warrant upon the Treasurer of the State against the appropriation herein made.

Sec. 3. That this appropriation being necessary to discharge the pressing demands and every day expenses of the court and its officers, and an emergency, and an imperative public necessity, exist for the immediate passage of this act, it shall therefore take effect and be in force from and after its passage.

Approved June 2, 1876.

Takes effect from and after its passage.

CHAPTER XXI.—*An Act to define the duties of Judges of the County Courts in certain cases therein mentioned.*

Section 1. *Be it enacted by the Legislature of the State of Texas,* That the County Judges of the several counties of this State are authorized and they are hereby required to perform all the duties heretofore required to be performed by the Chief Justices of this State, by an act entitled " An act supplementary to an act supplementary and amendatory of an act to regulate railroad companies," approved February 7, 1853; approved December 19, 1857; approved February 8, 1860.

Sec. 2. That all laws and parts of laws now in force and contravening the provisions of this act, be and the same are hereby repealed; that an imperative public necessity for the immediate passage of this act, and an emergency requiring that the same take effect and be in force from and after its passage, both exist, there being grave doubts as to whether there now exists any statute now in force in this State, whereby lands, belonging to individuals, may be condemned for railroad purposes, and many railroads in said State being liable to forfeit their charters, unless immediate relief, as herein contemplated, be granted; therefore that this act take effect and be in force from and after its passage.

Approved June 2, 1876.

Takes effect from and after its passage.

CHAPTER XXII.—*An Act to provide for a Special Term of the District Court in the Counties of Burnet and Menard.*

SECTION 1. *Be it enacted by the Legislature of the State of Texas,* That the Judge of the Seventeenth Judicial District is hereby authorized and directed to hold a special term of the District Court in the county of Burnet, at the county seat thereof, beginning on the third Monday in June, 1876, and may continue in session one week. In the county of Menard on the fourth Monday in June, 1876, and may continue in session two weeks.

SEC. 2. That the condition of affairs in the county of Menard, and the exigencies of the public service, require immediate relief, and it is therefore enacted, that this act take effect and be in force from and after its passage.

Approved June 5, 1876.

Takes effect from and after its passage.

CHAPTER XXIII.—*An Act to provide for Special Terms of the District Court in the Twentieth Judicial District.*

SECTION 1. *Be it enacted by the Legislature of the State of Texas,* That the Judge of the Twentieth Judicial District is hereby authorized and directed to hold special terms of the District Court in that Judicial District, at the times and places hereinafter stated.

SEC. 2. A special term shall be held in El Paso county at the court-house thereof, to begin on the last Monday in June, and to continue in session two weeks.

SEC. 3. A special term shall be held in Presidio county at the court-house thereof, to begin on the third Monday in July, and to continue in session two weeks.

SEC. 4. As it is necessary for the dispatch of the business in the said courts, it is hereby enacted that this act take effect and be in force from and after its passage.

Approved June 5, 1876.

Takes effect from and after its passage.

CHAPTER XXIV.—*An Act to make an appropriation to supply a deficiency in the appropriation for postage, to be used in the office of Secretary of State, for the fiscal year ending August 31, 1876.*

SECTION 1. *Be it enacted by the Legislature of the State of Texas,* That the sum of one thousand dollars, or so much thereof as may be necessary, be, and the same is hereby appropriated out of any money in the Treasury not otherwise appropriated, to pay for postage to be used in the office of Secretary of State during the remainder of the fiscal year ending August 31, 1876.

SEC. 2. Whereas, the appropriation for postage to be used in the office of the Secretary of State, for the fiscal year ending August 31, 1876, has been exhausted, and there being no appropriation for said purpose, and it being necessary that an appropriation be made for said purpose, to prevent delay in the business of said office, therefore, it is declared, that an emergency exists requiring this bill to take effect from and after its passage, and it is so enacted.

Approved June 8, 1876.

Takes effect from and after its passage.

CHAPTER XXV.—*An Act to amend Section Second of an Act concerning Divorce and Alimony, passed January 6th, 1841.*

SECTION 1. *Be it enacted by the Legislature of the State of Texas,* That section two of the foregoing recited Act shall hereafter read as follows, to-wit: the courts aforesaid are hereby invested with full power and authority to decree divorces from the bonds of matrimony in the following cases: That is to say, in favor of the husband, where his wife shall have been taken in adultery, or where she shall have voluntarily left his bed and board, for the space of three years, with the intention of abandonment. In favor of the wife, where the husband shall have left her for three years, with intention of abandonment, or where he shall have abandoned her and lived in adultery with another woman. In favor of either the husband or wife, when the other shall have been convicted, after marriage, of a felony and imprisoned in the State prison : *provided,* that no suit for divorce shall be sustained because of the conviction of either party for felony until twelve months after final judgment of conviction, nor then if the Governor shall have pardoned the convict : *provided,* that the husband has not been convicted on the testimony of the wife, nor the wife on the testimony of the husband.

NOTE.—The foregoing bill was presented to the Governor of Texas for his approval on the twenty-seventh day of May, A. D., 1876, and was not signed by him, or returned to the House in which it originated, with his objections thereto, within the time prescribed by the Constitution, and thereupon became a law without his signature.

(Signed)   A. W. DEBERRY, *Secretary of State.*

Takes effect ninety days after adjournment.

CHAPTER XXVI.—*An Act making appropriation of the Fourteenth Legislature for frontier defense available for payment of deficiency of previous year for same purpose.*

SECTION 1. *Be it enacted by the Legislature of the State of Texas,* That the appropriation made at the last session of the Fourteenth Legislature, for frontier defenses, is hereby made available for payment of deficiency in the appropriation of the previous year for the same purpose; and, whereas, a public necessity for the immediate passage of this bill exists, the same shall be in force from and after its passage.

Approved June 15, 1876.

Takes effect from and after its passage.

CHAPTER XXVII.—*An Act to organize the County Courts and define their powers and jurisdiction.*

SECTION 1. *Be it enacted by the Legislature of the State of Texas,* That there shall be established in each county in this State a Court of Record, styled the County Court; and there shall be elected by the qualified electors thereof, at the next general election for State and County officers, and every two years thereafter, one County Judge, who shall hold his office for the term of two years, and until his successor shall have been elected and qualified, and all vacancies in said office, shall be filled by the County Commissioners' Court of the county until the next general election.

SEC. 2. The County Judge shall keep his office at the county seat, and shall attend at said office from day to day, and shall not absent himself from the county for a longer period than twenty days without vacating his office, and not then without permission of the Commissioners' Court, which said court shall have power to grant County Judge leave of absence from the county not to exceed twenty days, which shall be entered on the minutes of the court; and there shall be begun and holden at the court-house of the respective counties throughout the State a term of the County Court for civil and probate business on the third Monday in January, March, May, July, September and November, and a term for criminal business on the first Monday in every month : *provided,* that the County Court of any county may change the times of holding court as herein provided by order duly entered on the minutes of said court, at some regular term thereof, and said order shall be published for two weeks prior to the time fixed for holding the term of the court as changed by said order, in some newspaper published in said county; and, if there be no such paper published in said county, then a copy of said order shall be posted by the Sheriff of the county at each place where Justices' Courts are held in the county, and at the court-house door, for two weeks, as aforesaid, and it shall be the duty of the County Clerk to make out and forward forthwith to the Secretary of State a certified copy of the order making such change; and all process returnable to the terms as fixed by this law shall be as valid, in case of a change of terms of holding court, as if made returnable to such term, and all parties shall be held bound to appear at such new term in the same manner as they would have been held to appear at the term from

2 GL

which the change was made: *provided, further*, that no such change of the times of holding said courts shall be made oftener than once in every two years, unless to obviate a conflict with the terms of the District Court, such change be rendered necessary by an act of the Legislature changing the times of holding District Court having jurisdiction in such county or counties; nor shall such change be so made as to require or permit the holding of any fewer terms of the county courts for both civil and criminal business than is now required by the Constitution of the State of Texas.

Sec. 3.   The County Court shall have exclusive original jurisdiction of all misdemeanors, except misdemeanors involving official misconduct, and except cases in which the highest penalty or fine to be imposed may not exceed two hundred dollars, and except in counties where there is established a Criminal District Court: *provided, however*, that nothing contained in this section shall be so construed as to prohibit the District Court from hearing and finally determining all charges of felony, whether the proofs develop a felony or a misdemeanor, and said courts shall have exclusive original jurisdiction in all civil cases where the matter in controversy shall exceed two hundred dollars in value, and not exceed five hundred dollars, exclusive of interest, and jurisdiction in the forfeiture and final judgment of all bonds taken in criminal cases, of which the County Court has jurisdiction and concurrent jurisdiction with the District Court when the matter in controversy shall exceed five hundred dollars, and not exceed one thousand dollars, exclusive of interest; but shall not have jurisdiction of suits to recover damages for slander or defamation of character; nor of suits for the recovery of lands; nor of suits for the enforcement of liens upon land; nor of suits in behalf of the State, for escheats; nor of suits for the forfeiture of charter of corporations and incorporated companies.   They shall have appellate jurisdiction in cases civil and criminal, of which Justices' Courts have original jurisdiction, but of such civil cases only where the judgment of the court appealed from, or the amount in controversy, shall exceed twenty dollars, exclusive of costs, and in criminal cases of which Mayors' and Recorders' Courts have jurisdiction, and after motion for new trial in the court below has been overruled, and notice of appeal given in open court.   In all appeals from Justices', Mayors' or Recorders' Courts, there shall be a trial *de novo* in the County Court, and when the judgment rendered, or fine imposed, or the amount in controversy shall not exceed one hundred dollars, exclusive of interest and costs, such trial shall be final; but if the judgment rendered, or fine imposed, or the amount in controversy, shall exceed one hundred dollars, an appeal therefrom may be taken to the Court of Appeals.   In all cases, civil and criminal, of which the County Court has exclusive or concurrent original jurisdiction, and in all cases appealed from Justices' Courts, if in said last named cases the judgment rendered or fine imposed, or the amount in controversy in the County Court shall exceed one hundred dollars, an appeal shall lie to the Court of Appeals, under the same rules and regulations as are prescribed by law for the regulation of appeals from the District to the Supreme Court of the State of Texas.   In all proceedings of administration and guardianship, an appeal shall lie to the District Court under such rules and regulations as are prescribed by the law regulating administrations of estates of decedents and wards.   In all counties where there is a Criminal

District Court, appeals in criminal cases from Justices', Mayors' and Recorders' Courts, and all other inferior courts and tribunals shall lie directly to such Criminal District Courts.

SEC. 4. The County Courts shall have the general jurisdiction of a probate court to probate wills, appoint guardians of minors, idiots, lunatics, persons *non compos mentis* and common drunkards; to grant letters testamentary, and of administration and guardianship; settle accounts of administrators, executors and guardians; transact all business appertaining to estates of deceased persons, minors, idiots, lunatics, persons *non compos mentis* and common drunkards, including the settlement, partition and distribution of estates of deceased persons; and to apprentice minors as provided by law.

SEC. 5. The County Court or Judges thereof shall have power to issue writs of mandamus, injunctions, attachments, sequestration, garnishment, certiorari, and all other writs necessary to the enforcement of the jurisdiction of said courts; and to issue writs of *habeas corpus* in all cases in which the Constitution has not conferred the power on the District Judge: *and provided further*, that no mandamus shall be granted on an *ex parte* hearing, and any peremptory mandamus granted without notice shall be deemed void: *and provided further*, that no writ of mandamus shall be issued out before the County Judge against any of the departments of the government.

SEC. 6. Whenever any Judge of a County Court shall be disqualified from trying or sitting in any case pending before him by reason of interest in such cause; or where he may be connected with any of the parties by consanguinity or affinity within the third degree; or where he may have been of counsel in the cause, it shall be the duty of such Judge, upon motion of any party interested in the cause, his agent or attorney, by an order entered of record, to remove such cause into the District Court of the county for adjudication therein; and it shall be the duty of the Clerk of the County Court immediately to make out a transcript of all entries in the minutes of the County Court in such cause, and file the same, together with the original papers of the cause, and a certified copy of the orders made therein, and a statement of the costs which have accrued, with the Clerk of the District Court; and the case shall stand for trial in the District Court as an original suit; and whenever in the case of any proceeding of administration or guardianship pending in any of the County Courts, the County Judge shall be subject to a like disqualification, such proceedings shall, on motion of the executor, administrator or guardian, or any person interested in the administration, or interested in the welfare of the ward, be in like manner transferred into the District Court of the county.

SEC. 7. All causes, both civil and criminal, and proceedings of administration and guardianship now pending in the several District Courts of this State, and all cases, civil and criminal, remaining on the docket of the several Criminal Courts which have been abolished by the adoption of the present Constitution, of which the County Courts have exclusive jurisdiction, are hereby transferred to the County Courts for trial; and it shall be the duty of the Clerks of the District Courts, upon the order of the District Judge made either in term time or in vacation, to certify the original papers and copies of all orders, a statement of the costs incurred in such causes, to the Clerk of the County Court, who shall immediately docket said causes, and they shall stand for trial the same as if originally instituted in said court: *provided*, that in all such causes and proceedings of administration and guardianship, when the Judge of the County Court may be disqualified to try the same, they shall remain in the District Court for trial and settlement: *provided further*, that all papers and records of the estates of deceased persons and minors shall be turned over to the custody of the Clerk of the County Court.

SEC. 8.   Prosecutions in the County Court may be commenced by information in writing, which information shall comply with Article 403, Part III, Title four, Chapter three of the Code of Criminal Procedure, filed with the County Clerk by the District or County Attorney, which information shall be based upon the affidavit of some credible person, which shall be filed with the information; or by an affidavit made by some credible person before the Clerk of the County Court, the County Judge, or the County or District Attorney, or Justice of the Peace, and filed with the County Clerk; upon which an information shall be prepared by the District or County Attorney and filed with the County Clerk before the case shall be called for trial; which information or affidavit shall charge the accused with some offense of which the County Court has jurisdiction; and when indictments certified to the County Courts for trial, informations or affidavits have been quashed, the person charged shall not be discharged if a new information or affidavit is filed against him; and, if the County Attorney requests, such person shall be held a reasonable time for such information or affidavit to be filed; and, upon the filing of the information or affidavit provided for in this section, the Clerk of the County Court shall issue a warrant for the arrest of the accused party; said warrant shall be in compliance with Article 216, Part III, Title two, Chapter two of the Code of Criminal Procedure, and the warrant shall be executed in the manner specified in said chapter.

SEC. 9.   The provisions of the Code of Criminal Procedure of this State and the several acts amendatory of and supplemental thereto, shall govern the practice and procedure in the County Courts, so far as the same are applicable and not in conflict with the provisions of this act.

SEC. 10.   Before each term of the County Court for criminal business, there shall be drawn in the manner which is now or may be hereafter prescribed by law, the names of a sufficient number of persons to serve as jurors at said term, and on the first day of the term or on the day on which said persons are summoned to appear, the names of all the jurors upon the venire shall be called, and thereupon two petit juries, to consist of six men each, shall be organized under the direction of the court, to be known as juries numbers one and two; and the juries so organized shall take the oath hereinafter prescribed; and in case any juror so summoned shall fail to attend or the number be reduced by challenge or other cause, the court shall require such additional number to be summoned as may be deemed necessary, so that said juries can be organized.   The oath administered to a juror in criminal cases shall be as follows: "You do solemnly swear, that in the case of the State of Texas against (A. B.), the defendant, you will a true verdict render, according to the law and evidence, so help you God."

SEC. 11.   All criminal cases shall be tried by a jury, unless waived by the defendant or his attorney, and in all cases where a jury has been empanneled and the defendant shall be convicted, a jury fee of three dollars shall be taxed against him, to be collected as other costs, and which when collected shall be paid out by the clerk in the manner provided in this act.

SEC. 12. If any party to a suit in the County Court shall desire to introduce in evidence any instrument of writing which is of record in the office of the Clerk of the Court in which said suit is pending, and the original of said instrument is lost, or said party be not able to procure the same, and said party shall account for the absence of the original in the manner required by law, and shall give the adverse party one day's notice in writing before the case is called for trial, stating in such notice the particular instrument or instruments of writing desired to be used, and the book and page where the same may be found of record, and the intention of said party to use the same in evidence; and said adverse party, or some other person for him, do not on the day after such notice is given, file an affidavit stating that he believes such instrument of writing to be forged, said party so desiring to use the same may prove the contents thereof by calling as a witness the Clerk of said Court, and have him read in evidence from the pages of the record book containing the same the said written instrument; and it shall not be necessary for said party to procure or file certified copies thereof with the papers of the suit.

SEC. 13. A jury in the County Court shall consist of six men, qualified jurors of the county, and in all cases civil and criminal in the County Court, each party shall be entitled to challenge three jurors without showing any cause therefor.

SEC. 14. Witnesses when summoned to attend court shall in civil cases be allowed a compensation of one dollar for each day's attendance and six cents per mile for every mile they may have to travel in going to and returning from the court-house at each term of the court; and no fine shall be imposed on a witness for non-attendance in civil cases, nor shall any attachment issue against his body for such non-attendance, until it is shown to the court by the affidavit of the party, his agent or attorney, causing the witness to be summoned, that the mileage and one day's compensation has been tendered the witness: *provided*, that if the party desiring the testimony of such witness shall swear that he is pecuniarily unable to make such tender of per diem and mileage, he shall not be deprived of such attachment; and that he believes his testimony is material.

SEC. 15. Witnesses in civil cases who may have been duly summoned, and who remain in attendance upon the court, whether they have been called to testify or not, may at any time during the term make an affidavit in writing before the Clerk, stating the number of days attendance and the distance they have been compelled to travel in going to and returning from the court, which affidavit shall be filed by the Clerk among the papers in the cause; and where a party has advanced the mileage and per diem as contemplated in the preceding section, the witness shall be required to make the affidavit as provided for by this section, upon the motion of any party having made said advance; and all witness fees and mileage shall be taxed in the bill of costs against the party cast in the suit: *provided*, that where a witness has been summoned and is not called to testify, his fees and mileage shall be taxed as a part of the costs, and shall be paid by the party causing him to be summoned.

SEC. 16. The said courts shall have the same power as District courts to punish contempts by fines or imprisonment, or both, in the discretion of the court.

SEC. 17. All suits in which answers are filed in due time, and in which a jury is not demanded, shall be tried or disposed of in the order in which they were filed, unless otherwise ordered by the court, with the consent of the parties or their attorneys.   On the first day of actual session of each term, all cases in which answers have been filed shall be called for the purpose of noting the demand of a jury in any of such cases; upon which call either party may demand a jury, and the Judge shall then fix some day for taking up the calendar of jury cases, and upon the calling of the appearance docket for default on default day either party to an appearance case may demand a jury.   The demand of a jury shall in all civil cases be accompanied by a deposit with the Clerk of three dollars as a jury fee, or by the affidavit of the party that he is unable, by reason of his poverty, to pay the costs of court; which jury fee shall be taxed in the bill of costs; but no jury fee shall be taxed in any case where a jury has not been demanded, and all cases in which a jury has been demanded shall be placed upon the calendar of jury cases, to be made up by the Clerk for the use of the Judge, (and a copy of said calendar shall be by the Clerk prepared for the use of the bar); and on the day fixed for taking up the trial and disposition of jury cases, the court shall proceed to try and dispose of the cases on said calendar in the order in which they were filed, unless otherwise ordered, with the consent of the parties or their attorneys.   Jurors in civil cases shall take the following oath: "You, and each of you, swear that in all cases between parties which shall be to you committed, you will give a true verdict therein, according to the law and the evidence given you, so help you God."

Sec. 18.   All civil cases in which service has been perfected as provided by the law regulating proceedings in the District Courts, are subject to be called on Wednesday, the third day of the term of the court; and unless the defendant, or party required to plead, shall have appeared and answered the petition, judgment may be entered by default.

Sec. 19.   All process, pleading, practice, evidence, procedure and appeals shall be governed by the laws and rules regulating proceedings in the District Courts, so far as applicable; and executions shall be issued by the Clerk of the County Court; and all laws now in force, regulating the mode of issuing executions out of the District Courts, and the mode and manner in which they shall be enforced, returned and recorded, shall be held to apply to executions issued from the County Court, so far as the same are applicable: *provided*, that execution may issue in fifteen days after the rendition of the judgment, and may be made returnable in sixty or ninety days from the date of its issuance.

Sec. 20.   On the first day of actual session of each term of the County Court, held for the disposition of civil business and matters in probate, the court shall, by order entered on the minutes, fix a day of the term for taking up probate business, and upon said day so fixed therefor, the said Court shall proceed to dispose of matters in probate, in the order in which the same shall have been arranged on a special docket of such matters for said term by the Clerk of said Court, (unless otherwise ordered by the Court).   The Judge of the County Court may in vacation grant temporary letters of administration or guardianship, and make such orders in reference to the custody and control of the property of estates as may be necessary for the preservation of the same, until the next term of the County Court, under such terms and restrictions as are prescribed by the laws regulating the administration of estates of decedents and wards.

Sec. 21.   All laws heretofore regulating the proceedings in District

Courts in matters of probate, except so much of said laws as confer power on the Clerk to act judicially in vacation, shall apply to and govern proceedings in the County Courts, until otherwise provided by law.

SEC. 22. The County Courts of each county in this State shall have a seal with a star of five points in the centre, and the words, "County Court of (insert the name of the county) county, Texas," engraved thereon; an impression of which seal shall be attached to all writs and other process, except subpœnas, issuing from said court, and shall be used in the authentication of all official acts of the Clerk; said seal shall be procured by the County Commissioners' Court of the county.

SEC. 23. All fines imposed on jurors, and all fines imposed for contempt of court, by any County Court of this State, and all jury fees imposed by this act, shall constitute a jury fund, to be paid to the County Clerk, and to be disposed of by him in the manner provided for in this act; and said Clerk and the sureties on his bond shall be liable for any misapplication of said fund by said Clerk, or for any failure of said Clerk to apply the same as directed by this act.

SEC. 24. On the last day of each term of the County Court, it shall be the duty of the Clerk of said court to make out a statement in writing, which shall set forth all moneys received by him for jury fees and fines, with the names of the parties from whom received, under this act, up to the date of such statement, and since his previous statement, if any such has been made; and also the name of each juror who has served at such term, the number of days he served, and the amount due him for such service, which statement shall be examined by the Judge holding such court, and if found to be correct, shall be approved and signed by him. Should said Judge consider said statement erroneous, he may make such corrections therein as he may deem necessary, and shall then approve and sign the same; which statement when so approved and signed shall be recorded in the minutes of the court.

SEC. 25. It shall be the duty of the Clerk of the County Court, after the statement provided for in the preceding section shall have been approved, signed and recorded, to pay each juror who had served at such term the amount due him for such service, if there shall be a sufficient amount of money in his hands, received under the provisions of this act, to pay all the jurors who served at such terms; but if there is not a sufficient amount in his hands for that purpose, then he shall pay to each juror his *pro rata* amount in proportion to his time of service, and shall give to each juror a certificate for the balance due him, which certificate shall be paid out of the County Treasury, and shall be a sufficient voucher for the Treasurer to pay the amount therein certified to be due.

SEC. 26. The County Courts shall have power to hear and determine all motions against Sheriffs or other officers for money received under execution or other process or order issued out of said court, which shall not have been paid to the party entitled to the same, his agent or attorney, on demand, or for other dereliction of duty; and also all motions against attorneys and counsellors at law, where the amount claimed is less than one thousand dollars, exclusive of interest, under the same rules and regulations as are prescribed by law for like proceedings in the District Courts.

SEC. 27. Should the Judge of any County Court not appear at the time appointed for holding the same, like proceedings shall be had as in the District Courts in such cases.

SEC. 28. All proceedings instituted and conducted in the County Court before the passage of this act, which would have been authorized by its provisions had this act been in force at the time said proceedings were instituted and conducted, shall have the same force and effect, and be as valid and binding on all parties undertaken to be affected thereby as if the same had been instituted after the taking effect of this act, and all official acts performed by the County Judge, or Clerk of the County Court, before the passage of this act which would have been authorized by its provisions had this act been in force at the time said official acts were performed, shall be as valid and binding on all parties undertaken to be affected thereby as if the same had been performed after the taking effect of this act.

SEC. 29. All laws and parts of laws in conflict with the provisions of this act, be, and the same are hereby repealed.

SEC. 80. An imperative necessity existing for the immediate passage of this act in order that the courts herein provided for shall go into operation, therefore this act shall be in force from and after its passage.

Approved June 16, 1876.

Takes effect from and after its passage.

CHAPTER XXVIII.—*An Act to amend an Act entitled " An Act to amend Article 382, Title II, Chapter 3 of the Penal Code, approved October 26, 1866, amendatory of an Act entitled ' An Act to establish the Penal Code,'" approved August 28, 1856.*

SECTION 1. *Be it enacted by the Legislature of the State of Texas*, That Article 382, Title II, Chapter 3 of the Penal Code be so amended as to read as follows:

ARTICLE 382. If any person shall go into any public place, or into or near any private house, or along any public street or highway near any private house, and shall by loud and vociferous or obscene, vulgar or indecent talking, or by swearing or cursing, or by exposing his person, or by rudely displaying any pistol or other deadly weapon in such public place, or upon such public street or highway, or near such private house, in a manner calculated to disturb the inhabitants thereof, he shall be fined in any sum not exceeding one hundred dollars.

Approved June 20, 1876.

Takes effect ninety days after adjournment.

CHAPTER XXIX.—*An Act to fix the amount of jury fees in the District, County and Justices' Courts.*

WHEREAS, An imperative public necessity exists for the immediate passage of a law fixing the amounts to be paid as jury fees by parties demanding juries in the District, County and Justices' Courts, as the said courts are to a great extent suspended for the want of such law; therefore,

SECTION 1. *Be it enacted by the Legislature of the State of Texas*, That in the trial of all causes in the District, County and Justices' Courts, the plaintiff or defendant shall, upon application made in open court, have the right of trial by jury; but no jury shall be empanneled in any civil case in any of said courts unless demanded by a party to the case, and a jury fee be paid by the party demanding a jury.

SEC. 2. That the jury fee to be paid as provided in the preceding section, shall be, in the District Court, the sum of six dollars; in the County Court, the sum of three dollars; and in the Justices' Courts, the sum of three dollars: *provided*, that such fees shall in all cases be paid to the Clerk of said courts, or to the Justices of the Peace, as the case may be, before entering on the trial of such cases, under such rules as may be prescribed by said respective courts, to be taxed in the bill of costs, as in other causes, and paid by the party cast in the suit: *and provided further*, that in no case shall any party be deprived of trial by jury where he or she may make affidavit that he or she is too poor to pay said jury fee.

SEC. 3. As an emergency exists, as stated in the preamble hereto, that this act take effect from and after its passage.

Approved June 21, 1876.

Takes effect from and after its passage.

CHAPTER XXX.—*An Act to permit the transfer of certain suits from one court to another.*

SECTION 1. *Be it enacted by the Legislature of the State of Texas,* That all suits now pending in the courts in original counties, from which a new county has been taken, in whole or in part, and the parties thereto reside in such new counties, may, by consent of parties or their attorneys, be transferred, either in term time or vacation, to the corresponding courts of such new counties; such transfer to be in the same manner as changes of venue are made when ordered.

Approved June 21st, 1876.

Takes effect ninety days after adjournment.

CHAPTER XXXI.—*An Act to require the Clerks of the District and County Courts of this State to provide and keep indexes and cross-indexes of the names of the parties to all causes in their courts, and to provide a penalty for their failure to comply with the provisions of this Act.*

SECTION 1. *Be it enacted by the Legislature of the State of Texas,* That the Clerks of the District and County Courts of the several counties in this State shall provide, and keep in their respective offices as part of the records of the same, full and complete alphabetical indexes of the names of the parties to all suits heretofore and hereafter filed in their respective courts; said indexes shall be kept in well bound books, and shall state in full the names of all the parties to such suits, and be indexed and cross-indexed so as to show the name of each party, under the proper letter; and reference shall be made opposite each name to the page of the minute book upon which is entered the final judgment in each case.

SEC. 2. Any clerk failing to comply with the provisions of this act shall, upon conviction therefor, before any court having jurisdiction, be fined not less than fifty dollars, nor more than one hundred dollars, for each offense; and the Judges of the several District Courts of this State are directed to give this act specially in charge to the Grand Jury.

SEC. 3.   The County Commissioners' Courts of the several counties in this State shall fix the compensation to be made to the said clerks for the performance of the duties required by this act, to be paid out of the general county fund; but no allowance or payment shall be made to any clerk for indexing suits filed during his term of office, and after the passage of this act.

Approved June 21, 1876.

Takes effect ninety days after adjournment.

CHAPTER XXXII.—*An Act to make persons liable for damages to the owner for buying stolen property after nightfall.*

SECTION 1.   *Be it enacted by the Legislature of the State of Texas,* That if any person within this State, shall purchase, trade, or barter for any personal property, after nightfall, and the same shall afterwards be proved to be stolen property such person so purchasing, or trading for said property, shall be liable to the true owner thereof in three times the value of the same, to be recovered in any court of the State, having competent jurisdiction of the case.

SEC. 2.   That nothing in this act shall be so construed as to relieve any person so offending from prosecution under the criminal laws of this State.

Approved June 22, 1876.

Takes effect ninety days after adjournment.

CHAPTER XXXIII.—*An Act to prohibit the sale, exchange or gift of intoxicating liquors in any county, Justice's precinct, city or town in this State that may so elect; prescribing the mode of election, and affixing a punishment for its violation.*

SECTION 1.   *Be it enacted by the Legislature of the State of Texas,* That it shall be the duty of the Commissioners' Court of each county in the State, upon the written petition of fifty qualified voters of said county, or upon such petition by twenty qualified voters of any Justice's precinct, town or city therein, to order an election to be held by the qualified voters of said county, Justice's precinct, town or city, as the case may be, to determine whether the sale of intoxicating liquors, and medicated bitters producing intoxication, shall be prohibited in such county, Justice's precinct, town or city, or not: *provided,* that nothing herein contained shall be construed to prohibit the sale of wines for sacramental purposes; nor alcoholic stimulants as medicines in cases of actual sickness, when sold upon the written prescription of a regular practicing physician, certifying upon honor that the same is actually necessary as a medicine.

SEC. 2.   It shall be the duty of such court, at its first session, after the filing of such petition with the Clerk thereof, to order an election to be held at the regular voting place or places within the proposed and prescribed limits, upon a day not exceeding thirty days from the date of said order; and said order shall express the object of said election. The Clerk shall post, or cause to be posted, at least five copies of said order at different public places in each Justice's precinct, town or city in which such election shall be held, for at least twenty days prior to the day of election. Said court shall appoint and qualify the proper officers under existing laws. At said election those who favor the prohibition of the sale of intoxicating liquors within the prescribed limits shall have written or printed on their tickets the words " For Prohibition;" and those who oppose it shall endorse on their tickets the words "Against Prohibition." The officers holding said election shall in all respects not herein specified conform to the existing laws regulating elections; and after the polls are closed, they shall proceed to count the vote ; and they shall, within ten days thereafter, make due report of said election to the aforesaid court.

Sec. 3.   Said court shall hold a special session on the eleventh day after the holding of the aforesaid election, or as soon thereafter as practicable, for the purpose of opening the polls and counting the votes; and if a majority of the votes cast are " For Prohibition," said court shall immediately make an order declaring the result of said vote, and absolutely prohibiting the sale of intoxicating liquors within the prescribed bounds, (except for the purposes specified in section one of this act), until such time as the qualified voters therein may, at a legal election held for the purpose, by a majority vote, decided otherwise; and said order of court so declaring the result of election and prohibiting the sale of intoxicating liquors, shall be published for four successive weeks in the newspaper having the largest circulation in the county ; and in such counties as shall have no newspaper, by posting said order at three public places within the prescribed limits. But if a majority voting at such election vote " Against Prohibition," the court shall make an order declaring the result, and have the same entered of record in the office of the Clerk of said court.

Sec. 4.   No election under the foregoing sections shall be held within the same prescribed limits in less than twelve months after an election under this act has been held therein ; but a failure to carry prohibition in a county shall not prevent such election being immediately thereafter held in a Justice's precinct, town or city of said county ; nor shall the failure to carry prohibition in a town or city prevent an election being immediately thereafter held in the same Justice's precinct; nor shall the holding of such election in any Justice's precinct in any way prevent the holding of an election for the entire county immediately thereafter.

Sec. 5.   When any such election has been held, and has resulted in favor of prohibition, and the aforesaid court has made the order declaring the result, and the order of prohibition, and has caused the same to be published as aforesaid, any person or persons who shall thereafter, within the prescribed bounds of prohibition, sell, exchange or give away, with the purpose of evading the provisions of this act, any intoxicating liquors whatsoever, or in any way violate any of the provisions of this act, shall be subject to prosecution, by information or indictment, and shall be fined in a sum not less than twenty-five nor more than two hundred dollars for each and every violation of any of the provisions of this act.

Sec. 6.   It is hereby made the duty of the District Judges to give this act in charge to the grand juries ; and it is made the especial duty of the County Attorneys, the County Judges, and all Justices of the Peace having jurisdiction in the premises to see that this act is rigidly enforced.   An officer failing to discharge his duties under this act in any respect shall be subject to indictment, and, if convicted, shall be fined not less than one hundred nor more than one thousand dollars. All fines collected under this act shall be paid into the County Treasury, and shall constitute a part of the school fund for the county, Justice's precinct, town or city in which the law is in force.

SEC. 7.   All laws and parts of laws in conflict with this act are hereby repealed.

Approved June 24, 1876.

Takes effect ninety days after adjournment.

CHAPTER XXXIV.—*An Act making an appropriation of forty thousand dollars to complete and finish the State Agricultural and Mechanical College.*

SECTION 1.   *Be it enacted by the Legislature of the State of Texas,* That the sum of forty thousand dollars, or so much thereof as may be necessary, be, and the same is hereby appropriated out of any money in the Treasury not otherwise appropriated, for the purpose of constructing and completing the bui(l)dings and improvements, and for providing the furniture necessary to put the State Agricultural and Mechanical College in immediate and successful operation.

SEC. 2.   The completion of the college building being an emergency requiring the speedy operation of this act, and an imperative public necessity existing, that this act take effect and be in force from and after its passage.

Approved June 24, 1876.

Takes effect from its passage.

CHAPTER XXXV.—*An Act to prevent the removal of rock, earth, sand, coal, slate, or minerals, from the premises of another, and prescribing a punishment therefor.*

SECTION 1.   *Be it enacted by the Legislature of the State of Texas,* That hereafter it shall be unlawful for any person to enter upon the land or premises of any citizen of this State and take or remove therefrom any rock, earth, sand, coal, slate, or mineral imbed(d)ed in the soil or lying upon the surface thereof, without the consent of the owner or his duly authorized agent.

SEC. 2.   Any person offending against the provisions of this act shall be guilty of a misdemeanor, and upon conviction thereof, before any court of competent jurisdiction of this State, shall be fined in any sum not less than three, nor more than ten times the value of the rock, earth, sand, coal, slate, or mineral, so taken and removed.

Approved June 24, 1876.

Takes effect ninety days after adjournment.

CHAPTER XXXVI.—*An Act to regulate the appointment and define the duties of Notaries Public.*

WHEREAS, An emergency exists which makes it necessary that a sufficient number of Notaries Public shall be immediately appointed in each of the counties of this State, to transact all the notarial business thereof; therefore:

SECTION 1. *Be it enacted by the Legislature of the State of Texas,* That there shall be appointed by the Governor, by and with the consent of two-thirds of the Senate, a convenient number of Notaries Public for each county in this State, not less than five nor more than twenty, who shall hold their offices for two years from the day of their qualification: *provided,* that the Notaries Public appointed during this session of the Legislature shall hold their offices until the termination of the first session of the Sixteenth Legislature.

SEC. 2. When a Notary Public is appointed to succeed another, his commission shall specify what Notary he succeeds.

SEC. 3. Every person who may be appointed a Notary Public, before he enters on the duties of his office, shall execute a bond, with good and sufficient security, to be approved by the Clerk of the County Court of his county, payable to the Governor and his successors in office, in the sum of one thousand dollars, conditioned for the faithful performance of the duties of his office; and shall also take and subscribe the oath of office prescribed by the Constitution, which shall be endorsed on said bond, with the certificate of the officer administering the same; said bond shall be recorded in the office of the Clerk of the County Court, and deposited in said office, and shall not be void on the first recovery, and may be sued on in the name of any party injured, from time to time until the whole amount thereof has been recovered.

SEC. 4. Every Notary Public who shall be guilty of any wilful neglect of duty or malfeasance in office may be indicted by the grand jury, and on conviction shall be removed from office; and whenever any Notary Public shall remove permanently from the county or precinct for which he is appointed, his office shall thereupon be deemed vacant.

SEC. 5. Every Notary Public shall provide a seal of office, whereon shall be engraved, in the center, a star of five points, and the words "Notary Public, County of ——, Texas," around the margin (the blank to be filled with the name of the county for which the officer is appointed), and he shall authenticate all his official acts therewith; and when any Notary Public shall vacate his office in any manner, his record books and all public papers in his office shall be deposited with the Clerk of the County Court of his county.

SEC. 6. Notaries Public may take the acknowledgment or proof of all instruments of writing in the manner provided by law, to entitle them to registration, and to give certificates of all such acknowledgments and proofs under their hands and official seals; they may take the examination and acknowledgment of married women to all deeds and instruments of writing conveying or charging their separate property, and their interest in the homestead, in the manner provided by law.

SEC. 7. Every Notary Public shall have power to administer oaths, and give certificates thereof under his hand and official seal. They may take the proof or acknowledgments of all instruments of writing relating to commerce and navigation, and also of letters of attorney and other instruments of writing, make declarations and protests, and certify under their hand and seal the truth of the matters or things done by virtue of their offices.

SEC. 8. Every Notary Public shall procure and keep a well bound book, in which shall be entered the date of all instruments acknowledged before him, the date of such acknowledgment, the name of the grantor or maker, the place of his residence or alleged residence, whether personally known or introduced, and if introduced, the name and residence or alleged residence of the party introducing him. If the instrument be proved by a witness, the residence or alleged residence of such witness, whether such witness is personally known to him or introduced, and if introduced, the name and residence of the party introducing him; the name and residence of the grantee. If land is conveyed or charged by such instrument, the names of the original grantee thereof shall be kept, and the county where the land is situated. The book herein required to be kept, and the statements therein required to be entered, shall be an original public record, and shall be transmitted by such Notary to his successor, and the same shall be open to inspection by any citizen at all reasonable times; and such Notary Public shall give a certified copy of any record in his office to any person applying therefor, on payment of all fees thereon.

SEC. 9. All declarations and protests made and acknowledgments taken by Notaries Public, and certified copies of their records and official papers, shall be received as evidence of the facts therein stated in all the courts of this State.

SEC. 10. Notaries Public shall have power to take the depositions of witnesses in the manner prescribed by law, to attest the oath of any person to a petition or answer in any suit, and when so attested shall be valid in all the courts of this State, and they shall be entitled to such fees for their services as shall be prescribed by law.

SEC. 11. Copies of all records, declarations, protests, and other official acts of Notaries Public, may be certified by their successors with whom they are deposited, and shall have the same authority as if certified by the Notary by whom they were originally made.

SEC. 12. When the Governor of the State shall make appointments of Notaries Public as required by the twenty-sixth section of article four of the Constitution, and said Notaries Public shall qualify, it shall be the duty of the Secretary of State to furnish to the Clerks of the County Courts such a printed list of all the Notaries Public in the State so appointed and qualified; and upon any subsequent appointment of such Notaries Public, it shall likewise be the duty of said Secretary of State to furnish a like list to said Clerk; and it shall be the duty of the Clerk of the County Court to preserve said list in his office for public inspection, and post a copy thereof on the court-house door.

SEC. 13. When a Notary is appointed, the Secretary of State shall forward the commission to the Clerk of the County Court of the county where the party resides, and the said Clerk shall immediately notify said party to appear before him in twenty days from the day of such notice and qualify according to law: *provided*, that if said party shall be absent from such county at the time of the reception of such commission by said clerk, then he shall have twenty days from his return to said county in which to appear and qualify. The Clerk receiving the commission shall endorse thereon the day on which the notice was given, and if the party does not qualify within the time limited, the appointment shall be void, and the Clerk shall certify on the back of the commission, under the seal of the court, that the party has failed to qualify, and return it to the Secretary of State.

SEC. 14. Any Notary Public who shall willfully fail, neglect, or refuse to comply with any of the requirements of this act, shall be deemed guilty of a misdemeanor, and upon conviction shall be fined in any sum not to exceed one hundred dollars, and not less than twenty-five dollars.

SEC. 15. The Clerk of the County Court shall be entitled to a fee of one dollar from every Notary Public who qualifies before him.

SEC. 16. That all laws or parts of laws in conflict with the provisions of this act be, and the same are hereby repealed; and that this act take effect and be in force from and after its passage.

Approved June 24, 1876.

Takes effect from its passage.

CHAPTER XXXVII.—*An Act to abolish the office of Notary Public as it existed prior to the adoption of the present Constitution.*

SECTION 1. *Be it enacted by the Legislature of the State of Texas,* That thirty days after the passage of this act, the office of notary public, as it existed prior to the 18th day of April, A. D. 1876, be, and the same is hereby abolished; and all commissions issued to Notaries Public prior to the said April 18th, 1876, by virtue of any law then in force, are revoked, and shall, after the expiration of the thirty days aforesaid, be of no force and effect.

SEC. 2. The Governor is hereby authorized and required to proceed immediately to the appointment of Notaries Public, under existing laws, in the several counties in this State, without reference to appointments made prior to the 18th of April, 1876.

SEC. 3. That on account of the public necessity of having Notaries Public appointed at once, and the emergency being that the Senate must pass on the nominations made by the Governor before adjournment, this act take effect and be in force from and after its passage.

Approved June 26, 1876.

Takes effect from its passage.

CHAPTER XXXVIII.—*An Act to provide for the public printing, binding and stationery, by contract.*

SECTION 1. *Be it enacted by the Legislature of the State of Texas,* That the Attorney General, Treasurer, and Secretary of State be, and are hereby constituted a Board of Public Printing, authorized and required to contract with any suitable person or persons, firm or firms, who are residents of and doing business in this State, to furnish such stationery as may be required by law or needed by any department of the State government, except the Judicial Department, and to print and bind the Laws and Journals of each House together with such printing and binding as may be ordered by each House, and to do such other printing and binding as may be required by law or needed by any department, except the Judicial Department, and except such as may be done at the Deaf and Dumb Asylum: *provided*, that said contract shall be for the term of two years, and until a new contract shall be made and approved: *and provided further*, that when printing is ordered in German, Spanish, or other language than English, a separate contract may be made for the work in each of such languages; and the Printing Board shall employ on such terms as they deem best, one or more competent translators to translate the laws and such other matter as may be required, into other languages than English, when necessary.

SEC. 2.   That the Secretary of State shall, every two years, advertise for thirty days in two or more, not exceeding five, weekly newspapers published in this State and having the largest circulation, for sealed proposals for furnishing such stationery and for doing such printing and binding, and shall in said advertisement, state a time and place when and where said proposals shall be received and opened, and contract awarded, not exceeding forty days from the date of the first publication of said advertisement; and he shall, in said advertisement, give such specifications and estimates of the probable amount of printing, binding and stationery that will be required, as may be practicable.   The proposals shall be for the public printing, and for stationery, separately; and the bid for printing shall include binding, blank books and such paper as may be necessary to be used in the execution of the work; and that for stationery shall include paper on which there is no printing; envelopes, and such other articles as are usually embraced in the term "stationery."   The proposals shall be sealed and addressed "To the Secretary of State," and shall be indorsed with the statement that they are proposals for public printing, or for stationery; and, when received, shall be filed carefully away by the Secretary of State in his office, and the seals thereof shall not be broken until the day named in the advertisement for awarding the contract; and shall be opened in the presence of the Printing Board and such bidders as may desire to be present.   The bids shall be examined by the Printing Board, a careful comparison made, and the contract awarded to the lowest and best responsible bidder whose bid shall be below such maximum rates as are hereinafter prescribed: *provided*, that each bid shall be accompanied by a guarantee, signed at least by two responsible citizens, guaranteeing that if the contract be awarded to the said bidder, that he or they will enter into contract, and give a good and efficient bond to carry out the same.

SEC. 3.   That the public printing shall be divided into five classes, as follows:

FIRST CLASS—The First Class shall include the printing and binding of the laws, journals, department reports, Governor's message and like documents; which shall be printed on white calendered No. 2 book paper, of uniform color, 24x38 inches in size, and weighing not less than forty-five pounds to the ream, on long primer type (except tabular work, which may be in such type smaller than long primer as the nature of the work and good taste may require), the pages to be fifty-seven ems long, including head and foot lines, and thirty-two ems wide, long primer measure, and not to contain less than 1800 ems; and when printed the laws and reports shall be neatly folded, stitched and covered; and the journals and message folded, stitched and trimmed.   Cover paper shall be thirty-five pounds to the ream.   The maximum prices for work of the First Class shall be: For paper, white and cover, $9 per ream, and no allowance shall be made for waste; composition, $1 per 1000 ems, printer's measurement; presswork, 16 pages to the form (unless the nature of the work requires a smaller number of pages), $1 per token of 240 impressions or less; binding, 50 cents per one hundred for folding, stitching and covering first signature of sixteen pages, and 25 cents per one hundred for each additional signature of sixteen pages or less; for folding, stitching and trimming, without covering, 40 cents per one hundred for first signature of sixteen pages, and 20 cents per one hundred for each additional signature of sixteen pages or less; *provided*, no matter shall be leaded, except by the express direction of the Printing Board.

SECOND CLASS.—Work of the Second Class shall consist of all blanks and printed stationery required by any department of the State Government, except the Judicial Department, and shall be on first class sized and calendered white wove paper, of such dimensions and weights as the nature of the work may require. The maximum rates for such work shall be as follows: For composition, 90 cents per 1000 ems, printer's measurement; for presswork, on forms the size of a flat cap sheet or less, 75 cents per token; on forms larger than flat cap, $1 per token; and a token shall be 240 impressions, or less, when the number of blanks ordered shall require a less number of impressions. The maximum rates for paper required for work of the second class shall be as follows: *Letter paper*—ten pounds to the ream, $4.20 per ream; twelve pounds to the ream, $5.05 per ream. *Flat cap paper*—twelve pounds to the ream, $5.05 per ream; fourteen pounds to the ream, $5.90 per ream; sixteen pounds to the ream, $6.75 per ream; eighteen pounds to the ream, $7.60 per ream; twenty pounds to the ream, $8.40 per ream. *Demy paper*—twenty-eight pounds to the ream, $11.75 per ream; thirty pounds to the ream, $12.60 per ream. *Folio post paper*—eighteen pounds to the ream, $7.60 per ream; twenty-two pounds to the ream, $9.25 per ream; twenty-four pounds to the ream, $10 per ream. *Medium paper*—twenty-eight pounds to the ream, $11.75 per ream; thirty-six pounds to the ream, $15 per ream. *Double flat cap paper*—twenty-eight pounds to the ream, $11.75 per ream; thirty-two pounds to the ream, $13.45 per ream; thirty-six pounds to the ream, $15 per ream; forty pounds to the ream, $16.80 per ream. *Super royal paper*—fifty-four pounds to the ream, $22.70 per ream. For ruling work of the Second Class, the maximum price shall be 40 cents per one hundred for each passage through the ruling machine. For binding work of the Second Class, the maximum price shall be: For pads of one hundred sheets each, quarter sheet cap, demy or folio, 20 cents per pad; half sheet cap, demy or folio, 25 cents per pad. For quarter binding, quarter sheet cap, demy or folio, 25 cents per quire; half sheet cap, demy or folio, 40 cents per quire. For half binding, quarter sheet cap, demy or folio, 50 cents per quire; half sheet cap, demy or folio, 75 cents per quire. For binding full skiver, quarter sheet cap, demy or folio, 60 cents per quire; half sheet cap, demy or folio, 90 cents per quire.

THIRD CLASS.—Work of the Third Class shall consist of blank books, either ruled and printed or ruled without printing. The paper used shall be sized and calendered, made of linen stock, and of the quality known among paper dealers as " P " paper; and the following shall be maximum rates: *Cap paper*—eighteen pounds to the ream, plain ruled, half bound, $1.25 per quire; do, printed heads, $1.75 per quire; do., plain ruled, extra full bound, $2 per quire; do., printed heads $2.50

per quire. *Demy paper*—twenty-eight pounds to the ream, plain ruled, half bound, $1.50 per quire; do., printed heads, $2 per quire; do., plain ruled, extra full bound, $2.50 per quire; do., printed heads, $3 per quire. *Medium paper*—thirty-six pounds to the ream, plain ruled, half bound, $2 per quire; do., printed heads, $2.50 per quire; do., plain ruled, extra full bound, $3 per quire; do., printed heads, $3.50 per quire. *Medium paper*—forty pounds to the ream, plain ruled, extra full bound, $4 per quire; do., printed heads, $4.50 per quire. *Super royal paper*—fifty-four pounds to the ream, plain ruled, extra full bound, $4.50 per quire; do., printed heads, $5 per quire.

FOURTH CLASS.—Work of the fourth class shall consist of the printing of bills, resolutions, committee reports and such other like work as may be ordered by the Legislature or either house thereof; and shall be on first class sized and calendered white wove flat cap paper of twelve pounds to the ream, printed on pica type, lines numbered in the margin, with space between the lines of the size of pica, the printing to be thirty-six ems pica wide and sixty-five ems in length. The maximum price for work of the fourth class shall be: for two hundred copies, or any number of copies less than two hundred ordered by either house of the Legislature, including composition, paper, press work and binding, $3.25 per page for as many pages as are contained in one copy thereof; and when more than two hundred copies of work mentioned in this class are ordered by either house of the Legislature, the printer shall be paid for the paper, presswork and binding only for such additional copies, at such rates as are contracted for, for work of the Second Class.

FIFTH CLASS.—The Fifth Class shall consist of the publication of executive proclamations, advertisements and like documents; and the maximum price shall be $1 per square of one hundred words for the first publication and 50 cents per square for each subsequent publication that may be ordered, and fractional parts of a square at proportionate rates, and each square shall contain not less than one hundred words.

SEC. 4. That when proclamations, advertisements, and like publications are authorized and required by law to be published in more newspapers than one, they shall be published under like rules: *provided*, that proclamations and like documents shall not be published in more than two newspapers in each Congressional District, and at different points, and shall not be inserted for a longer period than three months; and proposed amendments to the Constitution shall be published once a week for four weeks, commencing at least three months before the time specified by the Legislature for an election thereon, in one weekly newspaper in each county in which such a newspaper may be published; and all claims presented for publishing advertisements shall be accompanied by a copy of the advertisement as printed, and the affidavit of the publisher stating the dates when the same was published.

SEC. 5. That the maximum rates for stationery shall be as follows: *Legal cap paper*—eighteen pounds to the ream, seven dollars and twenty cents per ream; sixteen pounds to the ream, six dollars and forty cents per ream; fourteen pounds to the ream, five dollars and sixty cents per ream. *Foolscap paper*—sixteen pounds to the ream, six dollars and forty cents per ream; fourteen pounds to the ream, five dollars and sixty cents per ream. *Letter paper*—twelve pounds to the ream, four dollars and eighty cents per ream; ten pounds to the ream, four dollars per ream. *Note paper*—eight pounds to ream, three dollars and twenty cents per ream; six pounds to ream, two dollars and forty cents per ream; five pounds to ream, two dollars per ream. *Engrossing paper*—twenty-eight pounds demy, one-quarter sheets, seven dollars and twenty cents per ream; eighteen pounds cap, one-half sheets, eight dollars per ream. *Envelopes*—XX white or buff, number ten, plain, seven dollars and twenty cents per thousand; printed, eight dollars and eighty cents per thousand; XX white or buff, number six, plain, four dollars and eighty cents per thousand; printed, six dollars and forty cents per thousand; XX white or buff, number five, plain, four dollars per thousand. *Blotting paper*—one hundred and twenty pounds to ream, six dollars and forty cents per one hundred sheets; one hundred pounds to ream, five dollars and twenty cents per one hundred sheets. *Pencils*—the kind to be specified in bid, eight dollars per gross. *Red ink*—the manufacturer to be named in bid, two dollars and forty cents per dozen. *Mucilage*—quarts, seven dollars and twenty cents per dozen; pints, four dollars and eighty cents per dozen. *Steel pens*—brand to be named, two dollars per box. *Penholders*—five dollars and sixty cents per gross. *Rubber bands*—best, all sizes, two dollars and forty cents per box. *Mammoth ink and pencil erasers*—four dollars per dozen. *Rubber rulers*—twelve inch, one dollar and twenty cents each. *Wood rulers*—fifteen inch, eighty cents each. *Erasing knives*—eighty cents each. *Recording ink*—maker to be named in bid, quarts, fourteen dollars and forty cents per dozen. *Copying ink*—maker to be named in bid, quarts, nineteen dollars and twenty cents per dozen. *Inkstands*—C. H. number three, sixty cents each; glass, flat, eighty cents each. *Paper fasteners*—forty cents per box.

SEC. 6. That all printing and stationery not embraced within the specifications of this act shall be furnished by the contractors at rates in proportion to those fixed in the contract for work or stationery of like nature, to be approved by the Board of Public Printing.

SEC. 7. That at any time after a contract has been made and entered into with any person or firm as herein provided, the Legislature reserves the right to abrogate said contract, if said contract is not executed, or if said work is not performed in accordance with the provisions of this act; and to alter or amend by enactment the maximum rates for such printing and stationery; that the Board of Public Printing shall have power, and is hereby required, when the Legislature is not in session, to cancel the contract with the Public Printer whenever he shall fail to do the public printing as promptly as the exigencies of the public service demands; and it shall be their duty to let out a new contract in the manner herein provided; *provided, however*, such contract shall not be cancelled without the consent of the Governor and Comptroller thereto; and that nothing in the contract with the printer shall prevent the Deaf and Dumb Asylum from doing work for any of the departments.

SEC. 8. That there shall be printed not less than eight thousand copies of the laws of a general nature, and as many more as the Printing Board may require, not to exceed twelve thousand in all; and fifteen hundred copies of the special laws, including all acts for private relief; all acts incorporating towns and cities; all acts having a local application; all of a personal nature; and all acts incorporating private associations of every description, that may be passed at each session of the Legislature; and five hundred copies of the Journals of each house of the Legislature; and one thousand copies of the laws of a general nature in the Spanish language, and fifteen hundred copies in the German language; *provided*, that when printing is required in other languages than

English, fifty per cent. additional may be allowed for composition. There shall be printed, under the supervision of the Secretary of State, eleven hundred copies of the annual reports of the Comptroller of Public Accounts, Treasurer, Commissioner of the General Land Office, Superintendent and Financial Agent of the Penitentiary, Superintendent of the Lunatic Asylum, of the Asylums of the Blind, Deaf and Dumb; and the reports of all other officers who are required to report to the Governor or the Legislature; three hundred copies of which reports shall be delivered by the Secretary of State to the two houses of the Legislature, for their use, at as early a day as practicable after they are printed; three hundred copies shall be delivered to the officer making the report, for his use; and the remaining five hundred copies shall be kept by the Secretary of State for the public use; *provided,* that the Printing Board may change the number of any of said reports to be printed to not less than three hundred nor more than two thousand. There shall be printed such number of copies of the messages of the Governor and other documents as the Legislature, or either House, may order.

Sec. 9. That the Secretary of the Senate and the Chief Clerk of the House of Representatives shall cause the journals of their respective houses to be furnished to the printer contracted with to publish their proceedings, for the purpose of being printed; and, when printed, the manuscript journals shall be returned and filed in the archives of the Legislature; and the said Secretary and Chief Clerk, respectively, shall furnish to the said printer a comprehensive index of the same, which shall be printed at the end of the respective journals. It shall be the duty of the Secretary of State to cause copies of all laws and resolutions to be furnished to the printer contracted with, as early as possible after they severally shall have been approved or passed. He shall also furnish to the printer contracted with, a comprehensive index to the said laws, which shall be printed in like type and style to the index of the general laws of the Ninth Legislature.

Sec. 10. That the whole number of laws and journals, reports of public officers, and other public documents authorized to be printed, shall be delivered at the office of the Secretary of State; except such printing as may be ordered by the two houses of the Legislature, or either of them, for their use, which shall be deliverd to such persons and at such times as they or either of them may direct.

Sec. 11. That the laws and journals shall be delivered within sixty days after the last copy shall have been furnished to the printer contracted with to do the work. The reports of public officers shall be required to be delivered to the Governor by the respective officers making the same, in sufficient time to be delivered to the printer one month before the meeting of the Legislature; and if so furnished to said printer, shall be delivered by him to the the Secretary of State within the first week of said session; and if furnished less than one month before the meeting of the Legislature, or after, the same shall be delivered by said printer to the Secretary of State within one month after they are so furnished. The Secretary of State shall certify that the laws thus published are true copies of the originals in his office, and also certify the date upon which the Legislature adjourned; which certificate shall be appended to and printed at the end of each volume. The Secretary of State shall also superintend the printing of the same, and shall read and correct the proof; *provided, however,* that this requirement shall not dispense with the duty of the printer to furnish some competent person or persons also to read and correct the proof; *and provided further*, that should said laws be printed at any point away from the seat of government, the actual expenses of the Secretary of State, while attending at said place for the purpose of supervising the publication of the same, shall be paid out of the appropriation for public printing, and deducted from the amount due for the printing upon which this additional expense was incurred.

SEC. 12. That the person or persons with whom the Board shall enter into contract under the provisions of this act shall immediately enter into a bond, with two or more good sureties, in such sum as said Board of Public Printing may deem adequate for the protection of the State, payable to the State of Texas; conditioned that he or they will faithfully perform all the stipulations of their contract, and that they will also do and perform everything required of them as such contractors under this act; which bond shall be approved by said Board, and filed in the office of the Secretary of State. On breach of said bond, the same may be put in suit upon the order of the Governor, which suit may be brought in the county in which the seat of government may be located, and said bond shall not become void on the first recovery, but suit may be maintained thereon until the whole amount thereof be recovered; *provided*, that the current printing of the Legislature shall be done at the city of Austin.

SEC. 13. All accounts for printing done, or stationery furnished, under the provisions of this act (except that for the Legislature when in session), shall be audited as follows: The account shall be verified by the affidavit of the person or persons contracted with, or some one in their employ having an oversight of the work, that said account is just and correct, that the amount of work charged for has actually been performed, or the actual amount of stationery delivered, and that the prices charged in said account are in accordance with the stipulations of the contract, and be accompanied with a sample of the work done, and stationery furnished. After which it shall be examined by the practical printer and Printing Board, and if found correct, approved by said Board. Such claim, when thus examined and approved, shall be sufficient authority for the Comptroller to issue his warrant, to be paid out of the appropriations for public printing and stationery.

SEC. 14. That hereafter all accounts due for printing done, or for stationery used, in either house of the Legislature, shall, in addition to the requirements contained in the above section, be approved by the Chairman of the Committee on Public Printing, and the Chairman of the Committee on Contingent Expenses of the house ordering the work to be done, before being presented to the Printing Board; for which account, when thus approved, the Comptroller is authorized to draw his warrant, payable out of the contingent fund.

SEC. 15. That the Governor is hereby authorized to employ a practical printer, whose duty it shall be to examine all accounts for printing done and stationery furnished for the State, and certify to the accounts for the same; *provided*, that he shall not receive more than seventy dollars per month for his services.

SEC. 16. That the Secretary of State shall keep a record of his proceeding, and the proceedings of the Board of Public Printing; *provided*, that a majority of said Board shall be competent to do business; *and provided further*, that in contracting for the printing and stationery necessary for the immediate use of both houses of the Fifteenth Legislature, and for the departments of government, the Secretary of State shall not be required to advertise for proposals according to the manner herein prescribed, but shall give such notice as he shall deem necessary and proper, and contract for such printing and stationery as may be needed, until the full provisions of this act can be complied with.

SEC. 17.   That no member or officer of any department of the government, except translator, shall be in any way interested in said contracts: and all such contracts shall be in writing, and signed by the Board of Public Printing and contractors, and approved in writing by the Governor, Secretary of State, and Comptroller.

SEC. 18.   That "An Act to provide for the public printing by contract," approved March 14, 1874, and "An Act to provide for the proper auditing of the accounts of the Public Printer in certain cases," approved February 10, 1875, and all laws and parts of laws conflicting with the provisions of this Act, be, and the same are hereby repealed.

SEC. 19.   That an imperative public necessity exists for a suspension of the rules and immediate passage of this act; and there being no law in force, under which the necessary printing and stationery can be obtained for the Legislature and other departments of the government, the emergency requires that this Act shall take effect and be in force from and after its passage.

Approved June 27, 1876.

Takes effect from its passage.

CHAPTER XXXIX.—*An Act to authorize the United States Bonds now in the Treasury to the credit of the permanent school fund, to be disposed of, and the proceeds thereof invested in State Bonds; likewise to invest in the same manner the funds now in the Treasury to the credit of said fund, or that may hereafter be received from all sources.*

SECTION 1.   *Be it enacted by the Legislature of the State of Texas,* That the Board of Education (Governor, Comptroller and Secretary of State), are hereby authorized and empowered to dispose of the United States bonds now in the Treasury, or that may hereafter be received, to the credit of the permanent school fund, and invest the proceeds arising therefrom, in either the registered or coupon bonds issued by authority of this State: *provided,* it is the opinion of said Board that such investment will be advantageous to the interest of said school fund; and the funds now in the Treasury to the credit of said permanent school fund, or that may hereafter be received from any source, may in like manner be invested in State bonds.

SEC. 2.   That should said Board of Education esteem it advisable to make the investment authorized by the preceding section, it shall be the duty of said Board to collect from the State Treasury the semiannual interest as it becomes due on the bonds so purchased, and place the same to the credit of the available school fund account.

SEC. 3.   It being to the advantage of the school fund now in the Treasury that the same should be drawing interest, an emergency exists, that this act shall be in force from its passage; therefore, an imperative public necessity for the passage of this act.

Approved June 30, 1876.

Takes effect from its passage.

CHAPTER XL.—*An Act to amend an Act entitled " An Act to ascertain the amount due the teachers of the Public Free Schools of this State, for services rendered as teachers prior to the first day of July, eighteen hundred and seventy-three; and to provide for the payment of the same," approved April 27, 1874.*

SECTION 1. *Be it enacted by the Legislature of the State of Texas,* That Section five of an Act entitled " An Act to ascertain the amount due the teachers of the Public Free Schools of this State, for services rendered prior to the first day of July, 1873, and to provide for the payment of the same," approved April 27, 1874, be, and the same is amended so as to read as follows:

" SEC. 5. That in counties, in which, from any cause, the Treasurer of the School Board, or the County Treasurer, has failed to make the statements required by the fourth section of this Act, or where said statements, if made, are incorrect or defective, the holders of vouchers and claims for pay due teachers of Public Free Schools prior to the first day of July, 1873, may present said claims and vouchers to the County Commissioners' Court of the county in which the services were performed, and establish to the satisfaction of said Commissioners' Court the fact that said claims or voucher is justly due and unpaid; and said Court shall enter upon its minutes an order, stating that said claim is genuine and justly due said claimant, and upon presentation of said voucher or claim, approved or proven as is prescribed in the third section of this Act, accompanied by the order of said Commissioners' Court establishing the same, the Comptroller shall draw his warrant for the amount of said voucher or claim, as is provided in the second section of this Act; and all warrants issued under the provisions of this section shall draw interest at the rate of eight per cent. per annum, from the first day of January, 1875."

SEC. 2. That in view of the fact that there are many teachers who have long been deprived of their just dues by failure of the Treasurers of the School Boards to make their reports, an emergency exists that requires, and it is hereby declared, that this act take effect from and after its passage.

Approved July 6, 1876.

Takes effect ninety days after adjournment.

CHAPTER XLI.—*An Act to fix the times of holding the District Courts of the Eighteenth Judicial District of the State of Texas.*

SECTION 1. *Be it enacted by the Legislature of the State of Texas,* That the District Courts of the Eighteenth Judicial District of the State shall be holden at the times hereinafter specified, to-wit: In Brazoria county, on the third Monday in April and October of each year, and may continue in session three weeks. In Matagorda county, on the third Monday after the third Monday in April and October, and may continue in session two weeks. In Jackson county, on the fifth Monday after the third Monday in April and October, and may continue in session two weeks. In Wharton county, on the seventh Monday after the third Monday in April and October, and may continue in session three weeks.   In Fort Bend county, on the tenth Monday after the third Monday in April and October, and may continue in session three weeks.   In Waller county, on the thirteenth Monday after the third Monday in April and October, and may continue in session until the business is disposed of.

SEC. 2.   All writs and process returnable to any of the District Courts of the Eighteenth Judicial District, shall be returnable after the taking effect of this act, to the terms of said courts as herein defined, and shall be as valid as if returned to the terms of said courts as they existed before the passage of this act.

SEC. 3.   In order to meet the convenience of the people of the Eighteenth Judicial District in effecting the change of terms of courts made by this act, it is necessary, and is so enacted, that this act take effect and be in force on and after the tenth day of August next.

Approved July 6, 1876.

Takes effect from August 10, 1876.

CHAPTER XLII.—*An Act to provide for the payment of the bonds of the State of Texas, that will become due, and that are retirable in the years* 1876 *and* 1877, *and to make adequate provisions for the floating indebtedness of the State, and to supply deficiencies in the revenue by the sale of the bonds of the State, and to make an appropriation to carry into effect the provisions of the same.*

WHEREAS, Portions of the bonded debt of the State of Texas will become due in the years 1876 and 1877, and it is a case of imperative necessity and emergency that the same shall be provided for and paid at maturity, and at the same time that adequate provisions should be made for the floating indebtedness of the State, therefore, four-fifths of each House concurring by yeas and nays in the suspension of the rules requiring this act to be read on three several days therein, and two-thirds of all the members elected to each House concurring by yeas and nays in enacting that this act shall take effect from its passage, all of which is duly entered upon the journals:

SECTION 1.   *Be it enacted by the Legislature of the State of Texas,* That this act shall take effect from and after its passage.

SEC. 2.   That the Governor of the State is hereby authorized to have engraved the bonds of the State of Texas, of the denomination of one thousand dollars each, to the amount of eight hundred thousand dollars ($800,000), and also to have prepared, either in manuscript or from engraved plates, bonds of such denomination as the interest of the State and the parties purchasing may require, to the extent of eight hundred and seventy-five thousand dollars, to be known as registered bonds.

SEC. 3.   That said bonds shall be payable thirty years from the first day of July, A. D. 1876, to bearer, in gold coin of the United States, and shall bear interest at the rate of six per cent. per annum, payable semi-annually in gold coin of the United States, to-wit: on the first day of January and the first day of July of each year, and have coupons attached for each installment of interest which may become due, except the registered bonds herein provided for, which may be prepared without coupons.   The principal and interest of the eight hundred one thousand dollar coupon bonds shall be payable in the city of New York, through such agent or agents as the Governor of the State may select; but no agent shall receive more than one-fourth of one per cent. for paying said bonds or interest under this act; but the principal and interest of the registered bonds shall be payable in the city of Austin, at the office of the State Treasurer.

SEC. 4. That said bonds shall be signed by the Governor and Treasurer of the State of Texas, and countersigned and registered by the Comptroller, with the seal of the State thereto affixed.

SEC. 5. The Comptroller of Public Accounts shall sell the bonds provided for in this act, at such times and places, and in such amounts, as the Governor may direct; *provided*, the same shall not be sold for less than one hundred cents on the dollar, and shall cause the net proceeds arising from such sales to be deposited in the State Treasury.

SEC. 6. And it shall be the duty of the Governor to report to the Legislature the amount of bonds sold, to whom sold, the amount realized therefrom, the name of the agent or agents through whom sold, and the commission, if any, allowed the agent or agents on such sales.

SEC. 7. That the proceeds arising from the sales of bonds sold under the provisions of this act, shall be applied exclusively to the following purposes, using the money first realized to the payment of the debts now due, and so on to the other debts according to the respective dates at which they severally mature and are retirable, excepting that the two hundred and seventy-nine thousand dollars ($279,000), maturing July 1, 1876, are to be first provided for: First, for the redemption and payment of "revenue deficiency (ten per cent.) bonds," issued under act of May 19, 1871, maturing July 1, 1876, two hundred and seventy-nine thousand dollars, ($279,000); second, for the redemption and payment of the balance outstanding of (six per cent.) "bonds for funding State debt," issued under act of November 9, 1866, maturing January 1, 1877, one hundred and twenty-five thousand dollars, ($125,000); third, for the redemption and retiring of the balance of outstanding (ten per cent.) "bonds for funding State warrants," issued under act of May 30, 1873, retirable at the option of the Government at any time three years after the date of issue: *provided*, the Governor deem it advisable to retire the same, four thousand four hundred dollars, ($4,400); fourth, for the redemption and retiring of (ten per cent.) "bonds for funding State warrants," issued under act of May 2, 1874, retirable at the option of the Government at any time after July 1, 1877; *provided*, the Governor deem it advisable to retire the same, four hundred and ninety-nine thousand dollars, ($499,000); fifth, for the payment of "outstanding warrants on general revenue," forty-two thousand seven hundred and twenty-one dollars and twenty-nine cents, ($42,721.29), or as much thereof as may be necessary; sixth, for the payment of outstanding warrants on "school fund" account, and for claims yet to be audited, with interest due thereon, four hundred thousand dollars, ($400,000), or as much thereof as may be necessary; seventh, for the payment of "approved certificates of debt," outstanding, with interest thereon until paid, sixty thousand dollars, ($60,000), or as much thereof as may be necessary; eighth, for the payment of "interest due the Agricultural and Mechanical College fund," to February 1, 1876, forty-five thousand two hundred and eighty dollars, ($45,280); ninth, for the payment of outstanding (ten per cent.) interest Treasury warrants, issued prior to the 28th day of January, 1861, and for eight per cent.

bonds that should have been issued therefor, twenty thousand dollars, ($20,000), or as much thereof as may be necessary; tenth, "to supply casual deficiencies of revenue" for the support of the State Government (if necessary), as provided for by Section 49, Article III, State Constitution, two hundred thousand dollars, ($200,000). Total, one million six hundred and seventy-five thousand four hundred and one dollars and twenty-nine cents, ($1,675,401.29). After the payment of the several classes of indebtedness above enumerated, the balance, if any, shall be used for the retirement of the bonded indebtedness of the State in the same manner as the sinking fund is provided for by section nine of this act.

SEC. 8.   That the Treasurer of the State be and is hereby authorized and required immediately after the payment of the last preceding semi-annual installment of interest, to reserve and set apart out of the first money received in the Treasury, whether from taxes collected for the support of the government, or from a special interest tax, an amount of funds sufficient to pay the next succeeding semi-annual installment of interest, which may become due upon the bonds sold under the provisions of this act; and in the same manner he shall provide for the first semi-annual installment of interest due after the sale of any of the bonds sold under the provisions of this act, and also reserve and set apart from either of the same sources an amount sufficient to create a sinking fund of two per centum per annum for the ultimate redemption of the principal of the bonds so sold.

SEC. 9.   That whenever there is an amount of ten thousand dollars or more in the Treasury of the State to the credit of the sinking fund, it shall be the duty of the Treasurer of the State to give thirty days' notice in some daily newspaper of general circulation, published in the city of New York, and in one published at the Capital of the State, that he will receive sealed proposals for the purchase from the lowest bidder, of such amount of the bonds provided for in this act as the sinking fund in the Treasury shall enable him to purchase. The sealed proposals herein provided for shall be opened by the Treasurer in the presence of the Governor and Comptroller, and the sinking fund may be applied to the redemption of the bonds offered at the lowest rate. The bonds so purchased, if any, shall be burned at once, in the presence of the Governor, Comptroller and Treasurer of the State, who shall together sign a certificate certifying to the destruction of said bonds, in accordance with the requirements of this section, setting forth the numbers, dates and amount of each of said bonds so destroyed; said certificate shall be filed in the office of the Comptroller of Public Accounts.

SEC. 10.   The State of Texas hereby pledges her faith for the payment of the principal and interest of the bonds authorized by this act to be issued. All the provisions of section eight of this act shall forever be irrepealable until the principal and interest of the bonds provided for in this act shall have been fully paid and satisfied.

SEC. 11.   That the Treasurer of the State is hereby required to give notice in a newspaper of general circulation, published in the city of New York, and in a newspaper published at the State Capital, for at least thirty days prior to the maturity and the time fixed for the retiring of such bonds as are by law retirable, and are contemplated to be redeemed and retired by this act, that the same will be redeemed and retired by such agent or agents of the State as the Governor may appoint at the city of New York, for such bonds as are made redeemable there; and for those bonds made redeemable at the State Treasury, or where no place of redemption is specially named, that such bonds will be redeemed at the State Treasury; and all bonds not presented at the time specified in said notices, interest thereon shall cease. The bonds so redeemed and retired shall be destroyed in the same manner as bonds redeemed through the sinking fund, as provided by section nine of this act.

SEC. 12. Should the legal holder of any of the claims against the State for the payment of which this act provides, desire to take the bonds authorized to be issued by this act in payment or exchange for such claims, he may be permitted to do so; *provided*, he will allow the current market value of said bonds, should that be more than par; but in no instance shall said bonds be paid in redemption of any class of debt for whose payment this act provides at less than one hundred cents on the dollar, except herein otherwise provided. When parties holding claims for fractional amounts, so as to be unable to purchase one entire bond or more, such parties shall have the privilege to pay the difference in money, so as to purchase one or more bonds, as the case may be; *provided*, application for such purchase or exchange shall be made to the State Treasurer within sixty days after the passage of this act.

SEC. 13. That the sum of two thousand dollars, or so much of the same as may be necessary, is hereby appropriated out of any money in the Treasury not otherwise appropriated to pay the expenses of engraving and printing the bonds provided for by this act.

Approved July 6, 1876.

Takes effect from its passage.

CHAPTER XLIII.—*An Act to transfer and re-appropriate the unexpended balance remaining on hand of the appropriation to pay Supreme Court Clerks' fees in felony cases, appropriated under act of March 15, 1875, to pay Clerks of the Appellate Court for fees in felony cases.*

SECTION 1. *Be it enacted by the Legislature of the State of Texas,* That the balance remaining on hand of the appropriation under act of March 15, 1875, to pay Supreme Court Clerks' fees in felony cases, be, and the same is hereby transferred to, and re-appropriated to pay Clerk fees of the Appellate Court in felony cases, for the fiscal year ending August 31, 1876.

SEC. 2. That, whereas, it is necessary to pay such fees as they become due, to enable said clerks to pay as they go, an emergency exists for the immediate passage of this act, it shall, therefore, take effect and be in force from and after its passage.

Approved July 8, 1876.

Takes effect from its passage.

CHAPTER XLIV.—*An Act fixing the times for holding the District Courts in the Eighth Judicial District.*

SECTION 1. *Be it enacted by the Legislature of the State of Texas,* That the District Courts of the Eighth Judicial District shall be holden at the times hereinafter specified, to-wit: In the county of Hunt, on the first Mondays in January and July, and may continue in session four weeks; in the county of Delta, on the fourth Mondays after the first Mondays in January and July, and may continue in session two weeks; in the county of Hopkins, on the sixth Mondays after the first Mondays in January and July, and may continue in session four weeks; in the county of Kaufman, on the tenth Mondays after the first Mondays in January and July, and may continue in session four weeks; in the county of Rockwall, on the fourteenth Mondays after the first Mondays in January and July, and may continue in session one week; in the county of Collin, on the fifteenth Mondays after the first Mondays in January and July, and may continue in session six weeks.

SEC. 2.   That all process issued by or from said District Courts is hereby made returnable in conformity with the provisions of this act; and that all laws and parts of laws in conflict with this act, be, and the same are hereby repealed.

SEC. 3.   There being an imperative public necessity for the immediate passage of this law, that the courts of said Judicial District may be held in comformity with the provisions of this act, to meet the demands and conveniencies of the people of said District, that this act take effect and be in force from and after its passage.

Approved July 11, 1876.

Takes effect from its passage.

CHAPTER XLV.—*An Act to amend section one of an act entitled "An Act to authorize the United States Bonds now in the Treasury to the credit of the permanent School Fund, to be disposed of and the proceeds thereof invested in State Bonds; likewise to invest in the same manner the funds now in the Treasury to the credit of said fund, or that may hereafter be received from all sources," passed at the present session of the Legislature.*

SECTION 1.   *Be it enacted by the Legislature of the State of Texas,* That section one af the above recited act be, and the same is hereby amended so as to read as follows: That the Board of Education (Governor, Comptroller and Secretary of State), themselves, or by their duly constituted attorney or attorneys, are hereby authorized and empowered to dispose of the United States bonds now in the Treasury issued to the State of Texas, and belonging to the permanent School Fund, or that may hereafter be received to the credit of the permanent School Fund, and invest the proceeds arising therefrom, in either the registered or coupon bonds issued by authority of this State; *provided,* it is the opinion of said Board that such investment will be advantageous to the interest of said School Fund; and the funds now in the Treasury to the credit of said permanent School Fund or that may hereafter be received from any source, may in like manner be invested in State bonds.

SEC. 2.   It being to the advantage of the School Fund that the same should be invested so as to realize the largest rate of interest, an imperative emergency existing that this act should take effect from its passage, therefore, it is hereby declared that the same shall take effect and be in force from and after its passage.

Approved July 12, 1876.

Takes effect from its passage.

CHAPTER XLVI.—*An Act to fix the salaries of Special Judges and to prescribe rules for paying the same, and to make appropriation therefor.*

SECTION 1. *Be it enacted by the Legislature of the State of Texas,* That Special Judges, commissioned by the Governor of this State in obedience to the requirements of Section eleven, Article five, of the Constitution of 1870, and Section eleven, Article five, of the Constitution of 1876, shall receive the same pay as District Judges for every day they may have been heretofore necessarily occupied in going to and returning from the place where they may be required to hold court, as well as the time they are actually engaged in holding court.

SEC. 2. That the amount to be paid to such Special Judge shall be ascertained by dividing the salary allowed the regular Judge by three hundred and sixty-five, and then multiplying the quotient by the number of days actually served by the Special Judge.

SEC. 3. Upon the presentation of the account of such Special Judge, verified by his own affidavit, and certified by the regular Judge of the District or Clerk of the Court in which the services were performed, to the Comptroller of the State, showing the number of days that said Special Judge was necessarily occupied in going to and returning from the place or places where such special service was performed, and the number of days upon which such Special Judge presided under said appointment, and evidence that he was duly commissioned by the Governor; it shall be the duty of the Comptroller to draw his warrant upon the Treasurer of the State in favor of such Special Judge, for the amount found to be due him under the rules prescribed in this act.

SEC. 4. That warrants drawn by the Comptroller under this act, shall be paid by the Treasurer out of appropriations made for that purpose, and that the sum of ten thousand ($10,000) dollars, or so much thereof, as may be necessary, be, and the same is hereby appropriated out of any money in the Treasury not otherwise appropriated for the payment of the same.

SEC. 5. Whereas, many persons have been appointed special judges, and have performed services as such, and for which services they have received no pay; and, whereas, their claims are now long past due; and, whereas, it is an emergency that their just claims should be promptly paid, therefore, this act take effect and be in force from and after its passage.

Approved July 12, 1876.

Takes effect from its passage.

CHAPTER XLVII.—*An Act to amend an act entitled "An Act to provide for the supplying of lost records in the several counties in this State," approved April 14th, 1874.*

WHEREAS, Great inconvenience now exists in many of the counties in this State on account of the loss and destruction of county records; whereas, said inconvenience is likely to continue for the lack of legal provisions for supplying such lost or destroyed records; and whereas, the present emergency demands that there be provided at as early a day as practicable, all expeditious method of supplying such lost or destroyed records, therefore,

SECTION 1. *Be it enacted by the Legislature of the State of Texas,* That an act entitled "An Act to provide for the supplying of lost records in the several counties in this State," approved April 14th, 1874, shall be and the same is hereby so amended as hereafter to read as follows, to-wit:

"SECTION 1. *Be it enacted by the Legislature of the State of Texas,* That all deeds, bonds, bills of sale, mortgages, deeds of trust, powers of attorney and conveyances of any and every description, which are required or permitted by law to be acknowledged or recorded, and which have been so acknowledged or recorded; and any and every judgment of a court of record in this State, and which record and minutes of court containing such judgment have been or may hereafter be lost, destroyed or carried away, may be supplied by parol proof of the contents thereof—which proof shall be taken in the manner hereinafter provided."

SEC. 2. Any person having any interest in any such deed, instrument in writing, or judgment, the record or entry of which has been or may hereafter be lost, destroyed or carried away, may, in addition to any mode now provided by law for establishing the existence of such record, and the contents thereof, apply to the District Judge of the district in which such county, the records of which have been, or may hereafter be lost, destroyed or carried away, is situated, for a citation to the grantor in such deed, or to the party or parties interested in such instrument of writing, or to the party or parties who were interested adversely to the applicant at the time of the rendition of any such judgment, or who may be now interested, or the heirs and legal representatives of such parties, to appear at a term of the District Court to be designated in said citation, and contest the right of the applicant to have any such deed, instrument in writing, or judgment substituted and recorded; and service shall be, as now provided, for process from the District Court; and on hearing said application, if the court shall be satisfied of the existence of such deed, instrument in writing, record or judgment, and of the loss, destruction, or carrying away of the same, as alleged by the applicant, and the contents thereof, an order shall be entered on the minutes of the District Court to that effect, which order shall contain a description of the lost deed, instrument in writing, judgment or record, and the contents thereof, and a certified copy of such order may be recorded in the records of the county, and shall stand in the place of and have the same force and effect as the original of said lost deed, instrument in writing, judgment or record; and when duly recorded, may be used in evidence in any of the courts of this State with like effect as the original thereof.

SEC. 3. All certified copies from the records of such county, the record of which has been or may hereafter be lost, destroyed, or carried away, and all certified copies from the records of the county or counties from which said county was created, may be recorded in such county; *provided,* the loss of the original shall first be established.

SEC. 4. That when any of the original papers mentioned in section one of this act may have been saved or preserved from loss, the record of said originals having been lost, destroyed, or carried away, the same may be recorded again, and this last registration shall have force and effect from the date of filing for original registration; *provided,* said originals are recorded within three years next after such loss, destruction, or removal of the records; and certified copies from any record authorized by the provisions of this act to be made, may be received in evidence in all the courts of this State, in the same manner and with like effect as certified copies of the original record; *provided,* that when any judgment is substituted under and by virtue of this act, the time elapsing between the destruction and substitution of said judgment shall not affect any proceeding to a higher court, on appeal or writ of error; and said judgments, when so substituted, shall carry all the rights thereunder in every respect as the originals, especially preserving the liens from the date of the originals, and giving the parties the right to issue executions under the substituted judgments, as under the originals.

Sec. 5. Where any cause has been tried in any of the district courts of this State, and before the time has expired for taking the same to the Supreme Court by appeal or writ of error, as prescribed by law, and the principal records and papers in said cause have been destroyed by fire, or otherwise, either party may proceed to substitute a substantial record of said cause, which record shall contain a substantial statement of the pleadings, the exceptions to the rulings of the court, charge of the court, verdict of the jury, judgment of the court, and statement of facts, which record shall be agreed to by the parties or their attorneys, or in case the parties, or their attorneys, cannot agree, then the judge, before whom said cause was tried, shall make out such record, and certify that the same is a substantial record of the cause as tried before him, whereupon either party shall have the right to have said cause reviewed and determined by the Supreme Court, upon such substantial record, in the same manner as if the original record and papers had not been destroyed.

Sec. 6. In any case where judgment has been rendered in the District Court for the defendant, and notice has been given, or petition of error has been filed, or where suit has been brought, and before final judgment has been rendered, and the papers and records have been destroyed by fire or otherwise, without fault of plaintiff, the plaintiff shall have the right to bring a new suit, in which all the rights and equities of either party shall be determined *de novo,* and no law of limitation shall bar any of the rights and equities of either party that did not apply to the original suit; *provided,* that all suits in cases where the destruction occurred prior to the passage of this act, shall be brought within twelve months after the passage of this act, and in all other cases, the party shall file his suit within twelve months after the destruction of the papers; and in all cases of substitution of the record on appeal or writ of error, the substituted record shall be filed in the court that tried the cause within twelve months after the passage of this act, if said destruction occurred before the passage of this act; and in all other cases, within twelve months after the destruction of the papers and records.

Sec. 7. Whereas, an imperative public necessity exists for the immediate passage of this act, and an emergency that it go into effect at once, therefore, this act shall be in force from and after its passage.

Sec. 8. All laws and parts of laws in conflict with this act, be, and the same are hereby repealed.

Approved July 13, 1876.

Takes effect from its passage.

CHAPTER XLVIII.—*An Act to provide for holding a term of the District Court of Wharton county in August, 1876, for the trial of criminal causes.*

Section 1. *Be it enacted by the Legislature of the State of Texas,* That there shall be held a term of the District Court within and for the county of Wharton, for the trial of criminal causes, to commence on the third Monday in August, A. D. 1876, and may continue in session two weeks, unless business is sooner disposed of.

SEC. 2.   As an emergency exists, because of the number of prisoners charged with felonies, now in the county jail of said county awaiting trial, at a great cost and expense thereof to said county, which is largely in debt; therefore, this act shall take effect and be in force from and after its passage.

Approved July 14, 1876.

Takes effect from its passage.

CHAPTER XLIX.—*An Act prescribing the times of holding the District Courts in the Twenty-first Judicial District.*

SECTION 1.   *Be it enacted by the Legislature of the State of Texas,* That the District Courts of the Twenty-first Judicial District shall be holden as follows: In the county of Montgomery on the first Monday in February and September, and may continue in session four weeks.   In the county of Harris on the last Monday in March and October, and may continue in session until the business is disposed of.

Approved July 14, 1876.

Takes effect ninety days after adjournment.

CHAPTER L.—*An Act to provide for the transfer of business, civil and criminal, pending in the District Courts over which jurisdiction is given by the Constitution to the Justices' Courts, to the several Justices' Courts of this State.*

SECTION 1.   *Be it enacted by the Legislature of the State of Texas,* That all causes, civil and criminal, now pending in the District Courts of this State, over which jurisdiction is given by the Constitution to courts of Justices of the Peace, be transferred to the Justices' Courts of the respective counties in the manner hereinafter prescribed.

SEC. 2.   That immediately after this act shall take effect, the several District Courts of this State, or the judges thereof, in vacation, if any of such courts be not in session, shall, by an order entered of record in the minutes of such courts in each case, transfer all cases mentioned in the first section of this act pending in said courts to the Justice's Court of the precinct in which the county seats of the respective counties are situated; and the clerks of the several District Courts shall immediately make out a certified copy of the orders of the District Court in each of said causes, and file the same, together with all the original papers of the causes, and a certificate of the costs which have accrued, with the Justice to whose court the causes are transferred, as herein provided; and the several courts to which such causes are transferred shall have power to issue all process necessary to carry out the jurisdiction of such courts.

SEC. 3.   Should there be two Justices' Courts in any one of the precincts above mentioned, said cases shall be equally divided between the justices of such precinct, unless the parties or their attorneys shall otherwise agree ; said agreement to be in writing, signed by the parties thereto, and filed.

SEC. 4. All cases which have been taken up by appeal from the Courts of Justices of the Peace, whose jurisdiction were increased by special law, when the amount in controversy was more than five hundred dollars ($500) or less than twenty dollars ($20) shall remain for trial in the District Court.

SEC. 5. Whereas, a great public necessity exists for the immediate transfer of such business, it is hereby declared to be a case of emergency, and that this act take effect and be in force from and after its passage.

Approved July 19, 1876.

Takes effect from its passage.

CHAPTER LI.—*An Act to create the Twenty-Seventh Judicial District of the State of Texas.*

SECTION 1. *Be it enacted by the Legislature of the State of Texas,* That the counties of Collin and Grayson be and they are hereby created a Judicial District, to be designated and known as the Twenty-Seventh Judicial District.

SEC. 2. It shall be the duty of the Governor within ten days after the adjournment of the present session of the Legislature to issue his proclamation ordering the election of a Judge for said Twenty-Seventh Judicial District, who shall hold his office until the next general election for District Judges.

SEC. 3. That the District Court of said Twenty-Seventh District shall have the same jurisdiction and powers as is conferred by law upon the District Courts of this State.

SEC. 4. The District Courts of the Twenty-Seventh Judicial District shall be held at the times hereinafter specified, to-wit: In the county of Collin on the first Mondays in January and June, and may continue in session eight weeks. In the county of Grayson on the second Mondays in March and September, and may continue in session until the business is disposed of.

Approved July 19, 1876.

Takes effect ninety days after adjournment.

CHAPTER LII.—*An Act to provide for the change of venue in certain cases.*

SECTION 1. *Be it enacted by the Legislature of the State of Texas,* That all causes pending in the District Courts of this State wherein a change of venue has been taken as provided by law, by reason of the disqualification of the Judge to try and determine said causes, and said disqualification no longer exists, shall be removed to the county where the suit was originally instituted, upon the sworn application of the plaintiff or defendant, made to the District Judge of the county in which said causes are pending ; five day's notice of the application being given to the opposite party.

SEC. 2. There being an existing imperative necessity and emergency for the immediate passage of this bill, that the cases herein provided for may be at once transferred to the courts having jurisdiction of the same, that this act take effect and be in force from and after its passage.

Approved July 19, 1876.

Takes effect from its passage.

4 GL.

CHAPTER LIII.—*An Act to provide for refunding money paid into the State Treasury in certain cases.*

WHEREAS, Under the provisions of an act to provide for the sale of the alternate sections of lands, as surveyed by railroad companies and set apart for the benefit of the common school fund, approved April 24th, 1874, many citizens of the State of Texas have settled upon lands which they erroneously supposed to be portions of said alternate sections of land set apart for common school purposes; and, whereas, said citizens have by reasons of said error paid into the State Treasury a part of the purchase money for said lands, when in truth, and in fact, said lands so paid on by them were not a part of the lands set apart for said common school fund; and, whereas, there exists no legal remedy for these parties who have so paid, as aforesaid, and they having received no consideration for said payment so made; therefore,

SECTION 1. *Be it enacted by the Legislature of the State of Texas,* That any person or persons who may have heretofore purchased any land of the State supposed to have been set apart for the benefit of the school fund, and who cannot obtain a patent or title to the same, because the land designated by said purchaser, and for which the settler has paid the money into the Treasury, was not a part of the school fund of the State, shall have the right to recover the money so paid in the following manner: Said party, or his heirs or assigns, shall present to the Comptroller of Public Accounts the certificate given him by the County Surveyor in pursuance of the requirements of Section 7, of "An Act to provide for the sale of the alternate sections of lands surveyed by railroad companies, and set apart for the benefit of the common school fund," approved April 24th, 1874, and a certificate from the Commissioner of the General Land Office, stating that the land designated in said surveyor's certificate is not and was not at the time of the purchase a part of the said school fund; and also the receipt of the Treasurer showing the amount paid on said lands, and satisfactory evidence of the identity of the party in whose favor the claim is made; whereupon the Comptroller shall issue his warrant upon the State Treasury for the amount of money paid in by the purchaser.

SEC. 2. That since a majority of the persons above named are poor and unable to do without the use of their money thus erroneously paid into the State Treasury, there exists a sufficient emergency that this act take effect and be in force from and after its passage.

Approved July 19, 1876.

Takes effect from its passage.

CHAPTER LIV.—*An Act to authorize the refunding of moneys paid into the General Land Office, under the provisions of "An Act to authorize the location, sale and settlement of the Mississippi and Pacific Railroad reserve," passed August 26, 1856; and the provisions of a supplemental act, entitled "An Act supplemental to an Act to authorize the location, sale and settlement of the Mississippi and Pacific Railroad reserve," approved November 28, 1857, in all cases wherein the State failed to patent the lands for which such moneys were paid.*

SECTION 1. *Be it enacted by the Legislature of the State of Texas,* That all moneys paid into the General Land Office under the provisions of the supplemental act above recited, approved November 28, 1857, for lands in the Mississippi and Pacific Railroad reserve, to which the State failed to issue patent to the parties making such payment, shall be refunded to such party or parties, upon application, as hereinafter provided.

SEC. 2. It shall be the duty of the Commissioner of the General Land Office, upon application to him, made by any party or parties claiming to have made payments under the said supplemental act of November 28, 1857, and failed to receive patents to the land for which such payment was made, to investigate such claim, and when it shall appear that such claim is just, and that the money paid into the office of Commissioner of the General Land Office has not been refunded to the party or parties making such payment, and that the State of Texas is therefore justly indebted to the party or parties making such payments, he, the Commissioner of the General Land Office, shall issue to the party making application, or his legal representatives, an official certificate, showing the amount of money so paid and date of payment.

SEC. 3. Upon presentation to the Comptroller of Public Accounts of such certificate from the Commissioner of the General Land Office, properly authenticated, it shall be his duty to draw his warrant upon the State Treasurer, in favor of the party holding such certificate, for the whole amount originally paid into the General Land Office, as shown by the certificate of the Commissioner thereof, with interest thereon at the rate of eight per cent. per annum from the date of the original payment into the Land Office to the date of the said warrant on the State Treasurer. The sum of two hundred dollars, or so much thereof as may be required, is hereby appropriated out of any money in the Treasury not otherwise appropriated, to carry out the provisions of this act.

SEC. 4. In order that immediate relief may be granted under the provisions of this act in cases of extreme destitution and want, this act shall take effect from and after its passage.

Approved July 19, 1876.

Takes effect from its passage.

CHAPTER LV.—*An Act to organize Commissioners' Courts, and to define their jurisdiction and duties, and provide for vacancies therein.*

SECTION 1. *Be it enacted by the Legislature of the State of Texas,* That there shall be organized in each county in this State an inferior court, to be styled " The Commissioners' Court," which shall be composed of the County Judge and four County Commissioners.

SEC. 2. The County Judge shall be the presiding officer of said court, and shall be elected at each general election held for State and county officers, and shall hold his office for two years, or until his successor shall be appointed or elected and qualified.

SEC. 3. In each Commissioner's precinct there shall be elected at each general election, one County Commissioner, who shall hold his office for two years, or until his successor is qualified.

SEC. 4. The said courts shall have power, and it shall be their duty: 1st. To lay off their respective counties into precincts, not less than four nor more than eight, for the election of Justices of the Peace and Constables, and shall fix the times and places of holding the various Justices' Courts in their counties, and to establish places in such precincts where elections shall be held. 2nd. To establish public ferries whenever the public interest may require. 3rd. To lay out and establish, change and discontinue public roads and highways. 4th. To build bridges. 5th. To apportion hands and appoint road overseers. 6th. To exercise general control and superintend over all roads, ferries, highways and bridges in their counties. 7th. To provide court-houses, jails and all necessary public buildings. 8th. To allow and settle all county accounts and direct their payment. 9th. To provide for the support of paupers, and such idiots and lunatics as cannot be admitted into the Lunatic Asylum, residents of their county, who are unable to support themselves. 10th. To provide for the burial of paupers. 11th. And said courts shall have and exercise such other powers and jurisdiction as is now or may be hereafter prescribed by the Constitution and laws of this State.

SEC. 5.   The said courts shall have power to levy and collect a tax for county purposes, upon all subjects of taxation in their respective counties on which a tax may be levied by the State, but shall not levy more than one-half of the State tax in their respective counties for any one year for county purposes, except for the payment of debts already incurred, and for the erection and repair of public buildings, under such limitations and with such restrictions as may be prescribed by law and the Constitution of this State ; *provided*, that no tax levied for the purpose of paying debts incurred prior to the eighteenth day of April, A. D. 1876, shall exceed two and a half mills on the dollar ; and no tax levied for the erection of public buildings shall exceed two and a half mills on the dollar for any one year.

SEC. 6.   The said courts shall examine and adjust the accounts and books of the County Treasurer, and shall, quarterly, make up and cause a detailed statement of the receipts, expenditures and debts of their respective counties to be posted up in some conspicuous place in the office of the County Clerk ; *provided*, that said court shall, at the end of each year, make out a statement for the year of the receipts, expenditures and debts of their respective counties, and cause the same to be published in some newspaper printed in the county, if there be one; and if not, then to be posted in said Clerk's office as aforesaid, and at three other public places in the county.

SEC. 7.   Each Commissioners' Court of this State shall have a seal, whereon shall be engraved a star with five points, the words " Commissioners' Court, ——— county, Texas," (the blank to be filled with the name of the county), which seal shall be kept in the County Clerk's office, and shall be used in the authentication of all official acts of said court, or of the Clerk of said court, or of the presiding officer, in all cases where a seal may be necessary for the authentication of any of said acts.

SEC. 8.   The several County Clerks of the respective counties of this State shall be *ex-officio* Clerks of the several Commissioners' Courts ; and it shall be their duty to attend upon each term of the said courts ; to preserve and keep in their possession all books, papers, records and effects belonging to said courts ; to issue all notices, writs and process necessary for the proper execution of the powers and duties imposed upon such courts ; and shall perform all such duties as may be prescribed by law ; *provided*, that the duties herein provided for shall be performed by the District Clerks in those counties where no County Clerks have been elected, or where, by law, a single Clerk performs the duties of both District and County Clerk.

SEC. 9.   Each County Commissioners' Court shall have full power and authority to issue all such notices, citations, writs and process as may be necessary for the proper execution of the powers and duties imposed upon such courts, and to enforce its jurisdiction; and all notices, citations, writs and process issued by said courts shall be dated and signed by the Clerk, and when not otherwise directed by law, shall be executed at least five days before the return day thereof, which shall be specified in the same; *provided, however*, that subpœnas for witnesses, whenever necessary, may be executed and returned forthwith; and all such notices, citations and writs, other than subpœnas for witnesses, shall have the seal of such court impressed thereon, and may be directed to any lawful officer of the State, whose duty it shall be to execute and return the same.

SEC. 10. The Commissioners' Court shall have like power to punish contempts as the District and County Courts have, or may have, by law; *provided*, that said punishment shall be by fine or imprisonment, and in no case by fine exceeding twenty-five dollars, or by imprisonment beyond twenty-four hours; and in case of fine, the party to be held in custody until said fine be paid.

SEC. 11. The Commissioners' Court shall cause to be procured and kept in the Clerk's office suitable books, in which shall be recorded the proceedings of each term of the Court, which record shall be read over and signed by the County Judge, or the member of the Court presiding, at the end of each term, and attested by the Clerk. The Clerks shall also record all the proceedings of said Courts authorized to take place in the vacation between the terms; and such records so made in vacation shall be read over and signed on the first day of the proper court next after such proceeding took place.

SEC. 12. Any three members of the Commissioners' Court, including the County Judge, shall constitute a quorum; *provided, however*, that no county tax shall be levied unless at some one of the regular terms, and when a full court is present

SEC. 13. The regular terms of the Commissioners' Courts shall commence and be held at the court-house of their respective counties of this State, on the second Monday in February, May, August and November in every year, and may continue in session one week. Special terms of said courts may be called by the County Judge, or any three of the Commissioners, and may continue in session until the business is disposed of; *provided*, that at the called session of said courts the said Commissioners shall not receive pay for more than four days' service; *and provided*, the members of said Commissioners' Courts shall not receive pay for more than one called session for any one month.

SEC. 14. The County Judges and County Commissioners shall each receive the sum of three dollars per day for every day that they may be necessarily engaged in attendance on any regular term of said court, and the same amount for any special term, except as prescribed in the preceding section, to be paid out of the county treasury, upon the order of said court.

SEC. 15. All books, records, papers and effects belonging to the State Police Courts of the different counties of this State shall be transferred to the Commissioners' Courts established by this act; and the said Commissioners' Courts shall have and exercise all the powers conferred by law on County Courts as heretofore existing, which are not herein enumerated, and which are not in conflict with the provisions of this act.

SEC. 16. Neither the County Judges nor any of the Commissioners shall enter upon the duties of their offices until they shall have first taken the oath of office prescribed by the Constitution, and shall also take an oath that they will not be directly or indirectly interested in any contract with a claim against the county in which they reside, except such warrants as may issue to them as fees of office, before some officer authorized to administer oaths; which oaths, together with the certificate of the officer who administered the same, shall be filed and recorded in the County Clerk's office, in a book to be provided for that purpose.

SEC. 17.　In all cases where by law it shall be the duty of the Commissioners' Court to approve the bond of any of the officers of their several counties, it shall be their duty, whenever they shall become satisfied that said bonds, from any cause, are insufficient, to require new bonds or additional security to be given, as the case may require; and said court shall cause the officer whose bond is complained of to be cited to appear at a term of their court, not less than five days after service of said citation; and if any citizen shall be dissatisfied with the action of the Court approving the bond of any officer, or if any citizen or officer shall be dissatisfied with the action of the Court in the matter of requiring a new bond or additional security, as herein provided, an appeal may be made from the decision of said Commissioners' Court to the District Judge of the county, whose decision shall be final; and when said appeal is taken by a citizen, written notice shall be served upon the officer interested within ten days after the order of the court on said bond.

SEC. 18.　In cases of vacancy, other than County Judge, in any of said Commissioners' Courts, from any cause, it shall be the duty of the District Judge in which such county is situated, upon satifactory information of such vacancy, to appoint some suitable person living in the precinct where such vacancy occurs, to serve as Commissioner for said precinct until the next general election.

SEC. 19.　As public policy demands immediate organization of Commissioners' Courts in this State, and as these courts have now no rules of law defining their duties and powers; therefore, an imperative public necessity exists for the immediate passage of this act, and the same shall take effect and be in force from and after its passage.

SEC. 20.　That whenever a vacancy occurs in any Justice's precinct for Justice of the Peace or Constable, or when it becomes necessary to create a new precinct, in either case it shall be the duty of the County Commissioners' Court to fill the same by appointment until the next general election.

SEC. 21.　In case there is a regular established public hospital in the county, it shall be the duty of the County Commissioners to provide for the indigent sick in their county by sending such sick persons to a hospital; and when more than one public hospital exists in the county, indigent patients shall have the right to enter any such institution which such indigent patient may select.

SEC. 22.　That all laws and parts of laws in conflict with this act be and the same are hereby repealed.

Approved July 22, 1876.

Takes effect from its passage.

CHAPTER LVI.—*An Act to suppress lawlessness and crime in certain parts of the State, and to make an appropriation therefor.*

WHEREAS, In several counties in the Western part of the State the people are being depredated on, in person and property, by bands of criminal and lawless men too strong to be suppressed by the civil authorities unaided, and by bandits and robbers from Mexico; therefore, for the purpose of maintaining law and order, and giving security to that section against foreign invasion and domestic disturbance, and, for that purpose, to aid the civil authorities:

SECTION 1. *Be it enacted by the Legislature of the State of Texas*, That the Governor is hereby authorized and required to immediately organize a company of fifty men, rank and file, to-wit: Forty-two privates, four sergeants, and four corporals; and, in addition thereto, there shall be one captain, one first lieutenant, and one second lieutenant; and, in the aggregate, said company shall consist of fifty-three men, non-commissioned officers, and privates.

SEC. 2. That said company shall be mustered into the service of the State of Texas for the period of six calendar months, or longer should the Governor deem it necessary, in such manner as the Adjutant General may designate. Each officer, non-commissioned officer, and private thereof, shall furnish his own horse, saddle, bridle, rope, clothing, etc., for the entire term of service, and replace any or all of said articles, should it become necessary so to do.

SEC 3. That the State of Texas shall furnish said company with arms, ammunition, camp and garrison equipage, and rations of subsistence for the men, and forage for the horses, and with transportation necessary to move said supplies. The arms shall be issued and charged to the men, and, in case any of said arms shall be lost through neglect or by disobedience of orders, the value thereof shall be charged upon the rolls as a stoppage against the party losing the same; but, in no case, shall arms lost in the discharge of duty be so charged.

SEC. 4. The members of said company shall be allowed the following pay, to-wit: The captain, one hundred and sixty-six dollars per month; the first lieutenant, one hundred and thirty-three dollars per month; the second lieutenant, one hundred and twenty-five dollars per month; the sergeants, fifty dollars each per month; the corporals, forty dollars each per month; and the privates, forty dollars each per month. The payments shall be made at such times and in such manner as the Adjutant General of the State may prescribe.

SEC. 5. That said company shall be governed by the rules and regulations of the army of the United States and the articles of war, as far as the same may be applicable, and by such orders, rules and regulations as may be prescribed, from time to time, by the Governor and the Adjutant General of this State.

SEC. 6. That the officers, non-commissioned officers, and privates of said company shall be clothed with the powers of peace officers, and shall aid the civil authorities in the execution of the laws. They shall have authority to make arrests, and, in such cases, they shall be governed by laws regulating and defining the powers and the duties of Sheriffs when in discharge of similar duties. They shall, before entering upon the discharge of these duties, take an oath before some authority legally authorized to administer the same, that each of them will faithfully perform his duties in accordance with law. In order to arrest and bring to justice men who have banded together for the purpose of committing robbery or other felonies, and to prevent the execution of the laws, the officers, non-commissioned officers, and privates of said company, may accept the services of such citizens as shall volunteer to aid them; but, while so engaged, such citizens shall not receive pay from the State for their services.

SEC. 7.   When said company, or any member or members thereof, shall arrest any person or persons charged with the commission of a criminal offense or offenses, they shall convey said person or persons to the county or counties where he or they stand charged with the commission of an offense, and shall deliver him or them to the proper officer, taking his receipt therefor; and all necessary expenses thus incurred shall be paid by the State.

SEC. 8.   That the sum of forty thousand dollars, or so much thereof as may be necessary, be, and the same is herey appropriated, out of any moneys in the Treasury not otherwise appropriated, to carry out the objects of this act.

SEC. 9.   That the fact of the existence of bands of lawless men in counties of this State, of their having prevented the execution of the laws, and placed the good people in various counties in continual fear of the commission of outrages upon their persons and property, constitutes a public necessity and emergency that this act take effect, and it is hereby declared that the same go into effect and be in force from and after its passage.

Approved July 22, 1876.

Takes effect from its passage.

CHAPTER LVII.—*An Act supplementary to an Act entitled "An Act making an appropriation of forty thousand dollars to complete and finish the State Agricultural and Mechanical College," approved June 24, 1876.*

SECTION 1.   *Be it enacted by the Legislature of the State of Texas,* That the amount of forty thousand dollars appropriated by the above named act, to which this is a supplement, be and the same is hereby placed subject to the control of the Board of Directors of the Agricultural and Mechanical College of Texas; and the Comptroller is hereby authorized to draw his warrant or warrants on the Treasurer against said appropriation, on the order of the Board, signed by the presiding officer thereof.

SEC. 2.   Whereas, the buildings of the Agricultural and Mechanical College are in an unfinished condition, and it being necessary to have said buildings completed by the first of October next, therefore an emergency exists that this act shall take effect from and after its passage, and the same is hereby declared to take effect from and after its passage.

Approved July 28, 1876.

Takes effect from its passage.

CHAPTER LVIII.—*An Act to provide for settlements with the Comptroller of Public Accounts, by Sheriffs and other persons entrusted with the collection of taxes.*

SECTION 1.   *Be it enacted by the Legislature of the State of Texas,* That, whenever any Sheriff or other person entrusted with the collection of State and county taxes in any county in the State has had, prior to the passage of this act, the tax receipts and stubs destroyed by an overflow, he shall file with the Comptroller of Public Accounts his own affidavit stating that he has paid to the Comptroller, and to the County Treasurer of said county, all the money which he has collected for the State and county respectively, after deducting his legal commission for said collection; that all the tax receipts and stubs entrusted to him, and all other receipts, papers, books &c., connected therewith have been destroyed by overflow, giving the time and place, when and where said overflow occurred; and that the destruction of said receipts, stubs, papers, books, &c., was not occasioned by his neglect, procurement or consent, but was wholly accidental and could not have been prevented by any act on his part; and said Sheriff or other person entrusted as aforesaid with the collection of taxes, shall also file with the Comptroller the affidavits of two credible citizens of the county in which said destruction took place, setting forth the time and place, when and where said overflow occurred, and that they verily believe that said tax receipts and stubs were destroyed by said overflow, giving the reasons upon which they base their belief.

SEC. 2. That the Comptroller of Public Accounts, upon the filing in his office of the affidavits provided for in the foregoing section, and of the certificate of the Treasurer of said county, stating that the books of said Treasurer show that said Sheriff or other person entrusted as aforesaid with the collection of taxes, has paid to the County Treasurer of said county the amount which he claims to have paid said county, is authorized and hereby required to deliver to such Sheriff or other person entrusted with the collection of taxes, a full and complete release for the uncollected balance of State and county taxes the receipts and stubs for which were destroyed by said overflow.

Approved July 28, 1876.

Takes effect ninety days after adjournment.

CHAPTER LIX.—*An Act to provide for the publication of certain decisions of the Court of Appeals.*

SECTION 1. *Be it enacted by the Legislature of the State of Texas,* That the Court of Appeals be and is hereby authorized and required to appoint one or more Reporters of its decisions in criminal cases, and of such other of its decisions as may be required by law to be published. Such Reporters shall be subject to removal by said court, for any inefficiency or neglect of duty.

SEC. 2. It shall be the duty of the Reporter to prepare for publication, under the direction of said court, the said decisions thereof, and to cause the same to be printed and published with promptness, as fast as there shall be a sufficient number to form a volume; and to deliver to the Secretary of State, for the use of the State, four hundred copies of each volume of said reports.

SEC. 3. Each volume shall contain an average number of pages of the volumes of Texas Reports heretofore published, and each page shall contain the number of lines, and each line the same number of "ems" as are contained in each page of Moore and Walker's Reports, heretofore published. They shall be styled the Court of Appeals Reports, and shall be so styled on the title page and back thereof, and the numbers of the volumes shall be continued on consecutively. The name of the Reporter may be printed on the back, as on the volumes published by Moore and Walker.

Sec. 4. In payment for the four hundred copies of each volume, delivered as aforesaid, the said Reporter shall be entitled to receive the following compensation, viz: the sum of three dollars ($3.00) per page for as many pages as shall be contained in one copy of each volume so delivered; *provided*, that if the Reporter charge the profession over five dollars ($5.00) per volume, he shall be removed from office by the said court.

Sec. 5. As soon as the opinions are recorded, the originals, together with the records and papers in each case to be reported, shall be delivered to the Reporter by the Clerks of said court, who shall take the Reporter's receipt for the same; but the Reporter shall return to said Clerks the said opinions, records and papers, when he shall have finished using them.

Sec. 6. When the Reporter shall have delivered to the Secretary of State the copies of a volume of said reports, as required by this act, the Comptroller of Public Accounts shall draw his warrant on the State Treasurer for the amount of compensation due to such Reporter, based upon the certificate of the Secretary of State that the Reporter has delivered to him four hundred copies of ——— volumes of such reports, containing ——— pages, printed, published and bound, in accordance with the provisions of this act.

Sec. 7. That this act take effect from [and] after ninety days after the adjournment of this session of the Legislature.

Approved July 28, 1876.

Takes effect ninety days after adjournment.

CHAPTER LX.—*An Act to provide for revising, digesting and publishing the laws, civil and criminal, of the State of Texas.*

Section 1. *Be it enacted by the Legislature of the State of Texas,* That the Governor shall by, and with the advice and consent of the Senate, if in session, appoint a commission of five persons learned in the law, to make a complete revision and digest of the laws of the State of Texas, and embody the same in a bill, which shall be by the commission reported to the Governor, and by him laid before the next session of the Legislature, and said commission shall revise all the general statutes of the State in force, up to the time they shall make their report, and report to the Legislature which of said statutes in their opinion ought, and which ought not to remain in force, and shall suggest such omissions and contradictions as they shall find in said statutes, and the mode in which they can be reconciled, supplied or amended; and they shall arrange under appropriate chapters and sections all the different acts and parts of acts relating to the same subject matter which they shall deem ought to be continued or adopted, with such marginal and foot notes and explanations as they may deem essential to a clear understanding of the same; and shall execute and complete the revision in all respects in such a manner as in their opinion will render the general statutes most concise, plain and intelligible; and shall embody the result of their labors in two bills, one containing the entire body of civil statutes, and the other the entire body of the statutes relating to criminal law, both properly indexed.

Sec. 2. And it shall be the duty of the Governor, upon the receipt of said reports so made by said commission, to cause five hundred copies of the same to be printed at the expense of the State, in the same manner and under the same rules and regulations as are prescribed by law for other public printing, which said copies shall be filed, when printed, in the office of the Secretary of State for the use of the next Legislature.

SEC. 3. The commissioners herein provided for shall receive as compensation the same salary as District Judges, for the time they are necessarily engaged in the performance of their work, and the certificate of the Governor shall authorize the Comptroller, at stated times, to draw his warrant on the Treasurer for their payment.

SEC. 4. That the speedy revision and digesting of the statutes of the State being an imperative public necessity, and required by the State Constitution, and an emergency existing because of glaring defects in our laws, therefore this act shall take effect and be in force from and after its passage.

Approved July 28, 1876.

Takes effect from its passage.

CHAPTER LXI.—*An Act to provide for the detection and conviction of all forgers of land titles.*

SECTION 1. *Be it enacted by the Legislature of the State of Texas,* That every person who falsely makes, alters, forges or counterfeits, or causes or procures to be falsely made, altered, forged or counterfeited, or in any way aids, assists, advises or encourages, the false making, altering, forging or counterfeiting, any certificate, field notes, returns, survey, map, plat, report, order, decree, record, patent, deed, power of attorney, transfer, assignment, release, conveyance or title paper, or acknowledgment, or proof for record, or certificate of record, belonging or pertaining to any instrument or paper, or any seal, official or private, stamp, scrawl, mark, date, signature, or any paper, or any evidence of any right, title or claim of any character, or any instrument in writing, document, paper, memorandum, or file of any character whatever, in relation to or affecting lands, or any interest in lands, in this State, with the intent to make money or other valuable thing thereby, or with the intent to set up a claim or title, or aid or assist any one else in setting up a claim or title to lands, or any interest in lands, or to prosecute or defend a suit, or aid or assist any one else in prosecuting or defending a suit with respect to lands, or to cast a cloud upon the title, or in any way injure, obtain the advantage of, or prejudice the rights or interests of the true owners of lands, or with any fraudulent intent whatever, shall be deemed guilty of forgery, and be punishable by imprisonment in the State Penitentiary, at hard labor, not less than two, nor more than ten years.

SEC. 2. Every person who knowingly utters, publishes, passes, or uses, or who in any way aids, assists in or advises the uttering, publishing, passing, or using, as true and genuine, any false, forged, altered, or counterfeited certificate, field notes, returns, survey, map, plat, report, order, decree, record, patent, deed, power of attorney, transfer, assignment, release, conveyance, title papers, acknowledgment or proof for record, or certificate of record, belonging or pertaining to any instrument, or paper, or any evidence of any right, title or claim of any character whatever, or any instrument in writing, document, paper, memorandum, or file, or any official or private seal, or any scrawl, mark, date, or signature, in any way relating to, or having any connection with land, or any interest in land in this State, with the intent mentioned in the preceding section, or with any other fraudulent intent whatever, shall be deemed guilty, and be punishable in like manner as provided in the preceding section. And the filing, or causing or directing to be filed, or causing or directing to be recorded in the General Land Office of the State, or in any office of record, or in any court in the State, or the sending through the mail, or by express, or in any other way for the purpose of filing, or record of any such false, altered, forged, or counterfeited matter, documents, conveyances, papers or things, knowing the same to be false, altered, forged, or counterfeited, shall be an uttering, publishing and using, within the meaning of this section.

SEC. 3. Upon indictment under the preceding sections, to warrant a conviction, it shall only be necessary to prove that the person charged took any one step, or did any one act or thing in the commission of the offense, if from such step, act or thing, any of the intentions hereinbefore mentioned, or any other fraudulent intention may be reasonably inferred; nor shall it be any defense to a prosecution, under this act, that the matter, act, deed, instrument or thing, was in law, either as to substance or form, void, or that the same was not in fact used for the purpose for which it was made, or designed; and it shall only be necessary, in any indictment under this act to state with reasonable certainty the act constituting the offense, and charge in connection therewith, in general terms, the intention to defraud, without naming the person or persons it was intended to defraud, and on trial of such indictment, it shall be sufficient, and shall not be deemed a variance if there appear to be an intent to defraud the United States, or any State, Territory, county, city, town, or village, or any body corporate, or any public officer in his official capacity, or any copartnership or member thereof, or any particular person.

SEC. 4. If any person authorized by law to take the proof or acknowledgment of any instrument, document or paper whatever, affecting or relating to the title to lands in this State, wilfully and falsely certify that such proof or acknowledgment was duly made, or if any person fraudulently affixes a fictitious or pretended signature, purporting to be that of an officer or any other person, though such person never was an officer, or never existed, he shall be deemed guilty of forgery, and punished as provided in section one.

SEC. 5. Persons out of the State may commit, and be liable to indictment and conviction for committing, any of the offenses hereinbefore enumerated, which do not in their commission necessarily require a personal presence in this State, the object of this act being to reach and punish all persons offending against its provisions, whether within or without the State, and indictments under this act may be presented by the grand jury of Travis county, in this State, or in the county where the offense was committed, or in the county where the land lies, about which the offenses in this act were committed.

SEC. 6. The following rewards shall be paid to the person informing or prosecuting in the cases hereinbefore mentioned, viz. one hundred dollars for each person convicted and sentenced for either of the aforesaid offenses; and these rewards shall be paid out of the Treasury of the State, by warrant of the Comptroller, granted on the certificate of the judge who tried the case; and where there are two or more informers and prosecutors for the same offense, the reward shall be divided between them equally, or in such proportions as said judge determines.

SEC. 7. Whereas, the present evils and mischief which it is the design of this act to check are of a character so serious as to create an emergency and an imperative public necessity for this act to take effect and go into force at once, it is therefore enacted that this act go into force and take effect from and after its passage.

Approved July 28, 1876.

Takes effect from its passage.

CHAPTER LXII.—*An Act to validate certificates of acknowledgement of married women to deeds of conveyance, letters of attorney, and other written instruments.*

SECTION 1. *Be it enacted by the Legislature of the State of Texas,* That any certificate of acknowledgment of any married woman to any deed of conveyance, letter of attorney or other written instrument, purporting to convey, or to confer on others the power to convey her separate estate, or her interest in the homestead, heretofore taken by any Chief Justice, District Clerk, Notary Public, or other officer, authorized by the laws of this State to take such acknowledgment, whenever such certificate of acknowledgment is invalid, because the same is wanting in any word, or words, necessary to be contained in such certificate of acknowledgment, by the requirements of the statutes in such cases made and provided, shall nevertheless be as valid and as binding on the person or persons making such written instrument as if such certificate of acknowledgment was in strict conformity to law; *provided,* that said certificate shall show on its face, that the married woman was examined by the officer taking the acknowledgment, separate and apart from her husband, and, having the same fully explained to her, she declared that she had willingly signed the same, and that she wished not to retract it, or words to that effect; *and provided further,* that nothing contained in this act shall prevent the parties interested from setting up and pleading fraud.

Approved July 28, 1876.

Takes effect ninety days after adjournment.

CHAPTER LXIII.—*An Act to provide annual pensions for the surviving soldiers of the Texan Revolution, and the surviving signers of the Declaration of Texan Independence, and the surviving widows of such soldiers and signers.*

SECTION 1. *Be it enacted by the Legislature of the State of Texas,* That to every surviving soldier or volunteer who served in the war between Texas and Mexico in the army of the Republic of Texas at any time between the commencement of the revolution at Gonzales in 1835 and the first day of January, 1837; and to every surviving signer of the Declaration of the Independence of Texas, made at the town of Washington, on the Brazos, on the second day of March, 1836; and to every surviving widow of any such soldier or signer who remains and has always been unmarried since the death of such soldier or signer, there shall be and is hereby granted an annual pension of one hundred and fifty dollars.

SEC. 2. No person shall be entitled to receive the pension herein provided for, unless he or she shall be in indigent circumstances, proof of which shall be made as herein required.

SEC. 3. Any person designing to make application for a pension under the provisions of this act, shall file with the Clerk of the County Court a full statement of the facts which entitle him or her to receive the same, which statement shall be supported by the affidavit of the applicant and two other credible persons.

Sec. 4.   When the County Clerk receives such an application, properly verified, he shall file the same and docket it on the trial docket of the County Court, and give a notice of the same having been made by posting on the court-house door of the county for at least thirty days prior to the beginning of a term of the County Court.

Sec. 5.   The application shall be considered by the County Court in its regular order on the docket, and the State shall be represented by the District Attorney, or the County Attorney, or by some attorney appointed by the court.

Sec. 6.   The Court may hear evidence both in support of and contradictory to the application, and shall give or withhold the certificate as the facts may warrant.

Sec. 7.   If the Court is satisfied that the application states such facts as are required by this act to entitle the applicant to a pension, and that the facts so stated in the application are true, the Judge shall cause a certified copy of the application and the certificate of the court to the truth of the same to issue to the applicant.

Sec. 8.   Any person making application for a pension as provided for in this act, who shall fail to establish his rights thereto, shall pay the following fees, to-wit: To the County Judge, three dollars; to the attorney representing the State, four dollars; to the County Clerk, two dollars; and to the Sheriff, one dollar.

Sec. 9.   All applications are to be made under this act to the County Court of the county in this State where the applicant resides.

Sec. 10.   Upon presentation of the certificate of the County Court, as herein provided for, to the Comptroller, by the applicant for a pension, or his attorney, it shall be the duty of the Comptroller to enter the name of the applicant upon the roll of pensions.

Sec. 11.   It shall be the duty of the Comptroller, on the first day of January, the first day of April, and the first day of July, and the first day of October, of each and every year, to draw his warrant, accompanied by the affidavit of two witnesses as to the identity of the pensioner, and the certificate of the County Judge and County Clerk under seal of the court, that the pensioner is still living, on the Treasury, in favor of each person on the roll of pensioners for the sum of thirty-seven dollars and fifty cents, and upon presentation of this warrant at the State Treasury, the Treasurer shall pay the same out of any funds which may be appropriated for that purpose.

Sec. 12.   That the Comptroller of Public Accounts shall not issue his warrant in favor of any applicant for a pension under the provisions of this act, until he is satisfied that the applicant was in the service of the Republic of Texas, within the period of time specified in the Constitution, and he may be governed in his decisions by record or other credible and satisfactory evidence; and should the applicant have drawn a pension under the provisions of any former law, it may be taken by the Comptroller as proof in his or her case; but should he entertain doubts of the justness of the claim, he shall require further proof.

Sec. 13.   Whenever the Comptroller may be credibly informed that any pensioner has died or become pecuniarily able to support himself or herself, then that officer shall strike the name of such person from the roll of pensioners, and report to the Governor his reason for so doing.

SEC. 14. The pension granted under this act shall commence on the first day of July, 1876, and be paid in advance.

SEC. 15. No person who is not a resident of this State shall have the benefit of this act.

SEC. 16. The necessities of the old veterans creates such an emergency that this act shall take effect from and after its passage.

Approved July 28, 1876.

Takes effect from its passage.

CHAPTER LXIV.—*An Act to regulate the laying out, opening and classifying and working of public roads in the State of Texas, and fixing penalties for a violation of certain sections therein named.*

SECTION 1. *Be it enacted by the Legislature of the State of Texas,* That the Commissioners' Courts of the several counties of this State shall have full power, and it shall be their duty, to order the laying out and opening of public roads, when necessary, and to discontinue or alter any road whenever it shall be deemed expedient, as hereinafter prescribed; and it shall be their further duty to classify all roads running through their several counties, into first, second and third-class roads.

SEC. 2. First-class roads shall be clear of all obstructions, and not less than forty feet wide, with all stumps over six inches in diameter to be cut down to six inches of the surface, and rounded off; all stumps six inches and under in diameter to be cut smooth with the ground, all causeways laid out at least sixteen feet wide; *provided,* that Commissioners' Courts shall have power to order a first-class road in such places as may be necessary to be wider than forty feet and not to exceed sixty feet.

SEC. 3. Second-class roads shall be clear of all obstructions, and not less than thirty feet wide; stumps six inches and over in diameter to be cut down within six inches of the surface, and rounded off; and all stumps less than six inches in diameter to be cut smooth with the ground; all causeways to be laid out at least sixteen feet wide.

SEC. 4. Third-class roads shall be clear of all obstructions, and not less than twenty feet wide; stumps six inches and over in diameter, to be cut down to within six inches of the surface and rounded off; all stumps less than six inches in diameter to be cut down smooth with the ground, and all causeways laid out at least twelve feet wide.

SEC. 5. The Commissioners' Courts of the several counties shall lay off their respective counties into road precincts, and shall at their first regular meeting in each and every year appoint an overseer for each road precinct, and shall at the same time designate all the hands liable to work on public roads under the different overseers in their county; and in case any hand or hands liable to work on roads, shall not have been designated by said Court, the overseeer shall have power to summons them to work on the nearest public road to which they may live, as if they had been designated by the Court; *provided,* fifteen days' residence in the county be necessary to require the performance of said road service at the time said service is required; but if from any cause the Court should fail or neglect to perform the duties required in this section at its first meeting in the year, it shall be competent and legal for it to make such appointment and designation at a called meeting, or at any regular term ; and in case a vacancy should occur in any road precinct by the death, removal or other inability of any overseer of the road in the county, it shall be the duty of the County Judge, immediately upon information of the same, to appoint an overseer to fill such vacancy, who shall be notified of his appointment as in other cases, and whose duty it shall be to serve until the first regular meeting of the Court in the next succeeding year.

SEC. 6.   All public roads and highways that have heretofore been laid out and established agreeably to law, except such as have been discontinued, are hereby declared to be public roads, and the said Commissioners' Court shall in no instance grant an order on an application for any new road or to discontinue an original one, unless the persons making applications for the same or some one of them shall have given at least twenty days notice by advertisement of their intended application, posted up at the court-house door and two other public places in the vicinity of the route of the proposed new road, or the road proposed to be discontinued.

SEC. 7.   All applications for a new road, and all applications to change or discontinue an original one, shall be by petition to Commissioners' Court, signed by at least eight freeholders of the road precinct or precincts in which said road is desired to be made, or discontinued, or changed ; specifying in such petition the beginning and termination of such road proposed to be opened, changed, or discontinued.

SEC. 8.   All roads hereafter ordered to be made shall be laid out by a jury of freeholders of the county, to be appointed by the Commissioners' Court ; said jury shall consist of five persons, a majority of whom may proceed to lay out and mark the road so ordered, to the greatest advantage to the public, and as little prejudice to enclosures as may be, after taking the following oath before some person authorized to administer oaths, to-wit :   "I, —————, do solemnly swear (or affirm) that I will lay out the road now directed to be laid out by the order to us directed from the Commissioners' Court, according to law, without favor or affection, malice or hatred, to the best of my skill, knowledge and ability. So help me God."

SEC. 9.   No public road shall be surveyed or laid out upon or across any farm, lot or enclosure, without first obtaining the written consent of the owner or owners, his, her or their agent or attorney to the same, except as hereinafter provided.

SEC. 10.   If such written consent should be refused, it shall be the duty of the Commissioners' Court to appoint five disinterested freeholders of the county as commissioners, a majority of whom may act, to view the same and assess the damages incidental to the opening of the road of the first, second or third class, through any part of said farm, lot or enclosure, as proposed ; taking into consideration the advantages and disadvantages accruing to such person from the opening of such road, and report their action in writing and under oath at the next regular term of the Commissioners' Court.

SEC. 11.   If the owner or owners, his, her or their agent or attorney, of any enclosed land shall file in the Commissioners' Court a written protest against opening a road, viewed and marked out through the same, it shall be the duty of the Commissioners' Court to appoint five disinterested freehold citizens of the county as commissioners, a majority of whom may act, to review said road, assess the damages and report in manner and form as provided in the preceding section of this act.

SEC. 12. If in the judgment of the Commissioners' Court of the county, from the report of the commissioners aforesaid, the road should be deemed of sufficient importance, they may order the survey or opening of the same; *provided*, that said Commissioners' Court shall first order the payment of the damages assessed by said commissioners out of the County Treasury, and the County Treasurer shall have paid the same, or secured its payment by a special deposit in his office, of the amount, subject to the order of the person to whom the same shall be due; *provided*, that notification of such deposit be given by mail or otherwise.

SEC. 13. If no objection be filed, upon the report of the jury of view, the Court shall proceed to establish and classify such road, appoint an overseer, apportion hands and order the opening out of such road, as provided in the first, second, third and fourth sections of this act, as the case may be; and the overseer so appointed shall report his action upon the same at the first regular term of the Commissioners' Court in the next succeeding year, and he shall be liable to the fines imposed upon overseers of roads, for the non-performance of duty by the provisions of this act.

SEC. 14. It shall be the duty of the County Clerks of the various counties of this State to make out copies of all orders of appointments of juries of view and all overseers of roads in duplicate; and within ten days after such order of appointment shall have been made, he shall deliver such copies to the Sheriffs of their respective counties, endorsing on the back of the same the date of the issuance of the order; and all orders of appointments of overseers shall embrace the designation of hands liable to work under such overseer, embracing the boundaries of the precincts as laid off by the Court; and the Sheriff shall, within twenty days after the reception of the same, deliver to, or leave at the common residence of the overseer, or juror of view or review, a copy of the same, and make his return to the Clerk, endorsed on the duplicate the date of service; and the Clerks or Sheriffs failing to perform the duties herein required each shall forfeit and pay for every such failure the sum of ten dollars, which shall be recovered by judgment on motion of the District or County Attorney, in a court of competent jurisdiction of the county in which the defaulter may reside; and any juror, summoned as aforesaid to view or review a new road, or to change and establish roads, on his failure or refusal to perform the service herein required, shall forfeit and pay for every such failure, the sum of ten dollars, the same to be recovered by judgment, on motion of the District or County Attorney, in any court of competent jurisdiction of the county in which the defaulter may reside; said defaulter, in all cases, having three days' notice of said motion; *provided*, all reasonable excuses shall be heard and allowed; *and provided further*, that the said viewers or reviewers shall each be exempt from road duty as many days as they are engaged in performing the said services.

SEC. 15. All male persons between eighteen and forty-five years of age shall be liable, and it is hereby made their duty to work on, repair and clean out the public roads of this State, under such provisions and regulations as are hereinafter made, except ministers of the Gospel actually engaged in the discharge of their ministerial duties, and invalids, who shall be exempt.

SEC. 16. The overseers of the road shall have power to call out all persons liable to work on public roads, at any time, when it may appear necessary to work or repair the roads, or any part of them, in their precinct; *provided*, that no one person shall be compelled to work on more than one road, nor more than ten days in each year; *and provided further*, that every overseer shall work through his precinct at least twice in each and every year.

SEC. 17.   It shall be the duty of the overseer to give three days previous notice by summons in person, or in writing left at their respective places of abode, with some person of the family not less than ten years of age ; if no person ten years old can be found at the place of abode, then he shall post said notice on the door of the place of abode of such person or persons so notified, and who is liable to work on the road in his precinct, which notice shall designate the time and place of working on the road.   Each person liable to work on the road, when summoned to work by the overseer of the road shall take with him an axe, hoe, pick, or spade, or such tool as may be desired and directed by the overseer; *provided also*, that the overseer shall have power to appoint some one to warn the hands to work on the roads, and such person shall be exempt from working on the road as many days as he was actually engaged in warning the hands.

SEC. 18.   If any person liable to work on public roads, so summoned, shall fail to attend, or to send an able-bodied substitute to work in his place; or fail to pay to the overseer the sum of one dollar per day for each day said person may have been notified to work on the road; or, when attending, shall fail or refuse to perform his duties as required by this act, and by the overseer, such person shall be deemed guilty of a misdemeanor; and upon conviction of such failure, refusal, or neglect, before any court of competent jurisdiction, shall be fined the sum of one dollar for each and every day he may so fail to attend or refuse to work, together with all costs of suit in either case ; *provided*, all reasonable excuses shall be heard and allowed; *and provided further*, that a list of the defaulting road-workers, furnished by the overseer, shall be a sufficient showing to authorize any court of competent jurisdiction to issue writs against the parties liable ; upon the return or trial day of which, whether the defaulter was summoned verbally or by writing to work on the road, and if by writing, the testimony of the person leaving the notice shall be necessary, upon which judgment shall be had; *provided*, the written report of the overseer, sworn to by him, and filed with the court trying the same, shall be *prima facie* evidence in all cases of refusals, failures or neglects, to work on the road, whether notified by writing or otherwise ; and in no event shall the overseer be liable for costs, nor shall he be required to give bond in case he desires to take an appeal to a superior court.

SEC. 19.   If any overseer of a road shall fail, refuse or neglect to report any person who shall fail to attend, or neglect or refuse to perform his duty when lawfully summoned to work on roads, said overseer shall forfeit and pay for every such neglect, failure or refusal, the sum of five dollars, to be recovered before any Justice of the Peace having jurisdiction, in the same manner as in an action of debt, upon the complaint of any person liable to work on said road ; and the funds accruing from fines and forfeitures imposed by the provisions of this act, shall be used and applied to the improvement of the road in the road precinct in which the said defaulter resides.

SEC. 20.   When, to the overseer of the roads, it may appear expedient to make causeways and build bridges, the timber most convenient ay be used by paying the owner a fair compensation for said timber, to be paid out of the County Treasury. The earth necessary for said causeways shall be taken from both sides so as to make a drain on each side of the causeways; and he shall erect bridges across all such water courses, and other places as may appear to him necessary and expedient; and should there be a water course that requires a bridge dividing any two road districts, the overseer of each district shall meet at the same time and place with their hands, and the overseer chosen by the majority present, shall superintend the building of such bridges until finished.

SEC. 21. When it may be necessary to use a wagon to haul material for any bridge, causeway, or other purpose, or any plow or scraper in repairing the roads, the overseer of such road is authorized to exchange the labor of any hand or hands bound to work on such road, for the use of a wagon or wagons, teams, scrapers and plows to be employed as aforesaid; also to exchange labor for the making of index boards and mile posts.

SEC. 22. It shall be the duty of all overseers of public roads to measure such parts of roads as fall within their respective precincts or districts, in continuation, and set up posts of good lasting timber at the end of each mile leading from the court-house, or some other noted place or town, and to mark on said posts in legible figures the distance in miles to said court-house or other noted place; and when a post so erected shall be removed by any means whatever, the overseer of the road shall cause the same to be replaced by another, marked as the original one. It shall also be the duty of overseers of roads to affix at the forks of all public roads in their respective districts or precincts index boards with directions pointing towards the most noted places to which they lead; and on failure to put up mile posts marked as aforesaid, or index boards, within six months after their appointment, the overseer of such roads, for such failure and neglect, shall be liable to indictment; and on conviction thereof before any court of competent jurisdiction, shall be fined in the sum of five dollars and all costs of prosecution.

SEC. 23. If any person subject to road duty shall refuse to serve as overseer on any road in his road district, agreeably to the order of the court in the county in which he resides, he shall be deemed guilty of a misdemeanor, and on conviction thereof before any court of competent jurisdiction, shall be fined in a sum not less than ten nor more than forty dollars; *provided*, all reasonable excuses shall be heard and allowed by the court trying the same. And it shall be the duty of every person appointed by the Commissioners' Court as an overseer of roads, who is lawfully exempt from road duty, to notify the Clerk of the Commissioners' Court of his non-acceptance within ten days after his being notified of his appointment; and on failure to do so, it shall be an acceptance of his appointment; and it shall, moreover, be the duty of the Clerk to insert on the commission the duties required of overseers, in respect to their non-acceptance. And if any person so appointed shall notify the Clerk of his lawful exemption from road duty, the Clerk shall forthwith report the same to the County Judge, who is authorized and required to appoint a successor to serve for the residue of the time; and such new overseer, so appointed, shall be subject to the same penalties and forfeitures as the overseer appointed by the Commissioner's Court; and a copy of the order of the appointment made by the Commissioners' Court and certified to by the Clerk of said court, shall be sufficient evidence of the appointment of overseers in all cases of prosecutions under this act; *provided*, that no person shall be compelled to serve as an overseer more than one year in every three successive years, and shall not be required to serve on juries during the time he serves as overseer.

SEC. 24. If any overseer of a road shall fail, neglect or refuse to perform the duties as prescribed by this act; or if he should not keep the road, bridges and causeways, within his precinct, clear and in good order; or if he suffer them to remain uncleared and out of repair for twenty days at any one time, unless hindered by high water or other sufficient cause, to be judged of by the court, such overseers shall be deemed guilty of a misdemeanor, and on conviction thereof by any court of the county, of competent jurisdiction, he shall be fined not less than ten nor more than twenty-five dollars; said fines shall be paid into the County Treasury, as other fines and forfeitures, for the use of the road precinct under the control of such defaulting overseer.

SEC. 25. All fines recovered under the provisions of this act shall be paid over to the overseer of the road in the precinct where the penalty accrued, for which amount the overseer shall give his receipt, the money to be applied by him to the improvement and keeping in good repair of his road.

SEC. 26. Every person liable to work on roads, by calling on the overseer at any time before the day appointed to work on the roads, and paying to said overseer the amount for which he or they might be liable for failing or refusing to work on said road, taking said overseer's receipt for the same, shall be exempt from working for every such day paid for, and also exempt from any penalties for the same.

SEC. 27. The overseers of roads shall apply all moneys coming into their hands to the improvement of their roads, in an impartial manner, by hiring hands, and applying the work equally throughout his precinct; and should said overseer misapply, fail or refuse to apply, the money coming into his hands in manner as provided for in this section of this act, he shall, for such failure or refusal, be liable for double the amount so misapplied, to be recovered on motion as provided for in the nineteenth section of this act, and shall be precluded from holding any office in any county in this State until such moneys are fully accounted for; *provided*, all reasonable excuses shall be heard and allowed; *and provided, further*, that such moneys may be laid out by the overseer for repairing or building bridges in his precinct, as he may think best.

SEC. 28. It shall be the duty of all overseers of roads in the State to report in writing to the Commissioner's Court of their county, at its first regular session in each year, giving the number of hands and the names of the same in his precinct liable to work on roads, the number of days he has worked on his road, the condition the road is in, the amount of fines by him collected, all the funds received by him for his road and how and to whom the same were paid. And any overseer failing or refusing to make such report shall forfeit and pay five dollars for such failure or refusal, to be recovered on motion as provided for in the nineteenth section of this act, to be paid into the County Treasury for the use of the road where such penalty accrued, and shall pay over to said Court any money remaining in his hands.

SEC. 29. The County Clerks of the several counties of this State shall post up in their respective court-houses on the first day of each District Court held in his county, a list of the names and the precincts of all overseers of the roads in the county, and on neglect or failure to perform such duty, he shall forfeit and pay for each failure, ten dollars, to be recovered on motion made by the County or District Attorney in the District Court, and paid into the County Treasury.

SEC. 30. It shall be the duty of Judges of the District Courts of the several Judicial Districts in this State to give this act in charge to the Grand Jury, at the opening of every court held by them.

SEC. 31. In addition to being exempted from serving on juries during the term of their service, the overseers of roads shall receive as compensation for their services ten per cent. of all fines or moneys collected or received by them.

SEC. 32. And for the further and better providing for public roads in this State, any lines between different persons or owners of land, may, upon the condition herein provided for, be declared public highways, and left open and free from any and all obstructions for ten feet on either side of said lines; *provided*, that the trees marked and other objects used to designate the lines and corners shall not be removed.

SEC. 33. That whenever ten free-holders shall make application under oath, which said oath shall be filed in the County Clerk's office and taken before some person authorized to administer oaths, stating that it is necessary for the lines designated in said application to be declared public highways in order to give them a nearer, better and more practicable road to their church, mill, wood or timber, or county-seat, and give five days' notice in writing of such application to all parties along the line of such proposed highway, the Commissioners' Court may in their discretion, should they deem the same of sufficient public importance, issue an order declaring the lines between the parties designated as above required to be public highways; and when such order is made, shall issue a notice to the individual owners of the land designated in said application, to be served by the Sheriff or any constable of the county in the same way as other notices are served, stating that said designated lines are declared public highways, and within one year from the date of the service of such notice, each owner or owners of such land shall cause the same to be left opened as indicated; *provided*, that the Commissioners' Court shall not be required to keep said roads worked by the road hands, as in the case with other roads in the county.

SEC. 34. Each and every person notified as provided above, who shall refuse or neglect to leave open the line or lines, as above indicated, shall be guilty of a misdemeanor, and on conviction thereof, before any court of competent jurisdiction, be fined in any sum not more than twenty dollars, together with all costs for each and every month he, she or they, fail, refuse or neglect to leave open the lines designated and provided for in this act.

SEC. 35. The owners or owner of the land whose lines have been or may be declared public highways, and also any person through whose land a third class road may run, shall have the right to erect a gate or gates across such road or roads, said gate or gates to be ten feet wide, and hung so that no person on horseback can open and shut it without alighting from his horse, and any person who shall leave said gates open shall be guilty of a misdemeanor, and on conviction thereof, shall be fined ten dollars for each offense, and shall also be responsible to the owner for any damage that may be incurred thereby, to be recovered in any court of competent jurisdiction.

SEC. 36. The amount of damages to be allowed to the owners of said lands for opening of the lines as provided for in Sections 33 and 34 of this act, shall be assessed as is provided for in first, second and third class roads, in section ten of this act, to be paid by the parties making application for said road.

SEC. 37.   That all laws and parts of laws in conflict with the provisions of this act are hereby repealed.

SEC. 38.   The immediate working of the public roads is an imperative public necessity, and creates an emergency ; therefore, this act take effect and be in force from and after its passage.

Approved July 29, 1876.

Takes effect from its passage.

_____

CHAPTER LXV.—*An Act to amend an act entitled, "An Act regulating contested elections," approved May 8, 1873.*

SECTION 1.   *Be it enacted by the Legislature of the State of Texas,* That the second section of the above recited act, approved May 8, 1873, and entitled, "An Act regulating contested elections," shall be amended so as to read as follows, to-wit :

"Section 2.   If the contest be for the validity of an election for any district or county office, a copy of the notices and any other papers served on the parties shall be filed with the Clerk of the District Court of the county in which the residence of the party holding the certificate of election is; and when so filed, the entry of the trial of said contest shall be made upon the docket of said court, the same as in other causes, and said contest shall be tried at the next term of said court, and under the rules governing proceedings in other causes, except that the questions of fact which may be at issue between the contesting parties shall be passed upon by the court without the intervention of a jury ; and if on trial any vote or votes be found to be illegal or fraudulent, the court shall subtract such vote or votes from the poll of the candidate for whom cast, and after a full and fair investigation of the evidence shall decide to whom the office belongs; or should it appear that the election was illegally or fraudulently conducted; or that by the action or want of action on the part of the officers to whom were entrusted the control of such elections, such a number of legal voters were denied the privilege of voting as, had they been allowed to vote, might have materially changed the result ; or if it appear that such irregularities existed as to render the true result impossible to be arrived at, or very doubtful of ascertaining, to order a new election as the facts and necessities may require ; and the costs of the suit shall be taxed according to the laws governing costs in other causes; and such causes shall have the precedence over all other causes, both in the District Court and upon appeal in the Supreme Court ; *provided,* that if more than sixty days will have elapsed from the return day after such election, before the first day of any regular term of the District Court in which any contested election is pending, then, and in that event, it shall be the duty of the Judge of said District Court to hear the cause in the chambers at as early a day, to be fixed by him, as may be practicable, and he shall direct the District Clerk to give to the contesting parties at least ten days' notice of the time of hearing such cause.   And it shall be the duty of the officer in whose charge the custody of the several boxes containing the polls, tally lists and poll lists may be, at any time, upon application by either of the contesting parties in such causes, and the filing of an affidavit, that both of the duplicate poll lists or tally lists required by law, were sealed up in any of such boxes, to open the same, after having given at least five days' notice to the opposite party, of the application, and of the time and place when and where he will open said box or boxes; and to take therefrom one of the poll or tally lists, and to hold the same, subject to the examination of either of the said contesting parties; after which he shall immediately close up the said box or boxes, and securely seal the same. Or should either of the said contesting parties file his application with an affidavit of his inability to otherwise procure for examination any duplicate poll or tally list used at such election, to open the box containing the other duplicate, and to take the same therefrom and hold it subject to the examination of said contesting parties, and to immediately thereafter seal up the said box securely; *provided*, that the notice to the opposite party, above provided for, shall in all such cases be given.

SEC. 2. Whenever notice of contest and the answer thereto shall have been filed in the office of the District Clerk, it shall be the duty of the contestee to file with the said District Clerk a bond, with two or more good and sufficient securities, to be approved by the said Clerk, in an amount to be determined by said Clerk, but not less than double the probable amount of fees to be realized from the office during the term being contested for, said bond to be conditioned, in the event of the decision of the contest herein provided for, against him and in favor of the contestant, that he will pay over the said contestant whatever sum may be adjudged against him by a court having jurisdiction of the subject matter of said bond. And if any such contestee shall fail or refuse to file such bond before the time fixed by law for entering upon the discharge of the duties of the office in dispute, then, and in that event, it shall be the duty of the said District Clerk to notify the said contestant of the said failure or refusal, who shall thereafter have ten days in which to file a like bond, conditioned, in the event of the determination of the said contest against him, and in favor of the said contestee, to pay over to the said contestee whatever sum may be adjudged against him by a court having jurisdiction of the subject matter of said bond. Immediately upon the filing of said bond, it shall be the further duty of said District Clerk to certify the failure or refusal of the contestee to file the said bond, to the Governor, and the filing of said bond by the contestant; whereupon it shall be the duty of the Governor to issue a commission to the said contestant for the time pending said contest; *provided*, that it shall be the duty of the Governor to issue the commission to the said contestee at the time regularly provided for by the general election laws of the State, unless he has in the meantime been notified of his said failure to file the said bond hereinbefore provided for, in which event he shall withhold the issuance of such commission until after the time herein allowed the contestant to file his said bond has elapsed; but if the said contestant shall fail to file his bond within the time herein provided for, it shall be the duty of the said District Clerk to certify all the facts in the case to the Governor, who shall proceed to issue the said commission to the said contestee; *provided further*, that if any person, at the date of the passage of this act, shall have already have entered upon the discharge of the duties of any office, his right to which is being contested in any District Court in this State, he shall be required to file the bond hereinbefore provided for, within twenty days from the said passage of this act, and in the event of his failure or refusal to do so, it shall be the duty of the clerk of said court to give notice of such failure or refusal to the contestant, who shall thereafter be allowed ten days in which to file his bond, as hereinbefore provided for; and if he shall file said bond within the time above specified, it shall then be the duty of the said Clerk to certify all the facts in the case to the Governor, who thereupon shall annul the commission heretofore issued to the said contestant (contestee), who shall enter upon and discharge the duties of the office in dispute, pending the said contest. But if the said contestant shall fail or refuse to file his said bond, as herein provided for, then, and in that event, the said contestee shall remain in possesion of said office, and shall continue to discharge its duties, pending the said contest.

SEC. 3. That all the provisions of this act shall apply to election contests, now pending, as well as to those hereafter to be commenced.

SEC. 4. That all acts or parts of acts, now in force, in conflict with any of the provisions of this act, be, and the same are hereby repealed.

SEC. 5. That whereas, in a large number of the counties of this State, under the constitutional ordinance fixing the times for holding the District Courts of this State, no regular terms of said Courts can be held for many months; and whereas, in many of said District Courts there are election contests now pending in regard to various offices in the State; and whereas, the public interests are being made to suffer by reason of said contests, and the uncertainty thereby engendered as to who are properly entitled to said offices; and whereas, under the said constitutional ordinance the determination of these said election contests must otherwise be necessarily greatly delayed; therefore, an emergency exists which makes it very necessary for the public welfare that this act shall go into immediate operation; therefore, be it further enacted by the Legislature of Texas, that this act shall go into effect and be in full force from and after its passage.

Approved July 29, 1876.

Takes effect from its passage.

CHAPTER LXVI.—*An Act prescribing the times of holding the District Courts in the Twelfth Judicial District, and to attach certain counties therein named for judicial purposes.*

SECTION 1. *Be it enacted by the Legislature of the State of Texas,* That the District Courts of the Twelfth Judicial District be holden at the times hereinafter specified, to-wit: In the county of Coryelle on the first Monday in March and September, and may continue in session two weeks; in the county of Hamilton on the third Monday in March and September, and may continue in session one week; in the county of Comanche on the fourth Monday in March and September, and may continue in session one week; in the county of Brown on the fourth Monday after the first Monday in March and September, and may continue in session one week; in the county of Coleman on the fifth Monday after the first Monday in March and September, and may continue in session one week; in the county of Shackelford on the sixth Monday after the first Monday in March and September, and may continue in session one week; in the county of Stephens on the seventh Monday after the first Monday in March and September, and may continue in session one week; in the county of Young on the eighth Monday after the first Monday in March and September, and may continue in session one week; in the county of Jack on the tenth Monday after the first Monday in March and September, and may continue in session one week; in the county of Palo Pinto on the eleventh Monday after the first Monday in March and September, and may continue in session one week ; in the county of Hood on the twelfth Monday after the first Monday in March and September, and may continue in session one week; in the county of Sommerville on the thirteenth Monday after the first Monday in March and September, and may continue in session one week; in the county of Erath on the fourteenth Monday after the first Monday in March and September, and may continue in session one week ; in the county of Eastland on the fifteenth Monday after the first Monday in March and September, and may continue in session one week. For judicial purposes Reynolds shall be attached to Coleman; Callahan to Eastland, and that Throckmorton, Haskell and Jones be attached to Shackelford for judicial purposes.

SEC. 2. All writs of process issued previous to the passage of this act, shall be returnable at the terms specified in this act.

SEC. 3. There being a public necessity for a change in the times of holding the Courts in said district, and the condition of the district renders it necessary that this act take effect and be in force from and after the fifteenth day of August, 1876, and it is hereby so enacted.

Approved July 29, 1876.

Takes effect from August 15, 1876.

CHAPTER LXVII.—*An Act to fix the times for holding the terms of the District Court for the Seventeenth Judicial District, including the county of Mc-Culloch.*

SECTION 1. *Be it enacted by the Legislature of the State of Texas,* That the terms of the District Court of the Seventeenth Judicial District shall be held at the times and places hereinafter specified, to-wit:

SEC. 2. In the county of McCulloch on the first Monday in March and September, and may continue in session one week.

SEC. 3. In the county of San Saba on the second Monday in March and September, and may continue in session two weeks.

SEC. 4. In the county of Lampasas on the third Monday after the first Monday in March and September, and may continue in session two weeks.

SEC. 5. In the county of Burnet on the fifth Monday after the first Monday in March and September, and may continue in session two weeks.

SEC. 6. In the county of Gillespie on the seventh Monday after the first Monday in March and September, and may continue in session one week.

SEC. 7. In the county of Kimble on the eighth Monday after the first Monday in March and September, and may continue in session one week.

SEC. 8. In the county of Menard on the ninth Monday after the first Monday in March and September, and may continue in session one week.

SEC. 9. In the county of Mason on the tenth Monday after the first Monday in March and September, and may continue in session two weeks.

SEC. 10. In the county of Llano on the twelfth Monday after the first

Monday in March and September, and may continue in session until the business is disposed of.

SEC. 11.   That the county of Concho is hereby attached to the county of McCulloch for judicial purposes.

SEC. 12.   That the Clerks of the District and County Courts of San Saba county be, and they are hereby authorized and required, to deliver to the Clerks of the District and County Courts of McCulloch county, all books, papers, records and other property in their possession belonging to said county of McCulloch.   That the Clerks of the District and County Courts of Gillespie county be, and they are hereby authorized and required, to deliver to the Clerks of the District and County Courts of Kimble county, all books, papers, records and other property in their possession belonging to said county of Kimble.

SEC. 13.   That as the present law works a great hardship to the people of this district, and places an unnecessary burthen upon the people of McCulloch county, now organized, an emergency exists for the immediate passage of this act, it shall therefore take effect, and be in force, from and after its passage.

Approved July 29, 1876.

Takes effect from and after its passage.

CHAPTER LXVIII.—*An Act to transfer certain suits pending in the courts of the counties of this State, out of which new counties have been created, to the new counties so created.*

SECTION 1.   *Be it enacted by the Legislature of the State of Texas,* That in all cases where a civil suit may be now, or hereafter, pending in the District or County Court of any county of this State, out of the territory of which a new county has been, or may hereafter be made, in whole or in part, if the defendants, or any one of them, shall file a motion in the District or County Court, where such suit is or may hereafter be pending, to transfer the same to said new county, together with an affidavit stating that neither he nor any one of the defendants, should there be more than one defendant, in such suit, now resides in the territorial limits of the county where such suit is pending, and that neither he nor any one of the defendants resided in said territorial limits at the time of the institution of such suit; and shall further swear that, at the date of the filing of such suit, said defendant was a resident citizen within the territorial limits of the new county, stating the name of such new county; the court in which such suit is or may hereafter be pending, shall cause an order to be entered upon the minutes of the court, transferring the suit, together with all the papers on file belonging to or forming a part of said suit, to said new county; which suit shall be entered upon the docket of the court in the new county having jurisdiction of the same, and be tried in its order as other cases; *provided,* no such transfer shall be made, unless the party defendant shall first pay all cost incurred by the defendants in such suit; *and provided further,* that nothing herein contained shall be construed to apply to suits concerning land, where the land in controversy is situated in the territorial limits of the old county, where the suit is now, or may be hereafter pending.

SEC. 2.   As the new Constitution has changed the original jurisdiction of the several courts, created new courts, and abolished other courts; thereby making it necessary to the ends of justice that all laws upon the subject of transferring causes to the proper tribunal for trial and disposal, should go into effect immediately, it is therefore enacted that this act take effect and be in force from and after its passage.

Approved July 29, 1876.

Takes effect from its passage.

CHAPTER LXIX.—*An Act to amend section twenty-seven of "An Act authorizing the disposition and sale of the University lands," approved April 8, 1874, and to validate all sales of eighty acres to any one person.*

SECTION 1. *Be it enacted by the Legislature of the State of Texas,* That section twenty-seven shall hereafter read as follows: " In case any of the said University lands are not sold and taken up by actual settlers, as provided for in the act, to which this is amendatory, any other person may purchase the same at not less than the minimum price fixed by the Commissioners, and upon the same terms as actual settlers, and upon the same conditions contained in section thirteen of said act; *provided,* that no person shall purchase more than one hundred and sixty acres, and not less than eighty acres; *and provided further,* that if under the provisions of this section any improved lands should be sold, the purchaser thereof shall pay for the enhanced value of said land by reason of improvements, in addition to the appraised value thereof, which enhanced value shall be assessed under oath by two disinterested freeholders of the county where situated, and by them at the cost of the purchaser be reported to the Commissioner of the General Land Office, who shall add the same to the appraised value of said land under this act, and when other than a settler applies to purchase, his application shall be accompanied by his affidavit, stating that there is no actual settler on the land, and stating further whether it is improved or unimproved; *provided,* that all sales of University lands of not more than one hundred and sixty acres, and not less than eighty acres, made since the 8th day of April, 1874, if made in accordance with the provisions of this act, as now amended, shall be deemed as valid as if made after the passage of this act; *provided further,* that nothing herein contained shall be construed so as to validate any sale of land where more than one hundred and sixty acres were bought by any one person, nor where the purchaser has failed to settle upon the land in accordance with this act, and the act to which this is amendatory; *and provided further,* that should there be more than eighty acres of land in one body, the purchaser shall take the whole, not to exceed one hundred and eighty acres; *provided further,* that the provisions of this act shall extend to and include all University lands that have been sold and afterwards bought in by the State, or have in any manner reverted to and become the property of the State."

Approved July 29, 1876.

Takes effect ninety days after adjournment.

CHAPTER LXX.—*An Act prescribing the times of holding the District Courts in the Second Judicial District.*

SECTION 1. *Be it enacted by the Legislature of the State of Texas,* That the District Courts of the Second Judicial District shall be holden at the times hereinafter specified, to-wit: In the county of Rusk, on the first Mondays in January and July, and may continue in session six weeks; in the county of Panola, on the sixth Monday after the first Mondays in January and July, and may continue in session four weeks; in the county of Shelby, on the tenth Monday after the first Mondays in January and July, and may continue in session three weeks ; in the county of Sabine, on the thirteenth Monday after the first Mondays in January and July, and may continue in session two weeks; in the county of Harrison, on the seventeenth Monday after the first Mondays in January and July, and may continue in session until the business is disposed of.

SEC. 2.   That all writs of process, civil or criminal, heretofore issued by or from the courts in the counties of the second Judicial District, are hereby made returnable in conformity to the provisions of this act; *provided*, that nothing herein contained shall be so construed as to in any manner interfere with any term of the District Court in any county in said Judicial District that may be in session at the time this act goes into effect.

Approved July 31, 1876.

Takes effect ninety days after adjournment.

CHAPTER LXXI.—*An Act to declare the time when the Sixteenth and succeeding Legislatures of the State of Texas shall assemble.*

SECTION 1.   *Be it enacted by the Legislature of the State of Texas,* That the Sixteenth Legislature of this State shall assemble to hold its biennial session on the second Tuesday in January, A. D. one thousand eight hundred and seventy-nine, at 12 o'clock M., and the Legislature shall meet biennially thereafter on the same day until otherwise prescribed by law.

SEC. 2.   There being a provision in the new Constitution authorizing this Legislature to pass laws making appropriations necessary to carry on the government until the assemblage of the Sixteenth Legislature, and as the present session of the Legislature is rapidly drawing to a close, an imperative public necessity exists for the immediate passage of this act, and the same shall take effect from and after its passage.

SEC. 3.   All laws and parts of laws in conflict with this act be and the same are hereby repealed.

Approved July 31, 1876.

Takes effect from its passage.

CHAPTER LXXII.—*An Act to define drunkenness in officers of the State, county and corporations, and prescribing punishments therefor.*

SECTION 1.   *Be it enacted by the Legislature of the State of Texas,* That drunkenness in any officer of this State, holding any office of honor, trust or profit, shall be and is hereby declared to be an offense against the laws of this State.

SEC. 2.   Drunkenness under the provisions of this act shall consist in the immoderate use of any spirituous, vinous or malt liquors to such a degree as to incapacitate an officer from the discharge of the duties of his office, either temporarily or permanently.

SEC. 3.   Any State or district officer who shall be guilty of violating section two of this act, shall be subject to removal from office in the manner provided by law.

SEC. 4.   Any county or municipal officer who shall be guilty of drunkenness as herein provided, shall, for the first offense, upon trial and conviction before any court of competent jurisdiction, be fined in a sum of not less than five dollars nor more than fifty dollars; for the second offense, he shall be fined in the sum of not less than fifty nor more than one hundred dollars; and for the third offense, he shall be removed from his office, and shall be thereafter incompetent to hold the same office for the period for which he may have been elected.

Approved July 31, 1876.

Takes effect ninety days after adjournment.

CHAPTER LXXIII.—*An Act to provide for the election of a District Attorney in the first, twelfth, seventeenth, twentieth, twenty-third and twenty-fourth Judicial Districts of the State of Texas.*

SECTION 1. *Be it enacted by the Legislature of the State of Texas,* That a District Attorney shall be elected in the first, twelfth, seventeenth, twentieth, twenty-third and twenty-fourth Judicial Districts of the State of Texas, who shall perform all the duties required of those officers by law.

SEC. 2. There shall be an election held in all the counties composing the first, twelfth, seventeenth, twentieth, twenty-third and twenty-fourth Judicial Districts within ninety days after the passage of this act for the purpose of electing said officers, and the Governor shall issue his proclamation, commanding the same to be held in accordance with existing laws.

SEC. 3. That the public welfare demands the election of a competent prosecuting officer in said Districts, and that there exists an imperative public necessity and emergency that this act take effect and be in force from and after its passage, and therefore it is so enacted.

Approved July 31, 1876.

Takes effect from its passage.

CHAPTER LXXIV.—*An Act to amend an act entitled: "An Act supplementary to an act entitled: 'An Act to create the county of Ellis,' approved January 28, 1850."*

SECTION 1. *Be it enacted by the Legislature of the State of Texas,* That the act entitled: "An Act supplementary to an act entitled: 'An Act to create the county of Ellis,' approved January 28, 1850," be amended so as to read as follows:

"SECTION 1. That the boundaries of Ellis county be as follows, to-wit: Beginning on the west bank of the Trinity river, at a point which, by the meanderings of said river, will be one mile northwardly from Robert H. Porter's house. Thence on a straight line to Chamber's creek, at a point opposite the mouth of Mill creek. Thence south, sixty degrees; west to a point thirty-seven miles from the place of begi(n)ning. Thence north, thirty degrees; west, to the south-east corner of Johnson county. Thence north to a point directly west of the south-west corner of Dallas county. Thence east to the said south-west corner of Dallas county. Thence with the southern boundary line of said Dallas county to the Trinity river. Thence down said river, with the meanderings thereof, to the place of begi(n)ning."

SEC. 2. That the people living along the line proposed to be established by this act, are in doubt as to the county of their residence, said line not having been established, the same presenting difficulties in assessing and collecting the taxes, etc., along said line, and the Legislature being near its adjournment, therefore an imperative public necessity for the immediate passage of said bill, and an emergency that the same take effect immediately both exist that this act take effect and be in force from and after its passage.

Approved July 31, 1876.

Takes effect from its passage.

———

CHAPTER LXXV.—*An Act to provide for holding a special term of the District Court of Collin county, in November, 1876, for the trial of criminal causes.*

Section 1. *Be it enacted by the Legislature of the State of Texas,* That there shall be held a term of the District Court within and for the county of Collin, for the trial of criminal causes, to commence on the first Monday in November, A. D. 1876, and continue in session until the business is disposed of.

Sec. 2. As an imperative public necessity exists because of the number of prisoners charged with felonies, now in the county jail of said county, waiting for trial at great cost and expense to said county, this act shall take effect and be in force from and after its passage.

Approved July 31, 1876.

Takes effect from its passage.

———

CHAPTER LXXVI.—*An Act to regulate grand juries and juries in civil and criminal cases in the courts in the State.*

Section 1. *Be it enacted by the Legislature of the State of Texas,* That no person shall be qualified to serve as a juror on the trial of any cause, civil or criminal, unless he be a legal voter, a citizen of this State, a freeholder in this State, or householder in the county in which he may be called to serve; of sound mind and good moral character; *provided,* that an inability to read or write shall be a sufficient cause for challenge, without being charged to either party,

Sec. 2. All civil officers, undertakers, druggists, telegraph operators, attorneys and physicians in practice, millers engaged in grist, flouring and saw mills, persons over sixty years of age, ferry-men, railroad station agents, engineers, conductors and vice-presidents of railroad companies, when engaged in active discharge of duty, school-masters, publishers of newspapers and ministers of the Gospel in active discharge of their ministerial duties, and overseers of roads, are exempt from jury service, when claiming such exemption; *provided,* there shall also be exempted from jury service, in towns or cities having a population of fifteen hundred or more inhabitants, active members of organized fire companies, not exceeding twenty members for each one thousand inhabitants, of any incorporated town or city, as ascertained by the last United States census; *provided further,* that the members to be exempted shall be selected by their respective companies, and their names be handed to the clerks of the District and County Courts, before this exemption can be made available; *and provided further,* that if there be more than one organized fire company in any county, the whole number of exemptions under the provisions of this act, shall be divided equally between all the organized fire companies in such county.

Sec. 3. Every person is disqualified from serving as a juror in any cause, civil or criminal, pending in any court in this State, who may have been convicted of, or who may be under indictment for theft, or any felony, or who does not possess the qualifications prescribed for jurors in this act.

SEC. 4. The District Judge shall at each term of the District Court, appoint three intelligent citizens as Jury Commissioners, possessing the qualifications prescribed in this act for jurors, resident in different portions of the county, and freeholders therein, and able to read and write, and who have no suit in the District Court of such county, which requires the intervention of a jury. The Judge shall cause the Sheriff to notify said Commissioners of their appointment as such, and the day upon which they are to appear before said Judge; and he shall administer to the Commissioners the following oath: "You do swear faithfully to discharge the duties required of you as Jury Commissioners; that you will not knowingly elect any man as juryman whom you believe to be unfit and not qualified, that you will not make known to any one the name of any juryman selected by you, and reported to the court; that you will not directly or indirectly converse with any one selected by you as a juryman, concerning the merit of any case to be tried at the next term of this court, until after said cause may be tried or continued, or the jury be discharged.

SEC. 5. If any person appointed a Jury Commissioner shall fail or refuse to attend and perform the duties required, without a reasonable excuse, he shall forfeit and pay not less than twenty-five dollars nor more than one hundred dollars, nor shall the same person act as Jury Commissioner more than once in the same year, and any person acting as Jury Commissioner shall be exempt from jury service for one year thereafter.

SEC. 6. The Jury Commissioners, after they have been organized and sworn, shall retire to a jury room or some other apartment designated by the Judge; they shall be kept free from the intrusion of any person and shall not separate, without leave of the court, until they shall have completed the duties required of them. The Clerk shall furnish the Commissioners with the names of persons appearing from the records of the court to be exempt from serving on the petit jury at each term, and they shall also be furnished with the last assessment roll of the county.

SEC. 7. The Jury Commissioners shall select from the citizens of the different portions of the county, one hundred persons, or a less or greater number if so directed by the Judge, free from all legal exceptions, of good moral character, of sound judgment, well informed, and, so far as practicable, able to read and write, to serve as petit jurors at the next term of the District Court; they shall write the names of such persons on separate pieces of paper as near the same size and appearance as may be, and fold the same so that the name cannot be seen. The names of the persons so written and folded shall be deposited in a box, and after being well shaken and mixed, the Commissioners shall draw from said box the names one by one of thirty-six persons, more or less, as the Judge shall direct, for each week of the term of the court, and record the same as drawn upon as many sheets of paper as there are weeks of the term of the court, which shall be certified and signed by them, directed and delivered in open court to the Judge of the District Court in separate envelopes and endorsed, "the lists of standing juries." The lists shall be sealed in separate envelopes and endorsed respectively, "jurors for the first, second and ——— weeks of the court," the blanks to be filled by the number corresponding to the week of the court for which the jurors are chosen, and the Commissioners shall write their names upon the seals so that the contents cannot be seen without breaking the seals.

Sec. 8.   The Judge shall deliver the lists to the Clerk or one of his deputies in open court, and administer to the Clerk and all his deputies the following oath : "You do swear that you will not open the jury lists now delivered to you, nor permit them to be opened, until the time prescribed by law ; that you will not directly or indirectly converse with any one selected as a petit juror concerning any case pending and for trial in this court at the next term."   Should the Clerk subsequently appoint a deputy, he shall administer to him the like oath.

Sec. 9.   Within thirty days of the next term, and not before, the Clerk shall open the envelopes and make out a fair copy of the jury list for each week, and give the same to the Sheriff or his deputy, who shall, at least three days prior to the first day of the next term, summon the persons to attend on Monday of the week for which said persons were drawn as petit jurors, by giving personal notice to each juror, or by leaving written notice at the juror's place of residence, with a member of his family over sixteen years old ; and in either event, the Sheriff shall name the day and week said juror is required to appear. The lists shall be returned by the Sheriff on the first day of the term, with a certificate thereon of the date and manner in which each juror was summoned, from each of which lists twenty-four persons shall be selected for the week named in the list, from those summoned, in the order in which their names appear thereon, who shall compose the regular panels of that week.

Sec. 10.   A juror, legally summoned, failing to attend, without a reasonable excuse, may, by order of the court entered on the record, be fined in any sum not less than ten nor more than one hundred dollars.

Sec. 11.   The court may discharge the regular panel of a jury after they shall have served one week ; and any deficit in a panel shall be made up, when a selected juryman is excused or fails from any cause to attend on the day specified in the summons, from the original list returned by the Jury Commissioners, in the order in which their names are recorded in said list.

Sec. 12.   At the commencement of each term of the court at which jury causes may be tried, the Judge shall administer to the Sheriff and his deputies the following oath :   "You do swear that, without favor or affection, or without purpose to favor or injure the rights of any litigant, or of the State, or of any defendant, you will summon jurors in and for this county ; and that, to the best of your skill and judgment, you will select discreet, sensible, impartial men, when required to summon jurors not selected by the Jury Commissioners ; and that you will not, directly or indirectly, communicate or converse with any juryman touching the subject matter of any case pending for trial at the time ; that you will not, by any means, attempt to influence, advise or control a juryman in his opinion in any case under trial."

Sec. 13.   If, for any cause, the Jury Commissioners shall not be appointed, or shall fail to select jurors as herein provided, or the panel selected shall be set aside, or the jury lists returned into court shall be lost or destroyed, the court shall forthwith order proceedngs in conformity with the provisions of this act to supply for the term a sufficient number of jurors ; and, if necessary, appoint commissioners for that purpose.

SEC. 14. The Judge may, if he deem it expedient, make an order directing the Clerk to docket causes for the first day of the term, except appearance cases, in which there is a jury trial, and order the jury to be summoned to appear on that day; which order he may make and revoke at pleasure.

SEC. 15. Three Jury Commissioners, having the qualifications prescribed in this act for Jury Commissioners in the District Court, shall be appointed, summoned and sworn by each County Judge at the first term of the County Court held after the passage of this act, who shall, in accordance with the provisions prescribed for Jury Commissioners in the District Court, in this act, select jurors for all the terms of said court to be holden in the year 1876, and for the first term of said court to be holden in the year 1877, and the same proceedings shall be had in the County Court by the officers thereof and by said Commissioners, for procuring jurors and organizing petit juries for the trial of cases in the County Court, as are required by this act for similar proceedings in the District Courts; and the said County Judges shall, at the January and July terms of the County Courts, in the year 1877, and in every year thereafter, appoint, summon and swear three Jury Commissioners, who shall, in accordance with the provisions of this act, select jurors for all the terms of the County Courts to be holden within six months next after the adjournment of said January and July terms of said court; and the said County Judges may increase or reduce the whole number of jurors to be selected.

SEC. 16. The Clerk shall deliver to the Jury Commissioners, after their appointment, and before they enter on their duties, a list of those persons who have served for one week in any court of record of the county, within twelve months, if in the District Court, and within six months, if in the County Court, preceding, none of whom shall be selected by the Commissioners as jurors; *provided*, that the foregoing provisions of this section shall have no application to counties sparsely populated, if the Judge shall so direct; and the Commissioners shall also be furnished by the Clerk with a list of those under arrest, or on bail, against whom a criminal prosecution for theft or any felony is pending in the county; and also a list of all persons convicted of theft, or any felony known to the Clerk, none of whom shall be selected as jurymen.

SEC. 17. No jury shall be required in any civil case in the District or County Court, unless the party demanding a jury, if in the District Court, shall have deposited by nine o'clock A. M., of the day of the court set by the Judge for the trial of jury causes, a jury fee of five dollars if in the District Court, and three dollars if in the County Court; and all causes in which jury fees have been deposited shall be at once entered by the Clerk, in their regular order, on a "jury case trial docket;" said causes shall be tried or disposed of for the term in their regular order, except appearance cases, before those cases in which no jury has been demanded, and jury fee deposited; *provided*, that on the call for trial of a case in which a jury fee has been deposited, the party demanding a jury may waive it, in which event his jury fee deposit shall be refunded; but his case shall be tried in its order without a jury, as a jury trial docket case.

SEC. 18. Any party to a cause desiring a jury, who will, before nine o'clock A. M. of the day of the term set for the trial of jury cases, make oath before the Clerk that he has no money or property on which he can procure the amount required for a jury fee, and that he has not and cannot procure the jury fee deposit, shall be entitled to have his case tried by a jury in the same manner as if the jury fee had been paid.

SEC. 19.   No verdict shall be rendered in any cause in the District Court, whereby the rights of any citizen shall be affected, except upon the concurrence of all the jury (unless during the trial one or more jurors, not exceeding three, may die or be disabled from sitting; in which event the remainder of the jury shall have power to render the verdict); but when the verdict shall be rendered by less than the whole number, it shall be signed by every member of the jury concurring in it.

SEC. 20.   On the day the jurors shall be summoned to attend court, the panel for that week shall be called, and the names of such as attend, and are not excused by the court, shall be entered of record as the jurors of that week, and the Judge shall order the Sheriff to summon a sufficient number of good and intelligent citizens, having the qualifications of jurors as prescribed in this act, to supply the deficiency, if any, in the panel.

SEC. 21.   The Clerk shall write the names of all the jurors entered of record on separate slips of paper, as near the same size and appearance as may be, and when a jury is wanted for the trial of any case, the same shall be drawn from a box, after the slips of paper above mentioned shall have been deposited therein, and well mixed. The Clerk shall provide and keep for that purpose a suitable box with a sliding lid.

SEC. 22.   In all cases of jury trial, the Clerk shall draw from the box the names of twenty-four jurors, if in the District Court, or so many as there may be, if there be a less number in the box; and the names of twelve jurors, if in the County Court, or so many as there may be, if there be a less number in the box, and write them as drawn on two slips of paper, and deliver one slip to each party, if in a civil case, or, if in a criminal case, one to the Prosecuting Attorney, and the other to the defendant or his attorney, from which the plaintiff and defendant, or the Prosecuting Attorney and defendant, if in a criminal case, may each strike a number of names equal to the number of peremptory challenges allowed them by law; and they shall return the list to the Clerk, who shall, if in the District Court, call the first twelve names not erased, and, if in the County Court, call the first six names not erased, and swear them as a jury to try the case. But before either party shall be required to strike, those on the list shall be challenged for cause, and others drawn and placed as drawn upon the list, in place of as many as may be set aside for cause. In all cases when the jury shall be completed, the names of all jurors constituting a panel, not on the jury, shall be returned to the box, from which another jury may be drawn; and when from any cause it may be necessary to make up a jury, if there be not enough of the standing jurors remaining, or in attendance, the court shall order for the occasion a sufficient number of other jurors, possessing all the qualifications prescribed for jurors in this act, to be summoned by the Sheriff, to make up the deficiency in said jury; *provided*, that in summoning said jurors to supply said deficiencies, it shall not be lawful for the Sheriff or any officer to summon as a juror any person found in the court-house, or court yard, if they can be had elsewhere.

SEC. 23.   Whenever a special *venire* shall be ordered, the names of all the persons selected by the Jury Commissioners to do jury service for the term at which such *venire* is required, shall be placed upon tickets of similar size and color of paper, and the tickets be placed in a box which shall be well shaken up; and from this box the Clerk, in the presence of the Judge in open court, shall draw the number of names required for said special *venire*, and the names of the persons so drawn shall be attached to the writ of special *venire facias*, and the persons named shall be summoned by the Sheriff, or other lawful officer, by virtue thereof; *provided*, that when the whole number of jurors selected by the Jury Commissioners for any term of the court shall be less than the number required upon said special *venire*, the Judge shall order the Sheriff to summon a sufficent number of good and intelligent citizens, having all the qualifications of jurors prescribed in this act to supply the deficiency; *provided*, that in supplying the deficiency, it shall not be lawful for the Sheriff or any other officer to summon as a juror any person found within the court-house or yard, if they can be had elsewhere.

SEC. 24. The court may adjourn the whole or any part of the jury to any day of the term, but jurors shall not be paid for the time they stand adjourned.

SEC. 25. If the challenge to the array shall be sustained, the court shall order the whole panel to be discharged, and a new one to be summoned from the qualified jurors of the county; or a special jury may be summoned to try the cause of the party challenging.

SEC. 26. The fact that a juror is a witness in the case; that he is directly or indirectly interested in the case; that he is related, within the third degree, by consanguinity or affinity, to either of the litigants or to the defendant in any criminal case; or that he does not possess the qualifications of a juror enumerated in this act; or that he has served as a juror for one week in the District Court within six months preceding, or in the County Court within three months preceding; or that he is biased or prejudiced in favor of or against either party, or in favor of or against the defendant in a criminal case; or that he is unable to read or write; or that he is related within the third degree by consanguinity or affinity to the person injured by the commission of the offence with which the defendant in a criminal case is charged, or to the private prosecutor, if there be one; or that he served on the grand jury which found the bill of indictment; or that from hearsay or otherwise there is established in the mind of the juror such a conclusion, as to guilt or innocence of the defendant, as will influence him in his action in finding the verdict; shall be a good cause for challenge; *provided*, that where the requisite number of jurors, able to read and write, cannot be found, then the inability of a juror to read and write shall not be a good cause for challenge; *and provided further*, that no juror shall be sworn as a witness, after being accepted by the parties, sworn and impaneled as a juror, unless, by consent of the parties, such juror shall be discharged and the case be tried by the remaining jurors.

SEC. 27. Six men shall compose a jury in the courts of Justices of the Peace, and in all inferior courts of this State; and all jurors in such courts shall possess all the qualifications, and may be challenged for the same causes prescribed in this act; and in jury trials in such courts each party shall be entitled to three peremptory challenges.

SEC. 28. That at each term of the District Court, the Jury Commissioners appointed at that term shall, at the same time and place at which they shall select petit jurors for the next term, also select from the citizens of the different portions of the county, sixteen persons, to be summoned as grand jurors for the next term of the District Court, from whom the grand jury shall be formed, taking those who attend and are not excused by the court, as their names appear upon the list; and the deficiency, if any, shall be supplied under the direction of the court.   The persons so selected as grand jurors shall possess all the qualifications required by law for grand jurors, and shall also possess all the qualifications prescribed in this act for petit jurors, and persons summoned to supply any deficiency, shall possess the same qualifications.   The names of the persons selected as grand jurors by the Commissioners shall be written upon a piece of paper, and the fact that they were so selected shall be certified to and signed by the Jury Commissioners, who shall place said piece of paper so signed in an envelope, and seal the same and endorse thereon the words : "The list of grand jurors selected at —— term of the District Court," (the blank to be filled by the proper designation of the court).   The Commissioners shall write their names across the seal of said envelope and direct the same to the District Judge, and deliver it to him in open court, and the same proceedings shall be had by the Judge, Clerk and Sheriff, or other officer, as are prescribed in this act with reference to the list of petit jurors.

SEC. 29.   That all laws and parts of laws in conflict with the provisions of this act be and the same are hereby repealed.

SEC. 30.   Whereas, the jury laws now in force in this State are wholly inadequate to the public wants, thus creating an emergency; therefore, that this act take effect and be in force from and after its passage.

Approved August 1, 1876.

Takes effect from August 18, 1876.

CHAPTER LXXVII.—*An Act making an appropriation for per diem pay of the members, officers and employees of the Fifteenth Legislature.*

SECTION 1.   *Be it enacted by the Legislature of the State of Texas,* That the sum of thirty thousand dollars, or so much thereof as may be necessary, is hereby appropriated out of any moneys in the Treasury not otherwise appropriated, for the per diem pay of the members, officers and employees of the Fifteenth Legislature of the State of Texas.

SEC. 2.   That the certificate of the Secretary of the Senate, approved by the President thereof; or the certificate of the Chief Clerk of the House, approved by the Speaker thereof, shall be sufficient evidence to the Comptroller, upon which he shall audit the claims and issue his warrants upon the Treasurer for the respective amounts.

SEC. 3.   That an imperative public necessity exists for the passage of this law in order that the members, officers and employes may receive their per diem to enable them to perform their duties to the State, that this act take effect and be in force from and after its passage.

Approved August 2, 1876.

Takes effect from its passage.

CHAPTER LXXVIII.—*An Act to provide for transcribing county records in certain cases.*

SECTION 1.   *Be it enacted by the Legislature of the State of Texas,* That it shall be the duty of the County Commissioners' Court of any county in this State, when the records or indexes thereof of any county have become or may become defaced, worn, or in any condition endangering their preservation in a safe and legible form, to procure a good and well bound book or books, as the case may be, and require the County Clerk to transcribe, or have transcribed by a sworn deputy, the records contained in such book or books, in a plain, legible hand, and with some standard ink of a permanent black color ; and when so transcribed, they shall be carefully compared with the original record, by the said Clerk or sworn deputy so transcribing the same, assisted by some other sworn deputy.

SEC. 2. *Be it further enacted,* That when said record or records shall have been found to be truly and correctly transcribed, the County Clerk, with the sworn deputies so transcribing and verifying the same, shall certify under their official oath of office, at the conclusion of the record, with the impress of the seal of said court affixed on the same page, to the correctness of the same, reciting the number of pages contained in said book, from one to the highest number; after which, said transcribed record or records shall have all the force and effect in judicial proceedings in the courts of the State as the original records; *provided,* that the original book or books so transcribed shall be carefully kept and preserved by such Clerk, as other archives of his office ; *and provided further,* that the book or books so transcribed shall conform in all respects to the original record as indexed ; and also, that the designation of such transcribed book or books, whether by letter or number, shall not be changed from the original.

SEC. 3. That the County Clerk, or person making such transcript, shall be entitled to compensation therefor at the rate of ten cents per one hundred words, and for comparing and verifying the same, payable out of the county treasury, upon warrant issued under order of the Commissioners' Court.

Approved August 7, 1876.

Takes effect ninety days after adjournment.

CHAPTER LXXIX.—*An Act to define and regulate the duties of County Attorneys.*

SECTION 1. *Be it enacted by the Legislature of the State of Texas,* That it shall be the duty of each County Attorney to attend all terms of the District and County Courts, and all criminal prosecutions before Justices of the Peace when notified of the pendency of such prosecutions ; and, when not prevented by other official duties, to conduct all prosecutions for crimes and offences cognizable in such courts; to prosecute and defend all other actions in which the State or county is interested, and to perform such other duties as may be prescribed by the Constitution and laws of the State. They shall severally reside within the county for which they were elected, and shall notify the Attorney-General and Comptroller of Public Accounts of their post-office address.

SEC. 2. That the County Attorney shall be an attorney-at-law, duly licensed to practice in the District Court of this State, and shall, from time to time, give to the Attorney-General such information as he may require as to their official acts.

SEC..3. That the County Attorney shall give to the Assessor of Taxes, the Collector of Taxes, or the County Treasurer of his county, an opinion in writing, at their request, touching their duties concerning the revenue of the State or county ; and he shall give to the Clerk and

Sheriff of his county such advice in writing as he may deem necessary to insure the prompt collection of all money for which judgments may have been rendered in favor of the State or county.

SEC. 4.   That it shall be the duty of the County Attorney, upon the collection of any money for the use of the county or State, to deliver to the person paying the same receipts therefor.

SEC. 5.   That it shall be the duty of the County Attorney, on or before the last day of August of each year, to file in the office of Comptroller of Public Accounts an account in writing, verified by his affidavit, of all money received by him by virtue of his office during the preceding year, payable into the State Treasury; and he shall, within thirty days after its collection, pay into the State Treasury such money, after retaining the commissions allowed thereon by law.

SEC. 6.   That, in like manner, the County Attorney shall file with the County Treasurer a similar statement of all money received by him by virtue of his office, payable to the County Treasurer, and he shall within twenty days after collection pay the sum so received into the County Treasury, less his commissions.

SEC. 7.   That no County Attorney shall act as attorney or counsel for any party to an action wherein such party is charged with a crime, with a misdemeanor, or a breach of the penal statute; nor when the interest of such party is adverse to that of the State or county.

SEC. 8.   That each County Attorney shall keep in proper books, to be procured for that purpose at the expense of the State, a register of all his official acts and reports; and all actions and demands prosecuted or defended by him; of all proceedings had in relation thereto, and shall deliver the same over to his successor in office; and such books shall at all times be open to inspection by the Commissioners' Court.

SEC. 9.   That when it shall come to the knowledge of any County Attorney that any officer in his county entrusted with the collection or safe-keeping of any public funds is, in any manner whatsoever, neglecting or abusing the trust confided in him; or in any way failing to discharge his duties under the law, he shall institute such proceedings as are necessary to compel the performance of such duties by such officer, and to preserve and protect the public interests.

SEC. 10.   That it shall be the duty of the County Attorney to present to the court having jurisdiction, any officer, by information, for the neglect or failure of any duty enjoined upon said officer, when such neglect or failure can be presented by information, whenever it shall come to the knowledge of said Attorney that there has been a neglect or failure of duty upon the part of said officer; and it shall be his duty to bring to the notice of the grand jury all acts of violation of law, or neglect or failure of duty upon the part of any officer, when such neglect, violation or failure are not presented by information, and whenever the same may come to his knowledge.

SEC. 11.   That each County Attorney, before he enters upon the discharge of his duties, shall take and subscribe the oath of office prescribed by the Constitution, and shall execute a bond, with at least two solvent sureties, payable to the Governor and his successors in office, in the sum of twenty-five hundred dollars, to be approved by the County Commissioners' Court, conditioned that he will faithfully pay over, in the manner prescribed by this act, all moneys which he may collect, or may come to his hands for the State or county; which bond shall be, with the oath of office, recorded in the office of the County Clerk and deposited in the Comptroller's office, and which bond shall not be void on the first recovery, but may be sued on until the full amount of the penalty is recovered; *provided*, that all County Attorneys in this State, who have not heretofore qualified by giving the bond and taking the oath prescribed in this section, shall have sixty days after the passage of this act to give the bond and take the oath; and all official acts done by said County Attorney in accordance with the provisions of this act prior to giving the bond and taking the oath shall be held as legal and binding as if the Attorney had duly qualified as required by this act.

SEC. 12. Whenever any County Attorney shall fail to qualify and give bond as required by law, or shall fail or neglect to attend any term of the District, County or Justice's Court, it shall be the duty of the Judge of such court, or such Justice, to appoint some competent attorney to perform the duties of County Attorney, who shall be allowed the same compensation for his services as is allowed the County Attorney for the same; *provided*, however, that such appointment shall in no instance extend beyond the term of the court at which such appointment was made; *and provided further*, that said appointment shall be vacated upon the appearance of the County Attorney.

SEC. 13. Upon complaint being made before the County Attorney that an offense has been committed which the County Court or a Justice of the Peace has jurisdiction to try, it shall be the duty of said County Attorney to reduce the complaint to writing, and cause the same to be signed and sworn to by the complainant, and it shall be duly attested by said County Attorney. Said complainant shall state the name of the accused, if his name is known, and the offense for which he is charged shall be stated in plain and intelligible words; and it must appear that the offense was committed in the county where the complaint is filed; and the complaint must show, from the date of the offense stated therein, that the offense is not barred by limitation.

SEC. 14. The complaint specified in section thirteen of this act may be made before any Judge of the County Court, County Attorney or Justice of the Peace; and, for the purpose of carrying out the provisions of this act, the County Attorney is hereby authorized to administer an oath.

SEC. 15. It shall be the duty of the County Attorney, upon the filing of said complaint, to prepare an information in writing, which shall be in compliance with Article 403, Part third, Title four, Chapter three, of the code of criminal procedure.

SEC. 16. Whenever any credible person shall inform any County Attorney that an offense has been committed, and shall give the names of the person or persons who may have knowledge of an offense, it shall be the duty of said County Attorney, and he is hereby authorized and required, to issue a subpœna requiring said person or persons to appear before him, if the case is within the jurisdiction of the County or District Court, at a time and place named in such subpœna, to testify under oath in behalf of the State, without stating in the subpœna the nature of the offense or the party suspected; and for this purpose County Attorneys are hereby authorized to administer oaths. If the supposed case is one exclusively within the jurisdiction of a Justice of the Peace, the subpœna shall be returnable to the Justice of the Peace in whose precinct the offense was committed; and if said person or persons shall fail or refuse to obey said subpœna, it shall be the duty of said County Attorney, if he has reason to believe that the testimony is material, on his own motion, or upon the affidavit of any credible person, to make his application to the Justice of the Peace, or Clerk of the court having jurisdiction of the case, for an attachment to compel the attendance of said witness, to testify before the said County Attorney, or Justice of the Peace, as the case may be, at a time and place named in the attachment; *provided*, that if the information given by said credible person be in writing and under oath, the attachment shall issue as an original process, upon the written application of said County Attorney; and it shall also be the duty of the County Attorney to notify the Justice of the Peace to whom he sends such witnesses of all the information he has relative to the case; *and provided further*, in capital cases, the subpœna or attachment shall be made returnable to the County Judge before whom the examination shall take place.

SEC. 17.   Upon the appearance of said witnesses, it shall be the duty of the County Attorney, Justice of the Peace, or County Judge, as the case may be, to reduce their testimony to writing and cause the same to be signed by such witnesses; and if it appear therefrom that an offense has been committed, the County Attorney shall, upon said testimony, file an information in the court having jurisdiction of said offense, as is provided for in section thirteen of this act; or the Justice of the Peace shall issue his warrant thereon, if within his jurisdiction; *provided*, that nothing in this act shall be so construed to limit the power granted to magistrates and prosecuting officers under existing laws.

SEC. 18.   If said witness, upon his appearance before said County Attorney, shall refuse to testify, it shall be the duty of the County Attorney to reduce his questions to writing, and the reasons, if any, given by said witness for his refusal to testify, and report the same by motion in writing to the District or County Judge, in term time or vacation as the case may be, whereupon said witness may be fined and imprisoned by said Judge in like manner as District Judges are authorized to do in cases where witnesses refuse to testify before grand juries.

SEC. 19.   The County Attorney shall be entitled to the following fees, and no other, viz: In all cases of misdemeanor, where the defendant is prosecuted by the County Attorney, and is convicted, and no appeal is taken; or when, upon appeal, the judgment or sentence is confirmed, ten dollars, to be paid by defendant as other costs.   In all cases of felony above and including the grade of manslaughter, when the defendant is convicted and fails to appeal; or when, upon appeal, the judgment or sentence of the court from which the appeal is taken, is confirmed, fifty dollars; and in all other cases of felony, when the defendant is convicted and fails to appeal; or when, upon appeal, the judgment or sentence of the court below is confirmed, thirty dollars, to be paid by the State. On all fines, forfeitures or money collected for the State or county, recovered by him, the County Attorney shall be entitled to ten per cent. of the amount so collected; for services rendered in examining courts, in every felony case where the party is finally convicted, and no appeal is taken; or when the judgment of the court below has been affirmed, ten dollars; *provided*, that for services rendered since the eighteenth day of April, 1876, and prior to the passage of this act, County Attorneys shall be entitled to the same fees prescribed by this act.

SEC. 20.   The County Attorney shall not dismiss a case unless he shall file a written statement with the papers in the case, setting out his reasons for such dismissal, which shall be incorporated in the judgment of dismissal; *provided*, that no case shall be dismissed without the permission of the presiding Judge, who shall be satisfied that the reasons set out in the said statement are good and sufficient to authorize such dismissal.

SEC. 21. The County Attorney shall not take any fee, article of value, compensation, reward or gift, from any person whomsoever, to prosecute any case which he is required by law to prosecute; nor shall he take any fee, article of value, compensation, reward or gift, from any person whomsoever, in consideration of, or as a testimonial for his services in any case which he is required by law to prosecute, after such case has been tried or finally disposed of.

SEC. 22. That this act in view of the necessities for the prompt establishment of the judiciary system required by the Constitution; therefore an emergency exists for the immediate passage of this act, and it shall take effect and be in force from and after its passage.

Approved August 7, 1876.

Takes effect from its passage.

CHAPTER LXXX.—*An Act to ascertain the amounts due teachers for services rendered in the public schools from September 1, 1873, to January 1, 1876, and to provide for the payment of the same.*

SECTION 1. *Be it enacted by the Legislature of the State of Texas,* That the late Board of School Directors of each county shall constitute, and are hereby empowered to act as an Auditorial Board to audit all claims of teachers for services rendered in public schools of their respective counties, under the law and within the term specified in the caption of this act. In case of the refusal of any member of the late Board to act, the County Judge is hereby authorized to fill any vacancy; or if all the members of the late Board fail or refuse to act, then, in that case, to appoint a new Board.

SEC. 2. Each member shall be required to take an oath that he will faithfully perform the duties devolving upon him under this act.

SEC. 3. The Auditorial Board shall meet at the county-seats of their respective counties as soon as possible after the passage of this act and organize, when the Board will give thirty days' notice of the time of the meeting of the Board, by publishing said notice for thirty days in some newspaper published in the county; and if there is no newspaper published in the county, then by posting the same in ten public places in the county. At the expiration of the time, the Board will hold its sessions from day to day until they have passed upon such claims as may have been presented to them; *provided,* they shall not remain in session longer than six days.

SEC. 4. No claim shall be considered by the Board that has not been filed with said Board, or some member thereof, on or before the day set for their meeting.

SEC. 5. The Board, after the notice given as named in Section 3 of this act, shall proceed to pass upon all claims submitted to them under the requirements of this act, marking upon each, in writing and in figures, the amount due on each claim submitted.

SEC. 6. Having ascertained the amounts on all claims submitted, they shall aggregate the claims by school districts, indicating in the aggregate the amounts found to be due by each school district, respectively.

SEC. 7. In passing upon claims, the Board shall be governed strictly by the law and official instructions of the Superintendent of Public Instruction in force at the time the contract was entered into.

SEC. 8.   Having ascertained the amounts due from each district, they shall furnish the Commissioners' Court with a correct list of the several amounts due each claimant, together with a description, as far as practicable, of the bounds of each district.

SEC. 9.   It shall be the duty of the Commissioners' Court, upon the receipt of said list, to make the necessary levy up(on) the property of each district separately that is in arrears, to raise sufficient revenue to satisfy said claims of teachers and expenses incurred in the execution of this law.

SEC. 10.   It shall be the duty of the County Treasurer to report to the Commissioners' Court, the amount obtained from each district as soon as full returns have been made from any given district.

SEC. 11.   It shall be the duty of the Commissioners' Court, upon receipt of said report, from the County Treasurer to order warrants to be issued on the County Treasurer in favor of claimants for the full amount shown to be due, if there be sufficient funds on hand to pay all the claims; but if it appear that there is not sufficient funds to pay all the claims against the district in full, the said Court shall *pro-rata* the amounts due and draw warrants accordingly, taking receipt for the same in full or partially as the case may be.

SEC. 12.   The County Treasurer shall pay said warrants whenever presented, and hold the same as his voucher.

SEC. 13.   In the event the records of the late Board of School Directors show that there are no claims as herein specified outstanding and due teachers, then said Board shall not be required to reorganize; or if these records show that sufficient tax has already been levied to meet all of said outstanding claims, but not collected, it shall only be necessary for the late County Superintendent of Public Instruction to report to the Commissioners' Court, in writing, the action had by the Board of Directors in regard to the matter of levying the deficiency school tax, giving the limits of the school districts, the amounts of levy in each, and the amount due each teacher, and also such expenses necessarily incurred in the execution of this law, when the said Court shall proceed to make sufficient levy to satisfy said claims; *provided*, all persons having paid the amount of school tax assessed against him or her, or any part thereof, shall have a credit for the amount so paid.

SEC. 14.   The members of the Auditorial Board shall be allowed four dollars per day for every day they shall be engaged in the discharge of their duty as such Board, including the time in going to and returning from the county seat, and all other officers mentioned in this act, and the Collector of Taxes, shall receive such compensation as is now allowed by law for similar services.

SEC. 15.   The amounts necessary to defray the expenses of the execution of this law shall be included in the aggregate assessment against said district.

SEC. 16.   Whereas, an imperative public necessity exists for the passage of this law, in order that teachers may be paid the amounts due them, that this act be in force from and after its passage.

SEC. 17.   That all laws and parts of laws in conflict with the provisions of this act the same be and are hereby repealed.

Approved August 7, 1876.

Takes effect from its passage.

CHAPTER LXXXI.—*An Act to provide for and regulate Mechanics', Contractors', Builders', and other liens in the State of Texas.*

SECTION 1. *Be it enacted by the Legislature of the State of Texas,* That any person or firm, lumber dealer, artisan or mechanic, who may labor or furnish material, machinery, fixtures and tools, to erect any house, improvement, or to repair any building or any improvement whatever, shall have a lien on such house, building, fixtures or improvements, and shall also have a lien on the lot, or lots, or land, necessarily connected therewith, to secure payment for labor done, lumber, material, or fixtures furnished for construction or repairs. In order to fix and secure the lien herein provided for, the person or firm, contractor, mechanic, laborer, artisan or lumber dealer furnishing material, shall have the right at any time within six months after such debt becomes due to file his contract in the office of the County Clerk of the county in which such property is situated, and cause the same to be recorded in a book to be kept by the County Clerk for that purpose. If the contract, order or agreement be verbal, a duplicate copy of the bill of particulars shall be made, under oath, one to be delivered to the Clerk to be filed and recorded as provided for written contracts, and the other to be furnished to the party owing the debt. Both the contracts and accounts, when filed and recorded as above provided, shall be accompanied by a description of the lands, lots, houses, and improvements made, against which the lien is claimed. When such contract or account is filed and recorded, it shall be deemed sufficient diligence to secure the lien herein provided.

SEC. 2. The lien herein provided, if against land in the country, shall extend to and include fifty acres upon which such labor has been performed, or upon which the houses and improvements are situated. If in a city, town or village, it shall extend to or include such lot or lots upon which such houses, fixtures or improvements are situated, or upon which such labor was performed.

SEC. 3. The lien herein provided for labor performed or material furnished shall extend to the land designated, and the person enforcing the same may have the lot or lots and improvements sold altogether, or he may have the improvements sold only; and when the improvements are sold separately, the purchaser shall be by the officer making the sale placed in possession thereof, and he shall have the right to remove the same within a reasonable time from date of purchase; said sale to be upon judgment rendered by some court of competent jurisdiction foreclosing such lien and ordering sale of such property.

SEC. 4. But when lumber or material is furnished, labor performed, erection or repairs made upon a homestead, to fix a lien upon the same, it shall be the duty of persons, mechanics, artisans, lumber dealers or laborers, who shall perform any labor, or furnish any material upon or about the construction of any improvement or repairs upon a homestead, to make and enter into a contract in writing, setting forth the terms of said contract, which said contract in writing shall be signed by the husband and wife and acknowledged by her as required in making a sale of the homestead at the time when such improvements or repairs are to be made, or material furnished, or labor performed, and all such contracts shall be recorded in the County Clerk's office, in the county where such improvements are being made or land situated.

SEC. 5. The lien and contract mentioned in Section four shall inure to the benefit of mechanics, artisans, laborers and lumber dealers, and other material men, who shall have built, erected, repaired, improved or furnished material for a homestead.

Sec. 6.   Every mechanic, workman, or other person doing and performing any work or furnishing materials towards the erection, construction or completion of any building erected or improvement made under a contract between the owner of said building or other improvement and the original contractor, whose demand for work and labor performed, or material furnished toward the completion of said building or improvement has not been paid, may deliver to the owner of said building or improvement an attested account of the amount and value of said labor or materials thus furnished and remaining unpaid, and thereupon the owner shall retain out of the amount due such original contractor, if any, the amount of said labor or material furnished for the benefit of the party performing the work or furnishing the material; and a compliance with the provisions of this section shall be considered sufficient diligence to fix the liability of the owner of such building or improvement for the payment of such demand.

Sec. 7.   Whenever any such account shall be placed in the hands of such owner or his authorized agent, it shall be the duty of such owner or his agent to furnish his contractor with a true copy of said attested account; and if said contractor shall not, within ten days after the receipt of said copy of attested account, give the owner written notice that he intends to dispute said claims, he shall be considered as assenting to the demand, which shall be paid by the owner when it becomes due.   If said contractor shall dispute the claim of his journeyman or other person, for work and labor performed, or material furnished, as provided for in the preceding section, then such owner shall withhold the amount of said demand until the matter is adjusted between the parties by agreement, arbitration, suit or otherwise, when he shall pay over the amount to the party entitled to receive the same.

Sec. 8.   An Act entitled, "An Act to provide for and regulate mechanics', contractors,' builders' and other liens in the State of Texas," approved November 17, 1871, and all laws and parts of laws in conflict with this act, shall be and the same are hereby repealed.

Approved August 7, 1876.

Takes effect ninety days after adjournment.

CHAPTER LXXXII.—*An Act fixing the times of holding the District Courts in the Twenty-third Judicial District.*

Section 1.   *Be it enacted by the Legislature of the State of Texas,* That the District Courts of the Twenty-third Judicial District shall be holden at the times hereinafter specified, to-wit : In the county of Karnes on the first Monday in March and September, and may continue in session one week ; in the county of Live Oak on the first Monday after the first Monday in March and September, and may continue in session one week ; in the county of Bee on the second Monday after the first Monday in March and September, and may continue in session one week ; in the county of San Patricio on the third Monday after the first Monday in March and September, and may continue in session one week ; in the county of Refugio on the fourth Monday after the first Monday in March and September, and may continue in session one week ; in the county of Goliad on the fifth Monday after the first Monday in

March and September, and may continue in session two weeks; in the county of Calhoun on the seventh Monday after the first Monday in March and September, and may continue in session two weeks; in the county of Aransas on the ninth Monday after the first Monday in March and September, and may continue in session one week; in the county of Victoria on the tenth Monday after the first Monday in March and September, and may continue in session three weeks; in the county of DeWitt on the fourteenth Monday after the first Monday in March and September, and may continue in session three weeks.

SEC. 2. That in order to avoid conflict, and in order to facilitate the transaction of business in the courts of said district, an imperative public necessity exists for the passage of this act; therefore, this act shall take effect and be in force from and after its passage.

Approved August 9, 1876.

Takes effect from its passage.

CHAPTER LXXXIII.—*An Act supplemental to and amendatory of an act entitled " An Act regulating the government of the Agricultural and Mechanical College of Texas," approved March 9, 1875.*

SECTION 1. *Be it enacted by the Legislature of the State of Texas,* That each of the Board of Directors of the Agricultural and Mechanical College of Texas, except the Governor of the State, shall be allowed the sum of five dollars per day for each day they may have attended, or shall hereafter attend, the meetings of the Directors; and that they be allowed five dollars for each and every twenty-five miles traveled from their place of residence to the place of meeting; *provided,* that when meetings of the Board occur during sessions of the Legislature, the Lieutenant-Governor and Speaker shall not receive mil(e)age and per diem.

SEC. 2. That all laws and parts of laws in conflict with this act be and the same are here(by) repealed.

SEC. 3. There having been two meetings of said Board of Directors, and said Directors having expended their own private means in their attendance on the said meetings, an emergency and imperative necessity exists for the passage of this act, and that the same take effect from and after its passage.

Approved August 9, 1876.

Takes effect from its passage.

CHAPTER LXXXIV.—*An Act to regulate proceedings in the County Court pertaining to the estates of deceased persons.*

SECTION 1. *Be it enacted by the Legislature of the State of Texas,* That there shall be established in each organized county in this State a County Court, which shall be a court of record, and shall have the general jurisdiction of a Probate Court. Said court shall consist of a County Judge, who shall possess the qualifications, be elected, and hold office, as prescribed by the Constitution. The jurisdiction of said court shall be exercised as provided in this act, and wills shall be admitted to probate, and letters testamentary or of administration shall be granted: first, in the county where the deceased resided, if he had a domicil or fixed place of residence in the State; second, if the deceased had no domicil or fixed place of residence in the State, but died in the State, then either in the county where his principal property was at the time of his death, or in the county where he died; third, if he had no domicil or fixed place of residence in the State, and died without the limits of the State, then in any county in this State where his nearest kin may reside; fourth, but if he had no kindred in the State, then in the county where his principal estate may be situated. And the probate of wills and grant of letters of administration in any other than the proper county shall be void.

SEC. 2. Before granting letters testamentary, it must appear to the court: first, that the person is dead; second, that four years have not elapsed since his decease prior to the application; third, that the court has jurisdiction of the estate; fourth, that the will has been proved as prescribed by law; fifth, that the person to whom the letters are to be granted is named as executor in the will; sixth, that the person named as executor is not disqualified by law. The first three subdivisions of this section have no application when letters of administration have been previously granted in said court. Before granting letters of administration, it must appear to the court: first, that the person is dead; second, that four years have not elapsed since his decease prior to the application; third, that the court has jurisdiction of the estate; fourth, that the person to whom the letters are about to be granted is entitled thereto by law, and is not disqualified. All applications for the probate of wills, and for letters testamentary or of administration, shall be in writing and filed with the Clerk of the County Court. Upon the filing of any such application it shall be the duty of the Clerk to give at least ten days' notice thereof, by advertisement posted at the courthouse, and at two other public places in the county not in the same city or town; and proof that such notice has been given shall be made to the satisfaction of the court before any action shall be had on such application.

SEC. 3. A written will may be proved by the affidavit in writing of one of the subscribing witnesses thereto, taken in open court and subscribed by the witnesses. If all the witnesses are non-residents of the county, or those resident in the county are unable to attend court, it may be proved by the testimony of any one or more of them taken by deposition. If none of the witnesses are living, such a will may be probated on proof by two witnesses of the handwriting of the subscribing witnesses, and also of the testator, if he was able to write; which proof may be either by affidavit taken in open court and subscribed by the witness, or by deposition. If the will was wholly written by the testator, it may be probated on proof by two witnesses of his handwriting, which proof may also be made either by affidavit taken in open court and subscribed by the witnesses, or by deposition; such affidavits or depositions shall be filed in the court, and together with the will shall be recorded by the clerk; and in any suit that may afterwards be instituted to contest the validity of any such will, such record shall be evidence, if the witness or witnesses be dead or resident without the county. Any person interested in any such will may, within four years after it is admitted to probate, institute suit in the County Court to contest its validity; *provided*, that infants, *femes covert* and persons *non compos mentis*, shall have the like period after the removal of their respective disabilities; *and provided, also*, that any such will may be attacked for forgery or any other fraud, at the suit of any heir at law of the testator, or any other person interested in his estate, at any time within four years after the discovery of such forgery or other fraud; and infants, *femes covert*, and persons *non compos mentis*, shall have a like period after the removal of their disabilities.

SEC. 4. No noncupative will shall be proved within fourteen days after the death of the testator, nor until those who would have been entitled by inheritance, had there been no will, have been cited to contest the same if they please; nor shall any such will be probated after six months have elapsed from the time of speaking the pretended testamentary words, unless the same or the substance thereof shall have been committed to writing within six days after making such will; nor shall any such will be probated unless it be made in the time of the last sickness of the deceased, at his or her habitation, or where he or she hath resided for ten days next preceding, except when the deceased is taken sick away from home and dies before he or she returns to such habitation; nor shall any such will be probated unless it be proved by three credible witnesses that the testator or testatrix called on some person to take notice or bear testimony that such is his or her will, or words of like import; and whenever any such will may be probated, the evidence of the witnesses shall be committed to writing, sworn to and subscribed in open court by the witnesses, and shall be recorded by the clerk.

SEC. 5. When application is made for the probate of a will which has been probated according to the laws of any of the United States and territories, or of any country out of the limits of the United States, a copy of such will and of the probate thereof, attested by the clerk of the court in which such will was admitted to probate, and the seal of the court annexed, if there be a seal, together with a certificate from the Judge, County Judge or presiding magistrate, as the case may be, that the said attestation is in due form, may be filed and recorded in the court, and shall have the same force and effect as the original will, if probated in said court; *provided*, that the validity of such will may be contested in the same manner as the original might have been.

SEC. 6. Application for the probate of a will may be made by the testamentary executor, or by any person interested in the estate of the testator.

SEC. 7. When application is made for the probate of a will, any person interested in the estate of the testator may at any time before trial file his opposition thereto in writing, and on trial of the matter, all oral testimony shall be taken down in writing and subscribed by the witness or witnesses; copies of all testimony, and also of the testimony of witnesses taken by deposition, shall be admitted in evidence on the trial of the same matter in any other court when taken there by appeal or otherwise.

SEC. 8. When a will shall have been probated, it shall be the duty of the court to grant letters testamentary to the executor or executors appointed by such will, if any there be, or to such of them as are not disqualified, and are willing to accept the trust and qualify according to law, within twenty days after such probate.

SEC. 9. When any person shall die intestate, or when no executor is named in a will, or when the executor or executors named in a will are disqualified, or shall renounce the executorship, or shall neglect to accept and qualify within twenty days after the probate of the will, or shall neglect for a period of thirty days after the death of the testator to present the will for probate, then administration of the estate of such intestate or administration with the will annexed of the estate of such testator, shall be granted: first, to the surviving husband or surviving wife; second, to the next of kin, or the principal devisee or legatee of such intestate or testator, or to some one or more of them; and if none of these apply, or if applying they neglect to qualify for a period of twenty days after the order for their appointment, then to such other proper person or persons as will accept and qualify; *provided*, that no administration shall be had under this act, of any estate, unless it shall be shown to the court granting the administration that the intestate was in debt at the time of his death, and at the time of the filing of the application for letters of administration.

SEC. 10. Letters testamentary or of administration shall not be granted to any person who is under twenty-one years of age, or of unsound mind, or who has been convicted of any infamous crime; *provided, however*, that such letters may be granted to a surviving husband or wife who may be under twenty-one years of age.

SEC. 11. When the executor or executors named in a will are under age, and letters of administration, with the will annexed, have been granted to any other person or persons, such letters shall, at any time thereafter, be revoked on the application of such executor or executors, or any one of them, and letters testamentary issued to such executor or executors, or any of them, upon proof being made that he or they have attained the age of twenty-one years; and when two or more persons are named executors in a will, any one or more of whom are minors when such will is admitted to probate, and letters testamentary have been issued to such only as are of full age, such minor or minors, upon attaining the age of twenty-one years, shall be permitted to qualify and receive letters.

SEC. 12. Whenever any person named as executor shall have been absent from the State when the testator died or when the will was proved, whereby he was prevented from presenting the will for probate within thirty days after the death of the testator, or from accepting and qualifying as executor within twenty days after the probate of the will, or whenever he shall have been prevented by sickness from so presenting the will or so accepting and qualifying, he shall be allowed to accept and qualify as executor at any time within sixty days after his return to the State, or his recovery from sickness, upon making proof to the court that he was so absent or prevented by sickness; and if in the meantime letters of administration with the will annexed have been granted, such letters shall be revoked; *provided*, he shall have first caused the person to whom letters have been granted to be cited to appear before said court and show cause why said letters should not be revoked.

SEC. 13. When administration has been granted to any other person or persons than the surviving husband or surviving wife of the testator or intestate, upon application being made by him or her, such other person or persons shall be removed from the administration and letters of administration be granted to such applicant.

SEC. 14. When administration has been granted to any other persons than the surviving husband or the surviving wife, or the next of kin, or the principal devisee or legatee of the intestate or testator, upon application being made by the next of kin, or the principal devisee or legatee of such intestate or testator, or any of them, such other person or persons shall be removed from the administration, and letters shall be granted to such next of kin, or principal devisee or legatee, or to some one or more of them; *provided*, that said husband or wife, or next of kin, or the principal devisee or legatee of such intestate or testator, have not waived their right.

SEC. 15. Whenever letters of administration shall have been granted upon an estate, and it shall afterwards be discovered that the deceased left a lawful will, such will may be proved in the manner provided in this act; and if an executor is named in such will he shall be allowed to accept and qualify in the manner herein provided; but if no such executor be named, or if the executor named be disqualified, or shall renounce the executorship, or shall neglect to accept and qualify within twenty days after the probate of the will, or shall neglect for a period of thirty days after the discovery of such will to present it for probate, then administration, with the will annexed, of the estate of such testator shall be granted according to the provisions of this act; and whenever such executor shall accept and qualify, or whenever any person shall be appointed and qualified as administrator with the will annexed, the letters of administration previously granted shall be revoked; but all acts done by the first administrator, previous to the qualification of the executor or administrator with the will annexed, shall be as valid as if no such will had been discovered.

SEC. 16. When a will has been admitted to probate in any of the United States or the territories thereof, or of any country out of the limits of the United States, and the executor or executors named in such will have qualified, and a copy of such will and of the probate thereof has been filed and recorded in any court of this State under the provisions of the fifth section of this act, and letters of administration with such will annexed have been granted to any person or persons other than the executor or executors therein named, upon the application of such executor or executors, or any one of them, such letters shall be revoked, and letters testamentary shall be issued to such applicant, and if said executor or executrix, when he or she be a resident or non-resident, if no objection be made by creditors of said testator, shall have authority to sell and convey any property belonging to the estate of his testator that he may deem necessary without any action of the County Court.

SEC. 17. When application is made for letters of administration, any person may, at any time before the said application is granted, file his opposition thereto in writing, and may apply for the grant of letters to himself or to any other person; and upon the trial the court shall grant letters to the person or persons that may seem best entitled to them, having regard to the provisions of this act, without further notice than that of the original application.

SEC. 18. Whenever an estate is unrepresented by reason of the death, removal, or resignation of the executor or executors, or administrator or administrators, the court shall grant administration with the will annexed of the estate not administered, or administration of the estate not administered, as the case may be, in the same manner and under the regulations herein prescribed for the appointment of original administrators.

SEC. 19. Whenever an executor or administrator has been qualified in the manner required by this act, the certificate of the Clerk of the court, attested by the seal of said court, as to the qualification of said executor or administrator, shall be sufficient evidence of such appointment and qualification when it shall be necessary to make proof of such fact.

SEC. 20. Wills shall be probated, and letters testamentary or of administration with full powers shall be granted, only in open court at a regular term thereof, after application in writing and notice as hereinbefore required; but whenever it may appear to the County Judge that the interest of an estate requires the immediate appointment of an administrator, he shall either in open court or in vacation, by writing under his hand and the seal of the court, attested by the Clerk, appoint some proper person administrator *pro tem.*, with such limited powers as the circumstances of the case may require. Such appointment may be made without notice, shall define the powers conferred, and before being delivered to the person appointed shall be recorded in the minutes of the court, and the Clerk shall endorse thereon a certificate that it has been so recorded; and until such record and certificate are made, the appointment shall not take effect; such appoinment shall cease to be of force on the first day of the term of the court next after the date thereof, unless continued in force by an order entered on the minutes in open court; and in no case shall such appointment continue in force beyond the first day of the second term of the court next after the date thereof.

Sec. 21. Pending any contest relative to the probate of a will, or the granting of letters of administration, whether such contest be in the County Court or in any other court on appeal, it shall be the duty of the County Judge to appoint an administrator *pro tem.*, in the manner prescribed in the preceding section, and with such limited powers as the circumstances of the case may require; such appointment may continue in force until the termination of the contest and the appointment of an executor or administrator with full powers.

Sec. 22. Before the issuance of letters of administration *pro tem.* under the provisions of the two preceding sections, the person appointed shall take and subscribe an oath and enter into bond; which bond and oath shall be in substance the same as the bond and oath required of other administrators, varying the form to suit the particular case; and such bond and oath shall be filed and recorded in the like manner as other bonds of administrators.

Sec. 23. If there be more than one executor or administrator named in the letters, any one or more of them, on the neglect of the rest, may return an inventory as required by this act; and the executor or administrator so neglecting shall not thereafter interfere with the estate, or have any power over the same; but the executor and administrator so returning shall have thereafter the whole administration, unless within two months after the return, the delinquent or delinquents shall assign to the court some reasonable excuse which it shall deem satisfactory.

Sec. 24. When an administrator of the estate not administered has been, or shall be hereafter appointed, he shall succeed to all the rights, powers and duties of the former executor or administrator, except such rights and powers conferred on the former executor by the will of the testator as are different from those conferred by this act on executors generally; and such administrators shall have power to make themselves parties to all suits prosecuted by the former executor or administrator of the estate, and may be made parties to all suits prosecuted against the former executor or administrator of the estate. They shall have power to settle with the former executor or administrator of the estate, and to receive and receipt for all such portion of the estate as remains in their hands; they shall have power to bring suit on the bond or bonds of the former executor or administrator in their own name as administrators for all the estate that has not been accounted for by such former executor or administrator; and they shall proceed to administer such estate in like manner as if their administration was a continuation of the administration of the former executor or administrator, with the exceptions hereinbefore named; but such administrators shall, within one month after being qualified, return an inventory and list of claims in like manner as is required in this act for original administrators; and they shall also, in like manner, return additional inventories and lists of claims. And whenever an executor shall accept and qualify, after letters of administration shall have been granted, such executor shall, in like manner, succeed to the previous administrator; and he shall proceed to administer the estate in like manner as if his administration was a continuation of the former one, subject, however, to any legal directions of the testator in relation to the management of the estate.

SEC. 25. Whenever, under the provisions of this act, an administrator *pro tem.* shall have been appointed, and an executor shall afterwards be qualified, or an administrator appointed, such executor or administrator shall succeed and be made a party to all suits and actions prosecuted by or against such administrator *pro tem.*; and such executor or administrator shall have the right to settle with such administrator *pro tem.*, and receive and receipt for all the estate remaining in his hands, and shall have the right to sue, in like manner as is provided for in the previous section, on the bond of such administrator *pro tem.*, for all the estate not accounted for by him.

SEC. 26. Executors and administrators shall be removed by the County Judge, without notice, in term time, by an order entered on the minutes of the court in the following cases: First, when they neglect to qualify in the manner required by this act within twenty days after the will is probated, or the order is made for granting of their letters. Second, when they shall neglect to return to the court, within sixty days after receiving their letters, an inventory of the estate committed to their charge, so far as the same has come to their knowledge. Third, when they have been required to give a new bond, and neglect to do so within the time prescribed by the court. Fourth, when administrators absent themselves from the State for a period of three months, without the permission of the court.

SEC. 27. Executors and administrators may be removed by the County Judge, of his own motion or on the complaint of any person interested in the estate, after being cited to answer such complaint or motion, in the following cases: First, when they shall fail to make to the court any exhibit that they are required to make by the provisions of this act, or when they shall fail to comply with any order that the County Judge is authorized to make against them, under the provisions of the same. Second, when there shall appear sufficient grounds to believe that they have or are about to misapply, embezzle or remove from the State, the property committed to their charge. Third, when they are proved to have been guilty of gross neglect or mismanagement in the performance of any of their duties. Fourth, when they fail to obey any order of the court consistent with this act, in relation to the estate committed to their charge. In the cases enumerated in this section, on proof being made that the executor or administrator has removed from the State, or otherwise endeavored to elude the service of process on any such complaint or motion, the same may be heard and determined, though the citation be not served; and in all cases where an executor or administrator is removed, the causes of such removal shall be set forth in the order of removal.

SEC. 28. If any person named as executor shall have renounced the executorship, or shall have been removed therefrom, he shall not afterwards be appointed administrator of the estate; and whenever any person shall have been removed from the administration of an estate, he shall not afterwards be appointed administrator thereof.

SEC. 29. If at any time an executor or administrator shall wish to resign the administration of the estate that has been committed to his charge, he may present to the court from which his letters issued, a full and complete exhibit of the condition of the estate, together with his administration account—both of which shall be verified by affidavit—and also his application in writing for leave to resign; whereupon it shall be the duty of the clerk to make out a citation returnable to some regular term of the court, which citation shall state the presentation of such exhibit, account and application, the term of the court to which it is returnable, and shall require all those interested in the estate to appear and contest such account if they see proper. Such citation shall be published for at least twenty days in some newspaper printed in the county, if there be one; if not, then by posting copies thereof for a like period at three public places in the county. Proof of such publication may be made by the affidavit of the publisher or printer attached to a copy thereof. At the return term of such citation, or at some other term to which it may have been continued, upon the County Judge being satisfied that such citation has been published or posted, as the case may be, he shall proceed to examine such exhibit and account, and to hear all proof that may be offered in support of the same, and all objections and exceptions thereto; and shall, if necessary, re-state such accounts, and shall audit and settle the same.   If it shall then appear that such executor or administrator has accounted for all said estate according to law the County Judge shall order him to deliver the estate, if there be any remaining in his possession, to some person who has given bond for the same, in like manner as herein prescribed for administrators. Upon complying with such order, said executor or administrator shall be permitted to resign his trust and be discharged.

SEC. 30. Before the issuance of letters testamentary or of administration with the will annexed, the person named executor or appointed administrator with the will annexed, shall, before the Clerk or County Judge, or any officer authorized to administer oaths, take and subscribe an oath in form as follows: "I do solemnly swear that the writing which has been offered for probate is the last will of ———, so far as I know or believe, and that I will well and truly perform all the duties of executor of said will, or of administrator with the will annexed, of the estate of said ———."

SEC. 31. Before the issuance of letters of administration, the person appointed administrator shall, before the Clerk or County Judge, or any officer authorized to administer oaths, take and subscribe an oath in form as follows: "I do solemnly swear that ———, deceased, died without leaving any lawful will, so far as I know or believe; and that I will well and truly perform all the duties of administrator of the estate of said ———."

SEC. 32. Before the issuance of letters testamentary or of administration, the person named as executor or appointed administrator, shall enter into bond with at least two good and sufficient sureties, to be approved by and payable to the County Judge of the county, in such penalty as he may direct, not less than double the estimated value of the estate of the testator or intestate; *provided*, however, that when any testator shall direct in his will that no security shall be required of the person or persons named therein as executor or executors, letters testamentary shall be issued to such person or persons without any bond being required.

SEC. 33. The oath of an executor or administrator may be taken and subscribed, or his bond may be given, either in term time or vacation, at any time before the expiration of twenty days from the probate of the will or the order granting the letters, or before his letters shall have been revoked for a failure to do so within the time allowed, and all such oaths and bonds shall be filed and recorded by the clerk.

SEC. 34. The following form may be used for the bonds of executors and administrators:

The State of Texas, county of ———. Know all men by these presents, that we, A. B., as principal, and C. D. and E. F., as sureties, are held and firmly bound unto the County Judge of the county of ———, or his successors in office, in the sum of——— dollars, for the payment of which, well and truly to be made unto the said County Judge, we bind ourselves, our heirs, executors and administrators, jointly and severally, firmly by these presents, signed with our hands the ——— day of ———, A. D. 18—. The condition of this obligation is such, that whereas the above bound A. B. has been appointed executor of the last will and testament of J. C., deceased (or has been appointed by the County Judge of the county of ———, administrator, with the will annexed, of the estate of the said J. C., deceased; or has been appointed by the County Judge of the county of ———, administrator of the estate of J. C., deceased, as the case may be). Now if the said A. B. shall well and truly perform all the duties required of him under said appointment, then this obligation shall be null and void, otherwise to remain of full force and effect.

A. B.
C. D.
E. F.

SEC. 35. Whenever a married woman may be appointed as executrix, and shall wish to accept and qualify as such, she may jointly with her husband execute such bond as the law requires, and acknowledge the same before the County Judge or Clerk of the court, or any Notary Public of the county where the will was proved or letters were granted; and such bond shall bind her estate in the same manner as if she were a *feme sole;* and whenever an executrix may be a married woman she shall act as a *feme sole* in all matters pertaining to her said representative capacity; *provided,* that no married woman shall administer the estate of her former husband during the continuance of the second or subsequent marriage.

SEC. 36. Whenever a surviving husband or wife under twenty-one years of age shall wish to accept and qualify as executor or executrix, or administrator or administratrix, he or she may execute such bonds as the law requires, and acknowledge the same before the County Judge, Clerk of the Court, or any Notary Public of the county in which the will was proved or letters of administration were granted, and such bonds shall be as valid as if he or she were of lawful age.

SEC. 37. When the sureties upon an executor's or administrator's bond, or any one of them, shall die, or shall remove beyond the limits of the State, or shall become insolvent; or when in the opinion of the County Judge the sureties upon any such bond are insufficient, it shall be his duty, either in term time or vacation, to cause a citation to be issued and served upon such executor or administrator, requiring him to appear and show cause why he should not be required to give a new bond, on a day named in such citation, which may be in term time or vacation. And on the return of said citation served, the County Judge shall inquire into the truth of the matter, and if satisfied of the truth thereof, he shall require such executor or administrator to give a new bond.

Sec. 38. Any person interested in an estate may present a petition to the County Judge, representing that the bond of the executor or administrator is insufficient, whereupon it shall be the duty of the County Judge, either in term time or vacation, to cause a citation to be issued and served on such executor or administrator, requiring him to appear upon a day named in the citation, which may be either in term time or vacation, and show cause why he should not be required to give a new bond; and on the return of such citation served, the County Judge shall inquire into the truth of the fact alleged, and if satisfied of the insufficiency of the bond he shall require such executor or administrator to give a new bond; *provided*, that the administrator or executor shall pay all the cost of this proceeding when the bond is insufficient, and said administrator or executor shall not pay out any money or do any other official act after said service upon him until his new bond is approved.

Sec. 39. The sureties upon the bond of an executor or administrator, or any one of them, may at any time present a petition to the County Judge, praying that such executor or administrator may be required to give a new bond, and that he or they may be discharged from all liability for the future acts of such executor or administrator; whereupon it shall be the duty of said County Judge, whether in term time or in vacation, to cause a citation to be issued and served on such executor or administrator, requiring him to appear, on a day named in the citation, which may be either in term time or in vacation, and give a new bond; and whenever such new bond shall have been given and approved by the County Judge, such sureties shall be discharged from all liability under their bond for the future acts of such executor or administrator.

Sec. 40. In all cases where a new bond shall be required from an executor or administrator, under the provisions of this act, an order to that effect shall be entered in the minutes of the court, naming the time within which new bond shall be given; and until such new bond shall have been given and approved, the order shall have the effect to suspend the powers of such executor or administrator.

Sec. 41. The bond of an executor or administrator of any kind shall not become void on the first recovery, but may be put in suit and prosecuted from time to time until the whole amount thereof shall have been recovered. Such suit may be brought and prosecuted by any administrator of the estate not administered, in his own name as administrator, whenever the estate he represents has been injured by the breach of the bond of the executor or any previous administrator of the estate; or any other person or persons injured by a breach of any such bond may bring suit thereon in their own name, and any number of such persons may join in such suit.

Sec. 42. All suits on the bond of any executor or administrator shall be commenced and prosecuted within four years next after the death, resignation, removal or discharge of such administrator, and not thereafter; *provided, however,* that infants, *femes covert,* and persons *non compos mentis* shall have at least two years within which to institute such suits after the removal of their respective disabilities.

SEC. 43. Whenever letters testamentary or of administration shall be granted, the County Judge shall, by an order entered on the minutes of the court, appoint three or more disinterested persons and citizens of the county, any two of whom may act, to appraise the estate of the deceased. If from any cause such appointments be not made, or if the appraisers or any of them so appointed fail or refuse to act, or if from any other cause a new appointment is required, the County Judge shall by a like order, either in term time or vacation, appoint another appraiser or appraisers, as the case may require; and in all cases any two appraisers may act. Such appraisers shall each receive two dollars per day for every day they may be necessarily engaged, and all reasonable expenses.

SEC. 44. Every executor or administrator shall immediately after his appointment, with the assistance of any two or more of the appraisers appointed by the County Judge, make or cause to be made a full inventory and appraisement of all the estate of the testator or intestate, both real and personal, specifying in such inventory what portion of such estate is the separate property of the deceased, and what portion, if any, is represented as common property. The appraisement of the property specified in the inventory shall be sworn to and subscribed by the appraisers making the same before some officer of the county authorized by law to administer oaths; such executor or administrator shall also make and attach to such inventory a full and complete list of all claims due or owing to the testator or intestate, specifying what portion of such claims is the separate property of the deceased, and what portion, if any, is common property; such executor or administrator shall also make and attach to such inventory and list his affidavit in writing, subscribed and sworn to before some officer of the county authorized by law to administer oaths, that the said inventory and list is a full and complete inventory and list of the property and claims of his testator or intestate that has come to his knowledge.

SEC. 45. The inventory and list required to be made by the preceding section shall be returned to the court by the executor or administrator within sixty days after the date of his appointment, and may be returned either in term time or vacation; but when returned and approved it shall be noticed on the minutes of the court, and shall be recorded by the Clerk.

SEC. 46. Whenever other property or claims of the testator or intestate than such as may be included in the inventory and list which has been returned shall come to the knowledge of the executor or administrator, he shall make and return an additional inventory or list of such newly discovered property or claims, without delay, which said additional inventory and list shall be made, returned and recorded, in like manner as original inventories and lists; and any executor or administrator, on complaint of any person interested in the estate, shall be cited by the County Judge, and on good and sufficient proof being made that any property and claims of the estate have not been included in the inventory and list returned, shall be required to make and return an additional inventory and list thereof in like manner as original inventories and lists.

SEC. 47. Inventories, appraisements and lists of claims, taken and returned in accordance with the foregoing provisions of this act, may be given in evidence in any suit by or against the executor or administrator; but shall not be conclusive for or against him if it be shown that there is other property not inventoried; or that there are other claims than those named in such lists; or that the property or any part thereof, was *bona fide* sold for more or less than the appraisement; or was not separate or common property, as specified in such inventories and lists.

SEC. 48. When any inventory and appraisement has been returned in the manner hereinbefore provided, any person interested in the estate who may deem such appraisement unjust or erroneous, may apply to the County Judge for a new appraisement, notice of which application, together with a citation, shall be served on the executor or administrator, requiring him to appear at a regular term of the court and show cause why a new appraisement should not be made. On the return of such citation, served, the County Judge shall inquire into the truth of the facts alleged, and if satisfied that such appraisement was manifestly unjust or erroneous, shall appoint other appraisers and order a new appraisement to be made and returned in like manner as original appraisements. When such new appraisement is made and returned, and approved, it shall be recorded, and shall stand in the place of the original appraisement, which shall be as if never made; *provided*, that not more than one re-appraisement shall be made.

SEC. 49. It shall be the duty of the executor or administrator to take such care of the property of his testator or intestate, real and personal, as a prudent man would take care of his own property, and if there be any buildings or houses belonging to the estate, it shall be his duty to keep the same in tenantable repair, extraordinary casualities excepted: and all reasonable expenses incurred by the executor or administrator in taking such care of the property, or in making such repairs, on sufficient proof thereof, shall be allowed him by the County Judge.

SEC. 50. If there be a plantation or a manufactory belonging to the estate, and the disposition thereof be not specially directed by will, and if the same be not required to be at once sold for the payment of debts, it shall be the duty of the executor or administrator to carry on the plantation or manufactory, or rent the same, as shall appear to him to be most for the interest of the estate. In coming to a determination, he shall take into consideration the condition of the estate, and the necessity that may exist for future sale of such property for the payment of claims or legacies, and shall not extend the time of renting or hiring any of the property beyond what may consist with the speedy settlement of the estate; and any one who is interested in the estate, may, upon good cause shown after citation to the executor or administrator, obtain an order controlling his action in this particular.

SEC. 51. Whenever any property is hired or rented by an executor or administrator, under the provisions of this act, such renting shall be made at public auction to the highest bidder, after having given at least ten days' notice thereof by posting a copy of such notice at the courthouse and two other public places in the county where the same is to take place; *provided*, the executor or administrator may rent or hire privately, but shall be required to show, to the satisfaction of the Judge, that private renting was advantageous to the estate.

SEC. 52. Every executor or administrator shall use ordinary diligence to collect every claim due to the estate he represents, and to recover possession of all property to which the estate has a right; *provided*, there is a reasonable prospect that such claim can be collected on such property recovered; and if any executor or administrator shall neglect to use such diligence, he and his sureties on his bond shall be liable, at the suit of any person interested in the estate, for the use of the estate for the amount of such claims and the value of such property as may have been lost by his neglect to use such diligence.

SEC. 53. The naming an executor in a will shall not operate to extinguish any just claim which the deceased had against him; and in all cases where an executor or administrator may be indebted to his testator or intestate, he shall account for the debt in the same manner as if it were so much money in his hands; *provided*, however, that if said debt was not due at the time of receiving letters, he shall only be required to account for it from the date when it shall become due.

SEC. 54. Whenever an executor or administrator shall think it will be for the interest of the estate he represents to purchase any property, or take any claims for the use and benefit of the estate in payment of any debt due the estate, he may present a petition to the County Judge at a regular term of the court, representing these facts, and if the County Judge shall be satisfied that it will be for the interest of the estate to purchase such property or take such claims, he may make a decree authorizing such executor or administrator to make such purchase, either at public or private sale, or to take such claims for the use and benefit of the estate.

SEC. 55. When the mortgagee of any property shall die, the executor or administrator of such mortgagee shall be and he is hereby authorized, on receiving from the mortgagor, or any person for him, the amount due to the estate he represents, to release to the mortgagor the legal title to such mortgaged property, and such release shall be valid.

SEC. 56. At the first term of the court after the original grant of letters testamentary or of administration, it shall be the duty of the County Judge to fix the amount of an allowance to be made for the support of the widow and minor children, if there be either or any, of the deceased, which allowance shall be of an amount sufficient for their maintenance for the term of one year, and shall be paid by the executor or administrator to the widow, if there be one; *provided*, that in case the widow is not the mother of said minor children, the portion of said allowance necessary for the support of such minor children shall be paid to their guardian, in case they have any such guardian; otherwise, to be paid to such widow, either in money out of the first funds of the estate that may come to his hands, or in such personal effects of the deceased as such widow or guardian may choose to take at the appraisement, or a part thereof in each, as they may select. If there be no personal effects of the estate that such widow or guardian are willing to take for such allowance, or not a sufficiency of them, and if there be no funds, or not sufficient funds of the estate in the hands of such executor or administrator to pay such allowance, or any part thereof, then it shall be the duty of the County Judge, so soon as the inventory and list of claims are returned, to order a sale of so much of the estate for cash as will be sufficient to raise the amount of such allowance, or a part thereof, as the case may require; *provided*, however, that when any such widow and minor children shall have separate property adequate to their maintenance then no such allowance shall be made as is provided for in this section.

Sec. 57. At the first term of the court after an inventory and list of claims have been returned, it shall be the duty of the County Judge to set apart for the use and benefit of the widow and minor children, and unmarried daughters remaining with the family, if there be either or any, of the deceased, all such property as may be exempted from execution or forced sale by the Constitution or laws of the State, with the exception of any exemption of one year's supply of provisions; and in case there should not be among the effects of the deceased all or any of the specific articles so exempted, it shall be the duty of the County Judge to make an allowance in lieu thereof to the widow and children, or such of them as there be, which allowance shall be paid by the executor or administrator, either in money out of the funds of the estate that may come to his hands, or in any property of the deceased that such widow or children may choose to take at the appraisement, or a part thereof, or both, as they may select. If there be no property of the deceased that such widow or children are willing to take for such allowance, or not a sufficiency, and there be no funds, or not sufficient funds of the estate in the hands of such executor or administrator to pay such allowance, or any part thereof, it shall be the duty of the County Judge, on the application of such widow or children, to order a sale of so much of the estate for cash as will be sufficient to raise the amount of such allowance, or a part thereof, as the case may require. Such allowance shall be paid in the following manner: If there be a widow and no children, the whole to be paid to the widow; if there be a child or children and no widow, the whole to be paid to such child, or to be equally divided among such children; if there be a widow and a child or children, one-half to be paid to the widow, and the other half to such child, or to be equally divided among such children; *provided*, that if the estate of such decedent be not insolvent, nothing in this section contained shall be so construed as to prohibit the partition and distribution of said estate, except the homestead, among the heirs and distributees thereof, including the portion herein provided to be set aside for the use of the widow and children; *provided*, that an allowance for homestead shall not exceed five thousand dollars, and the allowance for other exempted property shall not exceed five hundred dollars, exclusive of one year's provisions. No property on which liens have been given by the husband and wife, acknowledged privately and apart from her husband, to secure creditors, shall be appropriated to make up the five thousand dollars or five hundred dollars aforesaid, until the debts secured by such liens shall be discharged.

Sec. 58. It shall be the duty of executors and administrators, within one month after receiving their letters, to publish in some newspaper printed in the county where the letters were issued, if there be one, a notice requiring all persons having claims against the estate of the testator or intestate to present the same within the time prescribed by law, which notice shall state the time of the original grant of letters testamentary or of administration, and shall be published once a week for four successive weeks; when no newspaper is printed in the county, a copy of such notice shall also be posted at the court-house; a copy of such printed notice, together with the affidavit of the publisher of the paper that it was published once a week for four successive weeks, sworn to and subscribed before any County Judge, Clerk of a court or Notary Public, and attested by his official seal, may be filed and recorded in the court from which the letters were issued, and a copy thereof may be given in evidence in any court in any action, whether by or against the executor or administrator; and a copy of the notice posted at the court-house, with a certificate of the Clerk that such notice was so posted, may be filed and recorded and a copy thereof be given in evidence in the like manner as provided for the printed notice.

SEC. 59. Every claim for money against a testator or intestate shall be presented to the executor or administrator within twelve months after the original grant of letters testamentary or of administration, or the payment thereof shall be postponed until the claims which have been presented within said twelve months and allowed by the executor or administrator, and approved by the County Judge or established by suit, shall have been first entirely paid; *provided,* that if the executor or administrator absent himself from the State or county, the time of such absence shall not be computed in estimating the twelve months in which claims against the estate shall be presented.

SEC. 60. If any executor or administrator fail to give the notice required by the fifty-eighth section of this act to be given, he shall be removed by the County Judge at any regular term of the court, on the complaint of any person interested in the estate, after being cited to answer such complaint.

SEC. 61. No executor or administrator shall allow any claim for money against his testator or intestate, nor shall any County Judge approve any such allowance, unless such claim is accompanied by an affidavit in writing that the claim is just, and that all legal offsets, payments and credits known to the affiant have been allowed; which affidavit, if made in the county where the letters were granted, may be made before any officer of the county authorized to administer [oaths]; if made in any other county of this State, it shall be made before some County Judge, Clerk of a court, or Notary Public, and shall be attested by his official seal; if made out of the State, it shall be made before some Notary Public, Clerk or Judge of a court of record having a seal, or Commissioner of Deeds for this State, and shall be attested by the seal of his office. If any such claim is allowed or approved without such affidavit, such allowance or approval shall be of no force or effect.

SEC. 62. No holder of a claim for money against the estate of a deceased person shall bring suit thereon against the executor or administrator unless such claim, properly authenticated, has been presented to such executor or administrator and he has refused to allow such claim for the whole amout, or a part thereof; or unless such claim has been presented to the County Judge and he has disapproved of the allowance made by the executor or administrator, or a part thereof. In any suit that may be brought by the holder of any such claim, if he fails to recover thereon a greater amount than has been allowed by the executor or administrator, or than has been approved by the County Judge, he shall be liable for all costs of such suit.

SEC. 63. When any claim for money against an estate shall be presented to the executor or administrator, if the same be properly authenticated in the manner required by this act, he shall endorse thereon or annex thereto a memorandum in writing, signed by him, stating the time of its presentment, and that he allows or rejects the claim, or what portion thereof he allows or rejects, as the case may be. If the claim, or a part thereof, be allowed by the executor or administrator, it shall then be presented to the County Judge within three months, if said County Judge be not absent from the State or county, either in term time or vacation, who shall endorse thereon or annex thereto a memorandum in writing signed by him, stating that he approves or disapproves of such allowance, or of what portion of such allowance he approves or disapproves. If all or any portion of the claim be so allowed and approved, the holder thereof shall be entitled to receive payment of the amount so allowed and approved in due course of administration. If such claim be rejected by the executor or administrator, either for the whole amount or a part thereof, or if the allowance or any part thereof made by the executor or administrator be disapproved of by the County Judge, the holder of such claim may within three months after such rejection by the executor or administrator, but not thereafter, bring a suit against the executor or administrator for the establishment thereof in any court having jurisdiction of the same; and on the trial of such suit the memorandum in writing of the executor or administrator, or of the County Judge, endorsed on or annexed to such claim, may be given in evidence to prove the facts therein stated without proof of the handwriting of such executor or administrator or County Judge, unless the same be denied under oath. No execution shall issue on a judgment obtained by the plaintiff in any such suit, but such judgment shall have the same force and effect as if the amount thereof had been allowed by the executor or administrator and approved by the County Judge; *provided*, that when a claim has been allowed by the executor or administrator and approved by the County Judge, the owner or holder thereof shall within ten days thereafter cause a memorandum of the amount, date of claim and date of allowance and approval, [to be] recorded in the office of the County Clerk on the claim docket, a book for which purpose shall be kept by the Clerk.

SEC. 64. When a claim for money against the estate of a deceased person, authenticated in proper form, shall be presented to the executor or administrator within the time prescribed by law, if such executor or administrator fail or refuse to endorse thereon or annex thereto a memorandum in writing, as the previous section requires, such failure or refusal shall be deemed equivalent to a rejection of the claim by the executor or administrator, and shall authorize the holder to bring a suit for the establishment thereof in like manner as if such claim had been so rejected; and such executor or administrator shall be removed by the County Judge at any regular term of the court, on the complaint of any person interested in such claim, after being cited to answer such complaint, and proof being made of such failure or refusal.

SEC. 65. When any person shall sell property and enter into bond or other written agreement to make title thereto, and shall depart this life without having made such title, the holder of such bond or written agreement, or his legal representatives, may file a complaint in writing in the County Court of the county where letters testamentary or of administration of such deceased person were granted, praying that the executor or administrator may be required to make titles agreeably to the title bond or other written agreement of the deceased; whereupon it shall be the duty of the Clerk of said court to issue a citation with a copy of the complaint to be served on the executor or administrator, and on the return thereof, served at some regular term of the court, the County Judge shall, if he find that such sale was legally made, order the executor or administrator to make titles according to the tenor of the bond or other written agreement, to the property so sold by his testator or intestate; whereupon it shall be the duty of such executor or administrator to make titles in compliance with such order; *provided, however*, that any person interested in such estate may at any time within two years after the making of any such order have the same annulled and set aside by a suit in the District Court, upon good cause shown why the same should not have been made; *provided, also*, that married women, minors, and persons of unsound mind so interested, shall have a like period of two years after the removal of their respective disabilities within which they may in like manner have such order annulled and set aside.

SEC. 66.   At the first term of the court after the expiration of twelve months from the time of the original grant of letters testamentary or of administration, it shall be the duty of the executor or administrator to return to the court an exhibit in writing, sworn to and subscribed by him, setting forth a list of all claims against the estate that were presented to him within twelve months after the said grant of letters testamentary or of administration, specifying which have been allowed by him, which have been rejected, and the date when rejected; which have been sued upon, and the condition of the suit; also setting forth fully the condition of the estate; and if any executor or administrator shall neglect to return such exhibit at the term of the court named above, it shall be the duty of the County Judge to revoke his letters and fine him in a sum not to exceed one hundred dollars; said fine and order of revocation to be remitted and set aside only on good cause being shown for said failure either in term time or in vacation, on the complaint of any person interested in the estate, upon notice to such executor or administrator; *provided*, that before any judgment imposing a fine upon such executor or administrator shall be made final, such executor or administrator shall be served with notice.

SEC. 67.   At the third regular term of the court, after the expiration of twelve months from the original grant of letters testamentary or of administration, it shall be the duty of the executor or administrator to return to the court a further exhibit in writing, sworn to and subscribed by him, setting forth a list of all suits that have been instituted against him since the return of the exhibit required by the sixty-sixth section of this act; the condition of such suits and all suits previously instituted, specifying which of said suits are upon claims presented to him within twelve months after such grant of letters, and which upon claims presented after the twelve months; also setting forth a list of all claims that have been presented to him since the expiration of the twelve months from said grant of letters, specifying which have been allowed by him and which have been rejected, with the date of the rejection; and he shall also, from time to time, after the said term, return to the court a further exhibit under oath, setting forth a list of all claims presented to and allowed or rejected by him since the return of his former exhibit, with the date of the rejection; and also of all suits instituted against him, and all judgments rendered upon suits against him since his former return.   Any executor or administrator who shall fail to return to the court any exhibit as required by this section, may, for cause, be removed by the County Judge with due notice, either in term time or vacation, on the complaint of any person interested in the estate.

SEC. 68.   All exhibits made by executors or administrators, showing a list of claims allowed and approved, or established against the estate they represent, or showing the condition of said estate, and an account of the moneys received and of the moneys paid out on account of said estate, returned to the court before the filing of the final account provided for in a subsequent section of this act shall be filed with the Clerk, and notice of such filing shall be posted by the Clerk on the court-house door of the county for, which said court is held; and no other action shall be had thereon until the expiration of at least twenty days from the posting of said notice, after the expiration of which time the County Judge shall, in term time, examine said exhibit, and if the same be found to be correct, render judgment of approval thereon, and order said exhibit to be recorded.

SEC. 69.   No claim for money against his testator or intestate shall be allowed by an executor or administrator, nor shall any suit be instituted against him on any such claim after an order for partition and distribution has been made, as provided for in a previous section of this act; but the holder of any such claim not barred by the laws of limitation, shall have his action thereon against the heirs, devisees or legatees of the estate, but they shall not be bound beyond the value of the property they may receive in such partition and distribution.

SEC. 70.   The provisions contained in this act respecting the presentation of claims shall not be so construed as to apply to the claim of any heir, devisee or legatee, when claiming in that capacity, nor to any claim that accrues against the estate after the granting of letters testamentary or of administration for which the executor or administrator has contracted, and any devisee or legatee may obtain from the County Judge of the court where the will was proved an order for the executor to deliver to him the property devised or bequeathed, whenever it shall appear to such County Judge that there will remain in the hands of the executor after such delivery a sufficient amount of the estate for the payment of all debts against said estate; *provided,* such devisee or legatee shall have first caused the executor and the other devisee or legatee, if any, and the heirs, if any of the estate is coming to them, to be cited to appear and show cause why such order should not be made.

SEC. 71.   The provisions of this act respecting the presentation of claims shall not be construed to apply to any claim of an executor or administrator against his testator or intestate that has not been allowed by some previous executor or administrator of the same estate; but any executor or administrator holding any such claims shall file them in the court from which his letters were granted before the expiration of six months after the original grant of letters, or the same shall be barred. The County Judge shall thereupon, in term time, proceed to examine such claims and hear all legal evidence that may be offered in support of them, and if satisfied from the evidence that such claims, or any of them, are just, he shall enter on the minutes of the court his approval of such of them as he may think just, and the substance of the testimony on which the claim was established shall be taken down in writing, and be certified to by the Judge and filed with the Clerk among the papers of the estate at the time of such approval; and the amount so approved shall be paid in due course of administration, unless within three months after such approval some person interested in the estate shall take an appeal from such approval to the District Court, in which case such account, or so much thereof as may be approved by a jury, shall be paid in due course of administration.   If such claims, or any of them, shall not be approved by the County Judge, the executor or administrator may appeal to the District Court in like manner, and such amount as may be approved by a jury shall be paid in due course of administration. If in any appeal under the provisions of this section the executor or administrator shall fail to establish the whole of his claim, he shall be liable for costs, but if he establish the whole amount of his claim, the costs shall be paid out of the estate of the testator or intestate.

SEC. 72. It shall be the duty of every executor or administrator, so soon as he shall ascertain that it is necessary, to apply to the County Judge, at some regular term of the court, for an order to sell so much of the property of the estate he represents as he shall think sufficient to pay the expenses of administration and the debts of the estate. Such application shall be in writing, and shall be accompanied by a statement in writing of the estimated expenses of administration, and of all the claims against the estate that have been presented to him, specifying what claims have been allowed by him, what rejected, and those upon which suit has been instituted against him, with the condition of such suit or suits; which statement shall be verified by affidavit; upon the presentation of such application and statement, it shall be the duty of the County Judge, if satisfied that there is a necessity for such sale, to order the same to be made; but no order for the sale of real property for the payment of debts shall be made either on the application of the executor or administrator of any heir, devisee, or legatee, or creditor of the deceased, unless notice of the application therefor shall have been given for thirty days before the first day of the term at which said order is made. Such notice shall be given by a general citation, to be issued by the Clerk of the court to all persons interested in the estate, to show cause why such sale should not be made; which citation shall be posted for thirty days in at least three public places in the county, one of which shall be the court-house door, and no two of which shall be in the same city, town or village.

SEC. 73. When any executor or administrator shall neglect to apply for an order to sell sufficient property of the estate he represents to pay the expenses of administration and the claims against the estate that have been allowed and approved, or established by suit, such executor or administrator shall be required by the County Judge, on application in writing of any creditor of the estate whose claim has been allowed and approved or established by suits; or any heir, devisee or legatee of the deceased, to present to the court at some regular term thereof a statement in writing like that provided for in the preceding section; and upon proof to the court by any such creditor, heir, devisee or legatee that a necessity exists for a sale to pay the expenses of administration and the debts of the estate, it shall be the duty of the County Judge to order such sale to be made; *provided*, the executor or administrator shall have been first cited and due notice of such application shall have been given.

SEC. 74. Whenever there is property belonging to the estate of a deceased person that is perishable or liable to waste, upon the application in writing of the executor or administrator, or any heir, devisee or legatee of the deceased, or any creditor of the estate whose claim has been allowed and approved, or established by suit, the County Judge, by an order entered on the minutes of the court, either in term time or in vacation, may direct the sale of such property or any part thereof; *provided*, the executor or administrator may sell at public or private sale, and for cash or on a credit not exceeding six months, any personal property belonging to the estate that is perishable or liable to waste; and he

shall keep a true account of the sales made, making a list thereof speci--
fying each article sold, the price for which it was sold, and the name of
the purchaser; and he shall be responsible for the sales having been
made at a fair price, and the circumstances authorizing such sale.

SEC. 75.   The County Judge, either in term time or in vacation, may,
by an order entered on the minutes of the court, direct the crops belonging to the estate of the deceased person, or any part thereof, to be
sold at private sale, upon the application in writing of the executor or
adminisistrator, or any heir, devisee or legatee of the deceased, or any
creditor of the estate whose claim has been allowed and approved or established by suit; *provided*, that no crops shall be sold under any such
order at a less price than their fair or market value; *and provided further*,
that the executor or administrator may sell the same without an order
of the court.

SEC. 76.   All sales for the payment of the debts owing by the estate
shall be ordered to be made of such property as may be deemed most
advantageous to such estate to be sold.

SEC. 77.   Any creditor of the estate of a deceased person holding a
claim secured by a mortgage or other lien, which claim has been allowed
and approved, or established by suit, may obtain at a regular term of
the court, from the County Judge of the county where the letters testamentary or of administration were granted, an order for the sale of
the property upon which he has such mortgage or other lien, or so much
of said property as may be required to satisfy such claim, by making
his application in writing and having a copy thereof served upon the
executor or administrator, with a citation requiring him to appear and
answer such application, and in case the lien shall be upon real property,
giving the notice of said application required to obtain an order for
the sale of such property.

SEC. 78.   When an application is made to the County Judge for an order
to sell any property belonging to the estate of a deceased person, for the
payment of debts, any person interested in such estate may, at any time
before an order is made thereon, file his opposition in writing to such
sale, or may make application in writing for sale of other property of
the estate, and upon the hearing of the matter in controversy the County
Judge shall make such order thereon as the circumstances of the case
may require, having due regard to the provisions of this act.

SEC. 79.   Whenever any property of an estate is ordered to be sold by
the County Judge, such order shall be entered on the minutes of the
court; shall describe the property to be sold, and shall specify the
terms of such sale.

SEC. 80.   Sales of personal property for the payment of debts may be
ordered either for cash or on such credit as the County Judge may direct,
and all sales of land for the payment of debts shall be made on a credit
of twelve months, except when such sales are ordered to raise the
amount of the allowance that may be made under the provisions of the
fifty-sixth and fifty-seventh sections of this act, or for the satisfaction of
a mortgage or other lien on said land, in which cases such sales shall be
made on such terms as the County Judge may direct.

SEC. 81.   All sales ordered by the County Judge shall be made to the
highest bidder, and at public auction, unless otherwise directed by the
will of the testator, or otherwise ordered by the County Judge under
some provisions of this act; *provided*, that the County Judge may direct the sale of real property to be made at private sale for cash or on a

credit, if it shall appear to be for the interest of the estate, but in all such cases before the County Judge shall order a confirmation of the sale it must be shown, in addition to the other requirements of this act, that the sale was made for a fair price.

Sec. 82. Whenever in a will power is given to an executor to sell any property of the testator, no order of the County Judge shall be necessary to authorize the executor to make such sale, and when any particular directions are given by a testator in his will respecting the sale of any property belonging to his estate, the same shall be followed, unless creditors or heirs may thereby be prejudiced in their rights; *provided*, that should the executor or executrix be a non-resident of this State, he or she shall have the same power under said will as though he or she resided in this State.

Sec. 83. Whenever a public sale of property is ordered under the provisions of this act, if the same be personal property, it shall be advertised at least ten days before the day of sale; if the same be land, it shall be advertised at least twenty days before the day of sale. The manner of advertising shall be by posting a notice of such sale at the court-house and at two other public places in the county where the sale is to be made, but not in the same city or town. All such public sales shall be made within the hours of 10 A. M. and 4 P. M.; in case the day set apart for such sale shall be insufficient to complete the same, such sale may be continued from day to day by giving public notice of the continuance at the conclusion of the sale of each day, and the continued sale shall commence and close within the same hours. All such public sales of personal property shall be made at such time and place as may be directed by the County Judge in the order of sales; all such public sales of land shall be made on the first Tuesday of the month at the court-house door of the county where the letters testamentary or of administration were granted, unless the County Judge shall deem it for the advantage of the estate to order the sale in the county in which the property is situated; and in all cases where such public sale is ordered to be made in any other county than that in which the letters testamentary or of administration were granted, such sale may be advertised in both counties.

Sec. 84. When any person shall bid off property offered for sale, rent or hire, at public auction by an executor or administrator and shall fail to comply with the terms of sale, renting or hiring, such property shall be re-advertised and sold, rented or hired, and the person so failing to comply shall be liable to pay such executor or administrator for the use of the estate, ten per cent. on the amount of his bid; and, also, the deficiency in price on the second sale, renting or hiring, if any such deficiency there be; to be recovered by such executor or administrator by action brought before a Justice of the Peace or in the District Court or County Court, according to the amount of such penalty or deficiency.

Sec. 85. When a sale of property is ordered under the provisions of this act, it shall be the duty of the executor or administrator to make such sale, or cause it to be made in obedience to the order at the earliest period; and when such sale has been made, it shall be the duty of the executor or administrator to return to the court that ordered the sale an account thereof, either in term time or in vacation, within thirty days after the day of sale. Such account shall be in writing, shall specify the property sold, the name of the purchaser, the price for

8 GL

which it was sold, and the terms of sale, and shall be sworn to and subscribed by such executor or administrator before some officer authorized to administer oaths; whenever such account of sale is returned, such return shall be noted in the minutes of the court; and at any time after the expiration of five days from the noting of such return in the minutes of the court, it shall be the duty of the County Judge to inquire into the manner in which such sale was made, and if satisfied that it was fairly made, and in conformity with law, he shall cause to be entered on the minutes of the court a decree confirming it and ordering the account of sales to be recorded by the Clerk, and a conveyance to be made to the purchaser of land by the executor or administrator; if not satisfied that such sale was so made, he shall cause to be entered in like manner a decree setting it aside and ordering a new sale to be made ; *provided*, that no sale of real estate shall be confirmed except at some regular term of the court. After any such decree or confirmation shall have been made, upon the purchaser complying with the terms of the sale, the executor or administrator shall execute and deliver to him a conveyance of the property so sold; if lands, reciting therein the decree confirming the sale and ordering the conveyance to be made, which conveyance of land so made shall vest the right and title that the testator or intestate had in the purchaser, and shall be *prima facie* evidence that all the requisites of the law have been complied with in making the sale, and such decree of confirmation of the sale of personal property shall in like manner vest the right and title thereof in the purchaser, and shall be like evidence that all the requisites of the law have been complied with in making the sale of such personal property.

Sec. 86. It shall not be lawful for any executor or administrator to take the estate of his testator or intestate, or any part thereof, at its appraised value, or to sell the same, or any part thereof, unless under the direction of the will or the order of the County Judge under the provisions of this act, or to become the purchaser, either directly or indirectly, of any property of the estate sold by him; and if any executor or administrator should either directly or indirectly become the purchaser of any of the property of his testator or intestate, at a sale made by him, upon the complaint of any person interested in the estate, and service thereof, and of citation on such executor or administrator, such sale shall be declared void by the County Judge, and such executor or administrator decreed to hold the property so purchased in trust as assets of the estate. Nor shall it be lawful for any executor or administrator, either directly or indirectly, to purchase for his own use any claim against the estate he represents; and if any executor or administrator should purchase any claim, upon the complaint in writing of any one interested in the estate, and service thereof with a citation on such executor or administrator, he shall be decreed by the County Judge to hold such claim in trust for the use of the estate, and he shall only be entitled to receive from the estate the amount he shall prove to have been paid by him therefor, such amount to be paid *pro rata* with other creditors of an equal degree.

Sec. 87. Whenever an executor or administrator sells property of the estate he represents on a credit, either under the direction of the will of the testator or under an order of the County Judge, he shall take the note of the purchaser for the amount of his purchase, with good personal security; and if land has been sold he shall also take a mortgage upon the property sold to secure the payment of the purchase money; *provided, however,* that said mortgage shall not be taken until the sale of said land shall have been approved by the court. And if the executor or administrator shall neglect to take such note, security and mortgage, and file the same for record before delivery of the deed, he and the sureties on his bond shall be liable, at the suit of any person interested in the estate, for the use of the estate for the amount of such sales; and whenever any executor or administrator shall rent or hire any property of his testator or intestate on a credit under the provisions of this act, and all notes taken for lands sold by an administrator or executor shall hold the vendor's lien on the land sold against all persons having notice, expressed or implied, in favor of the estate, whether the mortgage be recorded or not; he shall take the note of the person hiring or renting such property for the amount of the hire or rent, with good personal security, and if he shall fail to take such notice (note) and security, he and his sureties shall in like manner be liable for the amount thereof.

Sec. 88. The debts due from an estate shall be paid by the executor or administrator in the following order: First, funeral expenses and expenses of last sickness; second, all expenses of administration, including the allowance that may be made under the provisions of the fifty-sixth and fifty-seventh sections of this act, and the expenses incurred in the preservation, safe keeping and management of the estate; third, debts secured by mortgage, or having a lien, whether judgment or execution or otherwise, so far as the same can be paid out of the proceeds of the property subject to such mortgage or lien, and when more than one of such mortgages and liens, or any one of them, exists upon the same property, the oldest shall be first paid; fourth, all other debts; and no preference shall be given to debts secured by mortgage, or having a lien by judgment, execution or otherwise, further than regards the property subject to such mortgage or lien. When there is a deficiency of assets, debts of the fourth class shall be paid only *pro rata,* and no executor or administrator shall be allowed to pay any claims of the fourth class, whether the estate is solvent or insolvent, except with their *pro rata* amount of the funds of the estate that have come to hand; *provided,* that nothing in this section shall be construed to in any way impair or defeat the vendor's lien on the homestead or any other land, or any lien held by mechanics for work and material furnished in improvements on real estate, or any landlord's liens for rents and advances, and the lien for taxes due thereon; but if the estate is solvent the cost of enforcing the lien only may be paid out of the proceeds of the property on which the lien existed.

Sec. 89. Executors and administrators, whenever they have funds in their hands belonging to the estate they represent, shall pay: First, the funeral expenses and expenses of last sickness; second, expenses of administration, including the allowances that may be made under the provisions of the fifty-sixth and fifty-seventh sections of this act, and the expenses incurred in the preservation, safe-keeping and management of the estate, when such claims have been allowed and approved or established; and if they shall fail or refuse so to do when required by the holder of such claims, the person holding any such claim may obtain an order from the County Judge at a regular term of the court, directing such payment to be made, upon making proof that such executor or administrator has funds of the estate in his hands sufficient to make such payment, and fails or refuses to make it; *provided,* such executor or administrator shall have first been cited on the complaint of the holder of such claim, to appear and show cause why such order should not be made.

Sec. 90. Whenever any executor or administrator shall have in his hands the proceeds of a sale that has been made for the satisfaction of a mortgage or other lien, and such proceeds or any part thereof are not required for the payment of the expense of enforcing said lien in case the estate is insolvent, any debts against the estate that have a preference over such mortgage or other lien, it shall be the duty of such executor or administrator immediately to pay over such proceeds, or so much thereof as may not be required for the payment of the expense of enforcing said lien in case the estate is insolvent; any debts against the estate that have a preference over such mortgage or other lien to the creditor or creditors having a right thereto; and if any executor or administrator shall fail or refuse so to do, such creditor or creditors, upon proof thereof, may obtain an order from the County Judge, in like manner as is provided in the preceding section, directing such payment to be made; and in case of the sale of mortgaged property to satisfy the mortgage there be not money enough to pay the mortgage debt in full, then the balance unpaid shall stand as any other claim against the estate, to be paid in due course of administration.

Sec. 91. Upon the return of the exhibit mentioned in the preceding sections of this act, if it shall appear therefrom or by any other evidence that the estate is solvent, taking into consideration as well the claims presented before the expiration of twelve months from said granting of letters testamentary or of administration on which suit has been or can yet be instituted, as those so presented, allowed and approved, or established by judgment, and that the executor or administrator has in his hands sufficient funds for the payment of all the aforesaid claims, it shall be the duty of the County Judge to order immediate payment to be made of all the claims allowed and approved, or established by judgment. If he has funds in his hands, but if not sufficient for the payment of all the said claims, or if the estate be insolvent and he has any funds in his hands, it shall be the duty of the County Judge to order such funds to be applied to the payment of all claims having a preference, in the order of their priority, if they or any of them be still unpaid, and then to the payment *pro rata* of the other claims allowed and approved or established; taking into consideration also the claims that were presented within the twelve months, and in suit, or on which suit may yet be instituted.

Sec. 92. Claims for money against the estate of a deceased person, which may be presented to the executor or administrator after the expiration of twelve months from the original grant of letters testamentary or of administration, and allowed by him and approved by the County Judge, or established by suits, shall be paid by the executor or administrator at any time before the estate is finally closed, when he has funds of the estate in his hands over and above what may be sufficient to pay all debts of every kind against the estate that were presented within the twelve months and allowed and approved or established by suit, or that may be so established, and an order for the payment of any such claim, upon proof that the executor or administrator has such funds, may be obtained from the County Judge, in like manner as is provided in this act for creditors to obtain orders of payment.

Sec. 93. At the third regular term of court after the expiration of twelve months from the original grant of letters testamentary or of administration, or at any term of the court after that, any person interested in the estate may, by a complaint in writing, filed in the County Court, cause the executor or administrator to be cited to appear at a regular term of the court and make an exhibit in writing, under oath to the court, setting forth fully in connection with the previous exhibits, the condition of the estate he represents; and if it shall appear to the court by said exhibit or by other evidence that such executor or administrator has any funds of the estate in his hands subject to distribution among the creditors of the estate, it shall be the duty of the County Judge to order the same to be paid out to them according to the provisions of this act, or any executor or administrator may voluntarily present such exhibit to the court, and if he has any of the funds of the estate in his hands subject to distribution among the creditors of the estate, a like order shall be made.

SEC. 94.   At any time after the first term of the court, after the expiration of twelve months from the original grant of letters testamentary or of administration, the heirs, devisees or legatees of the estate, or any of them, may, by their complaint in writing, filed in the County Court, cause the executor or administrator, and the heirs, devisees or legatees of the estate to be cited to appear at a regular term of the court, and show cause why a partition and distribution should not be made among the heirs, devisees or legatees of the residue of the estate, if any there be after retaining in the hands of the executor or administrator a sufficient portion thereof to pay all debts of every kind against the estate that have been allowed and approved or established by suit, or that have been rejected by the executor or administrator, or not approved by the County Judge and may yet be established.   And if it shall appear to the County Judge after the service of such citation that there is any such residue of the estate, he shall order it to be so partitioned and distributed.

SEC. 95.   When all the debts known to exist of every kind against the estate of a deceased person have been paid, or when they have been paid so far as the assets of the estate in the hands of the executor or administrator will permit, the executor or administrator of such estate may present his account to the court, verified by affidavit, for settlement; or the County Judge shall cause him to be cited to present such account, either of his own motion or on the complaint of any person interested in the estate.   Upon the presentation of such account it shall be the duty of the County Judge, either in term time or in vacation, to order at least twenty days' notice to be given by publication in a newspaper, if there be one printed in the county, if not, then by posting such notice at the court-house and at two other public places in the county for at least twenty days.   Such notice shall state the presentation of said account, the term of the court when it will be acted on, and shall require all persons interested to appear and contest said account if they see proper.   The County Judge may order such other notice to be given as he shall deem expedient.   At the term of the court named in such notice, or at some subsequent term to which the same may be continued, upon proof being made that notice has been given in the manner required by this act, and the order of the County Judge, it shall be his duty, after examining said account with all the exceptions thereto, and hearing the evidence that may be offered in support of or against said account and exceptions, to re-state said account, if necessary, and to audit and settle the same ; and, upon the settlement of said account, if there is none of the estate remaining in the hands of the executor or administrator, he shall be discharged from his trust by an order of the County Judge; but if there is any of the estate remaining in the hands of the executor or administrator, and the heirs, devisees or legatees of the estate, or their assignees, or either or any of them, are present or represented in court, it shall be the duty of the County Judge to order a partition and distribution of the estate to be made among them, upon satisfactory proof being made that they are entitled to receive it.

SEC. 96.   Upon the settlement of the account of any executor or administrator, as provided for in the preceding section, if the heirs, devisees or legatees of the estate, or their assignees, or either or any of them, do not appear or are not represented in the court, and there are any funds of such estate remaining in the hands of the executor or administrator, it shall be the duty of the County Judge to order the same to be paid over to the Treasurer of the State; and if there shall be any property of the estate that has not been sold, or any debts due the estate that may be collected, it shall be the duty of the County Judge to order such property to be sold on a credit of twelve months, and such debts to be collected ; and at the first term of the court after the expiration of twelve months after such sale, and every six months thereafter, while the estate remains under the control of such executor or administrator, it shall be his duty to render to the court a full exhibit of the condition of such estate, verified by affidavit.   And whenever there shall be any funds of the estate in the hands of the executor or administrator, it shall be the duty of the County Judge to order the same to be paid to the Treasurer of the State ; *provided, however*, that while such estate, or any portion thereof, remains under the control of the executor or administrator, the heirs, devisees or legatees, or their assignees, or either or any of them, may obtain from the County Judge, at a regular term of the court, an order to have the same partitioned and distributed among them according to their respective interests in the same, upon causing the executor or administrator to be cited, and making satisfactory proof to the court of their right to the same ; and whenever such estate shall have been so partitioned and distributed and delivered over to the persons entitled thereto, or when the debts due such estate have been collected, so far as there is a reasonable prospect of collecting them, and the proceeds paid over to the Treasurer of the State, as herein required, such executor or administrator shall be finally discharged from his trust by an order of the County Judge, entered at some regular term.

SEC. 97.   Whenever an order shall be made by the County Judge for an executor or administrator to pay over any funds to the Treasurer of the State, under the provisions of this act, it shall be the duty of the Clerk of the court in which such order may be made to transmit to said Treasurer, by mail, a certified copy of such order within one month after said order shall have been made.   Whenever the Clerk mails such copy he shall take from the postmaster with whom it is mailed a certificate stating that such certified copy was mailed in his office, directed to the Treasurer of the State, at the seat of government of this State, and the date when it was mailed ; which certificate shall be recorded in the minutes of the court.   And any Clerk who shall neglect to transmit a certified copy of such order within the time prescribed, and to take such certificate and have it so recorded, shall be liable to a penalty of one hundred dollars, to be recovered by an action in the name of the State, before any Justice of the Peace of the county, on the information of any citizen of the county, one-half of which penalty shall be paid to the informer and the other half to the State.

SEC. 98. Whenever any executor or administrator shall pay over to the Treasurer of the State any funds of the estate he represents, under the provisions of this act, he may take from such Treasurer a receipt for such payment, with his official seal attached, and file the same, and have it recorded on the minutes of the court by which such funds were ordered to be paid, and a certified copy of such record shall be evidence of such payment.

SEC. 99. Whenever any funds of an estate shall have been paid to the Treasurer of the State, under the provisions of this act, any heir, devisee or legatee of such estate, or their assignees, or either or any of them, may recover the portion of such funds to which he or she would have been entitled, if the same had not been so paid to the Treasurer. Such recovery may be had in a suit against said Treasurer, before any court of competent jurisdiction in the county where the letters testamentary or of administration were granted; but in any such suit the plaintiff shall be liable for all costs of court; and in all cases where any funds belonging to the estate of a deceased person have heretofore been paid into the Treasury of the State, or when any title papers belonging to any such estate have been deposited with the Comptroller, such funds or title papers may be recovered in like manner by the person or persons who would have been entitled thereto, if the same had not been so paid over or deposited.

SEC. 100. Whenever any executor or administrator shall fail to pay to the Treasurer of the State any funds of the estate he represents that he has been ordered by the County Judge so to pay, within three months after such order has been made, such executor or administrator shall be liable to pay, out of his own estate, to the State Treasurer, damages thereon at the rate of five per cent. per month for each month he may neglect to make such payment after the three months from such order. The Treasurer of the State shall have the right, in the name of the State, to apply to the County Judge of the court in which such order was made to enforce the payment of such funds and damages, if any have accrued; and it shall be the duty of the County Judge to enforce the payment in like manner as other orders of payment are enforced by him; or the said Treasurer shall have the right to institute suit, in the name of the State, against such executor or administrator and the sureties on his bond for the recovery of the funds so ordered to be paid, and damages, if any have accrued; which suit may be instituted in any court of competent jurisdiction in the county where the letters testamentary or of administration were granted.

SEC. 101. In all cases where an order shall have been made by any County Judge under the provisions of this act for an executor or administrator to pay over money to any person other than the Treasurer of the State, and such executor or administrator shall neglect to make such payment when it is demanded by the person entitled thereto, his agent or attorney, such executor or administrator shall be liable on his official bond to the person in whose favor such order of payment was made for damages upon the amount he shall so neglect to pay, at the rate of ten per cent. per month for each and every month he shall so neglect to make such payment after the same was so demanded; such damages to be recovered by suit before any court having competent jurisdiction, against said executor or administrator and the sureties on his official bond.

SEC. 102. All applications for the partition and distribution of an estate under the provisions of this act shall be in writing, and shall be filed with the Clerk of the court to which the application is made. Upon the filing of any such application, it shall be the duty of the Clerk to issue a citation, returnable to some regular term of the court, which citation shall state the name of the person whose estate is sought to be partitioned and distributed, the term of the court to which such citation is returnable, and shall require all persons interested in the estate to appear and show cause why such partition and distribution should not be made; such citation shall be personally served by leaving a copy thereof with each person entitled to a share of the estate who is known and is a resident of this State, and if there be any persons so entitled who are not known, or who are not residents of this State, such citation shall be published for at least four successive weeks in some newspaper printed in the county, if there be one; if not, then it shall be published in like manner in one of the nearest newspapers published in the State. A copy of such publication and the affidavit of the publisher or printer attached thereto stating that it was so published shall be evidence of the publication.

SEC. 103. At the return term of any such citation as is provided for in the preceding section, or at some succeeding term to which the application may be continued by the court, if it shall appear that such citation has been served and published as required by law, the court shall proceed to ascertain who are the persons by law entitled to partition and distribution, and their respective shares; and if there are any persons so entitled who are known and are minors, and have no guardian in this State, or whose guardians are also entitled to a portion of such estate, the court shall appoint a guardian *ad litem* to represent them in the partition of the estate; and if there are any persons so entitled who are not known, or not residents of this State, and no person appears who is authorized to represent them, the court shall appoint an attorney to represent them in the partition of the estate, after which the court shall proceed to ascertain whether advancements have been made to any of the persons so entitled, their nature and value, and require the same to be placed in hotchpotch as required by the law governing descents and distributions, and also to ascertain what estate is liable to partition and distribution; the court shall then enter a decree which shall state the name and residence, if known, of each person entitled to a share of the estate, specifying those who are known to be minors, the names of their guardian or guardians *ad litem*, the name of the attorney appointed to represent those who are unknown, or are not residents of this State; the decree shall also state the proportional part of the estate to which each is entitled, and shall contain a full description of all the estate to be distributed; if the estate to be distributed shall consist only of money or debts due the estate, or both, the court shall fix the amount to which each is entitled, and order the payment and delivery thereof by the executor or administrator; but if the estate do not consist entirely of money or debts due the estate, or both, the court shall appoint three or more discreet persons as commissioners to make a partition and distribution of the estate, and shall order a writ of partition to issue commanding them to proceed forthwith to make such partition and distribution in accordance with the decree of the court, a copy of which shall accompany such writ; and also commanding them to make due return of said writ, with their proceedings under it, at some term of the court to be named in the writ.

SEC. 104. It shall be the duty of the commissioners of partition under this act to make a fair, just and impartial partition and distribution of the estate, in the following order: First, of the land or other property by allotment to each distributee of a part in each parcel, or of parts in one or more parcels, or of one or more parcels, either with or without the addition of a part or parts of other parcels, as shall be most for the interest of the distributees; *provided*, the said real estate is capable of being so divided without manifest injury to all or any of the distributees; and the said commissioners shall have power, if they think it necessary, to call to their aid one or more well qualified surveyors to run the lines of any lands, and also divisional lines thereof. If the real estate is not capable of a fair, just and equal division in kind, but may be made so by allotting to one or more of the distributees a proportion of money or other personal property to supply the deficiency or deficiencies, the commissioners shall have power to make as near as may be an equal division of the real estate, and supply the deficiency of any share or shares from the money or other property. The commissioners shall proceed to make a like division in kind, as near as may be, of the money and other personal property, and shall determine by lot, among equal shares, to whom each particular share shall belong.

SEC. 105. When, in the opinion of the Commissioners, the whole or any portion of any estate is not capable of a fair and equal division among the distributees, the said Commissioners shall make a special return of such property to the court, with the value thereof duly appraised by them. Upon such return being made to the court, any one or more of the distributees, at a regular term of the court, by the payment to the executor or administrator of the appraised value of the property so returned as incapable of division, or on the execution of his or their obligations with one or more good and sufficient sureties in favor of each of the other distributees for their share of the appraised value of such property, payable at such time, not exceeding twelve months from the date thereof, as the court may designate; *provided*, the court may think it for the interest of the distributees to allow a credit, shall have the right to take the said property. Should any one or more of the distributees take the said property as aforesaid, it shall be the duty of the court to enter a decree stating the facts, and on the entry of such decree the property shall vest as fully and absolutely in the person or persons taking the same as the deceased was vested therewith; *provided, nevertheless*, that when obligations are executed as aforesaid, a lien shall exist upon such property by operation of law, to secure the payment of such obligations; *provided, also*, that if any of the distributees shall file in the court his exception to the appraisement of the Commissioners before any of the distributees shall have so taken such property, a new appraisement of said property may be made by order of the court. If no distributee take the said property as aforesaid, the court shall order the sale of said property, either for cash or on a credit, as may be most for the interest of the distributees; and at such sale, if any distributee shall bid off any of said property he shall be required to pay or secure, as the case may be, only such amount of his bid as may exceed the amount of his share of such property; and the proceeds of sale, when collected, shall be distributed by the court among those entitled thereto.

SEC. 106. Said Commissioners having divided the whole or any part of the estate, shall make to the court a report in writing, subscribed and sworn to by them, containing a statement of the property divided by them, and also a particular description of the property allotted to each distributee and its value. And if it be real estate that has been divided, said report shall contain a general plat of such land, with the divisional lines plainly set down and the number of acres in each share. Upon the return of such report it shall be the duty of the court, at some regular term, to examine said report carefully, and if it be merely informal to cause said informality to be corrected; and if such division shall appear to have been fairly made according to law, and no valid exceptions are taken to it, the court shall approve it and order it to be recorded, but if said division shall not appear to have been so made, or any valid exceptions are taken to it, the court shall set aside said report and division and order a new partition to be made.

SEC. 107. When any portion of the estate to be partitioned lies in a distant county and can not be fairly partitioned without a view thereof, and it is inconvenient for the Commissioners to go and examine such property, they may report such facts to the County Judge in writing, whereupon he may at some regular term of the court, if satisfied that the said property cannot be conveniently divided, or that its sale would be more advantageous to the distributees, order a sale thereof for cash or on a credit of not more than twelve months, at his discretion; and when the proceeds of such sale shall have been collected they shall be distributed by him among those entitled thereto; but if no such proof be made, three or more Commissioners may be appointed in each county where any portion of the estate so reported is situated, and the same proceedings shall be had thereon as is provided in this act for Commissioners to make portion; *and provided*, that whenever any testator has by will instructed that no action be had in the courts in the settlement of his estate, and said testator does not in said will distribute his estate or provide a means of partitioning the same, the executor may, if he desires, file his final account and vouchers as provided in this act for administrators, in the court of the county in which the will was probated, and ask partition and distribution of the estate, and the same shall be partitioned and distributed in the manner herein provided for in case of ordinary administration.

SEC. 108. When any husband or wife shall die, leaving any common property, the survivor may at any time after letters testamentary or of administration have been granted, and an inventory of the estate of the deceased has been returned, make application to the court from which such letters were granted for a partition of such common property; and if he or she shall execute and deliver to said County Judge an obligation with good and sufficient sureties, payable to and approved by said County Judge, for an amount equal to the value of his or her interest in such common property, conditioned for the payment of one-half of all debts existing against such common property, then the County Judge shall proceed to make a partition of said common property into two equal moieties, one to be delivered to the survivor and the other to the executor or administrator of the deceased; and all the provisions of this act respecting the partition and distribution of estates shall apply to any partition made under the provisions of this section, so far as the same may be applicable; and whenever such partition may be made a lien shall exist upon the portion of such survivor to secure the payment of the obligation he may have given as aforesaid; and until a partition shall be applied for as herein provided, the executor or administrator of the deceased shall have the right and it shall be his duty to recover possession of all such common property, and hold the same in trust to be administered for the benefit of the creditors and others entitled thereto under the provisions of this act. After such partition any creditor of said common property may sue in his own name on such obligation, and shall have judgment thereon for the one-half of such debt as he may establish, and for the other half he shall be entitled to be paid by the executor or administrator of the deceased.

SEC. 109. In all cases where Commissioners to make partition are appointed under this act, the report of any three of them shall be sufficient. All such Commissioners shall receive two dollars each for every day they may be engaged, and all their reasonable expenses shall be paid them.

SEC. 110. In any case where the County Judge shall appoint a guardian *ad litem* for minors, or any attorney to represent the person absent from the State or unknown, under the provisions of this act, if such guardian *ad litem* or attorney shall neglect to attend to the duties of such appointment, the County Judge shall appoint others in their places by an order entered on the minutes of [the] court, and such guardian *ad litem* and attorneys shall be allowed by the County Judge a reasonable compensation for their services, which shall be paid out of the estate of the person they represent, and the County Judge may order execution to issue for the same.

SEC. 111. That all expenses incurred in the partition of estates shall be paid by the parties interested in the partition, each party paying in proportion to the share he may receive. The proportion of the estate allotted to each distributee shall be liable for his or her portion of the expenses, and if not paid the court shall have power to order execution therefor in the names of the persons entitled thereto.

SEC. 112. Any person or persons having a joint interest with the estate of a decedent in any property, real or personal, may make application to the County Court from which letters testamentary or of administration have been granted on said estate, to have a partition thereof; whereupon the court shall proceed to make a partition of said property between the applicant or applicants and the estate of the deceased; and all the rules and regulations contained herein in relation to the partition and distribution of estates shall govern partitions under this section, so far as the same may be applicable.

SEC. 113. When the report of any commissioners to make partition shall have been approved and ordered to be recorded, the court shall order the executor or administrator to deliver to the distributees their respective shares of the estate on demand, including all the title deeds and papers belonging to the same. If any distributee be a minor, his share shall be delivered to his guardian. If any minor distributee resident of the State of Texas shall have no guardian, the executor or administrator shall retain his share until a guardian shall be appointed; and he shall be allowed by the court reasonable compensation for taking care of the same. If any executor or administrator shall neglect to deliver to the person entitled thereto, his agent or attorney, when demanded, any portion of an estate so ordered to be delivered, such executor or administrator shall be liable to pay out of his own estate to the person so entitled damages on the amount of his share at the rate ten per cent. per month for each and every month he shall so neglect to deliver such share after such demand, which damages may be recovered by suit before any court of competent jurisdiction.

SEC. 114. If any person entitled to a portion of an estate shall not demand the same from the executor or administrator within six months after the report of the commissioners of partition has been approved and ordered to be recorded, the County Judge shall order so much of said portion as may be in money to be paid to the Treasurer of the State, and such portion as may be in other property the County Judge shall order the executor or administrator to sell on such terms as he may think best, and when the proceeds of such sale are collected he shall order the same to be paid to the Treasurer of the State; in all such cases allowing to the executor or administrator reasonable compensation for his services.

SEC. 115. The community property of the husband and wife shall be liable for all the debts contracted during marriage, except in such cases as are specially exempted by law. And in the settlement of community estates, it shall be the duty of the survivor, executor or administrator to keep a separate and distinct account of all the community debts allowed or paid in the settlement of such estates.

SEC. 116. Where the wife dies, her husband surviving, administration is unnecessary, except as to any separate estate which may have belonged to her. The husband continues to have the same power of disposition over the community property which he possessed during the continuance of marriage; but he shall be required to return an inventory and appraisement of all such property, and to file a bond, signed by two good and sufficient sureties, to be approved by and payable to the County Judge, in an amount equal to the value of the whole community property, to the effect that he will faithfully administer the same, and pay over one-half of the surplus, after the payment of the debts with which the whole is properly chargeable, to such person or persons as shall be entitled to receive it. And he shall be liable in such case to be called to account at any time after one year from the date of the bond, which bond shall be suable, recoverable, and in every other respect the same as the bond of the administrator. The surviving wife may retain the exclusive management and control of the community property of herself and her deceased husband in the same manner, and subject to the same rights, rules and regulations as provided above, until she may marry again; but upon a second marriage she shall cease to have such control and management of said estate, or the right to dispose of the same, as above provided; and said estate shall be subject to administration as in other cases of deceased persons' estate.

SEC. 117. Any person capable of making a will may so provide, by his or her will, that no other action shall be had in the County Court, in relation to the settlement of his or her estate, than the probating and registration of his or her will, and the return of an inventory of the estate; and in all such cases any person having a debt or claim against said estate may enforce the payment of the same by suit against the executor of such will, and when judgment is recovered against the executor, the execution shall run against the estate of the testator in the hands of such executor; *provided*, that no such executor shall be required to plead to any suit brought against him for money until the expiration of twelve months from the date of the probate of such will. But in cases where no bond and security has been required of such executor at the time of the probate of such will, any person having a debt, claim or demand against said estate, to the justice of which oath has been made by himself, his agent or attorney, or any person having an interest therein, whether in person or as representative of another, may, by complaint filed in the court where such will was probated, cause such executor to be cited to appear before such court, at some regular term, and on making it appear to the satisfaction of said court that such executor is wasting or misapplying said estate, and that thereby said creditor may probably lose his debt, or such person his or her interest in the estate, it shall be the duty of said court to order such executor to give bond, with two or more good and sufficient sureties, for an amount equal to double the full value of said estate, to be approved by and payable to the County Judge of the county, conditioned that said executor will well and truly administer such estate, and that he will not waste, mismanage or misapply the same; which bond may be recovered upon as other bonds given by executors and administrators; and should such executor fail to give such bond within ten days after the order requiring him to do so, then it shall be the duty of the County Judge to remove him from the executorship of such estate, and to appoint some competent person in his stead, whose duty it shall be to administer said estate according to the provisions of such will, and who, before he enters upon the administration of said estate, shall be required to give such bond as herein above provided for. And if such will does not distribute the entire estate of the testator, or provide a means for partition of said estate, the executor shall have the right to file his final account in the court in which the will was probated, and ask partition and distribution of the estate, and the same shall be partitioned and distributed in the manner provided herein for the partition and distribution of estates administered according to the provisions of this act.

Sec. 118. It shall be the duty of the County Judge of any county from which any county or part thereof has been or may hereafter be taken, to transmit all original papers relating to the settlement of estates of deceased persons, who were, at the time of their decease, residents of that part of the territory of the county which has been or may hereafter be taken to form any new county, to the Probate Court of such new county, upon the petition of any executor or administrator, or guardian, or a majority of the heirs of any such estate; and he shall also transmit, with such original papers, a transcript, certified under the seal of the court, of the records of all proceedings had in relation to such estates in his court; *provided*, that at the time of filing such petition the party filing it shall pay all fees due on account of such estate.

Sec. 119. Previous to the transmission of any such original papers, in the manner provided for in the preceding section, the Judge to whom such petition is presented shall cause a registry of all such original papers, as have not been recorded, to be made in his office, for which the same fee shall be allowed as is allowed for other recording.

Sec. 120. In all cases where the papers and proceeding relating to the settlement of an estate shall be transmitted to any court in the manner provided for in this act, such estate shall be proceeded in and settled in the Probate Court of such county in like manner as if the settlement of such estates had been originally commenced in such county, and the transcript of the record transmitted in the manner provided for in this act shall have the same force and effect in evidence as the record itself might or could have.

SEC. 121.   Executors and administrators shall be entitled to receive, and may retain in their hands, five per cent. upon all sums they may actually receive in cash, and the same upon all sums they may pay away in cash, in the course of their administration; *provided*, that no commissions shall be allowed for money received which was on hand at the time of the death of the testator or intestate, nor for paying out money to the heirs and legatees as such.   All reasonable expenses incurred by an executor or administrator in the preservation, safe-keeping and management of the estate, and all reasonable attorney's fees that may be incurred in the course of the administration, shall be allowed by the County Judge, on proof that there was a necessity therefor.

SEC. 122.   Whenever any executor or administrator shall file in the court receipts showing that he has disposed of any portion of the estate, under the provisions of this act, the court shall order the same to be recorded; and whenever he shall have so filed receipts showing that all of the estate has been disposed of by him, under the provisions of this act, he shall, provided the court approve said receipts and the account filed, be finally discharged from his trust by the County Judge; *and provided further*, when any person holding an allowed and approved claim against the estate does not come forward to receive payment for the same, the administrator or executor may deposit the money for the payment of said claim with the Clerk of the County Court, and take his receipt therefor.

SEC. 123.   Any person capable of making a will may so provide by his will that no other action shall be had in the County Court in relation to the settlement of his estate than the probate and registration of his will and the return of an inventory of the estate; but in all such cases any person having a debt against said estate may, by complaint in writing, filed in the court where such will was proved, cause all the persons entitled to any portion of such estate under the will, or as heirs at law, to be cited to appear before such court, at some regular term, and execute an obligation, with two or more good and sufficient sureties, for an amount equal to the full value of such estate, to be ascertained by the inventory, such obligation to be payable to the County Judge, and conditioned that the persons who execute the obligation shall pay all debts that may be established against such estate, in the manner herein provided; and on the return of such citations served, unless such persons so entitled to any portion of the estate, or some of them, or some other persons for them, shall execute such obligation to the satisfaction of the County Judge, such estate shall be settled under the direction of the court as other estates are required to be settled; but if such obligation shall be executed it shall be filed and recorded in said court, and no other action shall be had in said court in relation to such estate.   All costs of such proceedings shall be paid by the persons so entitled to such estate, according to their respective interests in it.   Every creditor of such estate shall have the right to sue on such obligation, and shall be entitled to judgment thereon for such debt as he may establish against the testator by a verdict of the jury in such suits, or such creditors may have their action against those in possession of the estate.

SEC. 124.   At any time after the return of the inventory of the estate of a deceased person, any one entitled to a portion of said estate, as heirs, devisee or legatee, or his or her guardian if he or she be a minor, may by a complaint in writing filed in the court where such inventory has been returned, cause the executor or administrator of the estate to be cited to appear at some regular term of the court and render an exhibit, under oath, of the condition of such estate; and on the return of such citation served, the person so entitled to such estate, or any of them, or any persons for them, may execute and deliver to the County Judge an obligation payable to him, with two or more good and sufficient sureties, to be approved by the County Judge, for an amount at least equal to double the appraised value of the estate as ascertained by the inventory, conditioned that the persons who execute such obligation shall pay all the debts against the estate not paid that have been allowed by the executor or administrator and approved by the County Judge, or that have been established by suit against the executor or administrator, or that may be established against the estate by suit in the manner herein provided; and may pay to the executor or administrator any balance that may be decreed to be due to him on his exhibit, in obedience to said citation; whereupon such obligation shall be filed and recorded in said court, and the court shall on the application of any of the persons so entitled to any portion of the estate, cause a partition and distribution of such estate to be made among the persons entitled thereto, in accordance with the provisions of this act respecting the partition and distribution of estates; and a lien shall exist on all of said estate in the hands of the distributees to secure the ultimate payment of the aforesaid obligation. Any creditor of such estate whose claim is yet unpaid and has been allowed by the executor or administrator previous to the filing of such obligation, and approved by the County Judge, or established by suit against the executor or administrator, previous to the filing of such obligation, shall have the right to sue on such obligation in his own name, and shall be entitled to judgment thereon for the amount of his claim; or any other creditor of such estate whose claim is not barred by the laws of limitation shall have the right to sue on such obligation, and shall be entitled to judgment thereon for such debt as he may establish against the estate by a verdict of the jury in such suit; or any of said creditors may sue the distributee, but no one of them shall be liable beyond his just proportion, according to the estate he may have received in the distribution.

SEC. 125. When a person dies, leaving a lawful will, all of his estate devised or bequeathed by such will shall vest immediately in the devisees or legatees; and all the estate of such person not devised or bequeathed shall vest immediately in his heirs at law; but all of such estate, whether devised or bequeathed or not, except such as may be exempted by law from the payment of debts, shall still be liable and subject in their hands to the payment of the debts of such testator; and whenever a person dies intestate all of his estate shall vest immediately in his heirs at law, but with the exceptions aforesaid shall still be liable and subject, in their hands, to the payment of the debts of the intestate. But upon the issuance of letters testamentary or of administration on any such estate, the executor or administrator shall have a right to the possession of the estate as it existed at the death of the testator or intestate, with the exception aforesaid; and it shall be his duty to recover possession of and hold such estate in trust, to be disposed of under the provisions of this act.

SEC. 126.   When complaint shall be made in writing to any County Judge that any person has the last will of any testator or testatrix, or any papers belonging to the estate of a testator or intestate, said County Judge shall cause said person to be cited to appear before him, either in term time or vacation, and show cause why he should not deliver such will to the court for probate, or why he should not deliver such papers to the executor or administrator, and upon the return of such citation served, unless such will or papers are so delivered, or good cause be shown to the court for not delivering the same, the County Judge, if satisfied that such person had such will or papers at the time of the complaint being filed, may cause him to be arrested and imprisoned until he shall so deliver them.

SEC. 127.   All the provisions in this act relative to an executor or administrator shall apply and extend to an executrix or administratrix, or executors or administrators respectively, unless expressly provided for; and whenever any party in the singular number or a male party is mentioned, the rule shall apply to a female, or to two or more having a joint interest, or jointly concerned, applying or called upon, so far as the rule can with propriety apply, or so far as is not otherwise directed.

SEC. 128.   Any one interested in the estate of a deceased person may at any time within two years after the settlement by the County Judge of any account of the executor or administrator of such estate, have the same revised and corrected by the District Court of the county in which the letters of such executor or administrator were granted, upon making proof before such District Court that there was any error or fraud in such account or settlement; provided, that he shall first obtain from the Clerk of the court in which such account was settled a transcript of all the papers relating to such account and settlement, and file the same with a petition in the office of the Clerk of said District Court, and cause such executor or administrator, or his legal representatives, to be cited as in other suits in said District Court.

SEC. 129.   All decisions, orders, decrees and judgments of the County Court under the provisions of this act, shall be entered on the records of the court by the Clerk at the time such decision, order, decree or judgment shall be made or rendered.

SEC. 130.   Any person who may consider himself aggrieved by any such decision, order, decree or judgment, shall have the right to appeal to the District Court of the county; provided, he shall, within fifteen days after such decision, order, decree or judgment shall have been made and rendered, filed with the Clerk of said Court a bond for costs and damages, with good and sufficient sureties, payable to the County Judge, in such sum as he shall require, and to be approved by said County Judge; conditioned that the appellant shall prosecute said appeal to effect, and perform the decision, order, decree, or judgment which the District Court shall make thereon, in case the cause shall be decided against him.

SEC. 131.   Upon such appeal bond being filed in the Clerk's office, it shall be his duty immediately to make out a certified transcript of the proceedings in the case and transmit the same to the District Court.

SEC. 132.   In case the Clerk of the County Court shall be unable, for want of time, to make out such transcript before the first day of the next term of the District Court of the county after such appeal is taken, then such transcript shall be transmitted to the next succeeding term of said court.

SEC. 133. In all cases where an executor or administrator shall neglect the performance of any duty required by this act, and shall be cited to appear before the court on account thereof, he and his sureties on his official bond shall be liable for all costs of such proceeding out of his own estate; and whenever an executor or administrator shall be removed for any of the causes set forth in this act, he and his sureties on his official bond shall be liable in like manner for all costs attending such removal.

SEC. 134. In all cases where a party shall file any application, complaint or opposition in the court, under the provisions of this act, and on the trial thereof he shall be defeated or fail in the object for which his application, complaint or opposition was filed, he shall be liable for all costs occasioned by the filing of his application, complaint or opposition.

SEC. 135. The County Judge shall have power to enforce obedience to all his lawful orders against executors or administrators, by attachment and imprisonment; *provided*, no such imprisonment shall exceed three days for any one offense, except in cases provided for in section one hundred and twenty-six of this act; he shall also have power to order the clerk to issue execution against the estate of an executor or administrator, in favor of any person to whom money has been ordered to be paid by such executor or administrator; such execution shall be made returnable in sixty days; shall be tested and signed by the Clerk, and sealed with the seal of the county, and may be directed to the Sheriff or other lawful officer of any county in the State; and all proceedings under such executions shall be governed by the laws regulating proceedings under executions issued from the District Court, so far as the same may be applicable.

SEC. 136. In all proceedings in the County Court arising under the provisions of this act, the depositions of witnesses may be taken and read in evidence, under the same rules and regulations as in the District Court, and all laws in relation to witnesses and evidence, which govern the District Court, shall apply to all proceedings in the County Court, under the provisions of this act, so far as they are applicable.

SEC. 137. In all cases, under the provisions of this act, where it is necessary to cite any person who is out of the limits of this State, and the manner of citing such person is not herein otherwise provided for, such person may be cited by publication in like manner as in suits in the District Court.

SEC. 138. Each Clerk of the County Court shall receive and file all applications, complaints, petitions and all other papers permitted or required to be filed in said courts under the provisions of this act, and shall endorse on each the date when it was filed, and sign his name to such endorsement; he shall issue all necessary notices, citations, writs and process from said court, without any order from the County Judge, unless such order is required by some provision of this act.

SEC. 139. Whenever complaint in writing and under oath shall be made to the County Judge by any person interested in the estate of a decedent, that the executor or admistrator of such estate is about to remove the same, or any part thereof, out of the limits of this State, such County Judge shall have power to order a writ to issue, directed to any lawful officer of this State, commanding him to seize such estate, or any part thereof, and hold the same subject to such further order as the County Judge may make on such complaint; *provided*, that no such writ shall issue unless the complainant shall give bond, with good and sufficient security, for such sum as the County Judge may require, payable to the executor or administrator, conditioned for the payment of all damages that may be recovered for the wrongful suing out of such writ.

SEC. 140. The County Judge of the several County Courts shall have like power to enforce all orders, decrees and judgments heretofore made and rendered in the Probate Court of their county, as they would have if such orders, decrees and judgments had been made or rendered by them under the provisions of this act.

SEC. 141. The rights, powers and duties of executors or administrators shall be governed by the principles of the common law, where the same do not conflict with the provisions of this act.

SEC. 142. In all cases where a County Judge may have been executor or administrator of an estate in the county where and at the time he was elected, or when a County Judge may wish to probate a will, and accept as the executor of the estate of a testator in the county where he officiates, or when he may be entitled to a distributive share of an estate that is to be settled in his court, any two of the County Commissioners shall have power to do all acts pertaining to the settlement, partition and distribution of such estates that might be done by the County Judge.

SEC. 143. There shall be begun and holden at the court-houses of the respective counties throughout the State a term of the County Courts on the third Monday in January, March, May, July, September and November of each year, for the transaction of all probate business provided for in this act.

SEC. 144. All proceedings in relation to the settlement, partition and distribution of estates of deceased persons, remaining unsettled in the District Courts of this State, shall be transferred to the County Court of the county having jurisdiction thereof, and shall be conducted and concluded under the provisions of this act.

SEC. 145. The executor or administrator, as soon as practicable after the appointment, shall sell, at public or private sale, all personal property belonging to the estate, except such bonds, securities and other personal property as may, in the opinion of the County Judge, be of a character not likely to waste or loss, and except property exempt from forced sale, specified legacies and personal property necessary to carry on a plantation or manufactory, giving such credit as he may deem most advantageous to the estate, not exceeding six months, and taking notes with one or more sufficient sureties, for the purchase money.

SEC. 146. If any testator direct his personal estate, or any part thereof, not to be sold, the same shall be reserved from sale, unless such sale be necessary for the payment of debts.

SEC. 147. The executor or administrator shall keep, or cause to be kept, a true account of the sales made, making a list thereof, specifying each article sold, the price for which it was sold, and the name of the purchaser, and shall annex to such list an affidavit, stating that it is a true account of the sales made by him at the time specified, and shall file it within thirty days after the sale. Such account shall be recorded after allowing one term for objections to be made.

SEC. 148. The law regulating sales under execution, so far as it relates to the advertisement and sale of personal property, and is not inconsistent with the provisions of this act, shall apply to the advertisement and public sales of such property, by an executor or administrator, the executor or administrator being substituted for the Sheriff or Constable, the estate for the debtor and persons interested in the administration only for the creditors.

SEC. 149. The executor or administrator may sell any of the personal property of the estate at private sale, if it appear to him to be for the interest of the estate, but he shall be responsible for its being sold for a fair price, and shall make return of such sale in thirty days.

SEC. 150. If the executor or administrator shall represent to the court, on oath, that there is wild stock belonging to the estate which he is unable to collect or command, the court may order that the same be sold at public auction, without taking an inventory or appraisement thereof, on such credit as the court may deem reasonable, not exceeding six months, taking notes with good and sufficient securities for the purchase money.

SEC. 151. Such sales shall be advertised, made, returned and confirmed in the same manner as the sales of real property.

SEC. 152. Where personal service is required under any of the provisions of this act, it means that the party shall be cited in the same manner which is provided in like cases for the service of citation in the District Court in civil cases.

SEC. 153. That whenever the bond of any executor or administrator shall have been approved by the County Judge, the Clerk shall make out a true copy of said bond, duly certified under seal of his office, and deliver the same to the County Judge, who shall note thereon the day he received the same, to be taken care of by said Judge, and by him delivered to his successor in office; and in case the original may be destroyed by fire or otherwise, said copy shall be received in evidence as the original, and have the same force and effect.

SEC. 154. That all laws and parts of laws in conflict with the provisions of this act are hereby repealed.

SEC. 155. That an imperative public necessity exists for the suspension of the constitutional rule requiring this bill to be read on three several days, and the fact that there being no laws in force regulating the proceedings pertaining to estates, creates an emergency requiring this act to go into effect immediately, it is therefore enacted that this act take effect and be in force from and after its passage.

Approved August 9, 1876.

Takes effect from its passage.

CHAPTER LXXXV.—*An Act to change and define the times of holding the terms of the District Courts in the Sixth Judicial District of the State of Texas.*

SECTION 1. *Be it enacted by the Legislature of the State of Texas,* That hereafter the terms of the District Courts of the Sixth Judicial District of the State of Texas shall be holden at the times hereinafter specified, to-wit: In the county of Fannin, on the third Monday of February and August, and may continue in session six weeks; in the county of Lamar, on the sixth Monday after the third Monday in February and August, and may continue in session seven weeks; in the county of Red River, on the thirteenth Monday after the third Monday in February and August, and may continue in session five weeks.

SEC. 2. That all writs and process returnable to said courts shall be returnable to the terms of said courts as herein defined, and all such writs and process as have been issued, executed and returned, shall be as valid as if no change had been made in said courts by the passage of this act.

SEC. 3. That no inconvenience may result to the people of the said Sixth Judicial District by the change in time of holding the courts therein, a public necessity and emergency exist, that this act take effect and be in force immediately upon and after its passage, and it is therefore so enacted.

Approved August 11, 1876.

Takes effect from its passage.

CHAPTER LXXXVI.—*An Act to define the Eighth Judicial District, and to fix the times of holding the courts therein.*

SECTION 1. *Be it enacted by the Legislature of the State of Texas,* That the counties of Rains, Hunt, Delta, Hopkins, Kaufman and Rockwall, be, and the same are hereby constituted the Eighth Judicial District.

SEC. 2. That the District Court in and for said county of Rains be holden on the twelfth Mondays after the first Mondays in January and July, and continue in session two weeks; in the county of Hunt, on the first Mondays in January and July, and may continue in session five weeks; in the county of Delta, on the fifth Mondays after the first Mondays in January and July, and may continue in session two weeks; in the county of Hopkins, on the seventh Mondays after the first Mondays in January and July, and may continue in session five weeks; in the county of Kaufman, on the fourteenth Mondays after the first Mondays in January and July, and may continue in session four weeks; in the county of Rockwall, on the eighteenth Mondays after the first Mondays in January and July, and may continue in session one week.

SEC. 3. All process heretofore issued or served, returnable in any of the counties of said Eighth Judicial District as heretofore prescribed by law, shall be considered as returnable at the times herein prescribed; and all such process is hereby legalized and validated, as if the same had been made at the times herein prescribed.

SEC. 4. That all laws and parts of laws in conflict with this act, be and the same are hereby repealed.

SEC. 5. That an imperative public necessity and an emergency exists for the holding the courts in the Eighth Judicial District, in accordance with the provisions of this act, therefore this act shall take effect and be in force from and after its passage.

Approved August 11, 1876.

Takes effect ninety days after adjournment.

CHAPTER LXXXVII.—*An Act to authorize sureties on the official bonds of county officers to require their principals in such bonds to give new bonds, and to provide for the giving of such new bonds in such cases.*

SECTION 1. *Be it enacted by the Legislature of the State of Texas,* That any surety on any official bond of any county officer in this State may apply to the County Commissioners' Court of the county to be relieved from his bond. And the Clerk of the County Court shall thereupon issue a notice to said officer, and a copy of the application, which shall be served upon said officer by the Sheriff or any Constable of the county; and upon the service of such notice, said officer so notified shall cease to exercise the functions of his office, except to preserve any records or property committed to his charge, and in case of Sheriffs and Constables, to keep prisoners, preserve the peace, and execute warrants for the arrest of persons charged with offenses; and said officer so notified shall give a new bond within twenty days from the time of receiving such notice, or his office shall become vacant.

SEC. 2. If a new bond be given and approved, the former surety or sureties shall be discharged from any liability for the misconduct of the principal, after the approval of such new bond.

SEC. 3. There being no law in force authorizing sureties on the official bonds of county officers, to obtain the relief provided for in this act, and justice to such sureties and the public good requiring that such provision should be made by law. a public necessity and emergency exist for the immediate passage of this law, and it is enacted that this act take effect and be in force from and after its passage.

Approved August 12, 1876.

Takes effect from its passage.

CHAPTER LXXXVIII.—*An Act to amend an act entitled, " An Act prescribing the times of holding the District Courts in the Twelfth Judicial District and to attach certain counties therein named for judicial purposes," approved July 29, 1876.*

SECTION 1. *Be it enacted by the Legislature of the State of Texas,* That section one of the above entitled act be so amended as hereafter to read as follows, to-wit: " That the District Courts of the Twelfth Judicial District be holden at the times hereinafter stated, to-wit: in the county of Coryell on the first Monday in March and September, and may continue in session two weeks; in the county of Hamilton on the third Monday in March and September, and may continue in session one week; in the county of Comanche on the fourth Monday in March and September, and may continue in session one week; in the county of Brown on the fourth Monday after the first Monday in March and September, and may continue in session one week; in the county of Coleman on the fifth Monday after the first Monday in March and September, and may continue in session one week; in the county of Shackelford on the sixth Monday after the first Monday in March and September, and may continue in session one week; in the county of Stephens on the seventh Monday after the first Monday in March and September, and may continue in session one week; in the county of Young on the eighth Monday after the first Monday in March and September, and may continue in session one week; in the county of Jack on the ninth Monday after the first Monday in March and September, and may continue in session two weeks; in the county of Palo Pinto on the eleventh Monday after the first Monday in March and September, and may continue in session one week; in the county of Hood on the twelfth Monday after the first Monday in March and September, and may continue in session one week; in the county of Somerville on the thirteenth Monday after the first Monday in March and September, and may continue in session one week; in the county of Erath on the fourteenth Monday after the first Monday in March and September, and may continue in session one week; in the county of Eastland on the fifteenth Monday after the first Monday in March and September, and may continue in session one week."

For judicial purposes the county of Reynolds is attached to Coleman county; Callahan county to Eastland county; Throckmorton, Haskell and Jones counties to Shackelford.

SEC. 2.   There being a public necessity for a change in the times of holding the Courts in said District, and the condition of the District renders it necessary that this act take effect and be in force from and after the fifteenth day of August, 1876, and it is so enacted.

Approved August 12, 1876.

Takes effect from August 15, 1876.

CHAPTER LXXXIX.—*An Act to authorize the Commissioner of the General Land Office to appoint a Surveyor.*

SECTION 1.   *Be it enacted by the Legislature of the State of Texas*, That the Commissioner of the General Land Office is hereby authorized and required to appoint a competent Surveyor, whenever he may deem it necessary to establish the lines and corners, in accordance with the provisions of "An Act authorizing the disposition and sale of the University Lands," approved April 8, 1874.

SEC. 2.   In view of the fact that the Commissioner of the General Land Office may need the services of said Surveyor at any time, an emergency exists for the immediate passage of this act, and it is therefore enacted that this act take effect and be in force from and after its passage.

Approved August 12, 1876.

Takes effect from its passage.

CHAPTER XC.—*An Act to provide for supplying lost records in certain cases.*

SECTION 1.   *Be it enacted by the Legislature of the State of Texas*, That in any county of this State, where the record books of land, the records of said county have heretofore been burned, lost or destroyed, and there is in the hands of, or owned by any person or persons, a part, or a complete abstract of the records of deeds, bonds, mortgages, and other conveyances to lands recorded in said books, the County Commissioners' Court of said county is hereby authorized and empowered to purchase said abstract from the owner thereof, upon such terms and conditions as the said Commissioners' Court and said owners of said abstract may agree; *provided*, that the individual or individuals who made said abstract shall make an affidavit that said abstract is a true and correct copy of the substance of the original record.

SEC. 2.   In case of the purchase of any such abstract as hereinbefore provided, the same shall be turned over to the custody of the Clerk of the County Court, and shall become a part of the records of said County Court, and it is hereby made the duty of said Clerk to keep up and continue said abstract in the same form, in a well bound book, to be procured for that purpose.

SEC. 3.   All copies from said abstracts, properly certified as being true, under the hand and seal of said Clerk, shall be received in testimony in all courts held in said county, as *prima facie* evidence of the contents of the original records of the contents of such original deeds, and said abstracts shall be constructive notice of the recording, date of recording and contents of such deeds therein noted; *provided*, that copies of said abstracts shall be received in evidence only in such cases and under the same rules and regulations in and under which copies of recorded deeds are permitted to be received in evidence.

SEC. 4. That said Clerk is hereby authorized and required to demand and receive, from any and all persons desiring him to examine the said abstract for them, the sum of fifty cents for each and every such examination, one-third of which fee he shall retain for his services, and the remainder he shall pay over to the County Treasurer at least once in every six months.

SEC. 5. As many counties in this State have had their land records burned, and no means exist to supply their loss; therefore, there exist an emergency and necessity for immediate legislation on the subject, it is therefore enacted that this act take effect and be in force from and after its passage.

Approved August 12, 1876.

Takes effect from its passage.

CHAPTER XCI.—*An Act to provide for the transferring of all criminal cases in which indictments have been found to the proper court having jurisdiction thereof.*

SECTION 1. *Be it enacted by the Legislature of the State of Texas,* That at the end of each term of the District Court of each county in this State, the District Judge shall make an order transferring all criminal cases over which the District Court has no jurisdiction to the several courts in the county having jurisdiction over the respective cases, and shall state in his order the cause transferred, and to what court they are transferred; *provided,* that all causes over which Justices of the Peace may have jurisdiction shall be transferred to a Justice of the Peace at the county seat; *and provided further,* that if it appear to the Judge that the offense has been committed in any incorporated town or city, the cause shall be transferred to a Justice in said city or town.

SEC. 2. The Clerk of the District Court shall deliver the indictments and all the papers relating to each case to the proper court or Justice, as directed in said order, and accompanying each case a certified copy of all the proceedings taken in the District Court in regard to the same; and also a bill of costs, showing what costs have accrued in the District Court; and the costs due in said account shall be collected in the court in which said causes are tried, in the same manner as if decided in the District Court.

SEC. 3. That all cases transferred under this act shall be entered on the docket of the court to which they are transferred, and the defendants arraigned and tried in the same manner as if said cause had originated in said courts.

SEC. 4. Whereas, many causes are now pending on the dockets of the various District Courts of the State which cannot be tried, because there is no existing law providing for the transfer of said causes to the respective courts having jurisdiction thereof; therefore, an imperative public necessity and emergency exist that this law go into immediate effect, and it is hereby enacted that the same go into effect and be in force from and after its passage.

Approved August 12, 1876.

Takes effect from its passage.

CHAPTER XCII.—*An Act to establish an Agricultural and Mechanical College of Texas, for the benefit of the colored youths and to make appropriations therefor.*

SECTION 1.   *Be it enacted by the Legislature of the State of Texas,* That there shall be established in this State at such point and in the manner provided for in this act, an Agricultural and Mechanical College for the benefit of the colored youths of this State.

SEC. 2.   The Governor is hereby authorized to appoint a Commission, consisting of three competent persons, who shall select a suitable place for the location of said Agricultural and Mechanical College, and make report thereof to the Governor as hereinafter provided for ; *provided,* that the site so selected shall contain not less than five hundred acres of land suitable for agricultural purposes.   The said Commissioners shall have authority to receive donations of land and money to aid in the erection and maintainence of said Agricultural and Mechanical College.   When said College shall have been located, it shall be known as the Agricultural and Mechanical College of Texas, established for colored youths, and shall be under the supervision and control of the Board of the Agricultural and Mechanical College, as established by an act of the Legislature, passed April 17, 1871.

SEC. 3.   The Governor shall appoint a competent Architect, who shall submit a plan and specifications of suitable buildings for said college, of capacity for the accommodation of at least one hundred students, to be approved by the Governor.

SEC. 4.   The said Commissioners shall proceed to make selection of said location, and report the same to the Governor at as early a day as practicable.

SEC. 5.   Upon the approval of the plans and specifications for said buildings by the Governor, the said Commissioners shall proceed to advertise for ninety days in two or more newspapers published in this State, for sealed proposals for the erection of said buildings, giving full particulars of the terms and conditions of such contracts, and the time and place when and where the bids therefor shall be opened and contracts awarded.

SEC. 6.   Contractors for the erection of said buildings shall be required to enter into bond with good and sufficient security payable to the Governor and his successors in office, to be approved by the Governor in a sum equal to double the amount of his or their bid, or bids, conditioned that such contractor or contractors will execute the work or furnish the material contracted for, in strict accordance with the terms and conditions of such contract.

SEC. 7.   The said Commissioners and Architect together, shall constitute a Board of Directors, or Building Committee, and shall have full management and control of the direction and execution of said contracts for the erection of said buildings, and shall make report of the progress of the same to the Governor at least once in each six months till the same is completed and received by the Governor.

SEC. 8.   The sum of twenty thousand dollars, or so much thereof as shall be deemed necessary to locate, erect, furnish and operate said college in accordance with the plans, specifications and estimates as shall be approved by the Governor, for the completion of the same be, and the same is hereby appropriated out of any money in the Treasury not otherwise appropriated.

SEC. 9. The said Commissioners shall be allowed each the sum of five dollars per day, and mileage at the rate of ten cents per mile for each day actually engaged, and each mile actually traveled, in the selection or locating of said college to be verified by their sworn statement respectively, and approved by the Governor, which sworn statement so approved shall be a sufficient voucher upon which the Comptroller shall draw his warrant on the Treasurer for such amount, and that for services to be by them rendered as a Board of Directors or Building Committee, such compensation as the Governor in his discretion shall allow; *provided*, that the Governor shall have and exercise his discretionary power to dissolve the said committee when in his judgment the same shall be necessary.

SEC. 10. That the class of citizens for whose benefit this act is to effect specially, shall enjoy the same at as early a day as practicable, a public necessity and emergency exists, that this act take effect and be in force from and after its passage.

Approved August 14, 1876.

Takes effect from its passage.

CHAPTER XCIII.—*An Act to amend the fifth section of an act concerning rents and advances, approved April 4, 1874.*

SECTION 1. *Be it enacted by the Legislature of the State of Texas,* That Section 5 of the above recited act shall hereafter read as follows :

SEC. 2 (5). Nothing in this act contained shall be so construed as to prevent landlords and tenants from entering into such stipulations or contracts in regard to rents and advances as they may think proper ; and should the landlord, without any default on the part of the tenant or lessee, fail to comply in any respect with his part of the contract, he shall be responsible to said tenant or lessee for whatever damage may be sustained thereby; and to secure such damages to such tenant or lessee, he shall have a lien on all the property in his possession not exempt from forced sale, as well as upon all rents due to said landlord, under said contract ; but if lands or tenements are rented by the landlord to any person or persons, such person or persons renting said lands or tenements shall not rent or lease said lands or tenements during the term of said lease to any other person without first obtaining the consent of the landlord, his agent or attorney.

Approved August 14, 1876.

Takes effect ninety days after adjournment.

CHAPTER XCIV.—*An Act to provide for a regular term of the District Court in Rains county.*

SECTION 1. *Be it enacted by the Legislature of the State of Texas,* That there shall be held, in the county of Rains, a regular term of the District Court, to begin on Monday, the twenty-fifth day of September, A. D. 1876, and continue in session two weeks ; and all process returnable to the regular term for said county, under the law as it heretofore existed, shall be returnable thereto.

SEC. 2. That an emergency and imperative public necessity exist, as no law now in force provides for a full term of the District Court in

Rains county; therefore, this act take effect and be in force from and after its passage.

Approved August 15, 1876.

Takes effect from its passage.

CHAPTER XCV.—*An Act to amend an act entitled, "An Act to provide for the organization of the State Lunatic Asylum, and for the care and maintenance of the insane," approved February 5, 1858.*

SECTION 1. *Be it enacted by the Legislature of the State of Texas,* That the eighth section of the act passed February 5, 1858, to which this is amendatory, shall read as follows:

"SEC. 8. If information in writing be given to any County Judge that any person in his county is a lunatic, or *non compos mentis,* and that the welfare of himself or herself or of others requires that he or she be placed under restraint, and said County Judge shall believe such information to be true, he shall order such person to be brought before him and twelve competent jurors of his county to be summoned, who shall be sworn to enquire and a true verdict render whether such person is of sound mind or not; whereupon, the matter shall be tried, and if the jury shall return a verdict that the person is not of sound mind, and that he or she should be placed under restraint, the same shall be recorded on the books of the County Court, and the County Judge shall thereupon order him or her to be sent to the lunatic asylum, unless some friend or legal representative (to whom the County Judge in his discretion may deliver such person) will give bond payable to the State, with sufficient security, to be approved by said County Judge, with the condition to restrain and take proper care of such person until the cause of confinement shall cease, or he or she is delivered to the Sheriff of the county, or other person, to be proceeded with according to law. Upon the trial and inquiry herein provided for, it shall be the duty of the County Attorney to appear for and represent the State, and the examination of the insane and the testimony of the witnesses shall be reduced to writing and filed. The proceedings of the County Judge in relation to insane persons shall be minuted in the record of his court appertaining to estates of deceased persons."

SEC. 2. That Section 9 of said act shall be amended so as to read as follows:

"SEC. 9. It shall be the duty of the County Judge, on ordering the person to be sent to the asylum, to ascertain and to state in the authenticated proceedings to be sent to the Superintendent of the State Lunatic Asylum: *First,* the age, nativity and civil condition of the lunatic; *Second,* the number of attacks, and how long the present one has existed; *Third,* whether the insanity is hereditary or not; *Fourth,* the number of his family, if he has one, and their ability to maintain themselves; *Fifth,* the value of his or her estate, if any; and *Sixth,* the ability of persons legally liable for his or her support; and he shall make an order specifying the amount which his guardian, if any, shall pay out of the estate of such person for his support in the asylum, and shall cause a minute to be made of the facts ascertained."

SEC. 3. That Section 10 of said act shall be amended so as to read as follows:

"Sec. 10. Before sending a patient to the asylum, the County Judge shall without delay cause authenticated copies to be made of the proceedings, evidence and decree of the original inquisition and of the record of all subsequent inquisitions and orders, to be forwarded by mail to the Superintendent of the Lunatic Asylum, and in all cases shall, before sending such person, ascertain from the Superintendent by application in writing that there is a vacancy. Thereupon the County Judge shall issue his warrant to the Sheriff or other suitable individual, ordering him to convey said person to the Lunatic Asylum, without delay, and when satisfied of the necessity for assistants, he shall prescribe in such warrant the number to be allowed, which in no case shall exceed two; and he shall see that the patient is provided with two good and full suits of summer and one of winter clothing."

Sec. 4. That Section 17 of the said act shall be amended so as to read as follows:

"Sec. 17. The custody and maintenance of all lunatics who shall be found to be indigent, as well those now in the asylum, as those to be hereafter admitted, shall be at the expense of the State, under the rules and restrictions as are prescribed herein. In cases where any patient is now in the custody and care of said asylum, if said patient is held and treated at the expense of the county from which he or she was sent, it shall be the duty of the Superintendent of said asylum, as soon as practicable after the passage of this law, to communicate by mail with the County Judge of said county, giving him the names of such persons so confined from said county; whereupon it shall be the duty of the County Judge to cause a jury of twelve men to be summoned before him and shall proceed to take the necessary evidence, to hear and determine whether such lunatic is a person without any means to support him or her, and whether any person in said county is legally liable to support said lunatic. Said jury shall be sworn to try the matter and a true verdict render; and said County Judge shall cause the testimony to be written down and filed, and the verdict of said jury to be recorded. And if said verdict shall be that said lunatic is in indigent circumstances, and without any property to support him or her, the County Judge shall certify the facts, together with a copy of testimony and the verdict of said jury to the said Superintendent of the asylum, and thereupon said lunatic shall be kept and maintained at the expense of the State."

Sec. 5. That in all cases, as provided for in Section 1 of this act, it shall be the duty of [the] County Judge to cause said jury to enquire, in addition to the matters to be enquired about, as set forth in said Section 1, whether such person, so found by the jury to be of unsound mind, is also a person without means to support him or her, and whether any person in said county is legally liable to support said lunatic; and it shall be the duty of said County Judge to certify all of said proceedings to the Superintendent of the asylum, and if it shall be found by the verdict of said jury that said lunatic is an indigent person, then, in that case, the expense and maintenance of such person shall be paid by the State. If it shall appear, upon such inquisition, that any person is legally liable for the support of such insane person, the facts shall all be certified to the Clerk of the District Court, who shall have authority to order the payment thereof by the person liable, and if the same be adjudged against the property of the patient or his or her guardian or legal representative, the payment thereof may be, as in other cases, enforced by execution; *provided*, that an appeal may be taken to the District Court from the order of the Clerk.

Sec. 6.   For all persons who are not indigent, the Superintendent may make a special contract at any rate not less than five dollars ($5) per week.   In all cases of indigent lunatics, the expenses of removing the patient from the asylum home and for the necessary clothing with which he shall be furnished by the asylum, shall be paid by the State.   The expenses of conveying indigent lunatics to the asylum shall be paid by the county; and the Sheriff or other person conveying said lunatic shall, in each case, make out and cause to be delivered to the County Judge for allowance, a statement, verified by affidavit, of the actual expenses incurred in the transportation of such lunatics to the asylum for payment; and the same shall be paid by the county.

Sec. 7.   In receiving patients into the asylum, preference shall be given, in all cases, to indigent patients.

Sec. 8.   Inasmuch as a number of indigent lunatics are being supported at the expense of many of the counties of this State, and as the Constitution requires that all such lunatics shall be supported at the expense of the State, an emergency and an imperative public necessity exists, requiring the immediate passage of this act; therefore, this act shall take effect and be in force from and after its passage.

Approved August 15, 1876.

Takes effect from its passage.

CHAPTER XCVI.—*An Act to provide for the holding of District Courts when the Judge thereof is absent, or is, from any cause, disabled or disqualified from presiding.*

Section 1.   *Be it enacted by the Legislature of the State of Texas,* That whenever on the day appointed for the beginning of a term of any District Court, or at any time before the expiration of the term or the completion of all the business of said court, the Judge of any District Court shall be absent from said court, or shall fail or be unable to hold said court, there shall be thereby no failure of the term of the court, and no failure to proceed with the business thereof, but it shall thereupon be the duty of the practicing lawyers in the court present thereat to choose from among their number a Special Judge of said court, who, upon taking the oath before the Clerk of said court to support the Constitution of the United States, and the further oath provided in Section 1 of Article 16, of the Constitution, shall have all the power and authority of a District Judge of said court during the continued absence or inability of the Judge thereof, and shall proceed to hold said court and conduct the business thereof as its lawful Judge.

Sec. 2.   That all the practicing lawyers in attendance at said court shall be entitled to participate in the election of said Special Judge, each lawyer having one vote, and a majority of all the lawyers present and participating in the election shall be necessary to the election of any Special Judge, and the said election shall be by ballot.   The said practicing lawyers shall compose an electoral body entitled to make and conduct said election, and the following mode thereof shall be legal and sufficient: Public proclamation shall be made by the Sheriff at the court-house door that the election of a Special Judge is to be made by the practicing lawyers of said court present thereat, after which the Clerk of the court shall make a roll or list of all such practicing lawyers present; and said lawyers shall proceed to organize and make the election of said Judge by ballot as aforesaid; and said lawyers shall have the right to organize and make such election, although the Sheriff and Clerk, or either of them, should fail or refuse to act, or their office be vacant. A record shall be made and entered on the minutes of the court of the election of said Judge, and said record must show : *First*— The names of all practicing lawyers present and participating in such election. *Second*—The fact that public proclamation was made at the court-house door that said election was about to take place. *Third*— The ballot or ballots polled at such election, with the result of each ballot, showing the number of ballots for each person. *Fourth*—That the oath prescribed in Section 2(1) of this act has been administered. And such proceedings, and the record thereof showing substantial compliance with the above, shall be evidence of the valid election of a Special Judge of said court. Such election may be made from time to time during the term of court to supply the absence, or failure, or inability of the Judge to act, and of any Special Judge of said court.

SEC. 3. That whenever any case is called in which the District Judge or the Special Judge chosen as hereinbefore provided, shall be a party or have interest, or have been attorney, or counsel, or otherwise disqualified from sitting in and trying the same, no change of venue shall be made necessary thereby; but the parties or their counsel shall have the right to select and agree upon an attorney of the court for the trial thereof.

SEC. 4. Said Special Judge shall be paid at the same rate of District Judges per day for his services, out of the State Treasury; such payment to be made on the certificate of the Clerk of the court to the Comptroller, of the record of such election and services, and an affidavit by the Special Judge to the correctness of the claim.

SEC. 5. To provide for the contingencies currently and frequently occurring in the conduct of the courts, an imperative public necessity and emergency exists for the immediate passage and taking effect of this act, and it is enacted that this act take effect from and after its passage.

Approved August 15, 1876.

Takes effect ninety days after adjournment.

CHAPTER XCVII.—*An Act to provide for the incorporation of associations that may be organized for the purpose of constructing railways, maintaining and operating the same, for prescribing and defining the duties and limiting the powers of such corporations when so organized.*

SECTION 1. *Be it enacted by the Legislature of the State of Texas*, That any number of persons, not less than ten, being subscribers to the stock of any contemplated railroad, may be formed into a corporation for the purpose of constructing, owning and maintaining such railroad, by complying with the following requirements, when stock to the amount of one thousand dollars for every mile of said road so intended to be built, shall be in good faith subscribed and five per cent. paid thereon.

SEC. 2. Such persons shall organize by adopting and signing articles of incorporations, which shall be submitted to the Attorney-General of this State, and if it shall be found by the Attorney-General of this State to be in accordance with the provisions of this act, and not in conflict with the laws of the United States and of this State, he shall attach thereto a certificate to that effect, whereupon said articles shall be recorded in the office of the recorder of deeds, in each county through or into which said railway is proposed to run, and in the office of the Secretary of State.

SEC. 3. Such articles shall contain: *First*—The name of the proposed corporation. *Second*—The places from and to which it is intended to construct the proposed railway, and the intermediate counties through whith it is proposed to construct the same. *Third*—The place at which shall be established and maintained the principal business office of such proposed corporation. *Fourth*—The time of the commencement and period of the continuation of such proposed corporation. *Fifth*—The amount of the capital stock of such corporation. *Sixth*—The names and places of residence of the several persons forming the association for incorporation. *Seventh*—The names of the members of the first Board of Directors, and in what officers or persons the government of the proposed corporation, and the management of its affairs shall be vested. *Eighth*—The number and amount of shares in the capital stock of such proposed corporation; *provided*, that such articles of association shall not be filed in the office of the Secretary of State, as aforesaid, until five per cent. of the amount of stock subscribed thereto shall have been actually paid in cash to the Directors named in such articles, nor until there is annexed thereto an affidavit made by at least three of the Directors named in said articles, that the amount of stock required by this section, to-wit: one thousand dollars per mile, has been subscribed, and that five per cent. on the amount has actually been paid in.

SEC. 4. When the articles shall have been filed and recorded as aforesaid, the persons named as corporators therein shall thereupon become and be deemed a body corporate, and shall thereupon be authorized to proceed to carry into effect the objects set forth in such articles in accordance with the provisions of this act. As such body corporate, they shall have succession, and in their corporate name may sue and be sued, plead and be impleaded. The said corporation may have and use a common seal, which it may alter at pleasure, may declare the interests of its stockholders transferable, establish by-laws, and make all rules and regulations deemed necessary for the management of its affairs in accordance with law. A copy of any articles of incorporation filed and recorded in pursuance with this act, or of the record thereof, and certified to be a copy by the Secretary of State, or acting Secretary of State, or recorder of deeds of any county in which the same has been recorded, shall be presumptive evidence of the incorporation of such company, and of the facts therein stated; *provided*, that in any suit in any court in this State, by or against any railway corporation, it shall not be necessary for either party to prove the act of incorporation, and the allegation that the corporation is an incorporated company shall be deemed *prima facie* true.

SEC. 5. The existence of the corporation shall date from the filing of the charter in the office of the Secretary of State, and the certificate of the Secretary of State shall be evidence of such filing. Any corporation organized under the provisions of this act, or any railroad corporation heretofore incorporated by special act of the Legislature and still in being, may amend or change its articles or act of incorporation in the same manner that this act requires for the original organization and incorporation of such corporation, to-wit: By filing, authenticated, as by this act required, the amendments or changes to the original charter with the Secretary of State; and in case of a corporation created by a special act of the Legislature, said corporation shall cause the changes or amendments to its charter, together with its original charter and such amendments as have been made by special act, recorded and authenticated as by this act required, to be filed with the Secretary of State, to be by him recorded as in the case of acts of incorporation under this act. And such changes or amendments shall be in force from the date of filing with the Secretary of State; *provided*, that where, by the special act or acts incorporating any railroad, any privileges, rights or benefits are conferred upon said railroad corporation, such as it could not claim, exercise or receive under this act, or the general laws of this State, if so organized under this act, such railroad corporation shall not be permitted so to change its charter or articles or act of incorporation as to relieve it from any of the requirements of said special act or acts conferring said rights, privileges or benefits; *and provided further*, that nothing in this act shall be construed so as to allow any railway company chartered under this act or under a special act of the Legislature, to alter or change any part of its charter requiring it to build its road through and to maintain passenger and freight depots in or near any town or city in this State, and within the time named in its charter; *provided further*, that any railroad company hereafter chartered under this act, shall make an actual survey of its route or line for a distance of twenty-five miles on its projected route, and shall designate the depot grounds along said first twenty-five miles before the road bed is begun, and no railway company shall change its route after being designated as aforesaid. And all railroad companies chartered as aforesaid shall, on the completion of the first twenty-five miles of its road bed, make a survey of the next twenty-five miles, and of each subsequent twenty-five miles as the preceding twenty-five miles shall be completed, and every subsequent twenty-five miles shall be controlled by the provisions applicable to the first twenty-five miles of the road; *provided further*, that whenever any such railway passes through any enclosure the necessary stock gaps for the protection of such enclosure from stock, shall be constructed by said railway.

SEC. 6. That all such companies, and all companies heretofore chartered by act of the Legislature, shall have the right to purchase lands and receive donations of the same, to aid in the construction of their road; the land so purchased or donated, except that used for depot purposes, reservations for the establishment of machine shops, turnouts and switches, to be alienated and disposed of in the same manner and time as is required where lands have been received from the State; and this provision shall apply to such roads as are prohibited by their acts of incorporation from purchasing or receiving donations of land.

SEC. 7. Any such railroad mentioned in the fifth section may, by amendment to its charter or act, or articles of incorporation, in the manner in said section indicated and required, project and provide for the locating, constructing, owning and maintaining a branch line to its original main or trunk line of railroad, from any point on its said original main or trunk line, to any other point in this State, by a branch line to the main line, making an angle with said main line of at least twenty-five degrees in the general course of said branch line, and also so projected that said branch line shall, in no case, be so located as to be or become such a line of railroad as that if the same were owned by another corporation the corporation owning the main line, or any one of the other branches thereof, would be forbidden by the Constitution and laws of this State from consolidating therewith, on account of the lines being parallel or competing lines ; *provided*, that any such corporation making such an amendment to its charter or act or articles of incorporation, as is authorized by this section, shall complete and put in good running order at least ten miles of its said branch line, in said amendment proposed, within one year from the making of said amendment, and an additional extent of at least twenty miles each and every succeeding year until the entire extent of the projected branch line is completed ; and in case of failure of any such corporation to comply with the requirements of this proviso, its corporate existence as to all the unfinished portion of said projected branch line shall immediately cease, and be incapable of resumption by any subsequent action of such corporation.

Sec. 8.   No such corporation shall be formed to continue more than fifty years in the first instance, but such corporation may be renewed from time to time in such manner as may be provided by law, for periods not longer than fifty years ; *provided*, that three-fourths of the vote cast by the stockholders of such corporation at any regular election for that purpose shall be in favor of such renewal, and those desiring a renewal shall purchase the stock of those opposed thereto, at its current value.

Sec. 9.   A copy of the by-laws of the corporation, duly certified, shall be recorded, as provided for the recording of the articles of associations in section two of this act; and all amendments and additions thereto, duly certified, shall also be recorded as herein provided, within ninety days after the adoption thereof.

Sec. 10.   Every such corporation organized under the provisions of this act shall have and maintain a public office or place at one of the termini or on the line of its road, in this State, for the transaction of its business, where transfers of all its stock shall be made, and in which shall be kept for public inspection, books, wherein shall be recorded the amount of capital stock subscribed, and by whom, the names of the owners of its stock, the number of shares held by each person, and the number by which each of said shares is respectively designated, and the amounts owned by them respectively, the amount of stock paid in, and by whom, the transfers of said stock, the amount of its assets and liabilities, and the names and places of residence of all its officers.   No transfer shall be valid until the transfer shall have been made on the stock and transfer books of the company.

Sec. 11.   All the corporate powers of every such corporation shall be vested in and be exercised by a Board of Directors, who shall be stockholders of the corporation, and shall be elected at the annual meeting of stockholders at the public office of such corporation within this State.   The number of such Directors, not less than seven nor more than nine ; the manner of their election and the mode of filling vacancies shall be specified in the by-laws, and shall not be changed except at the annual meetings of the stockholders.

Sec. 12.   A meeting may be called at any time during the interval between such annual meetings by the Directors or by the stockholders owning not less than one-fourth of the stock, by giving thirty days' public notice of the time and place of such meeting in some newspaper published in each county through or into which the said railway shall run or be intended to run ; *provided*, there be a newspaper published in each of the counties aforesaid; and if at any such special meeting so called, a majority, in value, of the stockholders, equal to two-thirds of the stock of such corporation shall not be represented in person or by proxy, such meeting shall be adjourned from day to day, not exceeding three days, without transacting any business, and if within said three days two-thirds in value of such stock shall not be represented at such meeting, then the meeting shall be adjourned and a new call may be given and notified as hereinbefore provided.

SEC. 13. At the regular annual meeting of the stockholders of any corporation organized under the provisions of this act, it shall be the duty of the President and Directors to exhibit a full, distinct and accurate statement of the affairs of the said corporation, and at any meeting of the stockholders, or a majority of those present, in person or by proxy, may require similar statements from the President and Directors, whose duty it shall be to furnish such statements when required in the manner aforesaid; and at all general meetings of the stockholders a majority in value of the stockholders of any such corporation may fix the rates of interest which shall be paid by the corporation for loans for the construction of such railway and its appendages, and the amount of such loans at any special meeting, by a two-thirds vote in value of all the stock, such stockholders may remove any President, Director or other officer of such corporation, and elect others instead of those so removed. All stockholders shall, at all reasonable hours, have access to and may examine all books, records and papers of such corporation.

SEC. 14. In case it shall happen at any time that an election of Directors shall not be made on the day designated by the by-laws of such corporation for that purpose, the corporation for such cause shall not be dissolved if within ninety days thereafter the stockholders shall meet and hold an election for Directors in such manner as shall be provided by the by-laws of such corporation; provided, that it shall require a majority in value of the stock of such corporation to elect any member of such Board of Directors, and a majority of such Board of Directors shall be citizens and residents of this State.

SEC. 15. There shall be a President of such corporation, who shall be chosen by and from the Board of Directors, and such other subordinate officers as such corporation, by its by-laws, may designate, who may be elected or appointed, and shall perform such duties and be required to give such security for the faithful performance thereof, as such corporation by its by-laws shall require; provided, that it shall require a majority of the Directors to elect or appoint any officer.

SEC. 16. The Directors of such corporation may require the subscribers to the capital stock of such corporation to pay the amount by them respectively subscribed in such manner and in such installments as they may deem proper. If any stockholder shall neglect to pay any installment as required by a resolution or order of such Board of Directors, the said Board shall be authorized to advertise said stock for sale, by publication once a week for thirty days, and then sell the same to the highest bidder, the proceeds to be credited to the delinquent stockholder.

SEC. 17. The stock of such corporation shall be deemed personal estate, and shall be transferable in the manner prescribed by the by-laws of such corporation. But no shares shall be transferable until all previous calls thereon shall have been paid, and it shall not be lawful for such corporation to use any of the funds thereof in the purchase of its

10 GL.

own stock, or that of any other corporation, or to loan any of its funds to any Director or other officer thereof, or permit them, or any of them, to use the same for other than the legitimate purposes of such corporation; *provided*, that nothing herein contained shall be so construed as to prevent lateral or branch roads, intended as feeders to the main line, or trunk road, from consolidating with and forming a part of the main or trunk line upon such terms and conditions as may be agreed upon by the companies owning the trunk and branch lines.

SEC. 18. In case the capital stock of any such corporation shall be found insufficient for constructing and operating its road, such corporation may, with the concurrence of two-thirds in value of all its stock, increase its capital stock from time to time to any amount required for the purpose aforesaid. Such increase shall be sanctioned by a vote, in person or by proxy, of two-thirds in amount of all the stock of such corporation, at a meeting of such stockholders, called by the Directors of the corporation for such purpose, by giving notice in writing to each stockholder, to be served personally, or by depositing the same in a post office, directed to the post office address of each of said stockholders severally, with necessary postage for the transmittal of the same prepaid, at least sixty days prior to the day appointed for such meeting, and by advertising the same in some newspaper published in each county through or into which the said road shall run or be intended to run (if any newspaper shall be published therein), at least sixty days prior to the day appointed for such meeting. Such notice shall state the time and place of the meeting, the object thereof, and the amount to which it is proposed to increase such capital stock; and at such meeting the corporate stock of such corporation may be so increased by a vote of two-thirds in amount of the corporate stock of such corporation, to an amount not exceeding the amount mentioned in the notice so given. Should the Directors of any such corporation desire at any time to call a special meeting of the stockholders for any other necessary purpose, the same may be done in the manner in this section provided, and if such meeting be attended by the owners of two-thirds in amount of the stock, in person or by proxy, any other necessary business of such corporation may be then transacted, except the altering, amending or adding to the by-laws of such corporation; *provided*, such business shall have been specified in the notices given, and the proceedings of any such meetings shall be entered on the journal of the proceedings of such corporation. Every order or resolution increasing the capital stock of any such corporation, shall be duly recorded as required in section two of this act.

SEC. 19. No person holding stock in any such corporation as executor, administrator, guardian or trustee, and no person holding such stock as collateral security, shall be personally subject to any liability as stockholders of such corporation; but the person pledging the stock shall be considered as holding the same, and shall be liable as a stockholder accordingly.

SEC. 20. Each stockholder of any corporation formed under the provisions of this act shall be held individually liable to the creditors of such corporation to an amount not exceeding the amount unpaid on the stock held by him, for any and all debts and liabilities of such corporation, until the whole amount of the capital stock of such corporation so held by him shall have been paid.

SEC. 21. If any such corporation shall be unable to agree with the owner for the purchase of any real estate required for the purpose of its incorporation, or the transaction of its business, or for its depots, station buildings, machine and repair shops, or for right of way, or any other lawful purpose connected with or necessary to the building, operating or running of said road, such corporation may acquire such title in the manner that may be now or hereafter provided for by any law of eminent domain.

SEC. 22. Any such corporation may, by their agents and employes, enter upon and take from any land adjacent to its road, earth, gravel, stone or other materials, except fuel and wood, necessary for the construction of such railway, paying, if the owner of such land and the railway can agree thereto, the value of such material taken and the amount of damage occasioned to any such land or its appurtenances; and if such owner and corporation cannot agree, then the value of such material and the damage occasioned to such real estate may be ascertained, determined and paid in the manner that may now or hereafter be provided by any law of eminent domain; but the value of such materials and the damages to such real estate shall be ascertained, determined and paid for before such corporation can enter upon or take the same.

SEC. 23. Every corporation formed under this act shall, in addition to the powers hereinbefore conferred, have power: *First*—To cause such examination and survey for its proposed railway to be made as may be necessary to the selection of the most advantageous route; and for such purpose, by its officers, agents or servants, may enter upon the lands or waters of any person or corporation, but subject to responsibility for all damages which shall be occasioned thereby. *Second*—To take and hold such voluntary grants of real estate and other property as shall be made to it in aid of the construction and use of its railway, and to convey the same when no longer required for the uses of such railway, not incompatible with the terms of the original grant. *Third*—To purchase, hold and use all such real estate and other property as may be necessary for the construction and use of its railway and the stations, and other accommodations necessary to accomplish the object of its incorporation, and to convey the same when no longer required for the use of such railway. *Fourth*—To lay out its road not exceeding two hundred feet in width, and to construct the same; and for the purpose of cutting and embankments, to take as much more land as may be necessary for the proper construction and security of the railway, and to cut down any standing trees that may be in danger of falling upon or obstructing the railway, making compensation in manner provided by law. *Fifth*—To construct its railway across, along or upon any stream of water, water course, street, highway, plank road, turnpike or canal, which the route of such railway shall intersect or touch; but such corporation shall restore the stream, water course, street, highway, plank road and turnpike thus intersected or touched, to its former state, or to such state as not unnecessarily to have impaired its usefulness, and keep such crossing in repair; *provided*, that in no case shall any railroad company construct a road bed without first constructing the necessary culverts or sluices as the natural lay of the land requires for the necessary drainage thereof. Nothing in this act contained shall be construed to authorize the erection of any bridge or any other obstruction across or over any stream navigated by steamboats or sail vessels at the place where any bridge or other obstruction may be proposed to be placed, so as to prevent th navigation of such stream; nor to authorize the construction of any railroad upon or across any street in any city or incorporated town or village, without the assent of the corporation of such city, town or village; *provided*, that in case of the constructing of said railway along highways, plank roads, turnpikes or canals, such railway shall either first obtain the consent of the lawful authorities having control or jurisdiction of the same, or condemn the same under the provisions of any eminent domain law now or hereafter in force in this State.   *Sixth*—To cross, intersect, join and unite its railways with any other railway before constructed at any point on its route, and upon the grounds of such other railway company, with the necessary turnouts, sidings and switches, and other conveniences in furtherance of the objects of its connections, and every corporation whose railway is or shall be hereafter intersected by any new railway, shall unite with the corporation owning such new railway in forming such intersections and connections, and grant the facilities aforesaid; and if the two corporations cannot agree upon the amount of compensation to be made therefor, or the points and manner of such crossings and connections, the same shall be ascertained and determined in manner prescribed by law.   *Seventh*—To receive and convey persons and property on its railway, by the power and force of steam or animals, or by any mechanical power.   *Eighth*—To erect and maintain all necessary and convenient buildings and stations, fixtures and machinery for the accommodation and use of passengers, freights and business interests, or which may be necessary for the construction or operation of said railway.   *Ninth*—To regulate the time and manner in which passengers and property shall be transported, and the compensation to be paid therefor, subject, nevertheless, to the provisions of any law that may now or hereafter be enacted.   *Tenth*—From time to time to borrow such sums of money as may be necessary for completing, finishing, improving or operating any such railway, and to issue and dispose of its bonds for any amount so borrowed, and to mortgage its corporate property and franchise to secure the payment of any debt contracted by such corporation for the purposes aforesaid; but the concurrence of the holders of two-thirds in amount of the stock of such corporation, to be expressed in the manner and under all the conditions provided in the eighteenth section of this act, shall be necessary to the validity of any such mortgage; and the order or resolution for such mortgage shall be recorded as provided in the second section of this act; and the Directors shall be empowered, in pursuance to any such order or resolution, to confer on any holder of any bond, for money so borrowed as aforesaid, the right to convert the principal due or owing thereon into the stock of such corporation at any time not exceeding ten years after the date of such bond, under such regulations as may be provided in the by-laws of such corporation.   And the provisions and privileges of the ten sub-divisions of this section shall extend to and apply as well to railway companies heretofore chartered by special acts of the Legislature as to those chartered under this act.

SEC. 24.   The rolling stock and all other movable property belonging to any such corporation shall be considered personal property, and shall be liable to execution and sale in the same manner as the personal property of individuals.

SEC. 25.   No such corporation shall issue any stock or bonds except for money, labor, or property actually received and applied to the purpose for which such corporation was organized.   All stock dividends and other fictitious increase of the capital stock or indebtedness of any such corporation shall be void.

SEC. 26. No such corporation shall consolidate its capital stock with any other railway owning a parallel or competing line, nor shall any corporation organized under this act consolidate by private or judicial sale or otherwise with any railroad company organized under the laws of any other State, or of the United States, and in no case shall any consolidation take place except upon sixty days' notice thereof given, which notice shall be given in manner and form as prescribed in the eighteenth section of this act.

SEC. 27. The President or Superintendent of any such corporation shall annually make a report, under oath, to the Comptroller of Public Accounts, or to the Governor, and to such other officers as may be designated by law, of all its actings and doings, which report shall include all matters relating to such corporation as may be now or hereafter prescribed by law.

SEC. 28. The Legislature shall have power to enact, from time to time, laws to prevent and correct abuses, and to prevent unjust discriminations and extortions in the rates of freight and passenger tariff, and to establish reasonable maximum rates of charges for the transportation of persons or property on any railway that may be constructed under the provisions of this act, and to enforce such laws by adequate penalties, to the extent, if necessary for that purpose, of forfeiture of the property and franchise of any such corporation.

SEC. 29. In all elections for Directors or Managers of such railway corporations, every stockholder shall have the right to vote in person or by proxy for the number of shares of stock owned by him for as many persons as there are Directors or Managers to be elected, or to cumulate said shares and give one candidate as many votes as the number of Directors multiplied by the number of his shares of stock shall equal, or to distribute them on the same principle among as many candidates as he may see fit; and such Directors or Managers shall not be elected in any other manner.

SEC. 30. In all cases when any corporation organized under this act, to induce aid in its construction, either by donation or subscription to its capital stock, shall desire to fix the rates for any period of time for the transportation of passengers or freights, such a corporation may adopt a resolution fixing such rates and the time for which the same is to be fixed, and have the same recorded in the office of the Recorder of Deeds, in the several counties through which said road is proposed to be run, and during the time for which they are fixed, said rates shall in no case be amended by said corporation or its successors; *provided*, that said rates shall not exceed the rates allowed by law.

SEC. 31. If any railway corporation organized under this act shall not within two years after its articles of association shall be filed and recorded as provided in the second section of this act, begin the construction of its road, and construct, equip and put in good running order at least ten miles of its proposed road, and if any such railroad corporation, after the first two years, shall fail to construct, equip and put in good running order at least twenty additional miles of its road each and every succeeding year, until the entire completion of its line, such corporation shall in either of such cases forfeit its corporate existence, and its powers shall cease as far as relates to that portion of said road then unfinished, and shall be incapable of resumption by any subsequent act of incorporation.

SEC. 32. Every corporation organized, or which may hereafter be organized by virtue of any law of this State, shall establish its domicil at some place within the State of Texas, and not elsewhere.

SEC. 33. There being no general law now in force in this State providing for the organization of railroad corporations, an imperative public necessity and emergency exists which requires the immediate passage and taking effect of this act, and it is therefore enacted that this act take effect and be in force from and after its passage.

Approved August 15, 1876.

Takes effect ninety days after adjournment.

CHAPTER XCVIII.—*An Act to carry into effect Sections twenty-two and twenty-three, Article sixteen, of the Constitution of the State of Texas, authorizing the passage of stock and fence laws.*

SECTION 1. *Be it enacted by the Legislature of the State of Texas,* That upon the petition of fifty freeholders of any county in the State, or upon the petition of twenty freeholders of any specified portion or sub-division of the same, which sub-division shall be described in said petition, setting forth clearly what character and description of stock other than horses, mules, jacks, jennets and all classes of horned cattle, which said freeholders desire may run at large in said county or sub-division, as the case may be, to the County Court of said county, asking for the enactment of a stock law, in accordance with the provisions of this act, the County Courts so petitioned shall order an election in the county or sub-division of the same, as the case may be, in accordance with the petition, at its first regular term thereafter, by giving thirty days' notice by advertisement, describing the kind of stock, as described in said petition, in the weekly newspaper of said county which has the largest circulation in the county, and if there be no newspaper in said county, notice shall be given in the following manner, to-wit: By posting a copy of such notice and description on the court-house door, and in each Justice's precinct, when in a county election, and when in an election of a sub-division of the county, in three public places in such sub-division.

SEC. 2. The freeholders being qualified voters of any county in the State, or sub-division of said county, may determine by a majority vote, at an election ordered for that purpose, whether the stock described in said petition shall run at large in such county or sub-division.

SEC. 3. The County Judge shall order an election to take place in the several voting precincts of his county, when the petition is for a whole county, and at such place or places within the sub-dvision to be affected by said election, as he may designate, if the petition is for a sub-division thereof, and he shall order said election to take place at a time named in said order, not less than thirty days after the date thereof, which election shall be carried on as in cases of the election of county officers, and the voters desiring to put this act in operation in their county or sub-division thereof, shall place upon their ballots the words, "For the stock law," and those opposed shall place upon their ballots the words, "Against the stock law."

SEC. 4. At the time of the issuance of the order of election, the

County Judge shall, if the election be for a sub-division of the county, designate proper persons, the same to be freeholders, to hold said elections, who shall have the power to appoint their own clerks, and it shall be the duty of the person or persons holding said election, on the tenth day after said election, to make due return of all the votes cast at their respective voting places or precincts in said county or sub-division thereof, for and against said proposition, to the County Judge of said county, who shall, in the presence of the County Clerk and at least one Justice of the Peace or two respectable freeholders of the county, count said returns and ascertain the result of said election; and if a majority of the votes cast at said election shall be in favor of the proposition, it shall be the duty of said County Judge to issue his proclamation declaring the result of said election, which proclamation shall be posted at the court-house door of said county, and said election and proclamation shall have the force and effect to put this act in full operation in said county or sub-division thereof, within thirty days after the issuance of said proclamation.

SEC. 5. That if at any such election the proposition be defeated, the vote shall not again be taken in said county or sub-division thereof for the period of twelve months; but at any time after the expiration of said period, the proposition may be again presented and voted upon; *provided*, that a failure to carry into effect the provisions of this act in said county shall not prevent such election being immediately held thereafter in a sub-division of the same; nor the failure to carry into effect the provisions of this act in a sub-division of the county shall not prevent such election being held immediately thereafter in the county in which said sub-division is situated.

SEC. 6. Should any stock not permitted to run at large enter within the enclosure of any owner or lessee of land entitled to the benefit of this act, without his or their consent, it shall be lawful for the owner or lessee of said enclosure to impound said stock, and it shall be the duty of the owner or lessee of said land to give notice immediately to the owner of said stock of their impounding and detention, and the owner of said stock shall be entitled to the possession of his or her stock on the payment of the expenses incurred in impounding and keeping said stock; *provided*, that in such county or sub-division said owners or lessees shall not be required to fence against stock not permitted to run at large; and any fence in said county or sub-division which is sufficient to keep out ordinary stock permitted to run at large under this act shall be deemed a lawful fence.

SEC. 7. It shall be lawful for the owner or lessee of such' enclosures as are contemplated in this act, to charge the following rates for impounding such stock as are contemplated in this act, to-wit: ten cents per day per head for hogs; ten cents per day per head for goats; and five cents per head per day for sheep; *provided*, that nothing in this act shall be so construed as to authorize the detention or impounding of any animals not absolutely within the enclosure; *and, provided further*, that if no owner can be found for any stock as contemplated in this act, it shall be the duty of him or them so impounding stock, as contemplated in this act, to proceed as with stray stock provided for in the estray law of the State of Texas; *and further provided*, that if the owner or agent of stock thus impounded, after being notified, shall fail or refuse to pay the fees for the same, the taker up may proceed to sell them, after having given notice as in Constables' sales, to the highest bidde for cash; and after paying said fees and expenses of sale, shall pay the balance to the owner or agent of said stock.

SEC. 8.   When such stock as are contemplated in this act shall have made their way into any such inclosures as are contemplated by the provisions of this act, and shall have committed any damage within such inclosures, after a proper assessment of such damage by two disinterested freeholders of the county, the owner or lessee of such premises may bring suit for damages, as otherwise provided by law, against the owner or owners of such stock, in any court of competent jurisdiction.

SEC. 9.   If any person whose fence is insufficient, under this act, shall, with guns, dogs or otherwise, maim, wound or kill any cattle, or any horse, mule, jack or jennet, or procure the same to be done, such person or persons so offending shall give full satisfaction to the party injured for all damages by such person or persons sustained, to be recovered as in other suits for damages; *provided*, this section shall not be so construed as to authorize any person in any event to maim, kill or wound, any horse, mule, jack, jennet or cattle belonging to another.

SEC. 10.   That all acts and parts of acts in conflict with this act, be, and the same are hereby repealed.

Approved August 15, 1876.

Takes effect ninety days after adjournment.

CHAPTER XCIX.—*An Act supplementary to " An Act to create and organize the county of Somerville," approved March* 13, 1875.

SECTION 1.   *Be it enacted by the Legislature of the State of Texas,* That whereas, there was an error in the spelling of the name of Somerville, said name having really been intended to be Somervell; therefore, this act hereby corrects such spelling, and hereafter said county now known as Somerville shall be known as Somervell county.

Approved August 15, 1876.

Takes effect ninety days after adjournment.

CHAPTER C.—*An Act making an appropriation to defray the contingent expenses of the first session of the Fifteenth Legislature.*

SECTION 1.   *Be it enacted by the Legislature of the State of Texas,* That the sum of fifteen thousand dollars, or so much thereof as may be necessary, be and the same is hereby appropriated out of any money in the State Treasury not otherwise appropriated, to pay the contingent expenses of the first session of the Fifteenth Legislature, and that the approval of the Chairman of the Committee on Printing and Contingent Expenses, countersigned by the President of the Senate and the Speaker of the House of Representatives, to the respective accounts against the two Houses, shall be sufficient authority for the Comptroller to draw his warrant upon the Treasurer for the several amounts charged against said fund.

SEC. 2.   Whereas, the appropriation to pay contingent expenses of the Fifteenth Legislature is now exhausted, there is an imperative public necessity that an appropriation should be made without delay; therefore, this act shall take effect and be in force from and after its passage.

Approved August 15, 1876.

Takes effect from its passage.

CHAPTER CI.—*An Act to encourage the construction of railroads in Texas by donations of lands.*

SECTION 1. *Be it enacted by the Legislature of the State of Texas,* That any railroad company heretofore chartered, or which may be hereafter organized under the general laws of this State, shall, upon the completion of a section of ten miles or more of its road, be entitled to receive, and there is hereby granted to every such railroad, from the State, sixteen sections of land for every mile of its road so completed and put in good running order ; *provided,* that no company whose road is of less than three feet gauge shall be entitled to receive any grant of lands under this section ; *provided, however,* that companies constructing railroads on the prismoidal plan shall be entitled to eight sections of land to the mile on the same terms as other roads ; *provided further,* that this act shall not be construed to renew or continue any right to companies who have failed or may fail to comply with the terms of their charters, with reference to the completion of portions of their roads in stated times ; *provided further,* that the provisions of this act shall not be so construed as to grant the aid herein provided for to any railroad that has already received or is otherwise entitled to receive aid from the State to the amount of sixteen sections of land to the mile.

SEC. 2. Any railroad company having completed and put in good running order a section of ten miles or more of its road, may give notice of the same to the Governor, whose duty it shall be to appoint some skillful engineer, if there be no State Engineer, to examine said section of road, and if, upon the report of said engineer under oath, it shall appear that said road is substantially built, and fully equipped for the transportation of both passengers and freight, and that the same is operated by steam, and is constructed of iron rails of not less than thirty pounds to the lineal yard ; *provided,* that rails for prismoidal roads shall not weigh less than twenty-two pounds to the lineal yard, and has been constructed in accordance with the provisions of its charter, or of the general laws under which it may be constructed, and of the general laws in force regulating railroads ; thereupon it shall be the duty of the Commissioner of the General Land Office to issue to said company certificates of six hundred and forty acres of land each, equal to sixteen sections to the mile of road so completed ; whereupon said company may apply to the District Surveyor of any land district in this State to survey such lands out of any of the unappropriated public land in his district ; said surveys shall be made in alternate sections, or half sections, as nearly square as practicable, one section for the company, and one for the State, for the benefit of the public school fund ; a map of all such surveys shall be returned with the field notes to the General Land Office, when the Commissioner of the General Land Office shall number contiguous surveys with even and odd numbers, and shall issue to the company patents for the odd sections of said surveys.

SEC. 3. All lands acquired by railroad companies under this act shall be alienated by said companies, one-half in six years and one-half in twelve years from the issuance of patents to the same, and all lands so acquired by railroad companies, and not alienated as herein required, shall be forfeited to the State and become a part of the public domain, liable to location and survey as other unappropriated lands ; *provided further,* that the State shall retain the right to regulate the rates of freight and passengers' fare by general law on all roads accepting a grant of land under this act.

SEC. 4.   That there being no law authorizing State aid in construction of railroads now in force, an imperative public necessity and an emergency exist for the immediate passage of this act, and it is hereby declared that this act take effect and be in force from and after its passage.

Approved August 16, 1876.

Takes effect ninety days after adjournment.

CHAPTER CII.—*An Act fixing the times of holding the District Courts of the Seventh Judicial District of the State of Texas.*

SECTION 1.   *Be it enacted by the Legislature of the State of Texas,* That the Spring terms of the District Courts of the Seventh Judicial District of the State of Texas shall be holden at the times hereinafter specified, to-wit: In the county of Smith on the second Monday in March, and may continue in session six weeks; in the county of Henderson on the sixth Monday after the second Monday in March, and may continue in session two weeks; in the county of Van Zandt on the eighth Monday after the second Monday in March, and may continue in session three weeks; in the county of Wood on the twelfth Monday after the second Monday in March, and may continue in session three weeks; in the county of Upshur on the sixteenth Monday after the second Monday in March, and may continue in session three weeks; in the county of Gregg on the nineteenth Monday after the second Monday in March, and may continue in session two weeks.   That the Fall terms of said courts shall be holden at the times hereinafter specified, to-wit: In the county of Smith on the second Monday in September, and may continue in session six weeks; in the county of Henderson on the sixth Monday after the second Monday in September, and may continue in session two weeks; in the county of Van Zandt on the eighth Monday after the second Monday in September, and may continue in session three weeks; in the county of Wood on the twelfth Monday after the second Monday in September, and may continue in session three weeks; in the county of Upshur on the second Monday in January, and may continue in session three weeks; in the county of Gregg on the third Monday after the second Monday in January, and may continue in session two weeks.

SEC. 2.   That an imperative public necessity and emergency exists to conform the times for holding the courts in said District to the laws of an act detaching Rains county therefrom; therefore, this act shall take effect and be in force from and after its passage.

Approved August 16, 1876.

Takes effect from its passage.

CHAPTER CIII.—*An Act to provide for the election of Justices of the Peace, and to define their powers and jurisdiction.*

SECTION 1.   *Be it enacted by the Legislature of the State of Texas,* That there shall be elected by the qualified electors of each Justice's precinct in the several counties of this State, at each biennial election, one Justice of the Peace, who shall hold his office for two years, and until his successor shall be elected and qualified; *provided,* that in any precinct in which there may be a city of eight thousand or more inhabitants, there shall be elected two Justices of the Peace.

SEC. 2. All vacancies in the office of Justices of the Peace shall be filled by the Commissioners' Court until the next general election for such offices.

SEC. 3. Justices of thr Peace shall have and exercise original concurrent jurisdiction with other courts in all cases arising under the criminal laws of this State, except misdemeanors involving official misconduct, in which the punishment shall be by fine and the maximum does not exceed two hundred dollars; and in civil matters of all cases where the amount in controversy is two hundred dollars or less, exclusive of interest, of which exclusive original jurisdiction is not given to the District or County Courts. They shall also have power to foreclose mortgages and enforce other liens on personal property where the amount in controversy shall not exceed two hundred dollars, exclusive of interest. They shall also have the power to take forfeitures of all bail bonds given for the appearance of any parties at their courts, regardless of the amount, where the conditions of said bonds have not been complied with. They shall also have the power to impose fines upon defaulting witnesses and jurors, not to exceed twenty-five dollars; *provided*, that no final judgment shall be entered against the parties to any bail bond, or against defaulting witnesses or jurors until such parties have been served with writ of *scire facias* requiring them to appear and show cause (at the next term after such forfeiture shall have been taken, or such fines imposed), why such judgment *nisi* should not be made final against them. They shall also have and exercise jurisdiction over all other matters not herein enumerated, that may be cognizable before a Justice of the Peace under the laws of this State.

SEC. 4. If any person shall make an entry into any lands, tenements or other real property, except in cases where entry is given by law, or shall make any such entry by force, or if any person shall wilfully and without force, hold over any lands, tenements or other real property, after the termination of the time for which such lands, tenements or other real property were let to him, or to the person under whom he claims, after demand made in writing for possession thereof, by the person or persons entitled to such possession, such person shall (be) adjudged guilty of forcible entry and detainer, or of forcible detainer (as the case may be), within the intent and meaning of this act. Any Justice of the Peace of any county in this State, shall have jurisdiction of any case arising under this section, and on complaint upon oath, of the party aggrieved, or his authorized agent, shall immediately issue his summons to the Sheriff or any legally authorized officer of his county, commanding him to summon the person against whom such complaint is made, to appear before such Justice, at a time and place named in such summons, not more than ten nor less than six days from the time of issuing such summons, which said summons shall be served at least five days before the return day thereof, by reading the same to the defendant, or by leaving a copy of the same with some person over the age of sixteen at his usual place of abode; and the said Justice shall also at the same time issue a precept to the Sheriff or other officer as aforesaid, commanding him to summon a jury of six men, freeholders and otherwise qualified jurors of the county to appear before him on the day set for trying said complaint, to hear and try the same, and if any of the jurors so summoned shall fail or refuse to attend or be challenged, then the said Justices may order the Sheriff or other legal officer to complete the number by summoning and returning others immediately. The Sheriff or other officer shall return to the said Justice the summons and precepts as aforesaid, on the day assigned for trial, and shall state on the back of said summons how the same was served, and on the back of said precept the names of the jurors if a jury has been demanded, and if the defendant does not appear and answer, the Justice shall proceed to try the said cause *ex parte*, or may in his discretion postpone the trial to a time not exceeding six days, and the said Justice shall issue subpœnas for witnesses, and shall proceed to try said cause as in other cases of trial before Justices of the Peace. The complaint shall describe the lands, tenements or other possessions in question so as to identify the same, and the Justice of the Peace shall keep a record of the proceedings had before him, and if the defendant shall be found guilty he shall give judgment thereon for the plaintiff to have restitution of the premises and damages at the rate of five dollars per day for every day after the notice in writing has been served on the defendant, and his costs; *provided*, this shall not deprive the plaintiff of a suit to recover rents and other damages, and shall award his writ of restitution; and if a verdict is given in favor of the defendant, judgment shall be given against the plaintiff for costs, and executions may issue therefor; and no writ of restitution shall issue until the expiration of two days from rendition of judgment.

SEC. 5. Every Justice of the Peace shall keep a docket in which he shall enter all examinations and trials for criminal offenses before him; the nature of the offense; the time when the examination was had; stating whether such trial was by jury or by himself; the verdict of the jury, if any; the judgment rendered by the Justice, and the time when it was rendered, and how the same was executed. He shall also keep a docket in which he shall enter: *First*—The titles of all suits commenced before him. *Second*—The time when the first process was issued against the defendant, when it was returnable, and the particular nature thereof. *Third*—The time when the parties, or either of them, appeared before him, either without citation or upon return thereof. *Fourth*—A brief statement of the nature of the plaintiff's demand or claim, and the amount claimed, and a brief statement of the nature of the defense made by the defendants (if any). *Fifth*—Every adjournment, stating at whose request and at what time. *Sixth*—The time when the trial was had, stating whether the same was by a jury or by the Justice. *Seventh* —The verdict of the jury (if any). *Eighth*—The judgment rendered by the Justice, and the time of rendering the same. *Ninth*—All applications for setting aside judgment or granting new trials, and the order of the Justice thereon, with the date thereof. *Tenth*—The time of issuing execution, the name of the officer or person to whom it was directed and delivered, and the amount of debt, damages and costs; and when any execution is returned he shall note such return on said docket, with the manner in which it was executed. *Eleventh*—All stays and appeals that may be taken, and the time when taken.

SEC. 6. If from any cause whatever, a Justice of the Peace shall vacate his office, all books and papers appertaining thereto shall be delivered to the person appointed and qualified to fill such vacancy, whenever demanded by him, who shall, upon receiving such books and papers, proceed with all judgments, executions and unfinished business connected with said office, in like manner as if the same had been commenced by himself. Any person or persons having the possession of any books or papers belonging or appertaining to the office of a Justice that has become vacant, who shall wilfully neglect or refuse to deliver them to the person appointed and qualified to fill such vacancy, when demanded by him, may, upon the motion of any person interested in such books or papers, be attached and imprisoned by order of the County Judge or any Judge of the District Court of the State, until he shall so deliver such books and papers; *provided*, that such motions shall be supported by affidavit, and three days previous notice thereof shall be given to the person or persons against whom such motion is made.

SEC. 7. Every Justice of the Peace qualified under the provisions of this act, shall demand of his predecessor all books and papers that may be in his possession belonging or appertaining to his office, and upon receipt of such books and papers said Justice shall proceed with all executions, judgments and unfinished business therein contained, in like manner as if the same had been commenced before himself; and any person or persons having possession of any such books or papers, who shall neglect or refuse to deliver them when so demanded, may be proceeded against in like manner as provided for in Section six of this act.

SEC. 8. Every suit in the court of a Justice of the Peace shall be commenced in the precinct in which the defendant, or one or more of several defendants, resides, except that suits for the possession of real property must be commenced in the precinct where the property, or a part thereof, is situated; suits for the recovery of rents must be commenced in the precinct where the rented premises, or a part thereof, are situated, or where the defendant resides, or where the cause of action, or a part thereof, accrued; or if the suit is for a tort, in the precinct in which the defendant resides, or in which the injury was inflicted. A defendant may be sued before a Justice of the Peace in the county or precinct in which the contract, by its terms, is to be performed, or in which the defendant resides. A suit against an executor, administrator or guardian to establish a demand for money against the estate which he represents may be commenced before the Justice of the Peace at the county seat of the county where the estate is administered, or in the precinct where the executor (or) administrator resides; *provided*, that all such suits shall be brought in the county where the administration or guardianship is pending. A suit against a private corporation created by or under the laws of this State may be commenced in any precinct where it has a place of business, or in which its chief officer resides, or in which the liability was incurred or the cause of action arose. A suit against a private corporation created by or under the laws of any other State or county must be commenced in a precinct in which there is property of such corporation, or in which there is an agency thereof, or in which the cause of action, or a part thereof, arose. A suit against the owners of a steamboat or other vessel may be commenced in any precinct where the boat or vessel may be found, or where the cause of action arose or the liability was contracted or accrued. If there be no Justice of the Peace qualified to try the suit in the precinct where the defendant resides, or in which he might be sued under the provisions of this act, the suit may be commenced before a Justice of the Peace of any other precinct in the county. A suit against a railroad or canal company, or an owner of a line of mail stages or coaches, for any injury to person or property upon the road, canal or line of stages or coaches of the defendant, or upon a liability as a carrier, may be brought in any precinct through which the road, canal or line of stages or coaches may pass, or in any precinct where the route of such railroad, canal, stages or coaches may begin or terminate. A person who has no fixed residence may be sued in any precinct in the county where he may be found. The residence of a single person is where he or she boards; *provided*, that residents of incorporated cities and towns may be sued before any Justice of the Peace within the limits of the corporation.

SEC. 9. Any party or parties to a suit before a Justice of the Peace shall be entitled to a change of venue to a Justice of the Peace at the county seat, unless he is similarly disqualified, in which event it shall be to the nearest Justice of the Peace in the county not subject to the same objection, or otherwise disqualified, on his or her or their affidavit, supported by two other credible persons, to the effect that they do not believe that the persons applying for such change of venue can have a fair and impartial trial before the Justice or in the Justice's precinct where the suit is pending.

SEC. 10. All process from a Justice of the Peace, except in criminal cases, shall be under the hand of such Justice, directed to some lawful officer, whose duty it shall be to execute and return the same. All such process shall be returnable, except in cases where it is otherwise provided for by law, to some regular term of such Justice's Court, and shall be served by leaving a copy thereof with the defendant at least five days before the return day, exclusive of the day of service, and when suit is brought against a private corporation, county, city or town, the copy of the citation shall be delivered to the chief officer or Director or managing agent of such private corporation, the Clerk of the County Court of such county, or Mayor of such city or town. The voluntary appearance of a defendant is equivalent to personal service of the citation and a waiver of all defects therein. Whenever in any civil suit before a Justice of the Peace, the plaintiff, his agent or attorney, shall make oath in writing before such Justice of the Peace, that the defendant is absent from this State, or that he is a transient person, so that the ordinary process of law cannot be served upon him, such Justice shall issue a citation, directed to some lawful officer, commanding him to cite the defendant to appear at a regular term of his Court, named in citation, to answer the plaintiff's complaint, stating the nature and amount thereof; such citation shall be returnable to the regular term of such Justice's Court therein named and shall be published in some newspaper printed in the county, if there be one, for at least three successive weeks before the return day; if there be no newspaper printed in the county, then it shall be published in like manner, in some newspaper printed in the nearest county where a newspaper is published. In cases of emergency any Justice of the Peace may depute any person of good character to execute any process, civil or criminal; *provided*, that in every such case, the Justice shall certify on the back of such process, that the person is so deputed by him, and the person so deputed shall take and subscribe an oath that he will execute such process according to law, which oath, with the certificate of the Justice that it was administered, shall be endorsed on or annexed to such process. In all suits brought in a Justice's Court against two or more defendants jointly liable, and where one or more of the defendants reside out of the county where suit is instituted, the Justice of the Peace before whom suit is brought shall issue process to the Sheriff or any Constable of the county or counties where such defendant or defendants are alleged to reside; and the officer to whom such process is directed shall serve the same as in other cases, and make his return to the court from which the process issued. Where there are two or more defendants in a suit, and one or more are served with process in due time, and others not so served, the plaintiff may either discontinue as to those not so served, and proceed against those that are, or he may continue the suit until the next term of the court, and take new process against those not served; and no defendant, against whom any suit may be discontinued, according to the provisions of this section, shall be thereby exonorated from any liability under which he was, but may, at any time, be proceeded against as if no such suit had been brought, and no such discontinuance entered as to such defendants; *provided*, that this section shall not be so construed as to allow a plaintiff to discontinue as to the principal and take judgment against the endorser or surety, who is jointly sued.

SEC. 11. Any Justice of the Peace before whom any suit or proceeding is pending may, for good cause shown by either party and supported by affidavit, continue the same to the next term of his court, and if such cause or proceeding is such as can be tried by such Justice at any other time than at a regular term, he shall have the like power to continue the same for a reasonable time. When both parties in any suit before a Justice of the Peace appear in person, or by agent or attorney, at the time appointed for the trial thereof, or at the time to which it may have been continued, if the amount in controversy shall not exceed ten dollars, or if the amount in controversy shall exceed ten dollars, and neither party shall make application to have the cause tried by a jury, the Justice shall proceed to hear the allegations and proofs of the parties, and the defendant, upon giving notice thereof to the plaintiff before the trial commences, shall be allowed to present and prove any claim or demand not exceeding two hundred dollars, exclusive of interest, against the plaintiff that is similar in its character to the claim or demand of the plaintiff, and the suit shall be determined by the Justice, as from the testimony shall seem to be right. If it shall appear from the testimony that the plaintiff is entitled to recover, judgment shall be entered in his favor for such amount as shall appear to be due him with costs; but if it shall appear from the testimony that the defendant is entitled to recover, then judgment shall be entered in his favor for such amount as shall appear to be due him (if any), with costs. If the amount in controversy shall exceed ten dollars, and either party shall make application to have the case tried by jury, then the same shall be so tried in like manner as hereinbefore provided, and upon the return of the verdict of the jury, the Justice shall enter judgment thereon with costs; *provided, however*, that whenever it shall appear on any such trial that the defendant's claim or demand was acquired after the commencement of the plaintiff's suit, the defendant shall be liable for all the costs.

SEC. 12. The pleading in a Justice's Court shall be oral, except where either party desires to plead any of the following matters, which must be contained in a written statement under oath, before the plaintiff announced ready for trial. *First*—That the suit is not commenced in the proper precinct. *Second*—That the plaintiff hath not legal capacity to sue. *Third*—That the party is not entitled to recover in the capacity in which he sues. *Fourth*—That there is another suit pending in this State between the same parties for the same cause of action, or counter claim. *Fifth*—That there is a defect of parties, plaintiff or defendant. *Sixth*—That a written instrument, purporting to be signed by him or by his authority, was not executed by him or by his authority. *Seventh*—That an endorsement or assignment of a written instrument was not made by the party by whom it purports to have been made, nor by his authority. *Eighth*—A denial of partnership, whether the same be on the part of the plaintiff or defendant. In all proceedings before a Justice of the Peace, in which either party may be entitled to a jury, and shall make application for one, such jury shall be composed of six men, and the Justice shall forthwith issue a writ, directed to some lawful officer of the county, commanding him to summon forthwith six legally qualified jurors to serve as a jury, and if any person so summoned shall fail or refuse to attend, he may be fined by the Justice three dollars, for the use of the county, for such failure or neglect, after being cited to do so, and not being able to show good cause for such failure or neglect. In all trials, whether civil or criminal, each party shall be entitled to three peremptory challenges, and also any number of challenges for cause, which cause shall be judged of by the Justice. If from challenges or any other cause, a sufficient number of persons are not in attendance, the Justice shall order some lawful officer to summon a sufficient number of qualified jurors to make up the jury.

SEC. 13.   When a jury is empanneled, the Justice shall administer to them an oath or affirmation in form as follows: " You and each of you do solemnly swear (or affirm as the case may be) that you will well and truly try the cause about to be submitted to you, and a true verdict render therein, according to the law and the evidence, so help you God." Whenever a jury has been summoned in a Justice's court, the same jury may be called on to try all causes before such Justice in which a jury is required on the same day, without the necessity of a new writ in each case; *provided, however*, that jurors shall be sworn for each cause. In all cases before Justices of the Peace, other than prosecutions for offenses against the laws of this State, the party applying for a jury shall, before the trial commences, pay a jury fee of three dollars, which shall be equally divided between the jury trying the cause, and if the party paying such fee shall recover judgment, the jury fee shall be taxed in the bill of costs, and when collected, shall be refunded to him; and in all cases, civil and criminal, before a Justice of the Peace, which shall be tried by jury, when the jury fee is not required to be paid before the trial commences, a like jury fee shall be taxed in the bill of costs, and when collected, shall be equally divided between the jurors who tried the same.

SEC. 14.   In all suits before a Justice of the Peace, it shall be his duty, on the application of either party, to issue subpœnas for witnesses residing in the county, and all such subpœnas shall be executed by the officer to whom they may be directed, by reading the same to the witness, and shall be returned on or before the time when the witness is required to attend, showing how the same has been executed. Justices of the 'Peace shall have power to enforce the attendance of witnesses, and compel them to give evidence in their courts, by attachment and imprisonment; *provided*, that in civil cases no witness shall be attached, fined or imprisoned unless he shall have refused to obey a subpœna after having been tendered his fees for one day's attendance before the day of the trial of any civil suit before a Justice of the Peace. Upon all trials before a Justice of the Peace, if any exceptions are taken to any deposition or evidence, the same shall be decided by the Justice. All witnesses who are subpœnaed to attend a Justice's court shall be entitled to receive one dollar per day for each day's attendance, which, if claimed by the witness at the time of trial, shall be taxed in the bill of costs against the party cast in the suit.

SEC. 15.   Whenever in any civil suit, before any Justice of the Peace, the evidence of a female is required, or the evidence of any witness residing in the county, who is unable by reason of age, infirmities or sickness to attend the court, or the evidence of a witness residing out of the county, the party interested may take the deposition of any such witness, by filing with the Justice before whom such suit is pending, interrogatories to such witness, and serving a copy of the same on the opposite party, his agent or attorney, with a notice that he intends to apply for a commission to take the answers of the witness to such interrogatories. Such notice and copy may be served by any lawful officer of the county, or by any other person, but when served by any other person than an officer, an affidavit shall be endorsed on or annexed to such notice by the person serving the same, stating the fact of the service of such notice, and a copy of interrogatories, which affidavit, unless disapproved, shall be evidence of such service; and the opposite party may file cross-interrogatories with the Justice at any time before the commission issued.

SEC. 16.   At the expiration of five days from the service of any such notice and interrogatories, on the application of the party who filed the same, his agent or attorney, it shall be the duty of the Justice to issue a commission, with a copy of the interrogatories and cross-interrogatories, if any have been filed, directed to some Notary Public, Clerk of the District or County Court of the county where such witness resides, requiring such Notary Public or Clerk to take the answers of such witness to the interrogatories and cross-interrogatories that accompany such commission, to cause the witness to be sworn to his answers, and to subscribe them; and every Notary Public or Clerk of the District Court to whom any such commission may be directed, shall execute the same according to the directions therein contained, and for that purpose he shall have like powers as Notaries Public and Clerks of the District Court have to execute commissions to take depositions, when issued from the District Court. He shall certify under his hand and official seal, the manner in which he has executed such commission, and seal up such certificate and answer with the commission and interrogatories, write his name across the seal of the envelope, direct the same to the Justice from whom the commission issued, and forward it either by mail or private conveyance. If sent by mail, he shall cause the Postmaster or his deputy, mailing the same, to endorse thereon that he received it from the hands of the officer who took such answers; if sent by private hands, the person delivering the same to the Justice shall make affidavit in writing before such Justice that he received the package from the hands of the officer who took such answers, and that it has undergone no change since. All evidence so taken and returned to any Justice's Court may be read in evidence on the trial of the suit on which it was taken, and shall have the same force and effect as if the witness were examined in open court; *provided*, the answers are responsive to the interrogatories; *and provided, also*, that the interrogatories and answers shall be subject to all legal exceptions; but when such depositions are filed with the Justice before the trial commences, no exceptions shall be heard as to the manner of taking and returning such depositions, unless they are taken before the

11 GL

trial commences.   All the rules of evidence prescribed for the government of District Courts, where the same do not conflict with the provisions of this act, shall govern the proceedings in Justice's Courts, so far as the same are applicable.

SEC. 17.   Any Justice may, for a good cause shown, supported by an affidavit in writing, grant a new trial in any civil suit tried before him, whenever he shall consider that justice has not been done in the trial of such case ; *provided, however*, that all applications for a new trial shall be made within ten days after the rendition of judgment; and one day's notice of the application shall be given to the opposite party, his agent or attorney ; *provided, also*, that not more than one new trial shall be granted to either party.   And in all cases where a new trial shall be granted, the cause shall be continued to the next term of the court. All judgments and final orders given by any Justice of the Peace, in any suit or prosecution, civil or criminal, shall be given in open court. Any person may appear before any Justice of the Peace and confess a judgment for any amount within the jurisdiction of a Justice of the Peace without the issuance of any citation; and all such confessions of judgment shall be recorded in like manner as other judgments.

SEC. 18.   When a defendant who has been served with a citation from a Justice of the Peace, according to law, shall neglect to appear at or before ten o'clock A. M. of the return day of the citation, at or before the same hour of any day to which the cause may have been continued, the Justice shall proceed in the following manner: *First*—If the plaintiff's cause of action is liquidated, and proved by any instrument in writing, purporting to have been executed by the defendant, the Justice shall, whether the plaintiff appear or not, after allowing the proper credits for all payments endorsed on such instrument in writing, render judgment by default against the defendant for the amount which shall appear by such instrument in writing to be due to the plaintiff, together with the costs of suit.   *Second*—If the plaintiff's cause of action is not liquidated, and the plaintiff appear in person, or by agent or attorney, the Justice shall proceed to hear his allegations and proofs, and shall determine the cause as shall appear from the testimony to be right; and if it shall appear, from such testimony, that the plaintiff is entitled to recover, judgment shall be rendered by default against the defendant, for such amount as the testimony shows the plaintiff to be entitled to, with costs ; but if it do not appear that the plaintiff ought to recover, judgment shall be given for the defendant, against the plaintiff, for costs. *Third*—If the plaintiff fail to appear at or before 10 o'clock A. M. of the return day of the citation, or at or before the same hour of any day to which the cause may have been continued, except in the case hereinbefore provided, the Justice may, upon motion of the defendant, his agent or attorney, render judgment of non-suit against the plaintiff, with costs.

SEC. 19.   Every Justice of the Peace shall have power, upon good cause being shown, supported by affidavit, to set aside a judgment by default or by non-suit, at any time within ten days after the same was rendered; *provided*, that one day's notice of such application shall be given to the opposite party, his agent or attorney, by the party applying, and in such case the suit shall be continued to the next term of such Justice's Court; *and provided further*, that all motions, where notice is required to the opposite party, shall be filed with the Justice of the Peace in writing. In all cases where a suit shall be brought before a Justice of the Peace for the recovery of specific articles, on the trial thereof, the jury or Justice, as the case may be, shall, if they find for the plaintiff, assess the value of such articles separately ; and if the plaintiff recover, judgment shall be rendered for the specific article or articles, if to be had, but if not, then for their value, and the Justice shall issue thereon his writ, directed to some lawful officer, commanding him to put the plaintiff in the possession of the article or articles so recovered, if to be found, but if not, then to proceed to make the value of such article or articles with the legal interest from date of judgment, and costs as under execution, and every Justice shall from time to time, when required by a party having a judgment in his court, issue such executions or other writs as may be necessary to enforce such judgment, until the same shall have been satisfied. No Justice shall render a judgment upon any attachment or sequestration unless the defendant shall have been cited either personally or by publication.

SEC. 20. All judgments hereafter rendered by any Justice of the Peace shall operate as a lien upon all the real estate of the defendant situated in the county where such judgment shall have been rendered, whenever a certified copy of such judgment shall be filed for registration in the office of the Clerk of the County Court of such county ; and it shall be the duty of such Clerk to record certified copies of such judgments as may be filed with him for registration at the earliest practicable period, in the book used in said office for the record of mortgages, and to cause a regular and alphabetical index to be made of the names of the plaintiffs and defendants in said judgments, and also a reference to the page on which such judgment is recorded.

SEC. 21. That any party, his agent or attorney, may appeal from any final judgment in any civil cause rendered by a Justice of the Peace to the County Court of the county in which such final judgment shall have been rendered, upon notice thereof being given in open court ; *provided*, that the amount of the judgment appealed from or the amount in controversy shall exceed twenty dollars, exclusive of costs ; *provided further*, that the party appealing shall, within ten days after the rendition of said judgment, file with such Justice a bond, with one or more good and sufficient sureties, in a sum at least double the amount of such judgment (if any) and interest and costs, payable to the appellee, conditioned that the party appealing shall prosecute his appeal to effect, or shall pay and satisfy the judgment or decree that may be rendered against the obligors in such bond ; and in all cases where an appeal shall be taken from a Justice's Court to the County Court, it shall be the duty of the Justice from whom such appeal shall be taken immediately to make out a transcript of all the entries made on his docket in such case and file the same, together with all the original papers of the cause, with the Clerk of the County Court on or before the first day of the term of such court next after such appeal was taken ; but if there is not time for such transcript and papers to be filed at such first term, then they shall be so filed at the next succeeding term of said court ; *provided, however*, there shall be no appeal from the Justices' Courts in actions of forcible entry and detainer and forcible detainer ; but either party in such cases being dissatisfied with the judgment of the court, may take the same to the County Court for trial *de novo* by writ of *certiorari*, by making affidavit in writing, setting forth sufficient cause to entitle him to said writ, and entering into bond with sufficient sureties within ten days after the rendition of such judgment, to be approved by the Clerk of said court, payable to the adverse party, conditioned that said party procuring said writ will prosecute the same with effect, and in case of failure, to pay all costs and damages occasioned by the proceedings under such writ of *certiorari*.

SEC. 22.   A Justice of the Peace may grant a stay of execution on any judgment for money rendered by himself on a civil suit for three months ; *provided*, the person against whom such judgment was rendered, shall with one or more good and sufficient sureties, to be approved by such Justice, appear before him and acknowledge themselves and each of them bound to the successful party in such sum as shall secure the amount of the judgment, interests and costs, which acknowledgment shall be entered by the Justice on his docket, and shall have the force and effect of a judgment against the person making the acknowledgment; upon which execution shall issue for the amount of the original judgment, interest and costs, in case the same shall not be paid on or before the expiration of such stay ; *provided, however*, that no such stay shall be granted unless the same is applied for within ten days after the entry of the original judgment.   All executions issued by a Justice of the Peace shall be directed to some lawful officer of the State, and shall be returnable to his court in sixty days.   It shall be the duty of the officer to whom any such execution is directed, to execute and return the same, on or before the return day thereof; and all the provisions of the laws regulating executions from the District Courts, where the same are not inconsistent with the provisions of this act, shall apply to and govern executions from Justices of the Peace, so far as the same are practicable.

SEC. 23.   No Justice of the Peace shall issue an execution in any case where the judgment may be for money, except in prosecutions for criminal offenses and for costs, before the eleventh day after the day on which judgment was rendered, unless the party in whose favor judgment was given, shall have filed an affidavit with the Justice, setting forth that he believes the party against whom the judgment was rendered, will within ten days sell or otherwise dispose of or remove his, her or their property out of the county; whereupon, it shall be the duty of said Justice to issue an execution forthwith. Upon service of any *certiorari* being made on a Justice of the Peace, he shall make out a certified copy of the entries in the cause on his docket, and transmit the same with the original papers to the County Court, on or before the first day of the term next thereafter.

SEC. 24.   When a stay of execution upon any judgment rendered in the Justice's court is taken, the same shall not prevent the taking of a writ of *certiorari ;* but the defendant shall have the right to take out his writ of *certiorari* to the Justice's court at any time within ninety days from the decision of the cause by the Justice of the Peace.   Every person who shall have a cause of action against another within the jurisdiction of a Justice of the Peace, who shall make oath in writing before such Justice that he is unable to pay the costs of such action, shall be entitled to all process necessary for the trial of such action, and to have a trial thereof free of costs.   No suit shall be brought before any Justice of the Peace where he may be interested, or where he may be related to either the plaintiff or defendant, within the third degree of consanguinity or affinity, but in all such cases suit shall be brought before the nearest Justice not so interested or related ; and in all cases pending before any Justice where he is thus disqualified from sitting in the case, any Justice in the county may sit and try the same.

Sec. 25. Each Justice of the Peace shall hold a term of his court once in each month, and may transact such business out of said term as is authorized by law; and the Justices of the Peace shall hold their courts at such times and places as may be prescribed by the Commissioners' Courts, and such Justices may hold their courts from day to day until all business shall be disposed of. Should the office of the Justice of the Peace within any county of this State become vacant by death, resignation or otherwise, it shall be lawful for any Justice of the Peace within said county to proceed to try and dispose of all such unfinished business as may be on the docket of such Justice who may have vacated his office as aforesaid, until a successor shall have been appointed and qualified. If, from sickness or absence from the county, any Justice of the Peace shall fail to hold a regular term of his court, then, and in that case, any other Justice of the Peace within the same county shall be and is hereby authorized to preside in the place and stead of such sick or absent Justice, and to discharge, perform and transact all such business as may be necessary during such absence. If from any cause whatever the regular term of a Justice's court should not be held at the time fixed by law, the business pending on the Justice's docket shall stand continued until the next regular term thereof, and all business not disposed of at a regular term of such court shall likewise stand continued until the next regular term thereof.

Sec. 26. Justices of the Peace shall have the same power, in cases within their jurisdiction, as Clerks of the District Court, to issue writs of attachments, sequestration and garnishment, and all laws regulating such writs in the District Court shall be held applicable to Justices' courts.

Sec. 27. The plaintiff in any civil suit, before process issues, or any time before final judgment, upon motion of the defendant, or any officer of the court interested in the costs accruing in such suit, may be ruled to give security for the costs; and if such rule be entered against the plaintiff, and he fail to comply therewith on or before the first day of the next term of the court, the suit shall be dismissed, unless the party ruled shall make and file an affidavit that he is unable to give such security. All bonds given as security for costs shall have the force and effect of judgments against all the obligors for the said cost. Executors and administrators of deceased persons' estates, and guardians, shall not be ruled to give security for costs in any suit to recover money due or property belonging to the estate; and no security shall be exacted of executors or administrators of deceased persons' estates in appeals taken in suing for such money or property, or in defending suits brought against such estates for money or property. Justices of the Peace shall keep a fee book in which shall be taxed all costs accruing in any suit, whether civil or criminal.

Sec. 28. Justices of the Peace shall be commissioned by the Governor to act as Justices of the Peace in their respective precincts, and also to act as Notaries Public. They shall also discharge all the duties of Coroner, except such as devolve upon Constables by Section 21 of the Constitution. They shall be authorized to solemnize the rites of matrimony.

Sec. 29. Upon complaint being made before any Justice of the Peace, or any other officer authorized by law to administer oaths, that an offense has been committed in the county which a Justice of the Peace has jurisdiction finally to try, the Justice or other officer shall reduce the same to writing, and cause the same to be signed and sworn to by the complainant, and it shall be duly attested by such Justice or other officer before whom it shall be made; and when made before such Justice, or when returned to him made before any other officer, the same shall be filed by him. Said complaint shall state the name of the accused, if his name is known, and the offense with which he is charged shall be stated in plain and intelligible words, and it must appear that the offense was committed in the county, and the complainant must show, from the date of the offense stated therein, that the offense is not barred by limitation.

Sec. 30. Whenever the requirements of the preceding article have been complied with, the Justice of the Peace shall issue a warrant for the arrest of the accused; said warrant shall be deemed sufficient if it contains the following requisites: *First*—It shall issue in the name of the State of Texas, and shall be deemed sufficient without regard to form. *Second*—It shall be directed to the Sheriff or any Constable, or some other person specially named, commanding him to take the body of the accused of an offense, to be dealt with according to law. *Third*—It must specify the name of the person whose arrest is ordered, if it be known; if not known, then some reasonable, definite description must be given of him. *Fourth*—It must state that the person is accused of some offense against the laws of the State, naming the offense. *Fifth*—It must be signed by the Justice, and his office be named in the body of the warrant or in connection with his signature.

Sec. 31. The Justice, when he has good cause to believe that an offense has been, or is about to be, committed against the laws of this State, may summon and examine any witness or witnesses in relation thereto; and if it shall appear, from the statement of such witness or witnesses, that an offense has been committed, the Justice shall reduce said statements to writing, and cause the same to be sworn to by such witnesses; and thereupon said Justice shall issue his warrant of arrest against such offenders; which warrant shall be returnable before said Justice at such time as he may direct, and if said Justice has final jurisdiction of the same, he shall proceed to try; otherwise he shall discharge the accused, if the law and the facts of the case warrant it; or if the offense charged is bailable, cause him to give bond for his appearance at the next term of the District or County Court; which bond, together with all the papers in the case, shall be returned to the Clerk of said court by said Justice.

Sec. 32. Witnesses summoned under the preceding article, who shall refuse to appear and make such statement of facts under oath, shall be guilty of a contempt of court and may be fined in any sum not exceeding one hundred dollars, and attachment may issue for such witnesses.

Sec. 33. A warrant of arrest may be executed by any Sheriff or Constable in any county in this State, or other person specially authorized by the Justice to execute the same, wherever the defendant may be found. Every peace officer is bound to execute all process and orders directed to him from a Justice of the Peace, and if he shall fail or refuse to do the same, he may be fined by said Justice for contempt of court in any sum not exceeding one hundred dollars. Bail is the security given by a person accused of an offense that he will appear and answer before the proper court the accusation brought against him. This security is given by means of a bail bond. A bail bond shall be sufficient if it contain the following requisites: *First*—That it is made payable to the State of Texas. *Second*—That the obligors thereto bind themselves that the defendant will appear before the proper court to answer the accusation against him. *Third*—That the offense of which the defendant is accused be distinctly named in the bond, and that it appear therefrom that he is accused of some offense against the laws of the State. *Fourth*—That the bond be signed by the principal and sureties, or in case all or either of them cannot write, then that they affix thereto their marks. *Fifth*—That the bond state the time and place, when and where the accused binds himself to appear and the court before which he is to appear. *Sixth*—That it shall show the amount of money for which the principal and his sureties are bound for. In stating the time, it is sufficient to specify the term of the court, and in stating the place, it is sufficient to specify the name of the court and of the county.

SEC. 34. Bail bonds may be taken by the Justice, or the officer having the defendant in custody, in all cases where the Justice has final jurisdiction over the case, but if the Justice has not jurisdiction finally to try the same, he shall take the bail bond in conformity with the code of criminal procedure.

SEC. 35. When the defendant is brought before the Justice, it shall be the duty of such Justice, unless a jury be waived, to issue a *venire facias* to the Sheriff or any Constable of his county, commanding him to summon a jury of six men for the trial of the case before him, who shall assess the fine; and when such jury shall be summoned they shall remain in attendance upon the court and sit as jurors in all cases that may come up for hearing, until discharged by said court, for which they shall be allowed one dollar each per day, to be paid out of the County Treasury, upon a certificate of such Justice of the number of days so served by them; *provided*, that if the defendant appear before such Justice and plead guilty to the charge or complaint against him, or a jury be waived, the Justice shall, if desired by the defendant, proceed to assess the fine without the intervention of a jury.

SEC. 36. Upon the conviction of a defendant, tried before any Justice of the Peace, a jury fee of three dollars shall be taxed against him and collected as other costs.

SEC. 37. In all cases where the defendant may be convicted before a Justice of the Peace of a misdemeanor, he shall be entitled to an appeal from the judgment of said Justice, to the County Court of the county where such judgment was rendered, and notice of such appeal shall be given in open court, upon the overruling of a motion for a new trial by such Justice.

SEC. 38. Whenever a defendant is desirous of appealing as provided in the preceding section, he shall file with the Justice a bond in double the amount of the fine and costs imposed upon him, conditioned that he shall prosecute his appeal with effect, and shall pay such fine and costs as shall be awarded against him by the County Court as well as other costs that may have been adjudged against him in the court below.

SEC. 39. Whenever complaint be made before any Justice of the Peace that an offense has been committed in any county other than the county in which the complaint shall be made, it shall be the duty of such Justice to issue his warrant for the arrest of the person named in such complaint, directed to the Sheriff or any Constable of his county, commanding such officer to bring the person named in said warrant before such Justice, whose duty it shall be to take bail of such person, if the offense charged be a misdemeanor, and send the bond so taken, to the Clerk of the County Court of the county where such offense is alleged to have been committed; but if the offense charged in said complaint be a felony, such Justice shall make his warrant returnable to any Justice of the Peace in the county where such offense was committed.

SEC. 40. Justices of the Peace shall be governed by the laws now in force in regard to proceedings in Justices' Courts in criminal and civil cases, where the same do not conflict with the provisions of this act.

SEC. 41. It shall be the duty of the Justice of the Peace to proceed with the trial of civil cases in regular order as they appear upon the docket; *provided*, that by consent of both parties any civil case may be set for trial for a day certain. The Justice of the Peace shall fix a time for the trial of criminal cases, either before or after the trial of civil cases, and give notice to the County Attorney, of the time fixed.

SEC. 42. That all laws and parts of laws in conflict with this act or any of its provisions be and the same are hereby repealed. ·

SEC. 43. Whereas, an immediate public necessity exists for conforming the jurisdiction and powers of Justices of the Peace to the new Constitution, and an emergency for the immediate passage of this law, therefore this act shall take effect and be in force from and after its passage.

Approved August 17, 1876.

Takes effect from its passage.

CHAPTER CIV.—*An Act to reserve from location, in the event of forfeiture, the public domain now reserved for the benefit of railroads or railroad companies.*

SECTION 1. *Be it enacted by the Legislature of the State of Texas*, That all reservations of the public domain for the benefit of any railroad or railroad company heretofore made by law, and the right to which reservation has lapsed since January 1, 1872, or may hereafter lapse, are hereby declared then to have been severed from the mass of the public domain, and in the event of forfeiture to the State, are, by this act, expressly reserved from location, except the three millions of acres of lands reserved for constructing a new State Capitol and other public buildings, and to actual settlers under the pre-emption laws of this State, and whenever a pre-emption survey of one hundred and sixty acres, or of eighty acres, shall be made for any settler, a like quantity shall be made adjoining said pre-emption survey, for the public free school fund of Texas. The settler having the pre-emption survey made shall pay to the surveyor the fees for both the pre-emption survey and the one for the school fund, and also the fees for recording the field notes of both surveys, and said field notes shall be returned to the General Land Office together; *provided*, that no right of any such railroad company to such reservation shall be in any manner impaired until a forfeiture has been judicially declared thereon.

SEC. 2. As this act cannot otherwise fully accomplish its purpose, an emergency exists, and it is hereby enacted that this act take effect and be in force from and after its passage.

Approved August 17, 1876.

Takes effect from its passage.

CHAPTER CV.—*An Act to provide for supplying the State Capitol buildings and Capitol grounds with water.*

SECTION 1. *Be it enacted by the Legislature of the State of Texas,* That the Governor, Comptroller and State Treasurer are hereby authorized and empowered to contract for the means of securing a lasting supply of water and fire hydrants for the Capitol buildings and Capitol grounds, at all seasons of the year, and also said water for two years, with such ornamental water fixtures as the said board, in its discretion, may select. Said contract shall not involve an expenditure of more than thirty-six hundred dollars.

SEC. 2. As the security of the public buildings and the preservation of the trees and shrubbery on the Capitol grounds require that the water supply contemplated by this act be at once secured, on account of said emergency and necessity this act shall take effect and be in force from and after its passage.

Approved August 17, 1876.

Takes effect ninety days after adjournment.

CHAPTER CVI.—*An Act to authorize the Clerk of the Court of Appeals to appoint a deputy.*

SECTION 1. *Be it enacted by the Legislature of the State of Texas,* That the Clerk of the Court of Appeals be and he is hereby authorized to appoint a deputy, whose duties shall be the same as those of the Clerk.

SEC. 2. As the present Clerk of the Court of Appeals is sick, and is at present unable to attend to the duties of his office, an emergency exists for the immediate passage of this act; it is therefore enacted that this act take effect and be in force from and after its passage.

Approved August 17, 1876.

Takes effect from its passage.

CHAPTER CVII.—*An Act to punish Drunkenness.*

SECTION 1. *Be it enacted by the Legislature of the State of Texas,* That any person who shall get drunk, or be found in a state of intoxication in any public place, shall be deemed guilty of a misdemeanor, and on conviction before a court of competent jurisdiction shall be fined in a sum not more than one hundred dollars for each and every such offense.

Approved August 17, 1876.

Takes effect ninety days after adjournment.

CHAPTER CVIII.—*An Act to fix the time of holding the next General Election.*

SECTION 1. *Be it enacted by the Legislature of the State of Texas,* That the next general election in the State of Texas shall be held on the first Tuesday next after the first Monday in November, A. D. 1878, and general elections shall be held every two years thereafter, at such places and under such regulations as may be prescribed by law.

SEC. 2. That all laws conflicting with the provisions of this act be and the same are hereby repealed.

Approved August 17, 1876.

Takes effect ninety days after adjournment.

CHAPTER CIX.—*An Act to better regulate grand juries and juries in civil and criminal cases in the courts of the State, and to amend Sections 9 and 17 of an act entitled: "An Act to regulate grand juries and juries in civil and criminal cases in the courts of the State," approved August 1, 1876.*

SECTION 1. *Be it enacted by the Legislature of the State of Texas,* That the Jury Commissioners appointed and serving as such at each term of the District Court, in addition to the other duties required of them by law, shall, at the same time and place at which they shall select jurors for the next term of the District Court, make out for the use of the Jury Commissioners of the County Court, a complete list of the names of all the persons selected by them as grand and petit jurors, and shall place said list in an envelope and seal the same, and write their names across the seal; and they shall address said envelope to the Jury Commissioners of the County Court of the proper county, and they shall deliver said envelope, without unnecessary delay, to the District Judge in open court.

SEC. 2. The District Judge shall, without unnecessary delay, deliver said envelope to the County Clerk or one of his deputies, and, at the time of delivery, administer to said Clerk or deputy, as the case may be, the following oath: "You do solemnly swear that you will, to the best of your ability, safely keep this envelope; and that you will neither open the same, nor allow it to be opened, except as provided by law; and that you will cause it to be delivered to the Jury Commissioners of the County Court next hereafter appointed in and for this county."

SEC. 3. At the first term of the County Court thereafter held, at which Jury Commissioners are appointed, it shall be the duty of the County Clerk to deliver said envelope to the Jury Commissioners or any one of them appointed at said term, and take a receipt therefor; and said receipt shall state whether the seal of said envelope be broken or not.

SEC. 4. After the Jury Commissioners appointed by said County Court shall have assembled for business, as provided by law, they shall open said envelope and read said list of names, and no person named on said list shall be selected as a juror by said Jury Commissioners.

SEC. 5. The Jury Commissioners appointed and serving as such at any term of the County Court, in addition to the other duties required of them by law, shall, at the same time and place at which they select jurors for the County Court, make out for the use of the Jury Commissioners for the District Court, a complete list of the names of all persons selected by them as jurors; they shall place said list in an envelope and seal the same, and write their names across the seal, and address said envelope to the Jury Commissioners of the District Court of the proper county, and deliver said envelope without unnecessary delay to the County Judge in open court.

SEC. 6. The County Judge shall, without unnecessary delay, deliver said envelope to the District Clerk or one of his deputies, and at the time of delivery administer to said Clerk or his deputy, as the case may be, the following oath: "You do solemnly swear that you will, to the best of your ability, safely keep this envelope, and that you will neither open the same, nor allow it to be opened, except as provided by law, and that you will cause it to be delivered to the Jury Commissioners of the District Court next hereafter appointed in and for this county."

SEC. 7. At the first term of the District Court thereafter held, it shall be the duty of the District Clerk to deliver said envelope to the Jury Commissioners, or any one of them, appointed at said term, and take a receipt therefor; and said receipt shall state whether the seal of said envelope be broken or not.

SEC. 8. After the Jury Commissioners, appointed at said term of the District Court, shall have assembled for business, as provided by law, they shall open said envelope and read said list of names, and no person named on said list shall be selected as a juror by said Jury Commissioners.

SEC. 9. It shall be the duty of the Jury Commissioners, in both the District and County Courts, before leaving the apartment in which they select jurors, to destroy said list of names, and it shall be unlawful for them, or any of them, to make known to any person the name of any person on said lists.

SEC. 10. That Section nine of an act entitled "An Act to regulate grand juries and juries in civil and criminal cases, in the courts of the State," approved August 1, 1876, be so amended as hereafter to read as follows:

"SEC. 9. Within thirty days of the next term, and not before, the Clerk shall open the envelopes and make out a fair copy of the jury list for each week, and give the same to the Sheriff or his deputy, who shall, at least three days prior to the first day of the next term, summon the persons to attend on Monday of the week for which said persons were drawn as petit jurors, by giving personal notice to each juror, or by leaving written notice at the juror's place of residence with a member of his family, over sixteen years old, and in either event the Sheriff shall name the day and week said juror is required to appear. The lists shall be returned by the Sheriff on the first day of the term, with a certificate thereon of the date and manner in which each juror was summoned, from each of which lists thirty persons, more or less, as the Judge may direct, shall be selected for the week named in the list, from those summoned and in attendance, and not excused by the Judge, in open court, in the order in which their names appear thereon, who shall compose the regular panel of that week.

SEC. 11. That section seventeen of an act, entitled, "An Act to regulate grand juries and juries in civil and criminal cases, in the courts of the State," approved August 1, 1876, be so amended as hereafter to read as follows:

"SEC. 17. No jury shall be required in any civil case in the District or County Court, unless the party demanding a jury shall have deposited by nine o'clock A. M., on the day of the court set by the Judge for the trial of jury causes, a jury fee of five dollars if in the District Court, and three dollars if in the County Court; and all causes in which jury fees have been deposited, shall be at once entered by the Clerk in their regular order on a "jury case trial docket." Said causes, except appearance, shall be tried, or disposed of for the term, in their regular order, before those cases in which no jury has been demanded and jury fee deposited; provided, that in civil cases filed before the passage of this act, parties desiring a jury shall not be required to pay the jury fee until the case be called for trial."

SEC. 12.   Whereas, there is an imperative public necessity existing for the immediate operation of the provisions of this act, " as well as an act entitled, 'An Act to regulate grand juries and juries, in civil and criminal cases, in the courts of the State,'" approved August 1, 1876, thus creating an emergency, thefore, that this act, " as well as the act to which this is supplementary," take effect, and be in force, from and after its passage.

Approved August 18, 1876.

Takes effect from its passage.

CHAPTER CX.—*An Act to amend an act entitled " An Act to organize the County Courts, and define their powers and jurisdiction," approved June 16, 1876.*

SECTION 1.   *Be it enacted by the Legislature of the State of Texas,* That Sections three and seven of the above entitled act be so amended as hereafter to read as follows :

"SEC. 3.   The County Court shall have exclusive original jurisdiction of all misdemeanors, except misdemeanors involving official mismisconduct, and except such misdemeanors as are punishable by fine only, and in the punishment of which the highest fine to be imposed may not exceed two hundred dollars; that in cases where the offense charged is within the jurisdiction of the County Court, the court shall hear and determine the case, notwithstanding the proof may show an offense not within but below the jurisdiction as herein conferred; *provided, however,* that nothing contained in this section shall be so construed as to prohibit the District Court from hearing and finally determining all charges of felony, whether the proofs develop a felony or misdemeanor, and said courts shall have exclusive original jurisdiction in all civil cases where the matter in controversy shall exceed two hundred dollars in value, and not exceeding five hundred dollars, exclusive of interest; and jurisdiction in the forfeiture and final judgment of all bonds taken in criminal cases of which the County Court has jurisdiction and concurrent jurisdiction with the District Court when the matter in controversy shall exceed five hundred dollars and not exceed one thousand dollars, exclusive of interest; but shall not have jurisdiction of suits to recover damages for slander or defamation of character, nor of suits for the recovery of lands, nor of suits for the enforcement of liens upon land, nor of suits in behalf of the State, for escheats, nor of suits for the forfeiture of charter of corporations and incorporated companies.   They shall have appellate jurisdiction in cases civil and criminal, of which Justice's Court have original jurisdiction, but of such civil cases only where the judgment of the court appealed from, or the amount in controversy, shall exceed twenty dollars, exclusive of costs, and in criminal cases of which Mayors' and Recorders' Courts have jurisdiction, and after motion for new trial in the court below has been overruled and notice of appeal given in open court.   In all appeals from Justices', Mayors' or Recorders' Courts, there shall be a trial *de novo* in the County Court, and when the judgment rendered or fine imposed, or the amout in controversy, shall not exceed one hundred dollars, exclusive of interest and costs, such trial shall be final; but if the judgment rendered, or fine imposed, or the amount in controversy, shall exceed one hundred dollars, an appeal therefrom may be taken to the Court of Appeals.   In all cases, civil and criminal, of which the County Court has exclusive or concurrent original jurisdiction, and in all cases appealed from Justices' Courts, if in said last named cases the judgment rendered or fine imposed, or the amount in controversy in the County Court, shall exceed one hundred dollars, an appeal shall lie to the Court of Appeals, under the same rules and regulations as are prescribed by law or the regulation of appeals from the District to the Supreme Court of the State of Texas. In all proceedings of administration and guardianship, an appeal shall lie to the District Court, under such rules and regulations as are prescribed by the law regulating administrations of estates of decedents and wards. In all counties where there is a Criminal District Court, appeals in criminal cases from Justices', Mayors' and Recorders' Courts, and all other inferior courts and tribunals, shall lie directly to such Criminal District Courts.

Sec. 2.   That Section 7 of said act shall hereafter read as follows:

"Sec. 7.   All causes, both civil and criminal, and proceedings of administration and guardianship, now pending in the several District Courts of this State, and all cases, civil and criminal, remaining on the dockets of the several criminal courts which have been abolished by the adoption of the present Constitution, of which the County Courts have original or appellate jurisdiction, are hereby transferred to the County Courts for trial, and it shall be the duty of the Clerks of the District Courts, upon the order of the District Judge, made either in term time or vacation, to certify the original papers and copies of all orders, a statement of the costs incurred in such cases, to the Clerk of the County Court, who shall immediately docket said causes, and they shall stand for trial the same as if they were originally instituted in, or appealed to, said Court; *provided*, that in all such causes and proceedings of administration and gurdianship, where the Judge of the County Court may be disqualified to try the same, they shall remain in the District Court for trial and settlement; *provided, further*, that all papers and records of the estates of deceased persons and minors shall be turned over to the custody of the Clerk of the County Court."

Sec. 3.   That Section 22 of said act shall hereafter read as follows:

"Sec. 22.   That the County Courts of each county in this State shall have a seal, with a star of five points in the centre, and the words, "County Court (insert the name of the county) County, Texas," engraved thereon, an impression of which seal shall be attached to all writs and other process, except subpœnas issuing from said court, and shall be used in the authentication of all official acts of the Clerk; said seal shall be procured by the County Commissioners' Court of the county.

Sec. 4.   The necessity for more definitely fixing the jurisdiction and powers of the County Courts, and giving the Clerks of said Courts the power to issue the writ of attachment, sequestration and garnishment, makes it an emergency that this act go into immediate effect; it is therefore declared that the same shall go into immediate force.

Approved August 18, 1876.

Takes effect from its passage.

CHAPTER CXI.—*An Act to provide for the levying, assessing and collecting of taxes to pay the interest and the principal of bonds heretofore issued by cities to aid in the construction of railroads and other works of internal improvement.*

SECTION 1. *Be it enacted by the Legislature of the State of Texas,* That all taxes collected under this act, or under an act entitled: "An Act to authorize counties, cities and towns to aid in the construction of railroads and other works of internal improvements," approved April 12, 1871, shall be applied solely to the objects for which they were levied, under the direction of the State Comptroller, as follows: *First*—To the payment of the expenses of assessing and collecting the same. *Second* —To the payment of the annual interest of such bonds, and not less than two per cent. of the principal; and if there be any excess on hand after making the above payments for the current year, it shall be used in the purchase and cancellation of said bonds.

SEC. 2. All taxes levied under this act, or the act of 1871, above referred to, shall be assessed and collected by the same officers whose duty it is to assess and collect the other municipal taxes, who shall receive the same rates of commission allowed for assessing and collecting the *ad valorem* tax of such city. The same remedies shall be used to enforce the assessment, collection and paying over of such taxes as are, or may hereafter, be provided by law to enforce the assessment, collection and paying over of other municipal taxes.

SEC. 3. The officer whose duty it is to collect the aforesaid taxes shall give bond, with two or more sufficient sureties, to be approved by the Mayor and Board of Aldermen of such city, in a sum fifty per cent. greater than the estimated annual amount of said taxes, which bond shall be payable to the State, and shall be conditioned for the faithful assessing, collecting and paying over of said tax into the State Treasury as provided by law; and the said Collector shall be amenable and subject to all laws enacted to secure the honest and faithful performance of the duties of Collectors of Taxes.

SEC. 4. It shall be lawful for the Collector to receive in payment of the taxes herein specified current money or the matured coupons of the bonds, for the payment of which such tax may have been levied.

SEC. 5. The Collector of Taxes levied under the provisions of the act above recited shall pay over to the State Treasurer, at the beginning of each and every month, all moneys or coupons he may have collected during the preceding month; deducting his legal commissions on the amount so paid, and shall make a report of his collections to the Mayor and City Council at its first regular meeting in each month.

SEC. 6. If it shall be ascertained at any time that the tax which has been levied for the payment of the city bonds issued under the provisions of the above recited act, is insufficient to pay the annual interest and two per cent. annually of the principal of such bonds, besides the expenses of assessing, collecting and paying over such tax, it shall be the duty of the Comptroller to inform the Mayor of said city of the fact, and it shall be the duty of the City Council, and they shall, upon such information, levy such additional tax and cause the same to be collected, as will be sufficient to make such payments; which levy shall be continued in force until the whole amount of principal and interest of said bonds shall have been fully paid.

SEC. 7. That all laws or parts of laws in conflict with the provisions of this act are hereby repealed.

SEC. 8. As the credit of the several cities in this State, and through them, the credit of the State, has been and is now suffering on account of the failure of such cities to collect the taxes levied to pay the interest upon the bonds issued under the provisions of the aforesaid act, and the consequent default in the payment of said interest, creates an imperative public necessity, and an emergency for the early enforcement of this act; therefore, this act shall be in force and take effect from and after its passage.

Approved August 18, 1876.

Takes effect ninety days after adjournment.

CHAPTER CXII.—*An Act to provide for the guardianship of persons and estates of minors, persons of unsound mind and habitual drunkards.*

SECTION 1. *Be it enacted by the Legislature of the State of Texas,* That the County Courts shall have power either in term time or vacation to appoint guardians of the persons and estates of minors, persons of unsound mind and habitual drunkards; transact business appertaining to such estates, and settle accounts of such guardians.

SEC. 2. Male persons under twenty-one years of age, and females under twenty-one years of age, and unmarried, are minors.

SEC. 3. The term, "persons of unsound mind," when used in this act, includes idiots, lunatics and insane persons. A habitual drunkard is one whose mind has become so impaired by the use of intoxicating liquors, or drugs, that he is incapable of taking care of himself or his property.

SEC. 4. The parents, or the survivors of them, except in certain cases, have a natural right and duty to take care of the persons of their minor children.

SEC. 5. The mode which the law provides for taking care of the persons and estates of minors, persons of unsound mind and habitual drunkards, is by the aid of a guardian, appointed by the County Court.

SEC. 6. The minor is called the ward of the guardian; and the latter is said to have the guardianship of the ward; or of his person, or of his estate, as the case may be.

SEC. 7. Incidental to the right and duty of the parent or guardian to take care of the person of a minor, it is their duty to see that he is educated in a manner suitable to his condition, and if necessary for his support, that he learn a trade or adopt some useful profession.

SEC. 8. Where the parents live together, the father is the natural guardian of the person of the minor children by the marriage, and is entitled to be appointed guardian of their estates.

SEC. 9. Where the parents do not live together, their rights are equal, and the guardianship of their minor children shall be assigned to one or the other, according to the circumstances of each case, taking into consideration the interest of the child alone.

SEC. 10. Where one of the parents is dead, the survivor is the natural guardian of the persons of the minor children, and entitled to be appointed guardian of their estates.

SEC. 11. When the surviving father or mother dies, he or she may appoint, by will or by written declaration, any person not disqualified, to be the guardian of the persons of his or her minor child or children;

and such person shall be entitled to be appointed guardian of their estates.

SEC. 12.   Where the minor is an orphan, and no one has been appointed by the surviving parent to be the guardian, the nearest ascendant in the direct line, if not disqualified, is entitled to the guardianship of the person of the orphan, and to be appointed guardian of his estate.

SEC. 13.   When there is more than one ascendant in the same degree, in the direct line, they are equally entitled, and the guardianship shall be given to one or the other, according to circumstances, taking into consideration the interest of the orphan alone.

SEC. 14.   In case the orphan has no ascendant in the direct line, the guardianship shall be given to the nearest of kin in the collateral line, who comes immediately after the presumptive heir or heirs of the orphan; and if there be two or more in the same degree, the guardianship shall be given to one or the other, according to circumstances, taking into consideration the interest of the orphan alone.

SEC. 15.   When an orphan arrives at the age of fourteen years, he becomes entitled to choose his own guardian, to be approved by the court, except where a guardian has been appointed by the lawful will of the parent; but if, after being personally cited, he fails to appear and choose a guardian, the appointment shall be made by the court.

SEC. 16.   The following persons cannot be appointed guardians: *First*—Minors, except the father and mother. *Second*—Persons whose conduct is notoriously bad.   *Third*—Persons of unsound mind. *Fourth* —Habitual drunkards.   *Fifth*—Those who are themselves, or whose father or mother are parties to a lawsuit, on the result of which the condition of the minor or part of his fortune may depend.   *Sixth*— Those who are debtors to the minor, unless they discharge the debt prior to the appointment.   The sixth subdivision does not apply to the father or mother.

SEC. 17.   All persons are parties to a proceeding for the appointment of a guardian for a minor.

SEC. 18.   It follows from the preceding section that any person has a right to appear and contest the appointment of a particular person, or to contest any proceeding which he deems to be injurious to the ward, or to commence any proceeding which he considers beneficial to him, being liable for the costs occasioned by him, in case of his failure.

SEC. 19.   A proceeding for the appointment of a guardian of the estate of a minor shall be commenced in the county where the parents reside.

SEC. 20.   If the parents do not reside in the same county, it shall be commenced in the county where the parent who has the custody of the child resides.

SEC. 21.   A proceeding for the appointment of a guardian of the person and estate of an orphan, or of either, shall be commenced in the county where the surviving parent resided at the time of his death, or where the orphan is found, or where his principal estate may be.

SEC. 22.   Where a minor or person of unsound mind resides out of the State, and owns property in this State, guardianship of the estate of such minor or person of unsound mind may be granted when it is made to appear that a necessity exists for such guardianship, in like manner as if said minor or person of unsound mind were a resident of this State; and the court making such grant of guardianship shall take all such action, and make all such orders in reference to the estate of said ward, for the maintenance and support, or education and care of said ward, out of the proceeds of said ward's estate, in like manner as if the ward had resided in this State, and guardianship of the person of said ward had been granted by the court, and the ward had been sent abroad by order of the court, for education or treatment.

SEC. 23.   A proceeding for the appointment of a guardian is commenced by written application.

SEC. 24.   Such application may be made by any person who is interested in the welfare of the minor.

SEC. 25.   At the term after notice shall have been given by citation duly posted, to all persons interested in the welfare of such minor, the application is ready for trial.

SEC. 26.   If application be not made by any person entitled to claim the guardianship, a proper person, who is not so entitled, may be appointed.

SEC. 27.   Before the appointment of a guardian of either the person or estate of a minor, over fourteen years of age, he shall be cited.

SEC. 28.   When it shall come to the knowledge of the County Judge that there is, within his county, any minor without a guardian of his person or estate, he shall cause a citation to be posted to all persons interested in the welfare of such minor, to show cause why a guardian for such minor should not be appointed.

SEC. 29.   On the return of such citation duly posted, and if the minor be fourteen years of age, of a citation duly served on him, the court shall appoint a guardian for such minor.

SEC. 30.   All citations which are not to be served on particular persons named shall be for all persons interested in the welfare of the minor, naming him.

SEC. 31.   The bond of the guardian of the person of a minor shall be in an amount to be fixed by the court, not to exceed one thousand dollars, to the effect that he will faithfully dischage the duties of guardian of the person of the minor.

SEC. 32.   The bond of the guardian of the estate of a minor shall be in an amount equal to double the estimated value of the property belonging to the estate, to the effect that he will faithfully discharge the duties of guardian of the estate of such minor according to law.

SEC. 33.   The surviving parent may provide, by will regularly probated, that a guardian appointed by the will shall not be required to give bond for the management of the estate devised by said will, and the direction shall be observed, unless it be made to appear at any time that such guardian is mismanaging the property, or about to betray his trust.

SEC. 34.   Where the same person is appointed guardian of the person and estate, only one bond shall be given, containing the substance required in Sections 31 and 32.

SEC. 35.   The guardian shall take an oath faithfully to discharge the duties of guardian of the person (or of the estate, or of the person and estate, as the case may be,) of the minor, according to law, which oath shall be endorsed on the bond.

SEC. 36.   Letters of guardianship shall consist of copies of the orders appointing the guardian and approving the bond, with the additional statement that they are given to prove the capacity of ———, to act as the guardian of the person (or of the estate, or of the person and estate, as the case may be).   Only one guardian can be appointed of the

12 GL.

person and estate of a minor; but one person may be appointed guardian of the person and another of the estate, where the applicants are equally entitled; *provided*, nothing in this section shall be held to prohibit the joint appointment of husband and wife.

SEC. 37.   The order for the appointment of a guardian for a minor shall specify whether it be of the person or estate, or of both person and estate.

SEC. 38.   The guardian of a minor continues in office, unless sooner discharged, according to law, until the minor arrives at the age of twenty-one years, or, being a female, marries.

SEC. 39.   Where a married woman may be appointed guardian, she may jointly with her husband, or without her husband, if he be absent from the State, execute such bond as the law requires and acknowledge the same before the Clerk ; and such bond shall bind her estate in the same manner as if she were unmarried, but shall not bind her husband as surety unless he sign and be approved as such.

SEC. 40.   A bond executed by a person appointed by a will, or surviving husband or wife, under twenty-one years of age, as guardian, shall be as valid as if he or she were of full age.

SEC. 41.   All bonds and official oaths shall be immediately recorded and filed.

SEC. 42.   Where it is not otherwise provided, a bond shall be required to be given and an oath to be taken at a time specified in the order within ten days, and at least one day before the adjournment of the court.

SEC. 43.   A surety may apply to be relieved from his bond, and upon notice to the guardian, he shall be required to give a new bond within ten days, and at least one day before the adjournment of the court, and in the meantime to refrain from acting as guardian, except to preserve the property committed to his charge.

SEC. 44.   If a new bond be given and approved, the former surety or sureties so applying shall be discharged from any liability for the misconduct of the principal after the approval of such new bond.

SEC. 45.   The remedy upon every bond filed in the County Court may be by petition and citation to the sureties, to show cause why judgment should not be rendered against them in that court; where the liability of the principal has not already been established, he shall be included in the suit.

SEC. 46.   Such remedy may be commenced within four years next after the death, resignation, removal or discharge of the guardian, and not after; *provided*, that infants, persons of unsound mind, married women, persons imprisoned under a sentence of a court for a term less than for life, and their representatives, shall have at least seven years within which to prosecute such remedy, after the removal of their respective disabilities, or after the death of one dying under disability.

SEC. 47.   The sureties on a bond are discharged when the whole penalty has been recovered, but not before.

SEC. 48.   It is the duty of the guardian, immediately after receiving letters, to collect and take into possession the personal property, books, title papers, and other papers belonging to the estate.

SEC. 49.   If the ward held or owned any property in common, or as part owner with another person, the guardian shall be entitled to possession thereof in common with the surviving part owner or part owners, in the same manner as the deceased was entitled thereto in his lifetime.

SEC. 50. It is the duty of every guardian, as soon as he shall have collected the estate, and within thirty days after taking the oath and giving bond, to return a true and perfect inventory of all the real and personal property, books, title papers, other papers and evidences of debt due, or to become due, belonging to the estate.

SEC. 51. The inventory shall describe the property, books and papers, and shall contain a list of the debts due, or to become due, to the ward, stating the names of the debtors, the date of the contract, the amount of interest due thereon, and the rates of interest.

SEC. 52. If any property, books, title papers, or other papers or evidences of debt, were held or owned by the ward in common with another or others, it shall be distinctly stated in the inventory what items thereof were so held, and the names and relationship of the surviving part owners, if any.

SEC. 53. Annexed to such inventory shall be the affidavit of the guardian that it is a full inventory and description of all the real and personal property, books, papers, evidences of debt, and of all debts due, or to become due, belonging to the estate, as far as he has been able to ascertain ; and that he was not bound or indebted to the ward in any contract, except as stated in the inventory (if at all).

SEC. 54. Where the guardian dies, the court, on application, shall appoint another.

SEC. 55. When a guardian wishes to resign, he shall, with such application, present to the court a full and complete account of the condition of the estate, and of his guardianship, verified by his affidavit.

SEC. 56. When such application is filed with the Clerk, a citation shall be issued as follows : First—It shall run in the name of " The State of Texas." Second—It shall be addressed to all persons interested in the guardianship of the estate of ————. Third—It shall state that ————, guardian of said estate, has filed an exhibit of the condition of the estate, an account of his guardianship, and an application for leave to resign. Fourth—It shall notify the persons to whom it is addressed to appear at a certain term of the court, commencing on such a day and month, and contest the account, if they see proper to do so. Fifth—It shall be dated and attested by the Clerk, with the seal of the court attached.

SEC. 57. Such citation shall be published at least once a week, for three successive weeks, in some newspaper in the county, if there be one regularly printed therein ; if not, then by posting copies thereof, twenty days before the term, at three of the most public places in the county, no two of which shall be within the same town or city.

SEC. 58. If it appear at the trial that such guardian has accounted for all the estate, according to law, the court shall make an order that he deliver the estate, if there be any remaining in his possession, to some person who shall have been, or may be, appointed in his place, and given bond and taken the oath of guardian. Upon compliance with such order and surrender of his letters of guardianship, the guardian shall be permitted to resign his trust and be discharged.

SEC. 59. Guardians shall be removed in the following cases, without notice, at a regular term of the court : First—When they neglect to return, within thirty days after qualification, an inventory of the estate, as far as the same (has come) to their knowledge. Second—When they have been required to give a new bond, and neglect to do so within the time prescribed. Third—When they have removed from the State.

SEC. 60. A guardian may be removed by the court, of its own motion, or on the motion of any person interested in the ward, after being cited to answer: *First*—When he fails to return any account which he is required to return by the provisions of this act. *Second*—When he fails to obey any order of the court or Judge, consistent with this act. *Third*—When there is good cause to believe that he has misapplied, embezzled or removed, or is about to misapply, embezzle or remove from the State the property committed to his charge, or any part thereof. *Fourth*—When he is proved to have been guilty of gross neglect or mismanagement in the performance of any of its duties. *Fifth*—Where he is proved to be disqualified under Section 16.

SEC. 61. When a guardian is removed, the order shall require the estate to be delivered up to some person who has been appointed in his stead, and who shall have previously given bond and taken the oath.

SEC. 62. The order of removal shall state the cause therefor, and shall require the guardian to surrender his letters of guardianship.

SEC. 63. When any person shall have been removed from the guardianship of an estate he shall not be afterwards re-appointed.

SEC. 64. If any guardian die or resign, or his letters be revoked, he or his legal representatives shall account for, pay and deliver to his successor, all property of every kind belonging to the estate of the ward, at such time and in such manner as the court shall order, and in case of a refusal to comply with an order of the court to that effect, the same may be enforced by attachment and punishment, as for contempt.

SEC. 65. Where a guardian succeeds a former guardian, he shall be required to account for all the estate which came into the hands of his predecessor, and shall be entitled to any order or remedy which the court has power to give, in order to enforce the delivery of the estate, and the liability of the sureties of his predecessor for so much as is not delivered. But he shall be excused if it appear that he has used due diligence and failed in whole or in part.

SEC. 66. Where a subsequent guardian proceeds against a former one and his sureties for neglect, he shall be entitled to recover the real damage only caused by such neglect.

SEC. 67. If there be more than one guardian, and letters of one or more of them be revoked, or surrendered, or one dies, the remaining guardian shall discharge all the duties required by law touching such estate, including the recovery from such other guardian and his sureties, or their representatives, of the part of the estate in his hands, or for which he is accountable.

SEC. 68. If any person appointed guardian fails to qualify within the time prescribed by the order of the court, or if a guardianship be vacant by reason of the death, resignation or removal of the guardian. the court, or the Judge thereof, in vacation, may appoint a receiver and make any order that may be necessary for the preservation of such estate, until a guardian be regularly appointed and qualified. Any such order made by a Judge in vacation shall be filed with the Clerk of the proper court and entered of record.

SEC. 69. The guardian or his heirs, executors, administrators or assigns, shall not dispute the right of the ward to any property that shall have come to his possession as guardian, except such property as shall have been recovered from the guardian, or there be a personal action pending on account of it.

SEC. 70. Where a guardian and his ward are residents of any other

State or Territory of the United States, or of the District of Columbia, or any other country, such guardian may file a full and complete transcript from the records of a court of competent jurisdiction where he and his ward reside, certified by the Clerk of the court in which the proceedings were had, under the seal of the court, if there be one, together with a certificate from the Judge, Chief Justice or Presiding Magistrate, as the case may be, that said attestation is in due form, showing that he has been appointed guardian of the estate of such ward; such transcript may be recorded, and the guardian shall be entitled to receive letters of guardianship of the estate of such minor situated in this State, upon filing a bond with sureties, as in other cases, in double the amount of the estimated value thereof.

SEC. 71. Upon the recovery of the property of the ward, if it be personal property, such guardian may remove it to the place of residence of himself and ward, unless such removal would conflict with the tenure of such property, or the terms and limitations under which it is held; and if it be real property, he may obtain an order for the sale of it, and remove the proceeds; such sale shall be made, returned and confirmed in the same manner as other sales of real estate by guardians.

SEC. 72. Any resident guardian having any of the estate of such ward, may be ordered to deliver the same up to such non-resident guardian.

SEC. 73. There shall be no removal of any of such property, until all the debts known to exist against the estate have been paid or secured by bond payable to, and approved by, the Clerk of the County Court.

SEC. 74. The benefit of the four preceding sections shall not extend to the residents of any State, Territory, District or country, in which a similar law does not exist in favor of the residents of this State.

SEC. 75. The guardian of the person is entitled to the charge and control of the person of the ward, and the care of his support and education, and his duties correspond to his rights.

SEC. 76. The guardian of the estate is entitled to the possession and management of all property belonging to the ward; to collect all debts, rents or claims due him; to enforce all obligations in his favor; to bring and defend suits by or against him. But in the management of the estate, the guardian is governed by the provisions of this act.

SEC. 77. It is the duty of the guardian of the estate to take care of and manage such estate in such manner as a prudent man would manage his own property; and he shall account for all such rents, profits and revenues as the estate would have produced by such prudent management.

SEC. 78. The guardian of the estate shall use due diligence to collect all claims or debts owing to the ward, and to recover possession of all property to which the ward has a title or claim; *provided*, there is a reasonable prospect of collecting such claims or debts, or of recovering such property; and if he neglect to use such diligence, he and his sureties shall be liable for all damages occasioned by such neglect.

SEC. 79. The guardian of both person and estate has all the rights and duties of the guardian of the person and the guardian of the estate.

SEC. 80. The guardian, as soon as practicable, after appraisement, shall sell at public or private sale, all the personal property belonging to the estate, except property exempt from forced sale, specific legacies, and personal property necessary to carry on a plantation or manufactory, giving such credit as he may deem most advantageous to the estate, not exceeding six months, and taking notes, with one or more sufficient sureties, for the purchase money.

SEC. 81.   The guardian shall keep, or cause to be kept, a true account of the sales made, making a list thereof, specifying each article sold, the price for which it was sold, and the name of the purchaser, and shall annex to such list an affidavit stating that it is a true account of the sales made by him at the time specified, and shall file it within thirty days after the sale.   Such accounts shall be recorded, after allowing one term for objections to be made thereto.

SEC. 82.   The laws regulating sales under execution, so far as it relates to the advertisement and sale of personal property, and is not inconsistent with the provisions of this act, shall apply to the advertisement and sale of such property by a guardian ; the guardian being substituted for the Sheriff or Constable, the estate for the debtor, and persons interested in the ward only, for the creditor.

SEC. 83.   The guardian may sell any of the personal property of the estate at private sale, if it appear to him to be for the interest of the estate ; but he shall be responsible for its being sold for a fair price, and shall make return of such sale within thirty days.

SEC. 84.   If the guardian shall represent to the court, on oath, that there is wild stock belonging to the estate, which he is unable to collect or command, the court may order that the same be sold at public auction, without taking an inventory or making an appraisement thereof, on such credit as the court may deem reasonable, not exceeding twelve months, taking notes bearing interest at the rate of ten per cent. per annum, from the day of sale, with good and sufficient security for the purchase money.

SEC. 85.   Such sale shall be advertised, made, returned and confirmed, the same as sales of real property.

SEC. 86.   If there be a plantation or manufactory belonging to the estate, and if the same be not required to be at once sold for the payment of debts, it shall be the duty of the guardian upon an order of the court to carry on such plantation or manufactory, or rent the same, as shall appear to the court to be for the best interest of the estate.   In coming to a determination, he shall take into consideration the condition of the estate, and the necessity that may exist for the future sale of such property for the payment of claims or legacies, and shall not extend the time of renting or hiring any of the property beyond what may consist with the speedy settlement of the estate.   And any one who is interested in the estate, may, upon good cause shown, after citation to the guardian, obtain an order controlling his action in this particular.

SEC. 87.   When the ward owns improved real property, it shall be the duty of the guardian of the estate annually to rent such property for the best price that can be obtained, taking good security for the payment of the rent, and that the tenant will not commit, nor permit any other person to commit waste on the demised premises.

SEC. 88.   If the ward own wild or unimproved real property, the guardian may let out the same on improvement leases, not to extend more than two years beyond the majority of the ward, taking security as provided in the preceding section.

SEC. 89.   If at any time the guardian shall have on hand any money belonging to the ward, beyond what may be necessary for his education and maintenance, such guardian shall, under the direction of the court, invest such money in bonds of the United States or of the State of Texas, or loan the same to such person as will give security therefor by mortgage or deed of trust on unincumbered real property in the county, for the highest rate of interest that can be obtained therefor; *provided*, whenever any guardian may have in his possession money belonging to his ward, he may make application to the County Court for an order to invest said money in real estate, for the benefit of his said ward; said application to be made, and notice of the same given in the same manner as applications to sell real estate belonging to minors; and if the court be satisfied, on the hearing of said application, that said investment will be beneficial to said ward, an order may be made and entered to that effect. At the next term of the court after the granting of said order, the investment aforesaid shall be inquired into, and if satisfied that said investment will benefit the estate of said ward, the court may approve the contract, and when titles of said real estate have been made to said guardian, he shall hold the same in trust for his said ward, and shall account for it in the same manner as other realty in his possession originally belonging to the estate of his said ward.

SEC. 90. If the money in the hands of the guardian cannot be invested as herein directed, the guardian shall be liable for the principal only.

SEC. 91. The guardian shall not be personally responsible for money loaned under the direction of the court, on security approved by the court, in case of the inability of the person to whom such money may have been loaned to pay the same, and the failure of the security, unless he has been guilty of fraud or negligence in respect to such loan.

SEC. 92. The guardian of the estate may receive property in payment of any debt due to the ward, in all cases where he shall be of opinion that the interests of the ward will be advanced thereby, being responsible for a prudent exercise of the discretion hereby conferred.

SEC. 93. Where different persons have the guardianship of the person and estate of the ward, the guardian of the estate must pay over to the guardian of the person, semi-annually, a sufficient amount of money for the education and maintenance of the ward, and on failure, shall be compelled to do so by order of the court, after being duly cited.

SEC. 94. The court may direct a guardian to expend, for the education and maintenance of his ward, a specified sum, although such sum may exceed the income of the ward's estate; but without such direction the guardian shall not be allowed, in any case, for the education and maintenance of the ward, more than the clear income of the estate.

SEC. 95. A guardian may pay any claim against the estate of his ward which he knows to be just, without the authentication thereof.

SEC. 96. When a judgment for the recovery of money is rendered in any court against a guardian, to be satisfied out of the property of the ward, the creditor, upon application to the County Court, is entitled to an order for its payment; if there be no funds in the hands of the guardian, and to await the receipt of funds from other sources would involve an unreasonable delay, an order shall be issued for the sale of property sufficient to pay the debt.

SEC. 97. If any guardian shall fail to pay any claim ordered to be paid, when demanded, upon affidavit of the demand and failure to pay being filed with the Clerk, an execution shall be issued for the amount ordered to be paid to such claimant, and costs, against the property of such guardian.

SEC. 98. If the execution be returned not satisfied, the claimant may institute suit against the sureties of the guardian, in the court where the guardianship is pending, referring to the official bond and the order for payment, the execution and the return thereon, requiring the sureties to appear and show cause why judgment should not be rendered against them for the amount of such claim, ordered to be paid as aforesaid.

Sec. 99.   Citation in such suit may be issued to any county in the State, and upon the return thereof, duly served, if good cause to the contrary be not shown, the court shall render judgment against the sureties for the amount of the claim ordered to be paid as aforesaid, and remaining unpaid, and ten per cent. damages thereon, together with interest and costs, and issue execution thereon.

Sec. 100.   Any person holding a claim against the estate, secured by mortgage or other special lien, may obtain an order for the sale of the property upon which he has such mortgage or other special lien, or so much thereof as may be required to satisfy the claim, by causing citation to be posted, and the guardian to be cited to appear at the next term of the court, and show cause why such order should not be made.

Sec. 101.   Where the income of the ward's estate and the proceeds of personal property sold are insufficient for his education and maintainance, or to pay debts against his estate, the guardian of the person or estate, or any person holding a valid claim, may apply for the issuance of an order for a sale of sufficient amount of the real estate to make up the deficiency.

Sec. 102.   Whenever it shall appear that the personal property or proceeds of previous sales are insufficient to pay the claims of creditors and legatees, and expenses of administration, an order shall be made, on the application of the guardian, or of any person interested in the ward, for the sale of enough real property to supply the probable deficiency.

Sec. 103.   Such sale shall be ordered to be made of the property which may be deemed most advantageous to the estate to be sold.

Sec. 104.   No order for the sale of real property for the payment of debts shall be made, unless notice of the application therefor shall have been published at least once a week for four weeks successively, or if there be no newspaper regularly printed in the county, by citation duly posted, to all persons interested in the ward, to show cause why such sale should not be made.

Sec. 105.   It is the duty of the guardian to apply for such order, whenever it appears that the proceeds of the personal property and previous sales of real property will be insufficient to pay the debts and expenses of guardianship.

Sec. 106.   If it should appear to the court that the discharge of such special lien, out of the general assets, would be beneficial to the estate, the payment may be ordered to be so made, instead of ordering a sale of the property.

Sec. 107.   All sales of real property, for the payment of debts, shall be made on a credit of twelve months, except where such sales are ordered for the satisfaction of a mortgage or other lien on the very property, in which case such sales shall be made on such terms as the court may direct, which shall be stated in the order of sale.

Sec. 108.   All sales of real property shall be made in the county where the guardianship is pending, unless the real property is situated in another county, in which case the court may order the sale to take place in such county.   And in all such cases the sale shall be advertised in both counties.

SEC. 109. The order of sale shall require the sales to be made, and account of sales returned before the next term of the court.

SEC. 110. The advertisement of the time and place ot the sale of real property shall be sufficient if it state: *First*—The time of the sale. *Second*—The place of the sale. *Third*—The property shall be so described as to distinguish it from like property. *Fourth*—The estate to which the property belongs. *Fifth*—That the same is sold under an order of the court, at what term made, for the payment of debts. *Sixth*—It shall be signed by the guardian officially.

SEC. 111. The law regulating sales under execution, so far as the same relate to the advertisement and sale of real property and the proceedings incidental thereto, and are not inconsistent with the provisions of this act, shall apply to the sale of such property by guardian, under an order of sale for the payment of debts, the guardian being substituted for the Sheriff, the ward for the debtor, and holder of mortgage for the creditor. The guardian shall keep or cause to be kept a true account of all sales made, making a list thereof, specifying each article sold, the price for which it was sold, and the name of the purchaser, and shall annex to such list an affidavit, stating that it is a true account of the sales made by him at the time specified, and shall file it within twenty (20) days after the sale. Such accounts shall be recorded after allowing one term for objections to be made thereto.

SEC. 112. The court may direct the sale of real property to be made at private sale, for cash or on credit, if it shall appear to be for the interest of the estate. But in all such cases, before the court shall order a confirmation of the sale, it must be shown that it was fairly made, and in conformity to law, and that the sale was made for a fair price.

SEC. 113 At the first term of the court, when such account of sale shall have been returned, the court shall inquire into the manner in which such sale was made ; and if it appear to have been fairly made, and in conformity to law, the court shall make an order confirming it, and directing conveyances to be made to the purchasers upon their compliance with the terms of the sale; if it does not appear to have been so made, an order shall be entered setting it aside and ordering a new sale, unless good cause shall have been shown in the meantime why such sale should not be made.

SEC. 114. The terms of sale of real estate in all cases, when made on credit, shall be that the purchaser give his note, bearing ten per cent. (interest) per annum from date, with good personal security, payable in the county, and secured by mortgage on the property purchased; *provided*, that said mortgage shall be executed at the time the conveyance is made by the guardian to said purchaser.

SEC. 115. The conveyance from the guardian to the purchaser, upon compliance with the terms of the sale, shall recite the decree of confirmation, and the recitation of the order of confirmation.

SEC. 116. If, from any cause, the guardian should fail to sell any real property ordered to be sold, at the time specified in the order, he shall report the facts to the court or Judge, accompanied by his affidavit of the truth thereof, and the court or Judge may appoint another day for such sale, and so on, from time to time, until the property is disposed of. When the order appointing another day is made by the Judge in vacation, the same shall be transmitted to the Clerk and be filed by him and entered of record.

SEC. 117. Where any guardian of the estate of a person or minor shall desire to remove the transaction of the business of the guardianship from one county in this State to another, he may be permitted to do so by an order duly entered.

SEC. 118.   Before such order shall be entered, the sureties of such guardian shall be cited to show cause, if any they have, why such removal should not be made; and the guardian shall file a certificate from the Clerk of the county to which the removal is proposed to be made, attested by the seal of the court, that he has filed in such court a certified transcript of all the proceedings in relation to the guardianship.

SEC. 119.   The guardian of the estate of a minor shall annually return to the court an account showing: *First*—Any property that may come to his knowledge or possession, belonging to his ward, which has not been previously inventoried *Second*—Any changes in the property belonging to the estate of the ward, which have not been previously reported.   *Third*—A complete account of receipts and disbursements since the last account. *Fourth*—The money on hand.   Annexed to such account shall be the affidavit of the guardian, that it contains a correct and complete statement of the matters to which it relates.

SEC. 120.   The guardian of the person, where there is a separate guardian of the estate, shall annually return an account, supported by his affidavit, showing the items of expenditure since the last account, for the education and maintenance of the ward.

SEC. 121.   Every account presented to the court by the guardian, shall, without being acted on, be continued until the next term of such court.

SEC. 122.   Notice of the filing of such account shall be given by citation to all persons interested in the ward, duly posted; if it purport to be a final account, the citation shall so state.

SEC. 123.   The account, with any objections made thereto, may be referred to an auditor, to be examined and re-stated.

SEC. 124.   The guardian must produce and file the proper vouchers for every item of credit claimed by him in his account, or support the same by satisfactory evidence.

SEC. 125.   If the account be found incorrect, it shall be correctly stated; and when so corrected, or if found correct, it shall be confirmed and entered of record.

SEC. 126.   A docket shall be kept, in which shall be entered a list of all guardians, the date of granting letters to each, the times at which each is required to return accounts, and whether or not such returns have been made.

SEC. 127.   There shall be put up in some conspicuous place in the office, twenty days before each term of the court, a list of all guardians who are required to return accounts at the next term of the court.

SEC. 128.   If any guardian fail to return accounts at the time prescribed by this act, he shall be cited to return the same at the next term of the court, and show cause for not having made the return according to law.

SEC. 129.   If the guardian fail to return such account after being cited, and to show good cause for not having made the return according to law, he shall be fined in any sum not exceeding five hundred dollars, for the use of the county, and he and his sureties shall be liable for all fines imposed, and damages sustained, by reason of such failure.

SEC. 130.   In the settlement of the account of the guardian, all debts due the estate which the court is satisfied could not have been collected by due diligence, and which have not been collected, shall be excluded from the computation.

SEC. 131. All necessary and reasonable expenses, incurred by the guardian in the preservation and management of the ward's estate, and all necessary and reasonable expenses incurred by him in collecting claims or debts due the ward, or in recovering property to which the ward has a title or claim, shall be allowed, on proof, to be paid out of the estate.

SEC. 132. Attorneys' fees are allowable as part of the expenses of the guardianship, for services in a controversy or controversies between the estate and other persons, and includes fees for advice or assistance in the guardianship. There may be a controversy without a suit.

SEC. 133. On the application of the ward, when he shall have become of full age, or, being a female, shall have married, it shall be the duty of the court to cite the guardian to appear and make a final settlement of the guardianship.

SEC. 134. A special guardian is one who is appointed by a court to take care of the interests of a minor in a suit or special proceeding which is pending or about to be commenced, and to which such minor or person of unsound mind is a proper party.

SEC. 135. A special guardian is appointed by the court, or the Judge or Justice thereof, in which the suit or special pleading is pending or about to be commenced, without notice.

SEC. 136. The duties and powers of the special guardian are the same, in such suit or special proceeding, as those of a general guardian would be.

SEC. 137. The special guardian gives bond and takes an oath to discharge his duties faithfully as a special guardian for the minor in the suit or special proceeding, and to pay over any money or deliver over any property which may come to his possession, according to the order of the court.

SEC. 138. A special guardian is not appointed if there be a general guardian, unless the latter is a party to the same suit or special proceeding in his own right, or has an interest therein adverse to that of the ward.

SEC. 139. The guardian of the person alone is entitled to no compensation.

SEC. 140. The guardian of the estate is entitled to five per cent. upon all sums that he actually receives or pays away in cash ; and if he manages a plantation or manufactory for his ward, the court may allow him a reasonable compensation for such service.

SEC. 141. If information be given to the Judge of the County Court that any person in the county is of unsound mind or a habitual drunkard, without a guardian, the court, if satisfied that there is good cause for the exercise of its jurisdiction, shall cause such person to be brought before it, and inquire into the facts by a jury, if the facts be doubtful.

SEC. 142. When any Sheriff or Constable shall discover any person who resides in the county to be of unsound mind, without a guardian, he shall give information thereof, and like proceedings shall be had as directed in the preceding section.

SEC. 143. If it be found by the jury that the person so brought before the court is of unsound mind, or incapable of managing his own affairs, the court shall appoint a guardian of his person and estate.

SEC. 144. The court may, if just cause appear at any time during the term at which an inquisition is had, set aside the same, and cause a new jury to be summoned to inquire into the facts; but when two juries concur in any case, the verdict shall not be set aside.

SEC. 145. The same person shall be appointed guardian of the person and estate of a person of unsound mind or habitual drunkard.

SEC. 146. The guardian of a person of unsound mind or habitual drunkard shall continue in office, unless sooner discharged according to law, until the ward shall be restored to sound mind or to correct sober habits, or shall die.

SEC. 147. All the provisions of this act relating to the guardianship of the persons and estates of minors, shall apply to the guardianship of persons of unsound mind and habitual drunkards.

SEC. 148. Within thirty days after filing bond and taking the oath, the guardian of a person of unsound mind or habitual drunkard, if such notice shall not have been previously given by a former guardian, shall cause to be published in some newspaper regularly printed in the county, if there be one, a notice that all claims for money not presented to him for allowance within one year from a certain day (which shall be the day on which the filing of the bond and taking the oath were complete), will be postponed until the claims presented within that time are paid; and he shall also, within said time, cause the same notice to be posted in three of the most public places in the county, not within the same city or town, one of which shall be the court-house door. Such notice shall be published at least once a week for four successive weeks.

SEC. 149. If the guardian of a person of unsound mind or habitual drunkard fail to cause notice to be given as prescribed in the preceding section, he shall be liable for any damage which any person may sustain by reason of the failure of such person to present his claim for allowance within the year, unless it appear that such person had notice of the grant of letters of guardianship.

SEC. 150. The term "within the year," and "after the year," as used in this act, mean within or after a year from the original grant of letters of guardianship.

SEC. 151. The provisions of this act relative to claims apply, not only to claims for money, but they also apply to claims for uncertain damages for injury or breach of contract, as well as to claims the amounts of which are susceptible of being ascertained by calculation.

SEC. 152. The provisions of this act relative to claims do not apply to legacies or to claims acknowledged by will. But a claim acknowledged by will may be resisted by a creditor, and reduced to the class of a legacy i proved not to have been really due.

SEC. 153. A claim is said to be "allowed" or "rejected" by the guardian, and to be "approved" or "disapproved" by the court; those terms referring, when used by the court, to the claim, and not to the action of the guardian.

SEC. 154. The guardian shall not allow, and the court shall not approve, any claim, except as provided for in Section 95 of this act, unless it be accompanied by an affidavit of the claimant "that the claim is just, that nothing has been paid or delivered towards the satisfaction of such claim, except what is mentioned or credited (if any), that there are no counter-claims known to affiant which have not been allowed (if any), and that the sum claim is justly due."

SEC. 155. Where the claim is not founded on an instrument in writing or an account, in addition to the statements required by the preceding section the affidavit must state the facts on which the claim is founded.

SEC. 156. Where a claim belongs to a corporation, the cashier, treasurer, or managing agent shall make the affidavit required to authenticate it.

SEC. 157. When an affidavit is made by an officer of a corporation, executor, administrator, trustee, assignee or attorney, it shall be sufficient to state in such affidavit "that he has made diligent inquiry and examination, and that he does verily believe that nothing has been paid and delivered towards the satisfaction of such claim, except the amount credited (if any), that there are no counter-claims which have not been allowed (if any), and that the sum claimed is justly due."

SEC. 158. A claim which the guardian held against the ward at the time of his appointment, or which has since accrued, is exhibited by being filed, verified by the affidavit of the guardian; after which it takes the same course as other claims.

SEC. 159. When a claim is presented to the guardian, properly authenticated, he shall endorse thereon or annex thereto a memorandum in writing signed by him, stating the time of its presentment, and that he allows or rejects it, or what portion thereof he allows, if any.

SEC. 160. The failure or refusal of a guardian to endorse on or annex to any claim presented to him, his allowance or rejection thereof shall be deemed to be a rejection; and in such case the costs, if the claim be established, shall be adjudged against the guardian, to be paid out of his own estate.

SEC. 161. After a claim has been presented to the guardian and allowed, the claimant shall file it with the Clerk of the County Court.

SEC. 162. When a claim, or a part thereof, has been rejected, the claimant, if he does not submit thereto, shall instiue suit thereon within ninety days after its rejection by the guardian, or the same shall be barred.

SEC. 163. At each term of the court all claims which have been allowed and filed shall be examined and approved or disapproved by an order duly entered; all claims which have been presented, whether allowed or approved or not, shall be assigned to their proper class. Claims may be referred by the court to an auditor, and the action of the court may be based upon his report.

SEC. 164. At each term of the court, in like manner, all claims which the guardian shall have been sued upon, and shall be established by suit, shall be examined and classed.

SEC. 165. When a guardian is sued upon a rejected claim, the endorsement thereon or annexed thereto of its rejection, shall be taken to be true without proof, unless it be denied under oath.

SEC. 166. Any person interested in the guardianship may appear and contest any of the claims, and shall be entitled to process to compel the attendance of witnesses, as in ordinary suits.

SEC. 167. Although a claim be properly authenticated and allowed, if the court be not well satisfied that it is just, it shall send for persons and papers, and may examine the claimant and the guardian under oath. If the court be not entirely convinced in such case by evidence other than the testimony of the claimant that the claim is just, it shall be disapproved. Suit may be brought to establish a claim which has been disapproved, within ninety days after such disapproval.

Sec. 168. The order of approval of a claim has the force and effect of a judgment.

Sec. 169. A claim is said to be legally exhibited: *First*—When it is properly presented to the guardian, and after being allowed by him is filed; or, *Second*—After being rejected by him, suit is commenced thereon.

Sec. 170. A claim is said to be established when it has been allowed by the guardian, and approved by the court; or, when in such suit thereon by the claimant, it has been sustained by the court.

Sec. 171. It is the duty of the guardian to report to the court a list of all judgments and special liens presented to him for allowance; and in like manner all suits for money pending against the ward at the time of the appointment and revived against the guardian, and all claims which have been presented or rejected.

Sec. 172. Claims which have not been legally exhibited within the year, may be exhibited at any time afterwards, before the estate is closed, or suit on such claims would be barred by the general law of limitations.

Sec. 173. The general law of limitations is interrupted: *First*—By filing a claim which has been allowed. *Second*—By presenting a claim, and commencing suit thereon within ninety days after its rejection or disapproval.

Sec. 174. Where a claim is lost or cannot be produced, the claimant may make an affidavit of the facts and present it to the guardian, or cause it to be filed with the same effect as the claim itself; but, in such case, the claim must be proved by disinterested testimony produced in court or taken by deposition, before it shall be approved.

Sec. 175. Where, by reason of a claim, being a claim against another person, or other like sufficient cause, it is inconvenient for a claimant to permit the same to remain on file, the court may, after such claim shall have been approved, order a copy thereof to be retained, and certified by the Clerk, and the original to be delivered to the claimant or his attorney.

Sec. 176. A docket shall be kept which shall be known as the claim docket. It shall be ruled at proper intervals from top to bottom, with a short note of the contents at the top of each column. One or more pages shall be assigned to each estate, in proportion to the probable number of claims which will be exhibited against it. In the marginal column shall be entered the names of the claimants, in the order in which their claims are filed, and when they are filed; the second column shall contain the amount of the claim; the third, its date; the fourth, when due; the fifth, the date from which it bears interest; the sixth, the rate of interest; the seventh, when allowed, in whole or in part, by the guardian; the eighth, the amount allowed; the ninth, the date of rejection; the tenth, the date of filing; the eleventh, when approved; the twelfth, the amount approved; the thirteenth, when disapproved; the fourteenth, the class to which the claim belongs; the fifteenth, when established by suit in the court; the sixteenth, the amount of judgment. When the entry is of any act in the court, the docket and the page shall be stated. An index shall be kept, showing the names of the wards, and the page on which the abstract of claims against them will be found.

SEC. 177. The court by which any person of unsound mind or habitual drunkard is committed to guardianship, may make order for the support of his family, and the education of his children.

SEC. 178. If any person shall be furiously mad, or so far disordered in his mind as to endanger his own person, or the person or property of others, it shall be the duty of his guardian, or other person under whose care he may be, and who is bound to provide for his support, to confine him in some suitable place until the first term of the County Court of his county, which shall make such order for the restraint, support and safe keeping of such person as the circumstances shall require.

SEC. 179. If any such person of unsound mind, as in the last section specified, shall not be confined by those having charge of him, or if there be no person having such charge, any Judge of the County, District or Supreme Court, or Justice of the Peace of the county, may cause such insane persons to be apprehended, and may employ any person to confine him in some suitable place until the court shall make further order thereon, as provided in the preceding section.

SEC. 180. The father and mother of persons of unsound mind and habitual drunkards, shall maintain them at their own charge, if able to do so; and the children and grandchildren of such persons shall maintain them at their own charge, if able to do so.

SEC. 181. The expenses attending the confinement of an insane person shall be paid by the guardian out of the estate of the ward, or by the person bound to provide for and support such insane person.

SEC. 182. In all cases of appropriations out of the County Treasury, for the support or confinement of any person of unsound mind, or habitual drunkards, the amount thereof may be recovered by the county from any person, who, by law, is bound to provide for the support of such person of unsound mind or habitual drunkard, if there be any such person able to pay the same.

SEC. 183. If any person shall allege under oath that a person declared to be of unsound mind or a habitual drunkard, has been restored to his right mind, or to correct, sober habits, the court shall inquire into the fact by a jury, if the fact be doubtful.

SEC. 184. If it be found that such person has been reformed or restored to his right mind, he shall be discharged from guardianship, and the guardian shall immediately settle his accounts and deliver up all the property remaining in his hands.

SEC. 185. In case of the death of any such ward, while under guardianship, the power of the guardian shall cease, and he shall immediately settle his accounts and deliver the estate to the person or persons entitled to receive it.

SEC. 186. The following papers shall be copied at length in the record, or in dockets specially provided for the purpose: *First*—All notices, whether published or posted, with the return thereon. *Second* —All wills and the testimony on which the same are admitted to probate. *Third*—All bonds and official oaths. *Fourth*—All inventories and appraisements. *Fifth*—All accounts of sales. *Sixth*—All reports, returns and accounts. Notices shall be copied in connection with the proceedings had upon the return thereof. Proper indexes shall be kept, in the names of the deceased persons and wards, referring to every order, proceeding and recorded paper.

SEC. 187. Every order made in term time or in vacation, shall state whether any opposition was made, and by whom made, if any. Orders made in vacation shall be filed with the Clerk and be entered of record.

Sec. 188. Certified copies taken from the record of all papers required to be recorded shall have the same effect as copies taken directly from the originals.

Sec. 189. The provisions of law regulating costs and security therefor, shall apply to costs in matters of probate, so far as the same are not controlled by the succeeding sections of this act.

Sec. 190. The costs incurred in the exhibition and establishment of claims shall be taxed as follows: *First*—If a claim which has been allowed be disapproved, the claimant shall pay the costs. *Second*—If a claim which has been rejected be established, the estate shall pay the costs.

Sec. 191. In all cases where a guardian or trustee shall neglect the performance of any duty required of him, and shall be notified to appear before the court on account thereof, he shall pay all costs of such proceedings out of his own estate.

Sec. 192. In all cases where a party shall make any application or opposition, and on the trial thereof he shall be defeated, he shall be liable for all costs occasioned by such application or opposition.

Sec. 193. The costs of partition and of distribution must be paid by the respective parties in proportion to their interests.

Sec. 194. When any person shall be found to be of unsound mind, the costs of the proceeding shall be paid out of his estate, or if that be insufficient, by the county.

Sec. 195. If the person be discharged, the costs shall be paid by the person at whose instance the proceeding was had, unless such person be an officer, acting officially under the provisions of this act, in which case the costs shall be paid by the county.

Sec. 196. Special guardians and attorneys appointed to represent absentees, shall receive a reasonable compensation, which the court shall determine, and order to be paid out of the shares of the persons whom they represent.

Sec. 197. Any person who may consider himself aggrieved by any decision, order or judgment of the court, or by any order of the Judge thereof, may appeal to the District Court as a matter of right without bond.

Sec. 198. An appeal is taken by causing an entry of notice thereof to be made on the record during the term at which such decision, order or judgment is entered; or if the order be made in vacation, by causing the entry of such notice to be made before the close of the next term.

Sec. 199. When such notice has been given, a certified transcript of the proceeding shall be made out and transmitted to the District Court. Such transcript shall not contain anything which does not relate to the order, decision or judgment appealed from. When notice of appeal has been given by the same person from more than one decision, order or judgment entered of record, in the same estate, at the same term, all of the appeals may be embraced in the same transcript.

Sec. 200. If there be not time to make out such transcript before the first day of the next term of the District Court after such appeal is taken, it shall be transmitted to said court within sixty days after such appeal be taken.

Sec. 201. The appeal shall not suspend the decision, order or judgment, except in the cases mentioned in the succeeding section, unless the appellant, within twenty days after the entry thereof, cause a bond to be filed in an amount fixed by the court at the time of entry of appeal, signed by one or more sureties, payable to and approved by the Clerk, to the effect that the appellant shall perform the orders and judgment which the District Court may make therein, in case the decision be against him.

SEC. 202. An appeal suspends the decision, order or judgment, without bond: *First*—When taken by a claimant from the disapproval of his claim. *Second*—When taken by the guardian or trustee, except where the controversy is respecting the rights of guardianship or the settlement of an account.

SEC. 203. When the certified copy of the judgment of the District Court is received, it shall be entered of record as the decision, order or judgment of the County Court.

SEC. 204. Where a certified copy of the order or judgment of the District Court is received, dismissing an appeal or quashing a supersedeas, it shall be entered of record, and the decision, order or judgment shall stand as if no appeal or supersedeas had been taken or obtained.

SEC. 205. Any person interested may, by a bill of review filed in the court in which the proceedings were had, have any decision, order or judgment rendered under this act, revised and corrected, on showing error therein. But no process or action under such decision, order or judgment shall be stayed, except by writ of injunction.

SEC. 206. A suit by bill of review must be commenced within two years after the proceedings were had that are sought to be reviewed, saving to persons *non compos mentis*, infants and *femme-coverts*, two years after their respective disabilities are removed.

SEC. 207. That acts and parts of acts in conflict with the provisions of this act be and the same are hereby repealed.

SEC. 208. There being no law in force in conformity with the Constitution relative to guardianships, therefore an imperative public emergency and necessity exists that this act be immediately passed and take effect from and after its passage, and it is so enacted.

Approved August 18, 1876.

Takes effect from its passage.

CHAPTER CXIII.—*An Act to provide for the resumption by the State of the possession and control of the State Penitentiary, at Huntsville, and of all the property and convicts belonging thereto, and to provide for the settlement of all matters between the lessees and State, growing out of the termination of the lease of said penitentiary, and to provide for the management and control of said penitentiary and convicts after the termination of said lease, and to make the necessary appropiations therefor.*

SECTION 1. *Be it enacted by the Legislature of the State of Texas,* That the Governor be and he is authorized and required at such time and in such manner as he may deem necessary or expedient to take and resume, in behalf of the State, the possession, control and management of the penitentiary, at Huntsville, and all the property and convicts belonging thereto, whether within or without the walls of said penitentiary, and upon such resumption, the lease heretofore made to A. J. Ward, E. C. Dewy, and Nathan Patton, and all the authorities and powers conferred thereby shall cease and determine, and said lessees shall upon demand turn over, surrender and deliver to such person or persons as may be designated by the Governor, the said penitentiary, its property and convicts.

13 GL

SEC. 2.   As soon as practicable after resuming possession of said penitentiary, the Governor shall, in behalf of the State, appoint and employ
such appraisers, accountants, arbitrators, and counsel to represent the
interests of the State, as he may think necessary, and take any and all
other steps which he may deem proper for the purpose of securing a
fair, just and equitable settlement of all claims, demands, accounts and
controversies of every character whatsoever between the State and said
lessees, growing out of or arising under or incident to the leasing of
said penitentiary to said lessees and the determination of said lease ;
provided, that in any settlement to be made the State shall not take any
property, real or personal, or any machinery, materials or other thing
belonging to the lessees, which under the lease the State is not required
to take unless such property, machinery, material or other thing be
necessary for or can be utilized in operating the penitentiary, or unless the taking of such property be necessary to liquidate indebtedness
of said lessees to the State, in which case the same may be received at
the appraised value ; and in making the settlement, property, real or
personal, may be exchanged, and the Governor may execute in the name
of the State any deeds or other conveyances required for this purpose.

SEC. 3.   If upon a settlement, as provided for in the preceding section, the State be found to be indebted to said lessees, and such settlement be certified by the appraisers and arbitrators, the Governor, if he
approve such settlement, shall direct the Comptroller to draw his warrant on the Treasurer in favor of said lessees for the amount of such
indebtedness ; *provided*, that said lessees, before being entitled to receive
such warrant, shall execute and file with the Comptroller a full release,
discharge and acquittance in substance, form and manner as may be directed by the Governor.

SEC. 4.   If no satisfactory settlement as contemplated by the preceding sections can be made, then either the State or said lessees, or
both, may bring suit in the District Court of Travis County for the enforcement and adjustment of any right or claim or the recovery of any
balances between the State and said lessees ; and appeal, or writ of error,
may be prosecuted from any final judgment or decree of said District
Court, as in other cases ; *provided*, that nothing contained in this section
shall be construed to prevent the State from suing said lessees or either
of them, or their or either of their sureties, on their bonds ; or from
adopting or pursuing any other or different legal measures for the enforcement of any claim or right in behalf of the State, of any character
whatsoever ; or for the recovery from said lessees of any property, sum,
balances or penalties, to which the State may be entitled ; *and provided
further*, that in no suit or proceeding in any court of the State, shall
the State be required to pay any costs or give any bond.

SEC. 5.   To defray the expenses attending the determination of the
lease and the settlement with the lessees, and to provide the means for
paying the lessees any balance that may, in an adjustment, be found in
their favor, or that may be established against the State by the judgment
of a court, the sum of five thousand dollars, or so much thereof as may
be necessary, be, and the same is hereby appropriated out of the State
Treasury ; and, upon the approval of said claims by the Governor, the
Comptroller shall draw his warrant on the Treasurer for the amount
thereof, and the Treasurer shall pay the same.

SEC. 6.   Upon the resumption of the possession and control of said
penitentiary, the Governor shall appoint three Commissioners, to hold

office for two years, each of whom shall receive an annual salary of two thousand dollars, to be paid quarterly out of the State Treasury, who, in conjunction with the Governor, shall take such measures and adopt such rules and regulations for the control and management of the penitentiary and the convicts belonging thereto as may be deemed best, not inconsistent with the laws prescribing the treatment and management of convicts; and such rules and regulations shall be binding upon all officers of the penitentiary, guards, employes, hirers of convict labor, and all others in any way connected with the penitentiary, or the convicts within or without the walls; and one of said Commissioners shall, at least twice in each month, visit the penitentiary and each place at which convicts may be employed; and said Commissioners shall meet and confer twice each month on matters pertaining to the penitentiary and its management, and shall, once in each month, make a full report to the Governor upon all such matters as he may require connected with the penitentiary and the management of the convicts, and discharge such other duties as may be required by the Governor, or by law; and said Commissioners may be removed at the discretion of the Governor.

SEC. 7. Upon the resumption of the State Penitentiary, under the provisions of this act, the Governor is hereby authorized and required as soon as possible to lease the same by public advertisement, for such time not to exceed fifteen years, and upon such terms and conditions as may be deemed best, special regard being had, as far as practicable, to the exaction of the penalty imposed by law on each convict, and to the protection, well being and humane treatment to which each convict is entitled at the hands of the State; and any lease made shall be subject to the approval or revocation of any Legislature of the State thereafter convening, and to any and all laws touching the penitentiary or convicts, thereafter passed, and any failure on the part of the lessee or lessees, to carry out, in good faith, any of the terms of such lease or to comply with any of the conditions and stipulations of any bond which may be given by them, shall operate as a forfeiture of all authority and powers under such lease, and the Governor may at once declare the same terminated, and again resume possession and control, as though such lease had not been made; and no lease shall be made by which the control of the prisoners, except as to a reasonable amount of labor, shall pass from the State or its officers to the lessees; and the State shall, in all cases, and under all circumstance, retain the absolute control of the persons of the convicts, put them to or withdraw them from any kind of labor; station and remove them at or from any point inside or outside of the prison; make or change at pleasure, all rules for the discipline and punishment of convicts; prescribe regulations for their food, clothing, nursing, instruction and guarding; and any lease made shall be subject to the reservation of these rights and powers on the part of the State, whether so stated in the lease or not; the object of these limitations being to prevent the State, under the guise of contract, from parting with the right to direct how, at any time and under all circumstances, convicts shall be lodged, fed, clothed, worked and treated; *provided*, that no convict shall be hired or leased to do any labor outside of prison walls, and detached from the prison when there is sufficient room for their accommodation within the walls of the penitentiary or penitentiaries of the State, and their labor can be utilized within said prison; *provided*, that if the Governor shall be unable to again lease the penitentiary as required in this section, the same shall be managed and controlled as the law may direct.

SEC. 8.   The right to hire or operate convicts outside the prison walls is hereby expressly given, but this right shall be exercised only under such rules, and with respect to such class or classes of convicts, as the Governor and Commissioners may prescribe.

SEC. 9.   For the purpose of providing the means with which to operate said penitentiary, feed, clothe, manage, guard and utilize the labor of the convicts, in case the possession and control of said penitentiary, its property and convicts shall, as hereinbefore provided, be resumed by the State, the sum of thirty thousand dollars, or so much thereof as may be necessary, be and the same is hereby appropriated, out of the State Treasury, to be paid out of any moneys not otherwise appropriated, on the warrants of the Comptroller, which warrants shall be issued only upon accounts approved by the Governor, or any two of said Commissioners, and the receipts and disbursements of all moneys shall be governed by such rules as the Governor and said Commissioners shall prescribe.

SEC. 10.   Whereas, the management of the penitentiary and convicts is wholly inadequate to the public necessities and wants, and an imperative public necessity existing for a change, thus creating an emergency therefor, that this act take effect and be in force from and after its passage.

Approved August 19, 1876.

Takes effect ninety days after adjournment.

CHAPTER CXIV.—*An Act to provide District and County Surveyors with offices in the various districts and counties of the State.*

SECTION 1.   *Be it enacted by the Legislature of the State of Texas,* That the District and County Surveyors of this State are authorized to rent some suitable building or room in which to keep their offices, in case the said Surveyors cannot be provided with offices in the court-houses of their respective counties.

SEC. 2.   The County Commissioners' Court shall make the necessary arrangement for paying the rent of an office rented by said Surveyors, upon satisfactory evidence showing that the rent was reasonable and the office necessary, and that there was no office provided for said Surveyors in the court-house of their county.

SEC. 3.   The fact that the Surveyors of some of the counties being without offices, except as provided through their own means, creates an emergency which requires that this act take effect and be in force from and after its passage, and it is so enacted.

Passed August 18, 1876.

Takes effect from its passage.

CHAPTER CXV.—*An Act to define the duties of persons subject to taxation by the laws of this State and fix the penalties for the violation of the same.*

SECTION 1.   *Be it enacted by the Legislature of the State of Texas,* That it is hereby made the duty of every person subject to taxation by the laws of this State, to make out and render a list of his, her or their taxable property, both real and personal, under oath, to the Assessor of Taxes, or before some officer authorized to take the acknowledgments of any instruments of writing for record, and it is also made the duty of each person rendering property for taxation to subscribe the oath of affirmation required to be subscribed to in section five of an act to define the duties, powers, qualifications and liabilities of Assessors of Taxes, and to regulate their compensation, passed by this session of this Legislature

SEC. 2. That any person who shall refuse or neglect to make out and render a list of his, her, or their taxable property when called upon in person by the Assessor of Taxes, or his deputy, or any person who shall fail or refuse to qualify to the truth of his, her or their statement, as prescribed in section five of the act referred to in section one of this act; or who shall fail or refuse to subscribe to the oath or affirmation as required in section five of the act above referred to, shall be guilty of a misdemeanor, and on conviction for each offence, shall be fined in any sum not less than twenty nor more than one thousand dollars.

Approved August 19, 1876.

Takes effect ninety days after adjournment.

CHAPTER CXVI.—*An Act to amend Section 1 of an act entitled: "An Act for the benefit of actual occupants of the Public Lands," approved May 26, 1873.*

SECTION 1. *Be it enacted by the Legislature of the State of Texas*, That Section 1 of an act entitled: "An Act for the benefit of actual occupants of the public lands," shall hereafter read as follows:

"SECTION 1. That any person who has occupied or shall occupy any portion of the public domain as a homestead, under any previous or existing law, shall have the same surveyed and the field notes returned to the Land Office within twelve months after settling upon the same, or as provided in Section 2 of this act, and such person, or his assignee or assignees, shall be entitled to a patent therefor upon filing in the Land Office an affidavit to the effect that such person, or his assigns, have occupied and improved said lands for three years in good faith, and has complied with the requirements of this act and paid all fees which affidavit shall be corroborated by the affidavit of two disinterested and credible citizens of the county in which the land is situated, all of which affidavits shall be subscribed and sworn to before the Clerk of the District or County Court, who shall certify to the same and the credibility of said citizens under the seal of his office; *provided,* that when in any county the affidavit required by the first section of said act to be made before a District Clerk, has been since the 18th day of April, 1876, made before a Clerk of the County Court, such affidavit and certificate of said Clerk, shall be sufficient and as valid in every respect as if such affidavit had been made before the District Clerk.

SEC. 2. Whereas, since the 18th day of April, 1876, the affidavit required by the first section of the act of which this act is amendatory has in many instances been made before County Clerks, instead of District Clerks, as required by said act, which creates an imperative public necessity for the immediate passage of this act, that the acts of County Clerks in such cases may be at once validated, therefore, this act take effect and be in force from and after its passage.

Approved August 19, 1876.

Takes effect from its passage.

CHAPTER CXVII.—*An Act to levy a tax on the privilege of keeping or harboring dogs, and to provide for the assessment and collection of the same.*

WHEREAS, There are in many localities in this State, a very large number of dogs, and there are strong indications of a prevalence to hydrophobia, from which much danger will result to the lives and property of citizens ; therefore,

SECTION 1. *Be it enacted by the Legislature of the State of Texas,* That the keeping of dogs shall be a privilege which shall be taxed as follows : Every owner or harborer of a dog, or dogs, shall pay one dollar ($1.00) on each dog, to be collected as other taxes of the State and county, and paid into the County Treasury for the use and benefit of public free schools in the county ; *provided,* that one dog to each family shall be exempt from taxation.

SEC. 2. That it shall be the duty of the Tax Assessors to enumerate and assess, as hereinbefore provided, every dog within his county, on the first day of January of each year, and the Tax Collector shall collect the same. The Assessor shall cause each person to state on oath the number and kind of dogs owned or harbored by him or her.

SEC. 3. That if any person shall keep a dog that has been assessed for taxes under this act, and shall fail to pay the tax on the same on or before the first day of January next after said assessment is made, he or she shall be guilty of a misdemeanor, and upon conviction thereof in any court of competent jurisdiction, shall be fined not less than five dollars ($5.00) and costs for each dog so kept. And it is hereby made the duty of County Attorneys to prosecute, upon his own motion, all delinquent tax-payers under this act.

SEC. 4. That in payment of the dog tax, the scalps of the cougar, panther, bear, wolf and catamount shall be received at two dollars ($2.00) for each scalp ; also, the scalps of leopards, American lions and sloths, and the scalps of the wild cat and red fox at one dollar ($1.00) each, and the grey fox at fifty cents each ; and the scalps of raccoons shall be received at twenty-five cents for each scalp ; *provided,* that the party presenting any of such scalps in payment of tax shall make affidavit before some officer authorized to administer oaths that the animal was captured and killed in the county.

SEC. 5. That whenever the Collector shall receive, in payment of any tax assessed under this act, any scalps, as provided in section four, he shall present the same to the County Treasurer, on or before the first day of January after the assessment was made. The County Treasurer shall credit the Collector with the amounts of said scalps on the basis of value as fixed for the same in section four of this act. And it shall be the duty of the Treasurer, in the presence of the Collector and at least one other commissioned officer of the county, to immediately destroy, or cause to be destroyed, all of such scalps so received by burning.

SEC. 6. That an imperative public necessity and emergency exist for the immediate passage of this act, and it is hereby declared that the same take effect from and after its passage.

Approved August 19, 1876.

Takes effect ninety days after adjournment.

CHAPTER CXVIII.—*An Act to validate the acts of the Commissioners' Courts throughout the State of Texas had from the 18th day of April, 1876, to the 15th day of August, 1876.*

SECTION 1. *Be it enacted by the Legislature of the State of Texas,* That the acts of the Commissioners' Courts had in the different counties of this State since the 18th day of April, 1876, to the 15th day of August, 1876, in the interests of their different counties are declared to be as valid and binding as if under the law defining duties and powers of Commissioners' Courts, passed by this Legislature on the 22d of July, 1876.

SEC. 2. That no inconvenience may result to the counties in which sessions of the Commissioners' Courts have already been held, a great public necessity and emergency exist that this act be of force and effect immediately upon and after its passage ; it is therefore so enacted.

Approved August 19, 1876.

Takes effect from its passage.

CHAPTER CXIX.—*An Act to provide for the election and qualification of County Treasurers and County Surveyors.*

SECTION 1. *Be it enacted by the Legislature of the State of Texas,* That at each regular biennial election for State and county officers in this State, there shall be elected in each county by the qualified voters thereof, a County Treasurer and County Surveyor, who shall take the oath of office, give the bond, and perform all the duties required by law.

SEC. 2. As there is no law providing for the election of County Treasurers and County Surveyors in the counties of this State, an imperative public necessity exists that this act take effect and be in force from and after its passage.

Approved August 19, 1876.

Takes effect from its passage.

CHAPTER CXX.—*An Act to establish and provide for the support and maintenance of an efficient system of Public Free Schools.*

SECTION 1. *Be it enacted by the Legislature of the State of Texas,* That the Governor, Comptroller, and Secretary of State, as the Board of Education, shall distribute the available school fund annually to the several counties of the State, on the basis of their scholastic population, prior to September first of each year, on which day each scholastic year shall begin.

SEC. 2. The Governor of the State shall be President of the Board of Education. A majority of said Board are authorized to perform all duties devolved by law on said Board.

SEC. 3. Said Board, if, in their judgment, the educational interests of the State require, may appoint some competent person as Secretary, who shall receive an annual salary of fifteen hundred dollars ($1500), to be paid out of the available school fund. He shall take the oath of office prescribed by the Constitution, and perform such duties as may be required by the Board.

SEC. 4. Said Board shall keep a complete record of all its proceedings, which shall be signed by the President of the Board at each session thereof. They shall cause to be filed all papers, reports, and documents transmitted to them by school officers or others, and keep a complete index thereof; they shall counsel and advise with county school officers and teachers, as to the best manner of conducting schools throughout the State, and shall give such instructions, not inconsistent with this act, to county school officers in the interest of common-school education as they may deem advisable. They shall, from time to time, address circular letters to county school officers, giving advice as to the best manner of conducting schools, constructing school-houses, furnishing the same, and procuring competent teachers. They shall cause to be printed, in pamphlet form, all school laws in force after this session of the Legislature, and a like publication after each session during which amendments may be made or new laws enacted, which shall be distributed to school officers and teachers throughout the State.

SEC. 5. They shall, one month prior to the meeting of each regular session of the Legislature, and ten days before the meeting of any special session having authority under executive proclamation to legislate on matter pertaining to public free schools, make a full report of the condition of public free schools throughout the State: the whole number of white and colored schools, which have been taught in each county in the scholastic year; the number of pupils, white and colored, in attendance receiving tuition free of charge; the number paying tuition; the number of white and colored children within scholastic age in the State; the number of scholastic age and less than eighteen years old, and how many of said number are unable to read; the number within scholastic age who have not attended school; the number within scholastic age unable to read; the amount of public free school fund; how its revenue for the previous year has been distributed and expended; the number of public free school-houses in each county, with a description of their kind and condition, together with such other information and suggestions as they may deem important for promoting education; which report shall be laid before the Legislature the first week of each session that may have power to legislate on school affairs. Whenever said reports are ordered to be published, two thousand copies shall be presented [printed], in pamphlet form, for furnishing the Legislature and such school officers and libraries in the State as the Board of Education may direct, and to Superintendents of each State and Territory.

SEC. 6. Said Board shall furnish to county school officers all blanks and forms necessary in making reports, or in carrying out such instructions as they may give them, not inconsistent with this act.

SEC. 7. Said Board shall require from school officers and teachers such reports necessary to school affairs and school funds as they may deem proper for collecting information for legislative consideration.

SEC. 8. On or before the first day of September of each year the Board of Education shall apportion the available school fund appropriated by the Legislature to the several counties in the State, according to scholastic population, upon the latest and most reliable data; and they shall issue certificates to the County Treasurer of each county for the amount of the available school fund to which said county is entitled, subject to the restrictions herein contained. They shall also furnish an abstract of said apportionment to the Comptroller of Public Accounts, and to each County Judge in this State a statement of the amount apportioned to his county.

SEC. 9. The Board of Education shall issue to school officers such instructions in the interest of public free schools as they may deem expedient, when not inconsistent with the provisions of this act.

SEC. 10. The Board of Education shall be allowed all necessary expenses for books, postage, and printing and stationery required for their office.

SEC. 11. Whenever, in this act, the words "school officers," or "officer," are used, the same shall be construed to include any officer of this State upon whom is devolved, by law, a duty pertaining to public free schools, as well as such officers as are created by this act.

SCHOOL FUND.

SEC. 12. One-fourth of the occupation and *ad valorem* taxes assessed since March 30, 1870, exclusive of the costs of collection; one-fourth of all the *ad valorem* and occupation taxes that may hereafter be collected, exclusive of the costs of collection; all poll taxes due since March 30, 1870, uncollected and which may be collected, exclusive of the costs of collection; all poll taxes hereafter to be collected, exclusive of the costs of collection; the interest arising on any bonds and funds, and all the interest derivable from the sale of lands hereinbefore set apart for the permanent school fund, belonging to the permanent school fund, and which now are or may hereafter come into the State Treasury, shall constitute the available school fund, and shall be appropriated for the establishment, support and maintenance of public free schools.

SEC. 13. All conveyances, devises and bequests of property, made by any one for the benefit of public free schools, for any county, city or town, shall, when not otherwise directed by grantor or devisor, vest said property in the County Judge of the county, or the Mayor of said city or town, and their successors in office, as the trustee for those to be benefited thereby, and the same shall, when not otherwise directed, be administered by said Judge or Mayor, subject to the approval of the Board of Education.

SEC. 14. The available public free school fund shall be distributed to school communities in the several counties, to be organized on the application of the parents and guardians of those to be benefited thereby to suit their convenience, without reference to geographical lines within the counties.

SEC. 15. The available public free school fund shall be appropriated in each county for the education alike of white and colored children, and each race shall receive its just *pro rata*, as far as practicable, in each county, according to the number of children of each race within scholastic age.

SEC. 16. No school in which sectarian religion is taught shall be entitled to any portion of the available public school fund, nor shall any form of religion be taught in any public free school in this State.

STATE COMPTROLLER'S DUTIES IN REGARD TO SCHOOL FUND.

SEC. 17. The Comptroller of the State shall keep a separate account of the amount of available school funds arising from every source; he shall, on or before the meeting of each regular session of the Legislature, report the amount of the available school fund that he may estimate will be received for the next two years, and which may be subject to appropriation for the establishment and support of public free schools, and the several sources from which they accrue; he shall draw his warrant on the State Treasurer in favor of any County Treasurer, or in favor of any County Collector of Taxes, in the manner and under the circumstances provided by this act for the amount of such fund due his county, on presentation of a certificate from the Board of Education issued to the County Treasurer, showing the amount to which such county is entitled, duly endorsed by the County Treasurer.

DUTIES OF STATE TREASURER PERTAINING TO SCHOOL FUND.

SEC. 18.   It shall be the duty of the Treasurer of the State to receive and hold as a special deposit all school moneys, and he shall keep a correct account of the several sources from which they accrue; he shall report to the Governor thirty days before the meeting of any session of the Legislature, which may have power to legislate regarding public school funds, and at such other times as the Board of Education may require, the condition of the permanent and available school fund; the amount of each in the Treasury, and the manner and amount of disbursement since his last report.   He shall pay out the available school fund whenever applied for, only on a warrant of the State Comptroller issued on certificates of the Board of Education, on each of which shall be endorsed the name of the party to whom it was payable.   He shall, under no circumstances, use any portion of the permanent or available school fund in payment of any warrant drawn against any other fund whatever.

SCHOLASTIC AGE.

SEC. 19.   All children between the ages of eight and fourteen years shall be entitled to the benefit of the available free school fund, under this act, without regard to race or color.

SCHOLASTIC CENSUS.

SEC. 20.   It shall be the duty of the Assessor of Taxes of the several counties in the State to take a careful census of the children in their counties, who will be of the age of eight and not over the age of fourteen years on the first day of September succeeding the taking of such census, which census shall contain the name, sex, age and race.   A separate census shall be made out and returned by the Assessor, embracing the population within scholastic age within the limits of each incorporate city and town in his county, which shall contain the same data required in making the general census.   All children known to the Assessor to contain an admixture of African blood shall be returned as colored.   Said list shall, after being sworn to by the Assessor, be returned to the Clerk of the County Court, together with two abstracts of the same, showing the number of children, white and colored, male and female, and such other data as may be required, on the forms furnished by the Board of Education, on or before the first day of July in each year; and shall not receive any compensation unless the same is properly made out and returned on said day.   One of the said abstracts shall be forwarded to the Board of Education, and the County Clerk shall retain the other and record it in a separate book, after it shall be approved by the County Judge.   The copy of said abstract shall be forwarded by the County Judge to the Board of Education immediately after the completion of the assessment of the county, as required by law, and prior to August first of each year. No allowance shall be made by the Comptroller for any assessment of taxes in any county until the County Assessor shall exhibit and file with him a certificate from the Clerk of the County Court of his county, that said census, reports and abstracts have been correctly taken, as required by law, approved by the County Judge, and filed by said Assessor.   And said Assessor shall receive for the enumeration of such scholastic population : for the first one thousand, four cents *per capita*, and two and one (half) cents for all numbers over one thousand for each and every child so enrolled on said lists, to be paid out of the common free school fund by the County Treasurer, on the certificate of the County Judge showing how much he may be entitled to receive. The County Clerk, for services required by this act, shall be allowed such compensation as may be allowed by the Board of Education, not to exceed one-eighth of the amount allowed for like labor under the other laws regulating the fees of office.

SEC. 21. Assessors, in taking a scholastic census, shall in all cases make careful inquiry as to the age of the child, availing themselves of all accessible information, and may, in their discretion, require the parent or guardian to answer under oath upon the question of age.

COUNTY TREASURER.

SEC. 22. The Treasurers of the several counties in this State shall be Treasurers of the available public free school fund for their respective counties ; and they shall be allowed only one per cent. commissions for disbursing the same, but shall be entitled to no commissions for receiving or collecting the same; *provided*, that should the Collector of Taxes of the county make default in paying over to the Treasurer on the certificate of the Board of Education, in a reasonable time, such Treasurer shall be allowed in settlement of his account such exchange for collecting the *pro rata* distributive portion of school fund due his county as may be allowed and certified to by the Board of Education.

SEC. 23. On receipt of notice from the Board of Education of the amount of State fund apportioned to the county, the County Treasurer shall execute bond for double the amount thus apportioned, with two or more good securities, to be approved by the County Judge, conditioned that he will safely keep and faithfully disburse the school fund according to law, and pay such warrants as may be drawn on said fund by competent authority. No certificate entitling said Treasurer to receive said *pro rata* of the school fund shall be issued by the Board of Education until a certificate has been received by said Board of Education from the County Judge, that the bond herein required of the Treasurer has been executed according to law, and that it has been filed and approved by the County Judge ; *provided*, that such bond, when once executed by the County Treasurer, shall entitle him to receive the *pro rata* of the school fund for his county annually, until otherwise ordered by the Board of Education.

SEC. 24. The County Treasurer shall keep a record of all school funds received by him, showing the year for which the same are to be disbursed, and shall credit school communities, after numbering and otherwise designating such communities, with such amounts as may be apportioned to them by the County Judge. All balances of the general fund not appropriated for the current year shall be carried over by the Treasurer as part of the general fund for the county for the succeeding year, and balances unexpended or unappropriated for a school community shall be carried over for the benefit of such school community if it be reorganized for the following year ; and if it be not reorganized, shall be added to the general fund for distribution for the general benefit of the county at large.

SEC. 25. That where there is any money or other property in the County Treasury to the credit of any school district, as constituted under the law repealed by this act, upon application to the County Judge by the trustees of any school community, incorporated city or town composing a part of said district, it shall be the duty of said County Judge to notify the trustees of the school communities composing the balance of said district to appear before him on a day named in said notice; and upon said date he shall enter up his order, making an equitable partition and distribution of said money and other property to the various communities, incorporated cities and towns, composing said original district; a copy of which order shall be delivered to the County Treasurer for his guidance, and the fund so distributed shall constitute a part of the available school fund for said communities; *provided*, that this section shall not be construed to authorize the sale of any real estate already appropriated or purchased for public school purposes, situated in an incorporated city or town, constituting a separate school district, until the consent of the municipal authorities has been obtained; *and provided further*, that out of said money in the County Treasury to the credit of any school district, the amount or amounts due teachers to 31st of August, 1876, under the law repealed by this act, shall be first paid before said money or property shall be partitioned and distributed to the various communities.

SEC. 26.   It shall be the duty of the Sheriffs or Tax Collectors of the several counties to pay over to the County Treasurers thereof all money collected by virtue of any school tax heretofore levied, and all persons who, while holding the office of Sheriff, have collected such money and have not accounted for the same, shall be liable on their official bonds therefor.   And all moneys in the hands of the Treasurers of the School Boards, of the Tax Collectors and the County Treasurer, that have been, or may hereafter be, collected or paid into the County Treasury, are hereby placed under the control of the County Commissioners' Court, and shall be paid out on warrants drawn by their order for such purposes as are now, or may hereafter be, provided by law.   And the County or District Attorney shall institute suit against any and all persons who fail or refuse to comply with the provisions of this section.

SEC. 27.   Upon receipt of a certificate from the Board of Education, countersigned by the Comptroller of Public Accounts, stating the amount of the available school fund to which any county is entitled, the Treasurer of such county shall present the same to the Collector of Taxes of his county, who shall pay the amount therein specified, from time to time, as taxes payable in the State Treasury, which payment shall be receipted for on the certificate, and also a receipt shall be given to the Collector; and when the whole is collected, the County Treasurer shall deliver the said certificate to the Collector of Taxes, in whose hands it shall be a voucher for so much money in his settlement with the Comptroller of the State.

BOARD OF SCHOOL EXAMINERS.

SEC. 28.   It shall be the duty of the County Judge to appoint a Board of School Examiners for his county, for each scholastic year, consisting of three well educated citizens of the county, who shall examine, before their employment, all teachers of public free schools, for which service they shall receive from each applicant examined by them three dollars. Every teacher, before being employed to teach any of the public free schools of this State, must obtain from the County Judge, on the report of the Board of School Examiners, a certificate of qualification; and no teacher can make a legal contract to teach a public free school without first obtaining such certificate.

SCHOOL COMMUNITIES.

SEC. 29. Parents and guardians, or next friend, of any minor, residents of any county of this State, on or after the first Monday of January, and up to the beginning of the next scholastic year, in order to avail themselves of the benefits of the available school fund for their county, for the scholastic year, beginning the next succeeding September, may organize themselves into school communities, embracing such population as may agree to avail themselves of the benefits of the available public free school fund, on the following terms, viz: They shall make out a list to be signed in person by such parents and guardians as desire to avail themselves of the available school fund; which list shall include the names and ages of children to be instructed, who may be within the scholastic age, on the first day of the next September, which names of children shall be made in alphabetical order, which list shall also include all minors within scholastic age in said community, who have no legal guardians; said list, together with an application to the County Judge, stating that they desire, in good faith, to organize a school at such place as they may designate, shall be filed with the County Judge; said application shall also show the capacity of the school houses, and school conveniences, if any. The Assessor, when taking the sholastic census, shall also ascertain to what community each child belongs; and if it appears that any child is not included in any community list, the County Judge shall assign such child to the most convenient and appropriate community, and set apart to said community such a child's *pro rata* of the fund.

SEC. 30. The application to establish a school, in case there be a school house reported, shall ask that the *pro rata* of the available school fund, properly due to the number of children reported, be credited to said school community.

SEC. 31. On receipt of such a petition from a school community, the County Judge shall compare the list of pupils presented in such application with the census made out by the County Assessor, and if the names of the children within scholastic age appear on said list, or if proof be made that they should have been placed on said list, and the County Judge be satisfied that the petition is in good faith, he shall enter an order, in a book kept for that purpose, sanctioning the establishing of said school community, and shall designate it by its name and number.

SEC. 32. School communities may be organized, when population will permit, for separate male and female schools, or for mixed schools, male and female, as the necessities and condition of each community may require. Three trustees shall be appointed by the County Judge for each community, who shall discharge such duties as are herein prescribed, or which may be prescribed by the Board of Education, and who shall see that the school for which they are trustees shall be conducted in accordance with the provisions and limitations of this act.

SEC. 33. After the receipt from the Board of Education of a certificate showing the amount of State school fund due the county for the next succeeding scholastic year, the County Judge shall apportion the same to the scholastic population of his county, according to the last census taken by the Assessor, as the same may have been corrected by inserting or omitting names, and direct the County Treasurer to credit the school communities, by number and name, with the amount of said school fund to which their scholastic population may be entitled in the aggregate.

Sec. 34.　The trustees of any school community, already provided with a school-house, desiring to avail themselves of the benefits of a public free school, shall employ a teacher holding a certificate of competency, issued by the Board of Examiners herein provided for, to teach school for such community at such time during the scholastic year as they may designate, having due regard for the convenience of the community: *provided*, however, that every school shall be taught, as nearly as practicable without intermission for the period contracted for with the teacher.

Sec. 35.　The trustees of each school community shall contract with the teacher to continue the school for the longest time they may be able to agree, for the benefit of the pupils within the scholastic age, for the *pro rata* of the school fund to which such community may be entitled, permitting said teacher to instruct, in said school, pupils over or under the scholastic age, and to teach branches not herein prescribed as the public school course of study, at such rates as he and the patrons may agree upon; *provided*, that no school with one teacher shall exceed forty pupils, except by the consent of the trustees.

Sec. 36.　The contract between the trustees and the teacher shall be in writing, and shall specify the number of months the school is to be taught, and the wages per month.　After being signed by the trustees and teacher, it shall be filed with the Clerk of the County Court, who shall safely keep the same; *provided*, teachers shall not receive more than one dollar and fifty cents per month for each pupil within the scholastic age in any school community.

Sec. 37.　The Board of Education shall provide teachers with a register, in which the names, age, studies, and daily attendance of pupils shall be recorded; and with the blank forms to enable them to make proper reports through the County Judge to the Board of Education about such matters as the Board of Education may instruct.

Sec. 38.　The amount contracted by trustees to be paid a teacher shall be paid on a check drawn by a majority of the trustees on the County Treasurer and approved by the County Judge.　The check shall, in all instances, be accompanied by the affidavit of the teacher that he is entitled to the amount specified in the check as compensation under his contract as a teacher.

Sec. 39.　A child within scholastic age entered at one public school shall afterwards receive no benefit of the school fund by attending another public school during the scholastic year.

Sec. 40.　A teacher's certificate shall be canceled on account of such misconduct or immorality as the Board of Trustees shall report to the County Judge disqualifying him, in their opinion, for the instruction of children.

Sec. 41.　County Judges shall be paid for the services required of them under this act such amount as may be allowed by the Board of Education, not to exceed one hundred dollars for any scholastic year, to be paid out of the available school fund.

Sec. 42.　When the nearest school community for children within scholastic age residing near a county line is situated in an adjoining county, such school community may receive such children, for whose tuition the teacher shall be paid by the County Treasurer of the county in which said children reside, on presentation of the account of the teacher, certified to by the Board of Trustees of the community school, and approved by the County Judge of the county in which the children reside. Such payment shall be made according to the *pro rata* of the school fund for distribution in the county where such children reside; and in all such cases, notice that said children are attending school out of the county of their residence shall be given, in writing, to the County Judge of the county in which they reside during the first four weeks of the session. Such notice, after being received by him, shall be filed with the Treasurer of the county in which said children reside.

TEACHERS.

SEC. 43. Any one desiring to teach a public free school shall, unless known to the County Judge, present a certificate from the Justice of the Peace of the precinct in which he or she desires to teach, or in which he or she may reside; or, in case the applicant has acquired no residence in this State, then some other certificate satisfactory to the County Judge, that he or she is a person of good moral character and of correct, exemplary habits. The County Judge shall thereupon, unless satisfied that some good cause exists for refusing such certificate, convene the County School Board of Examiners, and direct an examination of the applicant on the following branches, viz: Orthography, reading, writing, English grammar, composition, geography and arithmetic.

SEC. 44. On report by the Board that the applicant is competent to teach, the County Judge shall cause the same to be filed by the Clerk, and shall issue a certificate of competency to the teacher, authorizing him to contract with trustees of any school community to teach a school as contemplated by this act; which certificate shall be valid in the county where issued for the current scholastic year, and may be renewed by the County Judge for any subsequent year without examination, if the Judge be satisfied of the propriety of such renewal.

SEC. 45. The time for teaching public free schools shall be at such seasons of the year as may be fixed by the Trustees of each community, who, in determining the same, shall be guided by the convenience or interests of the parents and guardians, so as to secure the largest attendance of scholars with the least injury to home interests.

SEC. 46. Public free schools shall be closed on every Saturday, on Christmas and New Year's Day, on national or on State Thanksgiving Day, on the twenty-first day of April (the anniversary of the battle of San Jacinto), and on every national holiday. The session shall continue seven hours each day, and may continue longer by agreement with teacher and trustees.

SEC. 47. It shall be the duty of teachers to keep an accurate record of daily attendance of each pupil, and all other statistics required by the Board of Education necessary to make a complete report at the end of the term, which shall be filed with duplicate abstracts thereof with the Clerk of the County Court, one of which shall be forwarded by the County Judge to the Board of Education.

SEC. 48. Teachers, on the organization of their schools, shall determine the books of instruction to be used, subject to the approval of their community trustees, having due regard to the convenience of the parents with regard to books already purchased.

SCHOOL-HOUSES.

SEC. 49. When a school community, organized on the application of parents and guardians as herein provided, has no school-house, and a majority of its members are willing to assist, with their private means or labor, in building one, and shall donate a school-site for neighborhood public free school purposes, and deliver a deed therefor to the County Judge, executed to him and his successors in office in trust for public free school purposes, and shall pay for the registry of the same, they shall state the amount they propose to invest of their private means, and the value of the labor and material they propose to furnish free of charge for the erection of said house, and ask that the *pro rata* of the school fund to which the children in such community would be entitled may be set aside to assist in building said school-house. And the trustees of schoool communities, upon the order of the County Court, or the municipal authorities of any city or town constituting a separate school district, are hereby authorized and empowered, when deemed advisable, to sell any property belonging to said school community to the highest bidder, for cash or on time, as they may see proper; and apply the proceeds to the purchase of necessary grounds, or to the building, repairing or renting of school-houses.

SEC. 50. Upon receiving the application described in the foregoing section, the County Judge may enter an order granting said application; and notify the County Treasurer to credit such school community with the fund that may be apportioned thereto for building a school-house; *provided*, that the amount of money, labor, and material subscribed, together with the *pro rata* of the available school fund for one year to which said community would be entitled, would be sufficient to erect a comfortable school-house, with a capacity adequate to accommodate the children that may belong to said school community; *provided, also,* the community shall furnish one-half the amount necessary to build the house.

SEC. 51. Every school-house erected under the provisions of this act shall be erected under a contract for building, made with the school trustees of the school community who shall have control and direction of the work; and all accounts for labor and material furnished for said school-house shall be approved by them, and paid out of the fund apportioned to the school community for building purposes, on warrant of County Judge; but no such account shall be paid until the house is completed, unless the County Judge be fully satisfied, from securities deposited with the County Clerk for the use of the public school fund of the county, that the money, work, and material subscribed will be forthcoming when required in the progress of the work; *provided*, that nothing contained in this act shall be so construed as to prevent any school community from using the funds indicated in this section for being used in the purchase as well as the building of a school-house when the provisions of this section are complied with in reference to the title to the same.

SEC. 52. When the trustees of any school community not having a public school-house shall determine it to be to the interests of the community they represent to rent or lease a house for school purposes instead of building one, they are authorized to rent or lease the same for the scholastic year; the rent so contracted to be paid by the County Treasurer out of the school fund to which the children in such com--

munity would be entitled, upon the warrant of said trustees, approved by the County Judge; *provided*, the amount of rent so contracted shall not exceed six dollars per month for a suitable house, to be adjudged of by said trustees; which house so rented, for the time, shall be, as shall also each and every other community school-house, under the control of the trustees of the school community for school purposes, and for such other uses for the convenience of the neighborhood as may not interfere with school interests, but subject to the discretion of the school trustees. All school-houses erected under the provisions of this act shall be subject to the control of the trustees of the school community for whose benefit the same was erected; and, when deemed advisable, may be disposed of as provided for in section 49 of this act.

SEC. 53. A school-house, constructed in part by voluntary subscription by colored parents and guardians and for a colored school community, shall not be used, without the consent of the colored community assisting in its erection, for the education of white children; and a like rule shall protect the use of school-houses erected in part by voluntary subscription of white parents or guardians for the benefit of white children.

SEC. 54. In no case shall any school, consisting partly of white and partly of colored children, receive any aid from the available school fund, but the two races shall always be taught in separate public free schools.

SEC. 55. Any incorporated city or town in this State may have exclusive control of the public schools within its limits; *provided*, they determine so to do by a majority vote of the property tax-payers of said city or town; and the Council or Board of Aldermen thereof are invested with exclusive power to maintain, regulate, control and govern all the public free schools now established or hereafter to be established within the limits of said city or town; and they are furthermore authorized to pass such ordinances, rules and regulations not inconsistent with the Constitution and laws of this State, as may be necessary to establish and maintain free schools, purchase building sites, construct school-houses, and generally to promote free public education, within the limits of their respective cities or towns.

SEC. 56. When any such city or town shall, in good faith, elect to assume control and management of the public free schools within its limits, and shall have notified the State Board of Education, and the County Judge of the county in which it is situated, it shall receive from the Collector of Taxes in the county, on the certificate of the Board of Education, such a proportion of the public revenue in his hands as its scholastic population may entitle it to, which certificate shall be a voucher in the hands of the Collector of Taxes for so much money in his settlement with the State Comptroller. Such an additional amount as a city or town having control of public free schools may desire to raise by taxation for school purposes, shall be levied upon the taxable property in the limits of said town or city, in accordance with the usual assessment of taxes for municipal purposes; but such additional tax shall not exceed one per cent. on the city assessment of taxable property within its limits, and shall not be levied unless at an election, held for that purpose, two-thirds of those paying a tax on property in said city or incorporated town, to be determined by the last assessment rolls of said city or town, shall vote therefor. Schools thus organized and provided for by incorporated cities or towns shall be subject to the

14 GL

general laws of the State, so far as the same are applicable; but each city or town having control of schools within its limits shall constitute a separate school district, and may, by ordinance, provide for the organization of schools, and the appropriation of its school fund in such manner as may be best suited to a dense school population.

SEC. 57. The title to all houses, lands and other property, now owned or which may hereafter be purchased or acquired by a city or town for the benefit of public free schools, and all houses, lands or other property, purchased for the benefit of public free schools in the county, and lying within the limits of any town or city, which may have assumed control and management of the public free schools within its limits and conformity with law, shall be vested in the City or Town Council or Board of Aldermen, in trust for the sole use of public free schools established under this act; but no houses or lands so held in trust, or that may hereafter be acquired for the benefit of public education, shall be sold or otherwise diverted from the use herein indicated, without the consent of the State Board of Education.

SEC. 58. The apportionment of the available public free school fund to be made by the Board of Education for the scholastic year, begin-(n)ing September first, 1876, shall be made on the basis of the apportionment for the year ending August 31, 1875.

SEC. 59. For counties organized since September 1, 1875, the Board of Education, for the first scholastic year, shall apportion the available school fund on the most reliable data, as to population, accessible.

SEC. 60. The annual apportionment for the support of public free schools for the scholastic year subsequent to August 31, 1876, and prior to the scholastic year which will begin after the next regular session of the Legislature, shall be based on estimates, to be furnished by the State Comptroller, of available school funds that may be received for said year.

SEC. 61. For the scholastic year begin(n)ing September 1, 1876, school communities may organize and apply for the benefit of the available public free school fund at any time prior to January 1, 1877.

SEC. 62. County school officers, and school officers for cities and towns, under school laws in force prior to the passage of this act, shall continue to discharge the duties of their respective offices under existing laws in the disbursement of school funds already appropriated, until August 31, 1876, and shall make settlement with the County Judge in their counties, who shall cause to be turned over any balance, unexpended of school funds, to the County Treasurer, subject to the provisions of this act.

SEC. 63. Immediately on the passage of this act, five thousand copies of the same shall be published by the Board of Education, and at once, such number as the Board may direct, shall be sent to each County Judge in the State.

SEC. 64. On account of the emergency resulting from the necessity of immediately promulgating this act, that the people may be advised of their rights under the same, and in time to prepare for the next scholastic year, this act shall take effect and be in force from and after its passage.

Approved August 19, 1876.

Takes effect from passage.

CHAPTER CXXI.—*An Act to authorize the Commissioners' Court to procure buildings for the use of the County Courts in certain cases.*

SECTION 1. *Be it enacted by the Legislature of the State of Texas*, That the Commissioners' Courts in any of the counties in this State may provide buildings, rooms or apartments at the county seats, other than the court-house, for holding the sessions of the County Courts.

SEC. 2. There being a number of court-houses in this State too small in which to hold the terms of the District and County Courts, at the same time, a public necessity and emergency exist for the passage of this law; therefore, the same shall take effect from and after its passage.

Approved August 19, 1876.

Takes effect from its passage.

CHAPTER CXXII.—*An Act to amend the act of 8th of November, 1866, amending an act entitled: "An Act to establish a Penal Code," approved August 26, 1856.*

SECTION 1. *Be it enacted by the Legislature of the State of Texas*, That the act of the 8th of November, 1866, amending an act entitled: "An Act to establish a penal code for the State of Texas," approved August 26, 1856, be and is hereby amended so as to read as follows:

"SEC. 2. The owner or keeper of any horse, mare, gelding, mule, jack, jennet, colt or other animal diseased with glanders or farcy, be and is hereby required to keep the same in a safe and secure place, either in a lot or stable upon his or her own premises, at sufficient distance, and separate and away from any and all other stock, either his own or of any other person, liable to catch and communicate said disease, and shall keep the same in such close and separate confinement during the existence of said disease, and until the same is permanently cured; and any person who shall wilfully or knowingly fail or refuse to place said diseased animal in such confinement after the fact is made known to him that said animal is so diseased, shall be deemed guilty of a misdemeanor, and upon conviction thereof shall be fined in any sum not less than twenty-five dollars nor more than two hundred dollars, or be confined in the county jail for not less than ten days nor more than three months."

SEC. 3. Whereas, diseases are prevalent among horses in certain portions of this State, an imperative public necessity exists that this act take effect and be in force from and after its passage.

Approved August 19, 1876.

Takes effect from its passage.

CHAPTER CXXIII.—*An Act to regulate fees of committing magistrates and Sheriffs, in committing courts.*

SECTION 1. *Be it enacted by the Legislature of the State of Texas*, That in all cases where Justices of the Peace shall sit as committing magistrates, they shall be allowed such fees as are fixed by law, and twenty cents for each one hundred words for writing down the voluntary statement of the defendant, and for taking down the testimony in such cases; to be paid by the defendant, upon conviction for an offense less than a felony, as in cases of appeal from Justices' Courts. If convicted of a felony, such Justice of the Peace shall be entitled to and receive only ten cents for each one hundred words in such evidence and voluntary statement, not to exceed in any one case, for all his fees, more than five dollars, to be paid by the State upon the warrant of the Comptroller of Public Accounts, to be issued upon the bill of costs, duly sworn to by such Justice of the Peace, and attested by the Clerk of the court before which the case was finally tried, under his official hand and the seal of said court.

SEC. 2. That the Sheriff or Constable who may arrest the defendant, and attend upon the court during the investigation of any such cases, shall be allowed the same fees allowed them for similar services in cases tried in the Justice's Court, to be paid by the defendant or the State, as the case may be, in like manner as prescribed in the preceding section, upon the conviction of the defendant.

SEC. 3. As there are many cases now being tried by Justices of the Peace, as examining Courts, and as there are some doubts existing as to whether said officers will be entitled to receive any fees for such services, in the event that no bill of this kind be passed by this Legislature, and as the Legislature is nearing its adjournment, therefore an imperative public necessity for the immediate passage of this act, and an emergency that the same take effect from its passage, both exist; therefore this act shall take effect and be in force from and after its passage.

Approved August 19, 1876.

Takes effect ninety days after adjournment.

CHAPTER CXXIV.—*An Act making appropriations for deficiencies for the fiscal year, beginning September 1, 1875, and ending August 31, 1876, and previous years.*

SECTION 1. *Be it enacted by the Legislature of the State of Texas,* That the following sums, or so much thereof as may be necessary, be and the same are hereby appropriated out of any moneys in the Treasury not otherwise appropriated, for deficiencies incurred in the support of the State government for the fiscal year beginning September 1, 1875, and ending August 31, 1876, and previous years.

JUDICIARY.

For fees in felony cases, due Sheriffs, Clerks and District and County Attorneys in District and Justices' Courts for 1876 and previous years	$60,000 00
Fees in felony cases, due Justices of the Peace, and other peace officers, for 1876, and previous years	15,000 00
Salary of N. W. Battle, late Judge Criminal Court for the cities of Marlin, Waco and Calvert	478 00
For salary of Jas. Q. Chenoweth, late Judge Criminal Court for the cities of Clarksville and Bonham	1,652 95
J. L. Camp, for services as Criminal Judge in the cities of Jefferson, Marshall, etc., from 13th March, 1875, to August 31, 1875	1,633 00
For publishing Supreme Court reports	659 00

GENERAL LAND OFFICE.

For purchase of Spanish and Mexican law books, for use of translating department	161 50
For books, stationery and furniture	400 00
For vault for preservation of Spanish archives	300 00
For transcribing indexes	1,250 00

SUPREME COURT.

For contingent expenses..	$150 (
For fees due S. Ashe, late Sheriff of Harris county...........	50 £

ATTORNEY-GENERAL'S OFFICE.

For fees due Attorney-General in felony cases................	1,000 (

ADJUTANT-GENERAL'S OFFICE.

For pay to D. D. Cannedy, as State policeman, on approved account...	118 (
For pay for work on approved account for Henry Hinck...	7 ?

COMPTROLLER'S OFFICE.

For repairs on building, balance due Loomis and Christian	278 ?
For E. A. Stephens, Deputy Sheriff of Bexar county, expenses incurred in bringing taxes to the Treasury......	121 (

TREASURY-DEPARTMENT.

For stationery..	50 (

QUARANTINE.

For pay of health officers under quarantine laws, for services on the Gulf coast of Texas for 1876 and previous years..	9,000 (

PUBLIC BUILDINGS AND GROUNDS.

For amount due Fred Voigt...	1,535 (
To F. Voigt, to be used only for watering plants and shrubbery in the Capitol Grounds....................................	100 (
For gas for Governor's mansion....................................	110 (

EXECUTIVE OFFICE.

For telegraphing...................................	150 (

PENSIONS.

For amount due Dillard Cooper, under acts approved January 13, 1862, and November 29, 1871......................	850 (

MISCELLANEOUS.

For balance due Charles Hupperts on approved account...	20 (
For balance due J. Johnson on approved account.......... ...	52 (
For amount due on public debt certificates provided by law	60,000 (
For rent of buildings for storing arms and am(m)unition...	312 !
For William Raatz, for work done by order of Governor Davis, and approved by Auditorial Board	73 (
For Loomis and Christian, for material furnished, on approved account..	19 (
For Loomis and Christian, for material furnished, on approved account..	51 !
For John W. Harris, for services in the International case against the State...................	2,500 (
For Shelley and Walton, attorney's fees.......................	2,500 (
For account of R. C. Harrel, now owned by C. W. T. Welden, it being for pursuing criminal to Tennessee, capturing and returning him to jail at Bonham, Fannin county, Texas..	404 !

For amount due C. Johnson, for masonry on Capitol Grounds, to be paid on account approved by the Governor, Comptroller of Public Accounts, and Superintendent of Public Grounds................................... $2,196 75

For payment of workmen on Capitol Grounds, other than C. Johnson, to be paid out on account approved by the Governor, Comptroller of Public Accounts and Superintendent of Public Grounds............................. 1,585 16

DEAF AND DUMB ASYLUM.

For support of institution......... .... 2,000 00

Sec. 2. Whereas, an emergency and an imperative public necessity exists that the officers of the State of Texas, and the other creditors of the State, should be paid their just dues without delay; therefore this act shall take effect from and after its passage.

Approved August 19, 1876.

Takes effect from August 19, 1876.

CHAPTER CXXV.—*An Act to provide for the speedy assessment and collection of taxes upon land and real estate in cases when such property has been subject, by law, to taxation, but the assessment thereof has been omitted.*

Section 1. *Be it enacted by the Legislature of the State of Texas*, That in all cases where lands or real estate in this State have heretofore been subject to taxation for any year or years since the year one thousand eight hundred and seventy, but the rendition of and assessment thereof for any such year or years has been omitted, all such taxes, the rendition and assessment of which has been so omitted, shall be assessed upon such land and real estate, and collected in the manner hereinafter provided; *provided,* that all the lands in this State, and on which the taxes are unpaid, shall be assessed by the assessor of the county in which the land is situated, with all the taxes accrued thereon, in ratio to the taxation in the several counties of this State for the several years the taxes are unpaid, according to the average value of such lands in the several counties for the respective years said taxes are unpaid; and the same shall be a lien on the land until said taxes are paid, as required by this act.

Sec. 2. It shall be the duty of the Comptroller of this State, as soon as it will be possible for him to do so after the passage of this act, to make a separate list of all lands and real estate in each county for each year since the year one thousand eight hundred and seventy, which was not rendered and upon which taxes were not assessed for such year, but which was subject to taxation, by law, for such year; in preparing said lists he shall give the name of the original grantee, abstract number, number of acres and the rate of State and county taxes for such year, and shall forward the same to the Board of Equalization of the respective counties, with the verification that the said list is a true and correct statement of all the unrendered land and real estate in ——— county for the year ———, as shown by the records of his office. •

Sec. 3. Upon receipt of such list or lists by the Board of Equalization of such county, it shall be their duty to value each and every tract of land or parcel of real estate so mentioned and described in the said lists at their true and full value, as near as can be ascertained, for the year it was omitted to have been rendered.

Sec. 4. When the Board of Equalization shall have completed the valuation, they shall cause to be made out three separate rolls in the manner as may be prescribed by the Comptroller; they shall place one in the hands of the Collector of Taxes, forward one to the Comptroller of the State, and file one in the office of the County Clerk for the inspection of the public.

SEC. 5. Upon receipt of the rolls by the Collector of Taxes, he shall advertise in some weekly newspaper published in his county, and if no paper is published in his county by posting printed circulars in not less than eight public places in his county, for four consecutive weeks, that the rolls for the collection of taxes on unrendered land and real estate has been placed in his hands, and that unless the taxes are paid within thirty days after the last publication of said notice, he will proceed to collect the same as provided by law for the collection of delinquent taxes.

SEC. 6. The Collector of Taxes shall, at the expiration of the thirty days mentioned in Section 5 of this act, proceed to the collection of all unpaid taxes or unrendered land and real estate in his county in the same manner as provided by law for the collection of delinquent taxes, and shall charge and collect such fees and penalties the same as are allowed him for the collection of said delinquent taxes; *provided*, that the owner of such unrendered land and real estate, or his agent, shall, upon the payment of all taxes due upon the same since the first day of January, A. D. 1873, prior to the commencement of proceedings for the collection of the same by the Collector of Taxes under this section, receive a full and complete acquittance from all demands from the State for such delinquent taxes.

SEC. 7. That owing to the near approach of the close of this session of the Legislature, and that a law may be enacted to make taxation bear equally upon all property in this State, an imperative public necessity exists for the suspension of the rules, in order to immediately place this bill upon its final passage.

Approved August 19, 1876.

Takes effect ninety days after adjournment.

CHAPTER CXXVI.—*An Act supplemental to, and amendatory of an act, entitled: " An Act to make an appropriation for the fiscal year beginning September 1, 1875, and ending August 31, 1876, and previous years."*

WHEREAS, An imperative public necessity and emergency exists, that an act, entitled, " An Act to make an appropriation for the fiscal year, beginning September 1, 1875, and ending August 31, 1876, and previous years," passed at this session of the Legislature should take effect from and after its passage; therefore,

SECTION 1. *Be it enacted by the Legislature of the State of Texas,* That said above recited act do take effect and be in force from and after the passage of this amendatory act.

Approved August 19, 1876.

Takes effect from its passage.

CHAPTER CXXVII.—*An Act to provide for the issuance of patents for land in certain cases.*

SECTION 1. *Be it enacted by the Legislature of the State of Texas,* That the Commissioner of the General Land Office, be, and he is hereby authorized and required to issue patents upon locations made upon the islands of said State, in pursuance of the fifth section of the act entitled, "An Act to regulate the disposal of the public lands of the State of Texas," approved August 12, 1870; *provided, however,* that such locations shall have been made before the amendment of said section by the act entitled, "An Act to amend the first, third and fifth sections of an act entitled, 'An Act to regulate the disposal of the public lands of the State of Texas,' approved August 12, 1870;" approved May 16, 1871; *and, provided further,* that the land so located, shall, at some time prior to such location, have been offered for sale by said State.

Approved August 19, 1876.

Takes effect ninety days after adjournment.

CHAPTER CXXVIII.—*An Act to authorize and require the State Board of Education to invest the proceeds of the sale of University Lands now in the State Treasury, in six per cent. State Bonds.*

SECTION 1. *Be it enacted by the Legislature of the State of Texas,* That the State Board of Education is hereby authorized and required to invest the proceeds of the sale of University Lands now in the Treasury of the State in six per cent. State bonds.

SEC. 2. That whenever the interest on the bonds now belonging to the University Fund, together with the interest on the bonds contemplated in this act, shall amount to the sum of ten thousand dollars, it shall be the duty of the School Board to collect the same and invest it in the bonds of the State.

SEC. 3. Whereas, the importance of having the said University Fund at interest, creates an emergency; therefore, this act go into effect from its passage.

Approved August 19, 1876.

Takes effect from its passage.

CHAPTER CXXIX.—*An Act to prohibit the Judges of County Courts of this State from practising as attorneys or counselors-at-law in the County Courts and the Courts of Justices of the Peace of this State, and to affix a penalty for the violation of its provisions.*

SECTION 1. *Be it enacted by the Legislature of the State of Texas,* That it shall not be lawful for the Judge of any County Court of this State to practice as an attorney or counselor-at-law in any of the County Courts or Courts of the Justices of the Peace of this State, and any County Judge who may violate the provisions of this act shall be guilty of a misdemeanor, and upon conviction thereof, in any court of competent jurisdiction shall be punished by fine not less than one hundred nor more than five hundred dollars and in addition thereto, shall be removed from office.

SEC. 2. Whereas, no law now exists prohibiting County Judges practising as attorneys-at-law in the County and magistrate's Courts of this State, whereby much confusion results, thus creating an emergency, and an imperative public necessity that this act go into effect at once; therefore, this act shall take effect and be in force from and after its passage.

Approved August 19, 1876.

Takes effect from its passage.

CHAPTER CXXX.—*An Act to provide for the filling of vacancies in the offices of County Surveyor, County Treasurer and Hide Inspector in the counties of this State.*

SECTION 1. *Be it enacted by the Legislature of the State of Texas,* That whenever there shall be a vacancy in the offices of County Treasurer, County Surveyor and County Hide Inspector in any of the counties of this State, it shall be the duty of the County Commissioners' Court of the county in which such vacancy occurs is situated, to fill by appointment such vacancy or vacancies, such appointment to continue in force until the next general election; *provided,* that no person appointed to fill any of said vacancies shall exercise the duties of the office to which he may have been appointed until he shall have given the bond and taken the oath of office required of persons elected to such office.

SEC. 2. Inasmuch as there is no provision made by law for filling vacancies herein provided for, and inasmuch as there are vacancies now existing which should be filled, thereby creating an emergency; therefore, that this act take effect and be in force from and after its passage.

Approved August 19, 1876.

Takes effect from its passage.

CHAPTER CXXXI—.*An Act to amend Article seven hundred and twenty-one, of the code of criminal procedure.*

SECTION 1. *Be it enacted by the Legislature of the State of Texas,* That Article seven hundred and twenty-one of the code of criminal procedure be and the same is hereby amended so as hereafter to read as follows:

"ARTICLE 721. When the defendant appeals in any case of felony, he shall be committed to jail until the decision of the Appellate Court can be made; and if the jail of the county is unsafe, or there be no jail, the Judge of the District Court may, either in term time or vacation, order the prisoner to be committed to the jail of the nearest county in his district, which is safe; and such appeal may be prosecuted immediately to the term of the Appellate Court pending at the time the same is taken, or to the first term thereafter, without regard to the law governing appeals in other cases; the transcript of records in such appeals may be filed in the Appellate Court for trial, before the adjournment of the term of the District Court at which the case is determined, should the defendant so desire; *provided,* that in case the defendant shall make his escape from prison during the pending of the appeal, then the jurisdiction of the Appellate Court shall no longer attach in the case; and upon the fact of such escape being made to appear, the court shall, on motion of the Attorney-General, or counsel for the State, dismiss the appeal."

SEC. 2. Whereas, many felony cases now pending in the Court of Appeals, where the appellants have escaped from custody, and such cases are only encumbering the docket, an imperative public necessity exists this act be in full force and effect from and after its passage.

Approved August 21, 1876.

Takes effect from its passage.

CHAPTER CXXXII.—*An Act to provide for furnishing certain supplies herein named to the Lunatic, Deaf and Dumb and Blind Asylums.*

SECTION 1. *Be it enacted by the Legislature of the State of Texas,* That the Comptroller shall, on the first day of August of each year, and quarterly thereafter, advertise for sealed proposals for furnishing to the Superintendents of the Lunatic, Deaf and Dumb and Blind Asylums, certain supplies, as hereinafter named, for two weeks, in a daily newspaper published in the city of Austin and Galveston, prior to the day of opening said bids. Said advertisements shall state the articles for which bids shall be received, and bids shall be made separately as hereinafter named.

SEC. 2. Each bid shall be secured with such bond as the Comptroller may require, with two or more good securities, payable to the State, conditioned that the party to whom any contract may be awarded shall faithfully carry out the terms of his contract, and shall be liable to the State for any default of the same.

SEC. 3. On the day named for opening said bids, the Comptroller shall open the same in the presence of the Board of Trustees, and shall award to the lowest responsible bidder, the contract or contracts for which he may have bid.

SEC. 4. All bids shall be made for the term of three months, beginning September first of each year and quarterly thereafter.

SEC. 5. All supplies shall be furnished in accordance with contract, beginning September first and quarterly thereafter; and it shall be the duty of the Superintendents of the several asylums herein named, on the first day of August, November, February and May, of each year, to make out detailed estimates of such supplies as they will require for the ensuing three months, beginning on the first day of the following month, and to submit the same in duplicate to the Board of Trustees of their respective asylums. It is hereby made the duty of said Board to immediately examine said estimate and to approve the same, or any part thereof, as they may think necessary.

SEC. 6. Bids shall be made for the articles hereinafter named, separately, to-wit: Bids for fresh beef; bids for bacon and lard; bids for flour; bids for rice, peas, beans, grits and hominy; bids for soap, coarse and fine salt, vinegar, starch, soda, pepper and baking powders; bids for coffee and tea; bids for white and brown sugar; bids for molasses; bids for mackerel, prunes and dried apples, krout, brooms, candles and oil, canned goods, alcoholic stimulants and tobacco; bids for dry goods, hats, hose, shoes and under-shirts; bids for wood; *provided,* that the party to whom may be awarded the contract for wood, may deliver the amount required for a year, under such regulations as the Board of Trustees may direct.

SEC. 7. The Superintendents of the several asylums shall give an itemized receipt for all the articles delivered by the contractors of the same, and when approved by the Board of Trustees, the Comptroller shall draw his warrant upon the Treasurer for the amount, which amount shall be charged to the appropriate appropriations for the asylums furnished.

SEC. 8. The Superintendents of the several asylums shall furnish to the Comptroller a copy of the estimates that they may require for the ensuing three months, which shall be kept by him for the inspection of the public. Said estimates shall be itemized, stating the quantity ind quality of the articles needed, and as far as practicable the brands. The estimates for dry goods shall state the brands; for shoes, the quality and sizes needed; and for under-shirts, the quality.

SEC. 9. The Comptroller, in advertising for bids, shall specify the quality of the articles required and, as near as can be, shall specify the brands. If the Board of Trustees of said asylums, or any of them, shall find that a sufficient quantity of any articles, not enumerated in Section 6, shall be needed to justify its purchase by contract, it shall be their duty to report the fact to the Comptroller, who shall add said item or items to any bid, as required in Section 6, as he may deem best.

SEC. 10. It being important that the supplies for said asylums should be furnished as cheaply as possible to the State, an imperative public necessity exists; therefore this act take effect from and after its passage.

Approved August 19, 1876.

Takes effect from its passage.

_____

CHAPTER CXXXIII.—*An Act to create the Department of Insurance, Statistics and History.*

SECTION 1. *Be it enacted by the Legislature of the State of Texas,* That there is hereby created a Department of Insurance, Statistics, and History, which shall be charged with the execution of all laws now in force, or which may hereafter be enacted in relation to insurance, and insurance companies doing business in this State; also, with the execution of all laws relating to statistics and history, and do and perform such other duties as may be prescribed by law.

SEC. 2. The chief officer of said department shall be designated as the Commissioner of Insurance, Statistics, and History. He shall be a citizen of the State and experienced in matters of insurance, and be appointed by the Governor, by and with the advice and consent of the Senate, and shall hold his office two years from the date of his appointment, and until his successor shall have been appointed and qualified.

SEC. 3. Within fifteen days after notice of his appointment, and before entering upon the duties of his office, he shall take the oath of office prescribed by the Constitution of this State, and shall give a bond to the State of Texas in the sum of five thousand dollars, with two or more good and sufficient sureties, to be approved by the Governor, and conditioned for the faithful discharge of the duties of his office, which oath and bond shall be filed in the office of the Secretary of State.

SEC. 4. Said Commissioner may appoint a competent Clerk, who shall be subject to removal at the pleasure of the Commissioner, and who shall possess all the power and perform all the duties attached by law to the office of Commissioner, during the necessary or unavoidable absence of the Commissioner from the seat of government. The Commissioner shall be responsible for the acts of his Clerk, who shall before entering upon the duties of his position, take the oath required of the Commissioner in the third section of this act; he may also be required by the Commissioner to enter into bond with security, payable to said Commissioner, for the faithful performance of the duties of his said position.

SEC. 5. Said Commissioner shall receive an an(n)ual salary of two thousand dollars, and his Clerk an an(n)ual salary of twelve hundred dollars, which salaries shall be paid as other salaries are paid.

SEC. 6. Said Commissioner shall have a seal of office, the design which shall consist of a star with five points, with the letters composin the word, "Texas," arranged between the respective points thereof, sai seal not to be less than one and one-half and not more than two inche in diameter, and on the margin thereof, around the points of the sta shall be inscribed the words, "Department of Insurance, Statistics, an History," or an intelligible abbreviation thereof. A description of sai seal, with a certificate of approval by the Governor, shall be filed i the office of the Secretary of State, with an impression thereof, whic seal shall thereupon be and become the seal of office of the Commis sioner of the Department of Insurance, Statistics, and History.

SEC. 7. No person who is a director, officer or agent of, or directly o indirectly interested in any insurance company, except as insured, shal be Commissioner or Clerk; and no officer or agent of any insurance com pany, doing business in this State, shall be deputed to examine the a fairs of a company under this act.

SEC. 8. It is the duty of the Commissioner: *First*—To see that al laws of this State respecting insurance companies are faithfully exe cuted. *Second*—To file in his office every charter or declaration of or ganization of a company, with the certificate of the Attorney-Genera and on application of the corporators, to furnish them with a certifice copy thereof. *Third*—He shall, as soon as practicable in each year, cal culate or cause to be calculated in his office, by an officer or employee o his department, the net value, on the thirty-first of December of the previ ous year. of all the policies in force on that day, in each life insurance com pany doing business in this State, organized by authority of this State, anc of every life insurance company doing business in this State, that shal fail to furnish him, as hereinafter provided, a certificate of the Insurance Commissioner of the State by whose authority the company was organ ized, or by the State in which it may elect to have its policies valued and its deposits made; in case the company is chartered by the govern ment of the United States, giving the net value of all policies in forc in the company on the thirty-first day of December of the preceding year. *Fourth*—Calculations of the net value of each policy shall be based upon the American experience table of mortality, and four anc one-half per cent. interest per annum. And the net value of a policy a any time shall be taken to be the net single premium which will at tha time effect the insurance, less the value at that time of the future net premiums called for by the table of mortality and rate of interest des ignated above. *Fifth*—In case it is found that any life insurance com pany doing business in this State has not on hand the net value of al its policies in force, after all other debts of the company, and claims against it, exclusive of capital stock, have been provided for, it shall be the duty of the Insurance Commissioner to publish the fact that the then existing condition of the affairs of the company is below the standard of legal safety established by this State, and he shall require the com pany at once to cease doing new business, and he shall immediately in stitute proceedings, as required in this act, to determine what further shall be done in the case. *Sixth*—It is hereby made the duty of the Commissioner of Insurance, after having determined as above the amount of the net value of all the policies in force, to see that the company has that amount in safe, legal securities, of the description and character hereafter provided in this act, after all its debts and claims against it, exclusive of capital stock, have been provided for. *Seventh*—He shall ccept the valuation made by the Insurance Commissioner of the State under whose authority a life insurance company was organized, when such valuations have been properly made on sound and recognized principles, and legal basis as above; *provided*, the company shall furnish to the Insurance Commissioner of this State a certificate of the Insurance Commissioner of such State, setting forth the value calculated on the data designated above, of all the policies in force in the company on the previous thirty-first day of December, and stating that, after all other debts of the company, and claims against it at that time, were provided for, the company had, in safe securities of the character specified in this act, an amount equal to the net value of all its policies in force, and that said company is entitled to do business in its own State. *Eighth*—Every life insurance company doing business in this State during the year for which the statement is made, that fails promptly to furnish the certificate aforesaid, shall be required to make full detailed lists of policies and securities to the Insurance Commissioner of this State, and shall be liable for all charges and expenses consequent upon not having furnished said certificate. *Ninth*—For every company doing fire insurance business in this State, he shall calculate the re-insurance reserve for unexpired fire risks, by taking fifty per cent. of the premiums received on all unexpired risks that have less than one year to run, and a *pro rata* of all premiums received on risks that have more than one year to run; *provided*, that when the re-insurance reserve, calculated as above, is less than forty per cent. of all the premiums received during the year, the re-insurance reserve in this case shall be the whole of the premiums received on all of its unexpired risks. *Tenth*—In marine and inland insurance he shall charge all the premiums received on unexpired risks as a re-insurance reserve. *Eleventh*— Having charged against a company the re-insurance reserve, as above determined, for fire, inland and marine insurance, and adding thereto all other debts and claims against the company, he shall, in case he find the capital stock of the company impaired to the extent of twenty per cent., give notice to the company to make good its whole capital stock within sixty days; and if this is not done, he shall require the company to cease to do business within this State, and shall thereupon, in case the company is organized under authority of the State, immediately institute legal proceedings, as required in this act, to determine what further shall be done in the case. Any company having received the aforesaid notice of the Commissioner to make good its whole capital stock within sixty days, shall, forthwith, call upon its stockholders for such amounts as will make its capital equal to the amount fixed by the charter of said company; and, in case any stockholder of such company shall neglect or refuse to pay the amount so called for, after notice personally given or by advertisement in such time and manner as the said Commissioner shall approve, it shall be lawful for said company to require the return of the original certificate of stock held by such stockholder, and in lieu thereof to issue new certificates for such number of shares as the said stockholders may be entitled to in the proportion that the ascertained value of the funds of said company may be found to bear to the original capital of said company; the value of such shares, for which new certificates shall be issued, to be ascertained under the direction of said Commissioner and the company paying for the fractional parts of shares; and it shall be lawful for the Directors of such company to create new stock and dispose of the same, and to issue new certificates therefor, to any amount sufficient to make up the original capital of the company.   Whenever the capital stock of any joint stock, fire, fire and marine, or marine insurance company of the State becomes impaired, the Commissioner may, in his discretion, permit the said company to reduce its capital stock and the par value of its shares in proportion to the extent of impairment; *provided*, that in fixing such reduced capital, no sum exceeding twenty-five thousand dollars shall be deducted from the assets and property on hand, which shall be retained as surplus assets; *and, provided*, that no part of such assets and property shall be distributed to the stockholders; *and, provided further*, that the capital stock shall not be reduced to an amount less than that required by law for the organization of a new company; to examine, or cause to be examined every detail of the business of any company, transacting such business of insurance within this State, whenever in his judgment such examination is required by the interest of the policy-holders of such company.   *Twelfth*—It shall be the duty of the Commissioner of Insurance, after he has notified a life insurance company organized under authority of this State, to cease doing new business until the net value of its policies in force is equal to that called for by the standard of safety established by the State, at once to cause a rigid examination in regard to the affairs of such company; in case it shall appear that there is no fraud or gross incompetency or recklessness shown to exist in the management, he may, upon publishing the facts in the case, permit such company to continue in charge of its business for one year; *provided*, there is in his opinion, reason to believe that the company may eventually be able to re-establish the legal net value of its policies in force.   At the end of the year named above, he may renew the permission in case on examination he is satisfied that the company is likely to retrieve its affairs.   *Thirteenth*—In case the Commissioner does not permit the company to continue in the control of its old business, it is hereby made his duty to institute the necessary proceedings for the protection of its policy-holders in accordance with the laws of this State.   *Fourteenth*—To publish the result of his examination of the affairs of any company whenever he deems it for the interest of the public to do so, in one or more papers of this State.   *Fifteenth*—To suspend the entire business of any company of this State, and the business within this State of any other company during its non-compliance with any provisions of this or any other act relative to insurance, or whenever its assets appear to him insufficient to justify its continuance in business, by suspending or revoking the certificate granted by him, and to give notice thereof to the Insurance Commissioner or other similar officer of every State, and publish the same in such paper as he may think proper.   *Sixteenth*—To institute or cause to be instituted the necessary proceedings under the laws of this State, to close the affairs of any insurance company of this State which shall appear to him upon examination to be insolvent or fraudulently conducted.   *Seventeenth*—To report in detail to the Attorney-General, any violation of law relative to insurance companies, their officers or agents, or the business of insurance.   *Eighteenth*—To furnish to the companies required by law to report to him, the necessary blank forms for the statements required. *Nineteenth*—To preserve in a permanent form a full record of his proceedings, and a concise statement of the condition of each company or agency visited or examined.   *Twentieth*—At the request of any person, and on payment of fee, to give certified copies of any record or papers in his office, when he deems it not prejudicial to public interest so to do, and to give such other certificates as the law provides for. *Twenty-first*— To report annually to the Governor, on or before the thirty-first day of December, the name and compensation of his clerks, the receipts and expenses of his department for the year, his official acts, the condition of companies doing business in this State, and such other information as will exhibit the affairs of said department. *Twenty-second*—To send a copy of his annual report to the Insurance Commissioner or any similar officer of every other State, and to each company doing business in this State. *Twenty-third*—On request, to communicate to the Insurance Commissioner of any other State in which the substantial provisions of this act shall be enacted, any facts which by law it is his duty to ascertain, respecting companies of this State doing business within such other State. *Twenty-fourth*—It shall be his duty to see that no company is permitted to insure lives in this State whose charter authorizes it to do a fire, marine or inland business.

SEC. 9. The Commissioner, for the purposes of examinations authorized by law, has power, either in person or by one or more examiners by him commissioned in writing: *First*—To require free access to all books and papers within this State of any insurance company or the agents thereof, doing business within this State. *Second*—To summon and examine any person within this State, under oath, which he or any examiner may administer, relative to the affairs and condition of any company. *Third*—For probable cause to visit, at its principal office, wherever it may be, any insurance company not of a State in which the substantial provisions of the laws of this State shall be enacted, and doing business in this State, for the purpose of investigating its affairs and condition, and to revoke its certificate in the State if it does not permit an examination. *Fourth*—To revoke or modify any certificate of authority, when any conditions prescribed by law for granting it no longer exist. *Fifth*—The Commissioner has also power to institute suits and prosecutions, either by the Attorney-General or such other attorney as the Commissioner may designate, for any violation of this act; and the Commissioner shall be made a party to any proceedings for the closing up the affairs of any company when the same shall not be in the name of the State.

SEC. 10. Whenever, without justifiable cause, any person being within this State refuses to appear and testify before the Commissioner, when so required, or obstructs him in the discharge of his duty, he shall be punished according to law.

SEC. 11. Every instrument executed by the Commissioner of this State, or of any other State in which the substantial provisions of this act and the laws of this State shall be enacted, pursuant to authority confer(r)ed by this act, and authenticated by his seal of office, shall be received as evidence in this State, and copies of papers in his office certified by him and so authenticated, shall be received as evidence in this State, with the same effect as the original. Every such instrument so executed and authenticated by the Commissioner of this State shall be recorded in the same manner, and the same and its record shall have the like effect as if acknowledged or proved according to law. The impression of the seal may be directly on paper, with or without tenacious substance.

SEC. 12. There shall be paid by every company to whom this act applies, and doing business in this State, the following fees, to-wit:

Upon filing the declaration or certified copy of charter, twenty-five dollars; upon filing the an(n)ual statement, or certificate in lieu thereof, twenty dollars; for certificate of authority and certified copy thereof, one dollar; for every copy of any paper filed in his department, the sum of twenty cents per folio; and for affixing the official seal to such copy and certifying the same, one dollar; for valuing policies of life insurance companies, ten dollars per million of insurance, or any fraction thereof; for official examinations of companies under this act, the actual expenses incurred and ten dollars a day, not to exceed two hundred and fifty dollars; for countersigning and registering policies and annuity bonds, the reasonable expenses of custody, registration and issue. All fees received by the Commissioner under this act shall be paid over at the end of each month to the Treasurer of the State, and placed to the credit of general revenue.

Sec. 13. No transfer by the Commissioner of securities of any kind, in any way held by him in his official capacity, is valid unless countersigned by the Treasurer of the State. It is the duty of the State Treasurer: *First*—To countersign any such transfer presented to him by the Commissioner. *Second*—To keep a record of all transfers, stating the name of the transferee, unless transfer(r)ed in blank, and a description of the security. *Third*—Upon countersigning, to advise by mail the company concerned, the particulars of the transaction. *Fourth* —In his annual report to the Legislature, to state the amount of transfers countersigned by him.

Sec. 14. For the purpose of verifying the correctness of records, the Commissioner is entitled to free access to the Treasurer's record, required by Section 13, and the Treasurer is entitled to free access to the books and other documents of the Insurance Department relating to securities held by the Commissioner.

Sec. 15. That in event any number of insurance companies should associate together for the purpose of issuing or vending policies or joint policies of insurance, such association shall not be permitted to do business in this State until the taxes and fees due from each of said companies shall have been paid, and other conditions complied with; and any company failing or refusing to pay such taxes and fees, and to fully comply with the requirements of law, shall be refused permission by the Commissioner to do business in this State.

Sec. 16. It shall also be the duty of the Commissioner of Insurance, Statistics and History to obtain from every available source all reliable information and statistics relating to the population, wealth and general resources of the State; and particularly in regard to agriculture, stock raising, manufactures, mining, and other industries; also relating to commerce, exports and imports; also relating to internal improvements of all kinds, public and private, and such other subjects as may be of general interest or benefit to the State; and to enable the Commissioner to obtain such information and statistics, he is authorized to call on any and all State and county officers for such data, statistics and information as they may be able from their official position to afford; and it is hereby made their duty to fill up such blank forms as the said Commissioner may furnish to them, as far as it is possible for them to do so, and to return the same to the Department of Insurance, Statistics and History, within a reasonable time.

Sec. 17. The Commissioner shall embody all such reliable information and statistics as he may be able to obtain in accordance with the preceding section, in tabulated or other convenient form, and report the same to the Governor annually, who shall cause the same to be printed and distributed in such numbers as he and the said Commissioner may determine.

SEC. 18. It shall also be the duty of the Commissioner to keep in constant communication with the Department of Agriculture of the United States, and to ask and solicit from the chief officer thereof a due proportion of the seeds and plants annually distributed from said department, and when received, said Commissioner shall distribute the same among the most experienced, skillful and scientific farmers in different portions of the State, who will promptly and carefully report to said Commissioner the results of their practical experience with said seeds and plants; and whenever the chief officer of the Department of Agriculture shall so request, the Commissioner shall transmit to said department the results of such agricultural experiments, and such other information concerning agriculture in this State as may be accessible.

SEC. 19. It shall also be the duty of the Commissioner of Insurance, Statistics and History, to correspond with persons well informed in the early history of Texas, and to solicit and invite by printed circular, or otherwise, any reliable information, in the form of narrative or otherwise, respecting the incidents of the early history and settlement of the different portions of the State of Texas, for the future use of the historian; and the Commissioner shall revise and digest such information in proper form as near as practicable in chronological order, and shall record said revised and digested information in a properly bound book with indexes, and he shall carefully number and file the original documents in his office. He shall also keep a book in which he shall enter the names of persons furnishing information of incidents of early history with a condensed statement of the contents of each narrative or communication, and said Commissioner shall demand and receive from the Secretary of State, the Comptroller of Public Accounts, the Commissioner of the General Land Office, and from such other departments or officers as may have them in charge, all books, maps, papers, documents, memoranda and data, not connected with or necessary to the current duties of said departments or officers, as relate to the history of Texas as a Province, Colony, Republic and State, and carefully to classify, catalogue, number and preserve the same. The Commissioner shall also receive and preserve all historical relics, mementoes, antiquities and works of art connected with and relating to the history of Texas, which may be presented to the State, or otherwise come into his possession.

SEC. 20. It shall also be the duty of the said Commissioner to correspond with statistical, historical and agricultural societies beyond the State, and the Departments of other States, with the view of exchanging documents and data relating to the various interests sought to be fostered and advanced by the provisions of this act. He shall also endeavor to procure from Mexico the original archives which have been removed from Texas, and relate to the history and settlement thereof; and in case he cannot procure the originals, he shall endeavor to secure authenticated copies thereof; also any and all papers in Mexico, or elsewhere, relating to the early history of Texas.

SEC. 21. In addition to his other duties the said Commissioner shall have charge and control of the State Library, and of all the books,

15 GL

manuscripts and other articles therein contained. He shall preserve and cause to be bound the current files of not less than six nor more than ten leading newspapers in the State, for the future use of the historian. He shall make such regulations as he may deem proper, subject to the advice and approval of the Governor, concerning the management and use of the public library and the books therein contained, take special care that none are lost or damaged.

SEC. 22. It shall not be lawful for the Commissioner to permit any manuscripts, papers, documents, relics, works of art or other property under his charge, except bound volumes of books, to be taken from his custody, nor from the public buildings which are assigned for their display or preservation.

SEC. 23. The Commissioner shall procure and keep in the State library a complete set of the general laws of the United States, and of every State in the American Union; and from time to time make such purchases of books and other articles as may be directed by law.

SEC. 24. All papers and records now on file in the office of the Comptroller of Public Accounts, pertaining to insurance, and connected with the current duties of the Commissioner of Insurance, Statistics, and History, shall be transfer(r)ed and delivered to that officer as early as practicable after he shall have qualified under this act.

SEC. 25. In addition to the reports named in this act, it shall be the duty of the Commissioner to make such other reports of the business of his office, and the information therein collected and preserved, as the Governor may require; and all the reports made shall be by the Governor laid before the Legislature at its next session after they shall have been made and printed.

SEC. 26. The Commissioner of Insurance, Statistics, and History, shall be subject to removal for neglect of duty, drunkenness, breach of trust, incompetency or malfeasance in office, either by the address of two-thirds of each House of the Legislature, or by impeachment, in the same manner as is provided by the Constitution and laws for the removal of other officers.

SEC. 27. The Governor may fill any vacancy occurring in the office of Commissioner of Insurance, Statistics, and History, and report the name of the person so appointed to the Senate, if in session, or at the next succeeding session of the Legislature. Should the Senate fail to confirm the appointment made by the Governor, within ten days after being advised thereof, then the said office shall be deemed vacant, and a new appointment shall be made until the office is filled.

SEC. 28. In view of the injunction of the Constitution and the great importance to the whole State of the establishment of the Department of Insurance, Statistics, and History, and of the great public necessity of its being immediately put into practical operation, it is a case of emergency, and is hereby enacted that this act shall take effect from and after its passage.

Approved August 21, 1876.

Takes effect from its passage.

CHAPTER CXXXIV.—*An Act authorizing the Court of Appeals to appoint a Bailiff.*

SECTION 1. *Be it enacted by the Legislature of the State of Texas*, That the Court of Appeals or the Judges thereof shall be authorized to appoint a bailiff to attend before their court during its sessions and to execute its orders; he shall receive such compensation as may be allowed by said court, not to exceed four dollars per day, which compensation is to be paid out of the State Treasury.

SEC. 2. That there being no law in force to enable said court to appoint a bailiff to execute their orders, an imperative public necessity and emergency exists for the passage of this bill, and it is hereby declared that it shall take effect and be in force from and after its passage.

Approved August 21, 1876.

Takes effect from its passage.

CHAPTER CXXXV.—*An Act to define and punish barratry.*

SECTION 1. *Be it enacted by the Legislature of the State of Texas,* That the penal code of the State of Texas be and the same is hereby amended by inserting therein the following Articles:

"ARTICLE —. If any person shall wilfully instigate, maintain, excite, prosecute or encourage the bringing of any suit or suits at law, or equity, in any court in this State, in which the party has no interest, with the intent to distress or harass the defendant therein, or shall wilfully bring or prosecute any false suit or suits at law or equity, of his own, with the intent to distress or harass the defendant therein, he shall be deemed guilty of barratry, and shall be fined in any sum not exceeding five hundred dollars. and in addition thereto may be imprisoned in the county jail not exceeding one year."

Approved August 21, 1876.

Takes effect ninety days after adjournment.

CHAPTER CXXXVI.—*An Act to amend an act entitled: "An Act for the protection of the wool growing interests of the State," approved May 2, 1874.*

SECTION 1. *Be it enacted by the Legislature of the State of Texas,* That the first section of said act shall be so amended as to read as follows, to-wit:

"*Be it enacted by the Legislature of the State of Texas,* That if any person shall drive or graze upon any public road of this State or upon any land not owned or rented by himself, any sheep affected with the disease commonly known as the 'scab,' whereby any other flock of sheep should become diseased with 'scab,' by said driving or grazing, shall be deemed guilty of a misdemeanor, and, on conviction thereof, he shall be fined in any sum not to exceed one hundred dollars for each offense.

SEC. 2. That Sections 2, 3, 4, 5 and 6, of said act, be, and are hereby repealed.

Approved August 21, 1876.

Takes effect ninety days after adjournment.

CHAPTER CXXXVII.—*An Act regulating interest.*

SECTION 1. *Be it enacted by the Legislature of the State of Texas,* That on all written contracts ascertaining the sum due when no specific premium or rate of interest is expressed, interest shall be taken, recovered and allowed at the rate of eight per centum per annum, from and after the same is due and payable; and all open accounts, when no specific rate of interest is agreed upon, interest shall be taken, recorded and allowed at the rate of eight per centum per annum, from the first day of January of each year after the same are made.

SEC. 2.   The parties to any written contract may agree to, and stipulate for, any premium or rate of interest, not exceeding twelve per centum per annum on the amount or value of the contract, and the same may be taken, recovered and allowed.

SEC. 3.   All contracts or instruments of writing, whatsoever, which may in any wise, directly or indirectly, violate the foregoing provisions of this act by stipulating for allowing or receiving a greater premium or rate of interest than twelve per centum per annum for the loan, payment or delivery of any money, goods, wares, merchandise, bonds, notes of hand, or any commodity, shall be void and of no effect for the whole rate of interest so charged, stipulated or agreed to be paid and received, but the principal sum of money or the value of the goods, wares, merchandise, bonds, notes of hand or commodity may be received and recovered; *provided, however*, that no evidence of usurious interest shall be received on the trial of such causes, unless the same shall be specially pleaded and verified by the affidavit of the party wishing to avail himself of the provisions of this act.

SEC. 4.   That all laws and parts of laws in conflict with the provisions of this act be and the same are hereby repealed.

SEC. 5.   That the fact that the session is drawing near a close, and there being no law defining usury, in force, creates an emergency and necessity that this act be passed immediately and it is hereby declared that this act take effect from and after its passage.

Approved August 21, 1876.

Takes effect from its passage.

CHAPTER CXXXVIII.—*An Act to provide for the employment and hiring of county convicts, and prescribing the duties and fees of officers charged therewith.*

SECTION 1.   *Be it enacted by the Legislature of the State of Texas,* That any person or persons who may be convicted of any misdemeanor or petty offense in any of the courts of this State, and who shall be committed to jail in default of the payment of the fines and costs adjudged against him or them, shall be required to discharge such fines and costs by manual labor, in any manual labor work-house, or on any farm attached thereto, or on any road, bridge or other public work in the county where the conviction and committal were had.

SEC. 2.   If any person so convicted and committed be an artisan or mechanic, and be put to labor in any manual labor work-house, or on any bridge or other public improvement, such artisan or mechanic shall be allowed a reasonable compensation for such labor; but such compensation shall not be paid to such artisan or mechanic.

SEC. 3.   The preceding sections of this act shall not be so construed as to prohibit the employment of county convicts herein mentioned on other than public works, but it shall be lawful to hire out such person or persons to any individual, company or corporation.

SEC. 4.   Whenever the services of any county convict shall be desired, and contracted for under the provisions of this act, the person, company or corporation so desiring and contracting for such services shall execute bond, payable to the County Judge of the county, with sufficient sureties or surety, to be approved by said County Judge, for the prompt and faithful payment of the money that shall become due and payable for the services rendered or labor done by such convict or convicts, and that he or they will treat such convict or convicts humanely while in his or their employment; *provided*, that if any convict hired out under the provisions of this act shall escape from his employer, without any fault of such employer, before such convict shall discharge by his labor the fine and costs, the party hiring such convict shall not be liable on his, her or their bond on amount greater than the time worked by such convict before his escape; *provided*, that the convict is rearrested and again placed in the custody of the Sheriff or Constable; *and provided further*, that in any case any convict shall escape from such employer, he shall be deemed guilty of an offense, and, if recaptured, he shall, upon conviction by any court of competent jurisdiction, be fined in any sum not less than double the amount of the fine assessed against him in the first case, together with all costs of suit and recapture, and compelled to discharge the same by his labor, as provided for in the provisions of this act; and should any such convict, after a second conviction, comply faithfully with the terms of the contract, he shall be entitled to a deduction of twenty-five per cent. upon his labor on the second fine so imposed.

SEC. 5. Upon the breach of said bond it shall be the duty of the County Judge to cause said bond to be sued upon in any court having competent jurisdiction; and upon the recovery of a judgment against the principal and surety or sureties on said bond, and the collection of the amount of said judgment, the same shall be paid into the County Treasury.

SEC. 6. All moneys arising from hiring out or employing county convicts, shall be paid over to the County Judge, and by him paid into the County Treasury. But in every instance the county convict or convicts shall receive full credit for the amount of his labor, to be entered and counted in discharge of the fine and costs adjudged against him; and whenever his earnings shall be sufficient to pay in full the fine and costs adjudged against him, he shall be discharged.

SEC. 7. All fines collected under the provisions of this act shall be paid into the County Treasury, unless the destination of said fines or fine is otherwise fixed by law, and shall constitute a portion of the "Jury Fund," and all costs so collected shall be paid to the respective officers to whom they may be due.

SEC. 8. When convicts employed on public works or improvements, or in public work-houses, shall have paid the full amount of their fines and costs by their labor, then the County Judge shall issue a warrant in favor of each officer to whom costs may be due, for the amount of his costs, on the County Treasurer, and the same shall be paid, if there are sufficient funds in the Treasury for that purpose, out of the jury fund aforesaid. If there be not sufficient funds to pay the same, then said warrants shall be audited and registered, and paid whenever there are sufficient funds to pay the same, in the order of their registration.

SEC. 9. In order more effectually to accomplish the purposes of Section 1 of this act, it shall be the duty of the Commissioners' Court of each county in this State, wherever the public good may demand it, to provide for the erection of such work-houses in their respective counties as may be necessary to utilize the labor of county convicts; and they may, in addition thereto, purchase land for the establishment and carrying on of county farms by the labor of such convicts.

SEC. 10.   Such work-houses and county farms shall be under the control and management of the Commissioners' Court, under such rules and regulations as they may, from time to time, deem proper to adopt; *provided*, that no such rules or regulations shall be in contravention of any law in this State; *and, provided further*, that such rules and regulations shall have direct reference to carrying out the purposes of this act.

SEC. 11.   No county convict shall be allowed to work on any public work or improvement whatever where there may be danger of his escape; nor shall he be compelled to labor at any kind of business or in any avocation that would tend to impair his health or strength.

SEC. 12.   All persons hiring convicts under the provisions of this act, shall, in addition to the bond required in Section 4, obligate themselves to furnish said convicts, so hired, with good and wholesome food, with comfortable clothing, and medicine when sick; shall not require them to work at unreasonable hours, or for a longer time during any one day than other laborers, doing the same kind of labor, are accustomed to do.

SEC. 13.   The management and control of county convicts are confided to County Judges and the Commissioners' Courts; and all the duties herein required shall be performed as herein prescribed, or as may be hereinafter authorized; but said Judges and Commissioners' Courts shall always have the right to require the aid of the Sheriffs of their respective counties; and all lawful orders or process necessary to be issued and executed shall be executed by said Sheriffs.

SEC. 14.   Until otherwise provided by law, County Judges shall receive as compensation for their services the following fees, to-wit: For every contract of hire the sum of two dollars; for every bond required by this act, when prepared by County Judges, the sum of one dollar; for the examination and approval of each bond, the sum of fifty cents; said fees to be paid in every instance in advance, by the party or parties hiring such convicts; to be repaid to the contractor or employer, when demanded, out of the wages of such convict or convicts.

SEC. 15.   County Judges and County Commissioners' Courts shall cause a record of all their proceedings under this law to be recorded in well bound books, to be provided for that purpose; said record shall contain: *First*—A descriptive list of all persons known as "county convicts." *Second*—How such convict has been or is employed.   *Third*—The name of the party or parties hiring such convict.   *Fourth*—The time when and the price at which such convict has been employed.   *Fifth*—The amount paid or allowed for such employment or hire.   *Sixth*—The amount due by such convict as fine and costs.   *Seventh*—Such other information as may be necessary and required under the rules adopted by said Commissioners' Court.

SEC. 16.   The words, "county convicts," as used in this act, shall be understood to mean persons convicted of misdemeanors or petty offenses and committed to jail in default of the payment of the fine and costs adjudged against them.   The use of the "plural" shall include also the "singular," and *vice versa*, and the use of the "masculine" shall include the "feminine," and *vice versa*.

SEC. 17.   Whereas, in many counties of the State, criminals are confined at the expense of the counties, such as to create a public necessity and emergency therefor, be it enacted that this law go into effect from and after its passage.

Approved August 21, 1876.

Takes effect from its passage.

CHAPTER CXXXIX.—*An Act to amend Article 724 of an act entitled "An Act to adopt and establish a penal code for the State of Texas," approved August 28, 1856.*

SECTION 1. *Be it enacted by the Legislature of the State of Texas*, That Article 724 of an act entitled "An Act to adopt and establish a penal code for the State of Texas," approved August 28, 1856, be so amended as to hereafter read as follows, to-wit:

"ART. 724. The offense of burglary is constituted by entering a house by force, threats or fraud, at night, or in like manner by entering a house during the day, and remaining concealed therein until night, with the intent, in either case, of committing felony or the crime of theft."

SEC. 2. That owing to the near approach of the close of the session, an imperative public necessity exists for the suspension of the rules, in order to place this bill on its immediate passage.

Approved August 21, 1876.

Takes effect ninety days after adjournment.

CHAPTER CXL.—*An Act to regulate the practice of medicine.*

SECTION 1. *Be it enacted by the Legislature of the State of Texas*, That no person shall be permitted to practice medicine, in any of its branches or departments, in this State, without first having a certificate of qualification from some authorized Board of Medical Examiners, as hereinafter provided.

SEC. 2. That every person who may hereafter engage in the practice of medicine, in any of its branches or departments, in this State, shall, before entering upon such practice, furnish to the Clerk of the District Court of the county in which such practitioner may reside or sojourn, his certificate of qualification; and said Clerk shall enter the name of said person in a well bound book kept in his office for that purpose, together with the time when, the place where, and the person or persons by whom such certificate of qualification was given, after which he shall return the said certificate to the owner thereof; for which service said Clerk shall be entitled to receive from each, any and every such applicant the sum of one dollar.

SEC. 3. That the Presiding Judges of the District Courts of the several Judicial Districts shall, at the first regular term of their courts after this act shall become a law, or as soon thereafter as practicable, severally appoint a Board of Medical Examiners, for their respective districts, to be composed of not less than three practicing physicians of known ability, and having certificates of qualification for the practice of medicine under the "Act to regulate the practice of medicine," passed May 16, 1873, and said Board of Examiners to continue in office two years from and after their appointment; and they shall, immediately after accepting such appointment, select one of their number President, and one as Secretary, and adopt all necessary rules for the guidance and control of their meetings. It shall be the duty of said Board of Medical Examiners to examine all applicants for certificates of qualification to practice medicine, in any of its branches or departments, in this State, whether such applicants are furnished with medical diplomas or not, upon the following named subjects, to-wit: Anatomy, physiology, pathological anatomy and pathology, surgery, obstetrics, and chemistry; said examination to be thorough. When the said Board of Medical Examiners shall have been satisfied as to the qualifications of said applicant, they shall grant to him a certificate to that effect, which certificate shall be recorded with the Clerk of the District Court of the county in which said applicant may reside or sojourn, as provided in section two of this act, which certificate shall entitle him to practice anywhere in this State. Such Board of Examiners shall be entitled to receive the sum of fifteen dollars for each and every such applicant, to be paid by the applicant or party so examined; any two of them shall have authority to grant certificates, and whenever a vacancy occurs in any of said Boards, the same shall be filled by appointment by the Judge of the district in which such vacancy occurs.

SEC. 4. That said Boards shall meet regularly semi-annually at some central point in their respective districts, to conduct examinations and grant certificates, as hereinbefore provided, and they shall give at least one month's public notice of said meeting, by publication in some paper published in the judicial district, specifying the time and place thereof; *provided*, that any member of any of said Boards shall have authority to grant a temporary license or certificate to an applicant, upon examination, until the next regular meeting of the Board, at which time the temporary license shall cease, but the said applicant must apply for a thorough examination. Each and every one of such Boards shall procure a seal, as soon as practicable after their organization, which seal shall be impressed upon every certificate granted.

SEC. 5. That any person violating any of the provisions of this act shall be guilty of a misdemeanor, and on conviction thereof, before any court having competent jurisdiction, shall be fined in any sum not less than fifty dollars, and not more than five hundred ($500) dollars, for every such offense, one-half of such fine shall be paid to the prosecutor, and the other half into the County Treasury; and it shall be the duty of the Judge of each judicial district, at each term of the District Court in the respective counties composing his district, to charge the grand jury with the necessity of preserving this act inviolate, and to admonish them of their duty to find presentments against any and all persons guilty of its infraction; *provided*, that nothing in this act shall be so construed as to exclude or disqualify any person who may have been already qualified for the practice of medicine under the act of May 16, 1873; *provided*, that nothing in this act shall be so construed as to apply to those who have been regularly engaged in the general practice of medicine in this State, in any of its branches or departments, for a period of five consecutive years in this State prior to the first day of January, 1875; nor to those who have obtained certificates of qualification under said act; nor to females who follow the practice of midwifery, strictly as such.

SEC. 6. An act entitled, "An Act to regulate the practice of medicine," passed sixteenth of May, 1873, and all other laws or parts of laws in conflict herewith, are hereby repealed.

SEC. 7. It being important that the benefits of this act be realized at once, creates such imperative public necessity and an emergency as requires that it be of force and effect upon its passage, and it is so declared.

Approved August 21, 1876.
Takes effect ninety days after adjournment.

CHAPTER CXLI.—*An Act to provide for filling vacancies in the office of District Clerk.*

Section 1. *Be it enacted by the Legislature of the State of Texas*, That whenever vacancies occur in the office of District Clerk, from any cause, the same shall be filled by the District Judge of the district where such vacancy occurs; and the person so appointed shall hold his office until the next general election; the person so appointed shall give bond and qualify as if he were elected.

Sec. 2. That an imperative public necessity exists, and the emergency requires the immediate passage of this act, therefore be it enacted that this act take effect and be in force from and after its passage.

Approved August 19, 1876.

Takes effect from its passage.

CHAPTER CXLII.—*An Act to repeal Article 764 of an act entitled: "An Act to establish a penal code for the State of Texas," approved August 28, 1856.*

Section 1. *Be it enacted by the Legislature of the State of Texas*, That Article 764 of an act entitled, "An Act to establish a penal code for the State of Texas," approved August 28, 1856, be, and the same is hereby repealed.

Sec. 2. Whereas, the jails of the country are overburdened with parties charged with petty thefts, and the several counties in the State are daily increasing their indebtedness, in consequence of the necessity of the support of such criminals, therefore there exists a public emergency and necessity for immediate relief, and that this act go into effect and be in force from and after its passage.

Approved August 21, 1876.

Takes effect from its passage.

CHAPTER CXLIII.—*An Act to regulate procedure in relation to common uses of certain inclosed lands*

Whereas, Public policy and private economy encourage the inclosing of lands of separate owners in one inclosure for pasturage, therefore,

Section 1. *Be it enacted by the Legislature of the State of Texas*, That whenever lands of separate owners shall be in one inclosure for pasturage, exclusive of any interior inclosure, either with or without an agreement among any or all of such separate owners in relation to common pasturage of their respective portions of such pastoral premises, the District Court for any county in which all or part of such premises may be situated shall have jurisdiction to determine and enforce the pastoral rights of such owners, according to appropriate equity.

Sec. 2. In case of an agreement among any or all of such separate owners in relation to common pasturage of their respective portions of such pastoral premises, any interested party may proceed in court, in the usual way, for redress on account of alleged injury, either enforce the agreement, or to rescind it with other relief; and in the latter alternative, to procure equitable adjustment, including provision for the subsequent use of the premises.

Sec. 3. When the interests in such pasturage shall not be affected by contract, any interested party may proceed in court, in the usual way, to have the rights of pasturage apportioned among such separate owners ; and the proportions of common pasturage shall be equitable, with due appreciation not only of the values of the pasturages of the land so owned respectively, but also of the comparative values of corresponding portions of the inclosing work, and also of the actual values of contributions to such work in behalf of the separate interests in such pasturage.   In making such apportionment, the court if it should consider such aid necessary, would be authorized to have such values estimated by commissioners, to be appointed by the court, and sworn to perform their duties as prescribed in an order of the court.   The commissioners might have assistance by a surveyor, if the order should so provide ; and the costs of such commission, for allowance and payment, would be as provided by order of the court.   Any report of the commissioners would be subject to approval or rejection by the court. When approved, such report would be competent evidence in the trial of the case, without being conclusive, to be used in connection with other evidence.

SEC. 4.   This act applies to separate ownerships of land, as inclosed by any means that may be sufficient to prevent ordinary passing of the larger kinds of live stock, whether such hinderance be artificial or natural, in whole or in part, including a water boundary.   And this act recognizes the right of any owner of land to inclose it, not intruding on the premises of a separate owner, although his land be also inclosed, by using either artificial or natural means, or both kinds, adapted to prevent ordinary passing of such live stock, and so availing, when practicable, of the common right of a proprietor of land to use an adjacent water boundary for the purpose of inclosure.

SEC. 5.   That owing to the near approach of the close of the session, an imperative public necessity exists for the suspension of the rules, to put this bill on its final passage.

Approved August 21, 1876.

Takes effect ninety days after adjurnment.

CHAPTER CXLIV.—*An Act dividing Young and Bexar Territories into counties, and defining the boundaries thereof, and of certain other counties herein named.*

SECTION 1.   *Be it enacted by the Legislature of the State of Texas,* That the following named new counties shall be, and are hereby created out of Young and Bexar territories, and the boundaries shall be as follows:

The county of Lipscomb: Beginning at a monument on the intersection of the one hundredth meridian, and the thirty-six and a half (36½) degree of latitude, 1629 feet north of the 132nd mile post on the one hundredth meridian; thence west thirty miles to the thirtieth mile post on the 36½ degree of latitude ; thence south thirty miles and 1629 feet; thence east thirty miles to the 102nd mile post; thence north thirty miles and 1629 feet to beginning.

The county of Ochiltree: Beginning at the northwest corner of the county of Lipscomb ; thence west thirty miles to the sixtieth mile post; thence south thirty miles ; thence east thirty miles to the southwest corner of Lipscomb county; thence north thirty miles to place of beginning.

The county of Hansford: Beginning at the northwest corner of Ochiltree county ; thence west thirty miles to the ninetieth mile post ; thence south thirty miles; thence east thirty miles to the southwest corner of Ochiltree county; thence north thirty miles to the place of beginning.

The county of Sherman: Beginning at the ninetieth mile post, the northwest corner of Hansford county; thence west thirty miles to the one hundred and twentieth mile post; thence south thirty miles; thence east thirty miles to the southwest corner of Hansford county; thence north thirty miles to the place of beginning.

The county of Dallam: Beginning at the one hundred and twentieth mile post at the northwest corner of Sherman county; thence west about 47 miles to the 103rd meridian, and to a monument; thence south thirty miles; thence east forty-seven miles to the southwest corner of Sherman county; thence north thirty miles to the place of beginning.

The county of Hartley: Beginning on the 103rd meridian, and the southwest corner of Dallam county; thence east about forty-seven miles to the southwest corner of Sherman county and southeast corner of Dallam county; thence south thirty miles; thence west forty-seven miles; thence north thirty miles to the place of beginning.

The county of Moore: Beginning at the northeast corner of Hartley county and southwest corner of Sherman county; thence east thirty miles to the southwest corner of Hansford county; thence south thirty miles; thence west thirty miles to the southeast corner of Hartley county; thence north thirty miles to the place of beginning.

The county of Hutchinson: Beginning at the northeast corner of Moore county; thence east thirty miles; thence south thirty miles; thence west thirty miles; thence north thirty miles to the place of beginning.

The county of Roberts: Beginning at the northeast corner of Hutchinson county, and the southeast corner of Hansford county and southwest corner of Ochiltree county; thence east thirty miles to southeast corner of Ochiltree county and southwest corner of Lipscomb county; thence south thirty miles; thence west thirty miles to southeast corner of Hutchinson county; thence north thirty miles to the place of beginning.

The county of Hemphill: Beginning at the northeast corner of Roberts county, and the southeast corner of Ochiltree county and southwest corner of Lipscomb county; thence east thirty miles to the southeast corner of Lipscomb county, to the 102nd mile post on the 100th meridian; thence south thirty miles to the 72nd mile post; thence west thirty miles to the southeast corner of Roberts county; thence north thirty miles to the place of beginning.

The county of Wheeler: Beginning at the 72nd mile post, on the 100th meridian, the southeast corner of Hemphill county; thence west thirty miles to the southwest corner of Hemphill county and the southeast corner of Roberts county; thence south thirty miles; thence east thirty miles to the 42nd mile post, on the 100th meridian; thence north thirty miles to the place of beginning.

The county of Gray: Beginning at the northwest corner of Wheeler county and the southwest corner of Hemphill county; thence west thirty miles; thence south thirty miles; thence east thirty miles to the southwest corner of Wheeler county; thence north thirty miles to the place of beginning.

The county of Carson: Beginning at the northwest corner of Gray county and southwest corner of Roberts county and southeast corner of Hutchinson county; thence south thirty miles; thence west thirty miles; thence north thirty miles; thence east thirty miles to the place of beginning.

The county of Potter: Beginning at the northwest corner of Carson county and southwest corner of Hutchinson county, and southeast corner of Moore county; thence west thirty miles to southwest corner of Moore county and southeast corner of Hartley county; thence south thirty miles; thence east thirty miles to the southwest corner of Carson county; thence north thirty miles to the place of beginning.

The county of Oldham: Beginning at the northwest corner of Potter county, and southwest corner of Moore county and southeast corner of Hartley county; thence west about forty-seven miles to southwest corner of Hartley county, on the 103rd meridian; thence south thirty miles; thence east about forty-seven miles to southwest corner of Potter county; thence north thirty miles to the place of beginning.

The county of Deaf Smith: Beginning at the southwest corner of Oldham county, on the 103rd meridian; thence east about forty-seven miles to the southeast corner of Oldham county and southwest corner of Potter county; thence south thirty miles; thence west about forty-seven miles to the 103rd meridian; thence north thirty miles to the place of beginning.

The county of Randall: Beginning at the northeast corner of Deaf Smith county, and southeast corner of Oldham county and southwest corner of Potter county; thence east thirty miles to the southeast corner of Potter county and southwest corner of Carson county; thence south thirty miles; thence west thirty miles to southeast corner of Deaf Smith county; thence north thirty miles to the place of beginning.

The county of Armstrong: Beginning at the northeast corner of Randall, county, and southeast corner of Potter county and southwest corner of Carson County; thence east thirty miles to the southeast corner of Carson county and southwest corner of Gray county; thence south thirty miles; thence west thirty miles to southeast corner of Randall county; thence north thirty miles to the place of beginning.

The county of Donley: Beginning at the northeast corner of Armstrong county, and southeast corner of Carson county and southwest corner of Gray county; thence south thirty miles; thence east thirty miles; thence north thirty miles to the place of beginning.

The county of Collingsworth: Beginning at the northeast corner of Donley county, and southeast corner of Gray county and southwest corner of Wheeler county; thence east thirty miles to the southeast corner of Wheeler county, at the 42nd mile post on the 100th meridian; thence south thirty miles; thence west thirty miles to the southeast corner of Donley county; thence north thirty miles to the place of beginning.

The county of Childress: Beginning at the southeast corner of Collingsworth county, at the 12th mile post, on the 100th meridian; thence west 23 miles; thence south thirty miles; thence east about thirty-five miles, to the new west line of Hardeman county; thence north to Prairie-dog Town river; thence up said river to the initial monument on the 100th meridian; thence north to the 12th mile post, at the place of beginning.

The county of Hall: Beginning at the northwest corner of Childress county; thence west thirty miles; thence south thirty miles; thence east thirty miles to the southwest corner of Childress county; thence north thirty miles to the place of beginning.

The county of Briscoe: Beginning at the northwest corner of Hall county; thence west thirty miles; thence south thirty miles; thence east thirty miles; thence north thirty miles to the place of beginning.

The county of Swisher: Beginning at the northwest corner of Briscoe county; thence west thirty miles; thence south thirty miles; thence east thirty miles to southwest corner of Briscoe county; thence north thirty miles to the place of beginning.

The county of Castro: Beginning at the northwest corner of Swisher county; thence west thirty miles; thence south thirty miles; thence east thirty miles to southwest corner of Swisher county; thence north thirty miles to the place of beginning.

The county of Parmer: Beginning at the northwest corner of Castro county; thence west to the 103rd meridian and the southwest corner of Deaf Smith county; thence south with 103rd meridian thirty miles; thence east to the southwest corner of Castro county; thence north thirty miles to the place of beginning.

The county of Cottle: Beginning at the southeast corner of Childress county in the new west line of Hardeman county; thence west thirty miles; thence south to a point due west of the southwest corner of Hardeman county; thence east thirty miles to the new southwest corner of Hardeman county; thence north to the place of beginning.

The county of Motley: Beginning at the northwest corner of Cottle county; thence west thirty miles; thence south to a point thirty miles due west of the southwest corner of Cottle county; thence east thirty miles to the southwest corner of Cottle county; thence north thirty miles to the place of beginning.

The county of Floyd: Beginning at the northwest corner of Motley county; thence west thirty miles; thence south to a point thirty miles due west of the southwest corner of Motley county; thence east thirty miles to the southwest corner of Motley county; thence north to the place of beginning.

The county of Hale: Beginning at the northwest corner of Floyd county; thence west thirty miles; thence south to a point thirty miles due west of the southwest corner of Floyd county; thence east thirty miles to the southwest corner of Floyd county; thence north to the place of beginning.

The county of Lamb: Beginning at the northwest corner of Hale county; thence west thirty miles; thence south to a point thirty miles due west of the southwest corner of Hale county; thence east thirty miles to the southwest corner of Hale county; thence north to the place of beginning.

The county of Bailey: Beginning at the northwest corner of Lamb county; thence west to the 103rd meridian, at the southwest corner of Parmer county; thence south with the 103rd meridian to a point due west of the southwest corner of Lamb county; thence east to the southwest corner of Lamb county; thence north to the place of beginning.

The county of Cockran: Beginning at the southwest corner of Bailey county in the 103rd meridian; thence east to the southeast corner of Bailey county and southwest corner of Lamb county; thence south thirty miles; thence west to the 103rd meridian; thence north with said meridian to the place of beginning.

The county of Hockley: Beginning at the northeast corner of Cockran county, southeast corner of Bailey county and southwest corner of Lamb county; thence east thirty miles to the southeast corner of Lamb county and southwest corner of Hale county; thence south thirty miles; thence west thirty miles to the southeast corner of Cockran county; thence north to the place of beginning.

The county of Lubbock: Beginning at the northeast corner of Hockley county; thence east thirty miles; thence south thirty miles; thence west thirty miles to southeast corner of Hockley county; thence north to the place of beginning;

The county of Crosby: Beginning at the northeast corner of Lubbock county; thence east thirty miles to the southeast corner of Floyd county and southwest corner of Motley county; thence south thirty miles; thence west thirty miles to the southeast corner of Lubbock county; thence north thirty miles to the place of beginning.

The county of Dickens: Beginning at the northeast corner of Crosby county; thence east thirty miles; thence south thirty miles; thence west thirty miles to southeast corner of Crosby county; thence north thirty miles to the place of beginning.

The county of King: Beginning at the northeast corner of Dickens county; thence east thirty miles to the southeast corner of Cottle county; thence south thirty miles to the southwest corner of the new line of Knox county; thence west thirty miles to the southeast corner of Dickens county; thence north thirty miles to the place of beginning.

The county of Stonewall: Beginning at the southeast corner of King county; thence west thirty miles to the southwestern corner of Cottle county and southeast corner of Dickens county; thence south thirty miles; thence east thirty miles to southwest corner of new line of Haskell county; thence north thirty miles to the place of beginning.

The county of Kent: Beginning at the northwest corner of Stonewall county; thence west thirty miles; thence south thirty miles; thence east thirty miles to the southwest corner of Stonewall county; thence north thirty miles to the place of beginning.

The county of Garza: Beginning at the northwest corner of Kent county; thence west thirty miles; thence south thirty miles; thence east thirty miles; thence north thirty miles to the place of beginning.

The county of Lynn: Beginning at the northwest corner of Garza county; thence west thirty miles, to the southwest corner of Lubbock county; thence south thirty miles; thence east thirty miles; thence north thirty miles to the place of beginning.

The county of Terry: Beginning at the northwest corner of Lynn county; thence west thirty miles; thence south thirty miles; thence east thirty miles to southwest corner of Lynn county; thence north thirty miles to the place of beginning.

The county of Yoakum: Beginning at the northwest corner of Terry county; thence west to the southwest corner of Cockran county, on 103rd meridian; thence south thirty miles with said meridian; thence east to the southwest corner of Terry county; thence north thirty miles to the place of beginning.

The county of Fisher: Beginning at the northwest corner of Jones county—new corner; thence west thirty miles; thence south thirty miles; thence east thirty miles; thence north thirty miles to the place of beginning.

The county of Scurry: Beginning at the northwest corner of Fisher county; thence west thirty miles; thence south thirty miles; thence east thirty miles; thence north thirty miles to the place of beginning.

The county of Borden: Beginning at the northwest corner of Scurry county; thence west thirty miles; thence south thirty miles; thence east thirty miles to the southwest corner of Scurry county; thence north thirty miles to the place of beginning.

The county of Dawson: Beginning at the northwest corner of Borden county; thence west thirty miles; thence south thirty miles; thence east thirty miles to the southwest corner of Borden county; thence north thirty miles to the place of beginning.

The county of Gaines: Beginning at the northwest corner of Dawson county; thence west to the southwest corner of Yoakum county in the 103rd meridian; thence south with said meridian thirty miles; thence east to the southwest corner of Dawson county; thence north thirty miles to the place of beginning.

The county of Andrews: Beginning at the southwest corner of Gaines county in the 103rd meridian; thence east to the southeast corner of Gaines county; thence south thirty miles; thence west to the 103rd meridian; thence north with said meridian to the place of beginning.

The county of Martin: Beginning at the northeast corner of Andrews county and the southeast corner of Gaines county; thence east thirty miles to the southeast corner of Dawson county; thence south thirty miles; thence west thirty miles to the southeast corner of Andrews county; thence north thirty miles to the place of beginning.

The county of Howard: Beginning at the northeast corner of Martin county and the southeast corner of Dawson county; thence east thirty miles to the southeast corner of Borden county; thence south thirty miles; thence west thirty miles to the southeast corner of Martin county; thence north thirty miles to the place of beginning.

The county of Mitchell: Beginning at the northeast corner of Howard county and southeast corner of Borden county; thence east thirty miles to the southeast corner of Scurry county; thence south thirty miles; thence west thirty miles to the southeast corner of Howard county; thence north thirty miles to the place of beginning.

The county of Nolan: Beginning at the northeast corner of Mitchell county and the southeast corner of Scurry county; thence east thirty miles to the southeast corner of Fisher county and the new southwest corner of Jones county, and the new northwest corner of Taylor county; thence south thirty miles to the new southwest corner of Taylor county; thence west thirty miles to the southeast corner of Mitchell county; thence north to the place of beginning.

The county of Callahan shall be bounded as follows: Beginning at the southwest corner of Stephens county and the southeast corner of Shackelford county; thence west thirty miles; thence south thirty miles; thence east thirty miles; thence north thirty miles to the place of beginning.

The boundary of Eastland county line shall be hereafter as follows: Beginning at the southwest corner of Stephens county and southeast corner of Shackelford county, and northeast corner of Callahan county; thence South thirty miles to the southwest corner of Eastland county and southeast corner of Callahan county.

Taylor county shall hereafter be bounded as follows: Beginning at the northwest corner of Callahan county and the southwest corner of Shackelford county and the southeast corner of Jones county; thence west thirty miles to the southwest corner of Jones county; thence south thirty miles; thence east thirty miles to the southwest corner of Callahan county; thence north thirty miles to the place of beginning.

The county of Jones shall hereafter be bounded as follows: Beginning at the southwest corner of Shackleford county and northwest corner of Callahan county; thence west thirty miles; thence north thirty miles; thence east thirty miles; thence south thirty miles to the place of beginning.

Haskell county shall hereafter be bounded as follows: Beginning at the southwest corner of Throckmorton county; thence west thirty miles; thence north thirty miles; thence east thirty miles to the southwest corner of Baylor county and the northwest corner of Throckmorton county; thence south thirty miles to the place of beginning.

Knox county shall hereafter be bounded as follows: Beginning at the southwest corner of Baylor county and the northwest corner of Throckmorton county; thence west thirty miles; thence north thirty miles; thence east thirty miles to the southwest corner of Wilbarger county and northwest corner of Baylor county; thence south thirty miles to the place of beginning.

Hardeman county shall hereafter be bounded as follows: Beginning at the southwest corner of Wilbarger county; thence west thirty miles; thence north to the Prairie-dog Town River; thence down said river to the western boundary line of Wilbarger county; thence south with said line to the place of beginning.

SEC. 2. The county of Hemphill is named in honor of John Hemphill, the first Chief Justice of the Supreme Court of Texas. The county of Wheeler is named in honor of Royall T. Wheeler, the second Chief Justice of the Supreme Court of Texas. The county of Lipscomb is named in honor of Abner S. Lipscomb, one of the associate Justices of the first Supreme Court of Texas. The county of Collingsworth is named in honor of James Collingsworth, the first Chief Justice of the Republic of Texas. The county of Ochiltree is named in honor of W. B. Ochiltree, a distinguished Texan Judge. The county of Sherman is named in honor of Sidney Sherman, a distinguished soldier of San Jacinto. The county of Moore is named in honor of Commodore E. W. Moore, of the Texas Navy. The county of Hockley is named in honor of G. W. Hockley, who was Adjutant and Inspector-General at the battle of San Jacinto. The county of Martin is named in honor of Wyly Martin, the President of the Consultation. The county of Potter is named in honor of Robert Potter, a distinguished Texan in the days of the Republic. The county of Carson is named in honor of Samuel P. Carson, Secretary of State under the Republic. The county of Fisher is named in honor of S. Rhoads Fisher, a distinguished officer of the Republic. The county of Castro is named in honor of Henry Castro, a distinguished pioneer and colonizer of Texas. The county of Swisher is named in honor of James G. Swisher, who commanded a company at the storming of Bexar, in 1835, and was one of the signers of the Declaration of Texas Independence. The county of Briscoe is named in honor of Andrew Briscoe, who commanded a company at the battle of Concepcion, in 1835. The county of Childress is named in honor of George C. Childress, the author of the Declaration of Texan Independence. The county of Hansford is named in honor of John M. Hansford, one of the Judges during the Republic. The county of Hutchinson is named in honor of Anderson Hutchinson, one of the Judges during the Republic. The county of Dallam is named in honor of James W. Dallam, a laborious lawyer of the Texan Republic. The county of Oldham is named in honor of Williamson S. Oldham, Sr., a distinguished jurist and orator of Texas. The county of Gray is named in honor of Peter W. Gray, the learned and incorruptible Judge, the able advocate and unflinching patriot. The county of Donley is named in honor of Stockton P. Donley, one of the Supreme Judges of Texas. The county of Scurry is named in honor of Wm. R. Scurry, who fought and died as a soldier should. The county of Randall is named in honor of H. Randall, who fell in battle at the head of his brigade. The county of Mitchell is named in honor of two brothers, Asa Mitchell, a member of the Consultation, and Eli Mitchell, who fired the first cannon in the Texas Revolution, at Gonzales. The county of Howard is named in honor of Volney E. Howard, a distinguished orator and Congressman from Texas. The county of Nolan is named in honor of Philip Nolan, the great pioneer and scout, who explored Texas in 1800. The county of Deaf Smith is named in honor of Erastus Smith, the intrepid spy, who served his country so well in the Revolution of 1836. The county of Lubbock is named in honor of Tom Lubbock, Colonel of the Terry Rangers. The county of Crosby is named in honor of Stephen Crosby, one of the Commissioners of the General Land Office. The county of Garza is named in honor of the family of that name, who were one of the first thirteen families who came from the Canary Islands and founded San Antonio. The county of King is named in honor of W. King, one of the heroes who fell at the Alamo. The county of Stonewall is named in honor of the immortal T. J. Jackson. The county of Kent is named in honor of R. Kent, one of those who made the Alamo glorious. The county of Dawson is named in honor of Nicholas Dawson, who commanded the Texas troops at the Salado massacre in 1842. The county of Lynn is named in honor of G. W. Lynn, one of those who baptized the altar of Texas with his life-blood at the Alamo. The county of Lamb is named in honor of Lieutenant Lamb, who fell at San Jacinto. The county of Hale is named in honor of Lieutenant J. C. Hale, who fell at San Jacinto. The county of Floyd is named in honor of D. Floyd, whose name is inscribed on the monumental stone of the Alamo. The county of Motley is named in honor of Dr. William Motley, who was mortally wounded in the battle of San Jacinto. The county of Cottle is named in honor of G. W. Cottle, who fell fighting for Texas at the Alamo. The county of Borden is named in honor of Gail Borden, an early Texas pioneer, afterwards distinguished in the scientific world. The county of Dickens is named in honor of J. Dickens, who sacrificed his life on the altar of Texas liberty at the Alamo. The county of Yoakum is named in honor of Henderson Yoakum, the historian of Texas. The county of Cockran is named in honor of —— Cockran, a private, who died at his post of duty in the Alamo. The county of Terry is named in honor of Frank Terry, whose name is inseparably linked with that other glorious name, "Texas Ranger." The county of Bailey is named in honor of —— Bailey, a name which cannot be entirely defaced from the monument of the Alamo. The county of Hall is named in honor of Warren D. C. Hall, who was Adjutant-General of the Texas army in 1835. The county of Andrews is named in honor of Richard Andrews, the first Texan who fell in the Revolution, and who was killed at the battle of Concepcion, on the 28th of October, 1835. The county of Hartley is named in honor of the two brothers, O. C. and R. K. Hartley, distinguished members of the Texas bar. The county of Roberts is named in honor of John S. Roberts, one of the signers of the Declaration of Texas Independence, and other distinguished Texans of the

16 GL

same name. The county of Armstrong is named in honor of several early Texas pioneers of that name. The county of Parmer is named in honor of Martin Parmer, an eccentric Texan of the olden time, and one of the signers of the Declaration of Texas Independence. The county of Gaines is named in honor of James Gaines, an old Texan and valuable citizen.

SEC. 3.   That the law creating Wegefarth county, and all laws and parts of laws in conflict with this act, be and the same are hereby repealed.

SEC. 4.   That the counties of Collingsworth, Donley, Gray, Wheeler, Roberts, Hemphill, Lipscomb, Hall, Ochiltree and Childress, be and the same are hereby attached to the county of Clay, for judicial, surveying and all other purposes.

SEC. 5.   That the counties of Bailey, Lamb, Hale, Motley, Cottle, Floyd, Briscoe, Swisher, Castro, Parmer, Deaf Smith, Oldham, Hartley, Moore, Hutchinson, Hansford, Sherman, Dallam, Potter, Carson, Randall and Armstrong, be and the same are hereby attached to the county of Jack, for judicial, surveying and all other purposes.

SEC. 6.   That the counties of King, Dickens, Crosby, Lubbock, Hockley, Cockran, Stonewall, Kent, Garza, Lynn, Terry and Yoakum, be and the same are hereby attached to the county of Young, for judicial, surveying and all other purposes.

SEC. 7.   That the counties of Fisher, Scurry, Borden, Dawson, Gaines, Andrews, Martin, Howard, Mitchell and Nolan, be and the same are hereby attached to the county of Shackleford, for judicial, surveying and all other purposes.

SEC. 8.   Whereas, these counties are unorganized and unattached to any organized counties, and there is no judicial authority having jurisdiction over this part of the public domain, to try offenders for any offenses committed therein, an imperative public necessity exists for the immediate passage and operation of this act; therefore, that it take effect and be in full force from and after its passage.

Approved August 21, 1876.

Takes effect ninety days after adjournment.

CHAPTER CXLV.—*An Act to amend Article 757 of an act entitled, " An Act to adopt and establish a penal code for the State of Texas," approved August 26, 1856; November 12, 1866.*

SECTION 1.   *Be it enacted by the Legislature of the State of Texas,* That Article 757 of the above recited act shall hereafter read as follows, viz: "Theft of property, under the value of twenty dollars, shall be punished by imprisonment in the county jail for a term not exceeding one year, during which time the prisoner may be put to hard work, and by fine not exceeding five hundred dollars, or by such imprisonment without fine."

SEC. 2.   That all laws and parts of laws in conflict with the provisions of this act be, and the same are hereby repealed.

Approved August 21, 1876.

Takes effect ninety days after adjournment.

CHAPTER CXLVI.—*An Act to regulate taxation and to fix the rate of the same.*

SECTION 1.   *Be it enacted by the Legislature of the State of Texas,* That there shall be levied and collected an annual direct *ad valorem* State tax of one-half ($\frac{1}{2}$) of one per cent. of the cash value thereof, estimated in lawful currency of the United States, on all real property situate, and all movable property owned in this State (except so much thereof as is exempted from taxation by the laws of this State), on the first day of January, A. D. 1877, and on that day in every year thereafter, one-fourth ($\frac{1}{4}$) of the aforesaid tax shall be for the benefit of public schools, and three-fourths ($\frac{3}{4}$) for the support of the State Government, and the payment of the interest on the public debt, as may be directed by law; *provided*, the cost of assessing and collecting shall be paid *pro rata* out of each fund.

SEC. 2. That there shall be levied on and collected from every male person between the ages of twenty-one and sixty years, resident within this State, on the first day of January, 1877, and on that day in every year thereafter (Indians not taxed and persons insane excepted), an annual poll tax of two dollars each, one dollar for the use and benefit of public free schools, and one dollar for general revenue purposes.

SEC. 3. That there shall be levied on and collected from every person, firm, company or association of persons, pursuing any of the following named occupations, an annual tax (except when herein otherwise provided) on every such occupation or separate establishment, as follows: For selling spirituous, vinous or other intoxicating liquors in quantities less than one quart, two hundred and fifty dollars; in quantities of a quart and less than five gallons, one hundred and fifty dollars; *provided*, this section shall not be so construed as to include any wines, liquors or alcohol, sold by druggists exclusively for medical purposes; for selling in quantities of five gallons and over, two hundred dollars; for selling beer exclusively, fifty dollars; from every wholesale merchant, an annual tax of fifty dollars; from every first-class retail merchant, an annual tax of thirty dollars; from every second-class retail merchant, an annual tax of twenty dollars; and from every third-class retail merchant, an annual tax of ten dollars; and from every fourth-class retail merchant, an annual tax of five dollars. A wholesale merchant is one whose annual purchases amount to one hundred thousand dollars or more; a first class retail merchant is one whose annual purchases amount to less than one hundred thousand dollars and more than fifty thousand dollars; a second class retail merchant is one whose annual purchases amount to less than fifty thousand dollars and more than twenty-five thousand dollars; a third class retail merchant is one whose annual purchases amount to less than twenty-five thousand dollars and more than twelve thousand dollars, and a fourth class retail merchant is one whose annual purchases amount to less than twelve thousand dollars. A merchant is any person or firm engaged in buying and selling goods, wares or merchandise of any kind whatever. From every traveling person selling or bartering patent rights, fifty dollars; from every traveling person selling patent or other medicines, five hundred dollars; and no traveling person shall so sell until said tax is paid; *provided*, this tax shall not apply to persons traveling and selling patent medicines to merchants and druggists by the wholesale; from every fortune-teller, one hundred dollars; from every spiritualist, clairvoyant, mesmerist or medium, so-called, who plies his or her vocation for money, ten dollars for each and every county; from every person, firm or association of persons engaged in discounting and shaving paper, or engaged in business as money brokers, in any city or town exceeding five thousand inhabitants, an annual tax of one hundred dollars; and from every other such person, firm or association of persons, an annual tax of twenty-five dollars; *provided*, that no such person, firm or association of persons who have paid a tax for dealing out stocks or bills of exchange, shall be so taxed. From every owner or operator of daguerrean, photograph or such like gallery, by whatsoever name called, if in any incorporated city or town of less than five thousand inhabitants, ten dollars; if more than five thousand inhabitants, twenty dollars; and if elsewhere, five dollars. From every auctioneer doing business in a city of ten thousand inhabitants or over, an annual tax of fifty dollars. From every auctioneer in a city of five thousand inhabitants and less than ten thousand, forty dollars. From every auctioneer in a city of two thousand inhabitants and less than five thousand, thirty dollars. From auctioneers in all other towns or villages, twenty dollars. From every person, firm or association of persons following the occupation of ship merchandise, ten dollars. From every keeper of a public ferry, an annual tax of ten dollars. From every keeper of a toll bridge, an annual tax of ten dollars. From every person, firm or association of persons, selling upon commission, if in a city of more than five thousand inhabitants, an annual tax of fifty dollars; in all other cases, twenty-five dollars. From land agents there shall be collected an annual tax of ten dollars. The term, "land agent," shall be construed to mean any person or member of a firm or association of persons performing for compensation any of the following services: purchasing or selling real estate for others; purchasing or selling land certificates for others; examining into land claims for others. But this term, "land agents," shall not be so construed as to levy any tax in addition to the tax levied on attorneys-at-law. This shall not be construed to tax more than one member of any firm doing business as land agents. For every person practicing law, ten dollars; *provided*, that attorneys-at-law shall only pay county occupation tax in the county of his residence. For every practicing physician having a permanent home in this State, ten dollars; and for every physician or surgeon having no permanent home in this State, ten dollars in each county where he may practice his profession. For every dentist, ten dollars. For every billiard, bagatelle, pigeon-hole or Jenny Lind table, or anything of the kind used for profit, fifty dollars. For every nine or ten pin alley, without regard to any number of pins, used for pleasure or profit, fifty dollars. For every foot pedler, ten dollars in each and every county. For every pedler with one horse or one pair of oxen, in each and every county, twenty-five dollars. For every pedler with two horses or two pair of oxen, fifty dollars, in each and every county in which he may pursue such occupation; *provided*, that nothing herein contained shall be so construed as to include traveling vendors of fruits or fruit trees, or earthenware. For every theatre or dramatic representation for which pay for admittance is demanded or received, five dollars, or one hundred and twenty-five dollars per quarter; *provided*, that theatrical or dramatic entertainments given by performers for instructions only, or for charitable purposes only, shall not be herein included. For every circus where equestrian performances or acrobatic feats are exhibited, for which pay for admittance is demanded or received, for each performance thereof, notwithstanding more than one such may take place daily, one hundred dollars; and for every bull fight, between men and bulls or dogs and bulls, fifty dollars for each such performance, if exhibited for pay; for every menagerie, wax work or exhibition of any kind where a separate fee for admission is demanded or received, twelve dollars for every day on which fees for such admissions are received ; for every concert where a fee for admittance is demanded or received, six dollars; *provided*, that entertainments given by the citizens of any city or town for charitable purposes are excepted ; for every livery or feed stable, one dollar for each stall, and one dollar for each hack, buggy or other vehicle; from every person, firm or association of persons, dealing in stocks or bills of exchange in any city or town exceeding ten thousand inhabitants, an annual tax of one hundred dollars; in any city or town of five thousand inhabitants and less than ten thousand, an annual tax of fifty dollars ; in any city or town of one thousand inhabitants and less than five thousand, an annual tax of twenty-five dollars; in any city or town of less than one thousand inhabitants, an annual tax of ten dollars ; from every life insurance company doing business in this State, an annual tax of two hundred dollars, and in every county in which they may do business, ten dollars, as county taxes; from every fire and marine insurance company doing business in this State, an annual tax of two hundred dollars, and in every county in which they may do business, five dollars, as county taxes; the State tax due from insurance companies shall be paid by the company to the Comptroller of Public Accounts, whose receipt, under seal, shall be issued to the company, certified copies of which shall be evidence of payment of State tax, and the County Collector's receipt shall be authority to work in any county in this State for which said company has a receipt; from every person, firm or association of persons dealing in lightning rods, two hundred dollars, and in every county in which they may do business, the further sum of ten dollars for the use of the county; from every person, firm or association of persons keeping a barber shop, one dollar for every chair therein at which a barber works; from every person, firm or association of persons following the occupation of cotton broker, in a city of more than five thousand inhabitants, an annual tax of fifty dollars; in all other cases twenty-five dollars; from every pawnbroker, an annual tax of forty dollars; from all sewing machine agents, the sum of one hundred dollars to the State, and twenty-five dollars to each county in which they do business.

Sec. 4. The Commissioners' Court of the several counties of this State shall have the power of levying taxes equal to one-half of the amount of the State tax herein levied, except on occupations in which there is a specific rate of taxation payable to the county, is fixed in this act; *provided*, that any one wishing to pursue any of the vocations named in this act for a less period than one year, may do so by paying a *pro rata* amount of such occupation for the period he may desire; *provided, further*, that no such occupation license shall issue for a less period than three months; *and provided further*, that the receipt of the proper officer shall be *prima facie* evidence of the payment of such tax ; *and provided further*, that the provisions of this act shall not be deemed to affect the provisions of any law specially authorizing any Commissioners' Court to levy a different rate of tax; *and provided, further*, that the tax herein authorized to be levied by the County Commissioners' Courts shall not be construed to authorize said courts to levy a higher rate of tax than ten dollars on life insurance companies, and five dollars on fire and marine insurance companies.

Sec. 5. That any license taken out which has not expired at the date of this act taking effect, shall avail the party to whom the same was granted for the full time for which such license was issued.

SEC. 6.   That the taxes levied by this act are hereby made payable in the currency or coin of the United States; *provided*, that all *ad valorem* county tax may be paid in jury and county scrip of their respective counties.

SEC. 7.   That it shall be the duty of every person, firm, corporation or association owning any property subject to taxation by the laws of this State, on the first day of January of each and every year, to render and return the same for the purposes of taxation, as is required by law.

SEC. 8.   That all laws and parts of laws in conflict with the provisions of this act are hereby repealed.

SEC. 9.   Whereas, the day of adjournment has been set for next Monday, the twenty-first instant; and whereas, the finances of the State demand the passage of a law fixing the rate of taxation, therefore, an emergency and public necessity exists for the immediate passage of this act.

NOTE.—The above bill was not approved by the Governor, nor was the same returned to the house in which it originated with his objections thereto, but was filed by the Governor in the office of Secretary of State on the 21st day of August, 1876, at 11 o'clock and 10 minutes A. M., being before the Legislature adjourned, and becomes a law without the approval of the Governor, and takes effect ninety days after the adjournment of the Legislature.

A. W. DEBERRY, *Secretary of State.*

CHAPTER CXLVII.—*An Act to make appropriations for the support of the State Government for the fiscal years ending August* 31, 1877, 1878, *and for additional period of time, ending December* 31, 1878.

SECTION 1.   *Be it enacted by the Legislature of the State of Texas,* That the following sums, or so much thereof as may be necessary, be and the same are hereby appropriated out of any moneys in the Treasury not otherwise appropriated for the support of the State Government for the fiscal years ending August 31, 1877, 1878, and for additional period of time, ending December 31, 1878:

EXECUTIVE OFFICE.

	Years ending August 31,		December 31,
	1877.	1878.	1878.
For salary of Governor.............	$4,000 00	$4,000 00	$1,333 33
For salary of Private Secretary..	1,800 00	1,800 00	600 00
For salary of Clerk.................	1,200 00	1,200 00	400 00
For telegraphing	400 00	400 00	133 33
For books and stationery........	400 00	400 00	133 33
For postage.........................	250 00	250 00	83 33
For porter hire, Executive office and office of Secretary of State..............................	480 00	480 00	160 00
For gardener........................	400 00	400 00	133 33
For repairs and furniture, Governor's mansion...............	500 00	500 00	83 33
For wood, lights, etc., Executive office......	200 00	200 00	66 66
For gas for mansion...............	200 00	200 00	66 66
For contingent fund..............	200 00	200 00	66 66

	Years ending August 31, 1877.	August 31, 1878.	December 31, 1878.
For recovering fugitives from justice..............................	$15,000 00	$15,000 00	$5,000 00

STATE DEPARTMENT.

For salary of Secretary of State	$2,000 00	$2,000 00	$666 66
For salary of Chief Clerk.........	1,800 00	1,800 00	600 00
For salary of two Clerks.........	2,400 00	2,400 00	800 00
For salary of extra Clerk to copy laws for printer...............	250 00	....	....
For postage............................	1,250 00	1,000 00	333 33
Freight and express charges.....	250 00	250 00	83 33
Contingent expenses...............	50 00	50 00	16 66
For books and stationery.........	500 00	500 00	166 66
For wood..............................	100 00	100 00	33 33
For lights.............................	50 00	50 00	16 66
For printing...........................	30,000 00	....	....

TREASURY DEPARTMENT.

For salary of Treasurer...........	$2,500 00	$2,500 00	$833 33
For salary of Chief Clerk........	1,800 00	1,800 00	600 00
For salary of Bookkeeper.........	1,650 00	1,650 00	550 00
For salary of Assistant Clerk...	1,200 00	1,200 00	400 00
For salary of night watchman...	900 00	900 00	300 00
For porter hire, Treasurer's and Comptroller's Departments	480 00	480 00	160 00
For books and stationery.........	300 00	300 00	100 00
For wood and lights...............	150 00	150 00	50 00
For postage............................	200 00	200 00	66 66
For contingent fund.................	100 00	100 00	33 33

COMPTROLLER'S OFFICE.

Salary of Comptroller..............	$2,500 00	$2,500 00	$833 33
Salary of Chief Clerk..............	2,000 00	2,000 00	666 66
Salary of Bookkeeper..............	1,800 00	1,800 00	600 00
Salary of Assistant Bookkeeper..	1,250 00	1,250 00	416 66
Salary of Chief Tax Clerk.........	1,650 00	1,650 00	550 00
Salary of Warrant Clerk.........	1,800 00	1,800 00	600 00
Salary of Assistant Warrant Clerk.............................	1,200 00	1,200 00	400 00
Salary of Delinquent Tax Clerk	1,600 00	1,600 00	533 33
Salary of Assistant Delinquent Tax Clerk.........	1,200 00	1,200 00	400 00
Salary of additional Clerks......	12,000 00	12,000 00	4,000 00
Telegraphing	50 00	50 00	16 66
Wood.........	250 00	250 00	83 33
Postage, current correspondence and forwarding assessment rolls...............................	1,500 00	1,500 00	500 00
Furniture for office.................	300 00	....	....
Contingent expenses and repairs of rooms.................	250 00	150 00	50 00
Books and stationery..............	1,000 00	1,000 00	333 33
(Publishing), printing and binding abstract of land titles...	30,000 00	....	....

GENERAL LAND OFFICE.

	Years ending August 31, 1877.	1878.	December 31, 1878.
Salary of Commissioner...........	$2,500 00	$2,500 00	$833 33
Salary of Chief Clerk..............	2,000 00	2,000 00	666 66
Salary of Spanish Clerk...........	1,800 00	1,800 00	600 00
Salary of Receiving Clerk.........	1,600 00	1,600 00	533 33
Salary of Examining Clerk......	1,500 00	1,500 00	500 00
Salary of Calculator...............	1,500 00	1,500 00	500 00
Salary of first Assistant Clerk...	1,500 00	1,500 00	500 00
Salary of two Abstract Clerks...	3,000 00	3,000 00	....
Salary of two Filing Clerks........	2,500 00	2,500 00	833 33
Salary of two Corresponding Clerks..............................	2,800 00	2,800 00	933 33
Salary of principal Patent Clerk	1,400 00	1,400 00	466 66
Salary of fifteen Assistant Clerks	15,750 00	15,750 00	5,250 00
Salary of Chief Draftsman......	1,800 00	1,800 00	600 00
Salary of Compiling and Abstract Draftsman........................	1,500 00	1,500 00	....
Salary of four Compiling Draftsmen............	6,000 00	6,000 00	2,000 00
Salary of ten Assistant Draftsmen...............	12,000 00	12,000 00	· 4,000 00
Salary of one night watchman..	500 00	500 00	166 66
Salary of one porter..............	400 00	400 00	133 33
Stationery, books and furniture	3,000 00	3,000 00	1,000 00
Postage	500 00	500 00	166 66
Wood................................	250 00	250 00	83 33
Contingent expenses.............	150 00	150 00	50 00
For building fence around the Land Office.....................	350 00	....	....
For extending file room...........	500 00	....	....

LUNATIC ASYLUM.

Salary of Superintendent.........	$2,000 00	$2,000 00	$666 66
Salary of Assistant Superintendent...................	1,200 00	1,200 00	400 00
Salary of Steward..................	1,200 00	1,200 00	400 00
Salary of Matron...................	500 00	500 00	166 66
Salary of ten male wards, $25 per month.....................	3,000 00	3,000 00	1,000 00
Salary of eight female wards, $25 per month...............	2,400 00	2,400 00	800 00
Salary of four seamstresses, $20 per month.....................	960 00	960 00	320 00
Salary of five laundresses, $20 per month.....................	1,200 00	1,200 00	400 00
Salary of one night watchman..	480 00	480 00	160 00
Salary of one day watchman...	300 00	300 00	100 00
Salary of one gardener...........	360 00	360 00	120 00
Salary of two assistant gardeners, $15 per month.................	360 00	360 00	120 00
Salary of one scavenger...........	360 00	360 00	120 00
Salary of one chief cook..........	360 00	360 00	120 00

| | Years ending August 31, | | December 31, |
	1877.	1878.	1878.
Salary of one assistant cook.....	$300 00	$300 00	$100 00
Salary of one cook for officers, private patients and sick...	300 00	300 00	100 00
Salary of one carpenter...........	480 00	480 00	160 00
Purchase of medical stores, etc.	500 00	500 00	166 66
Purchase of clothing, dry goods	4,000 00	4,000 00	1,333 33
Purchase of bedding.........	200 00	200 00	66 66
Purchase of groceries, provisions and wood.........	20,000 00	20,000 00	6,666 66
Repairs of buildings...............	500 00	500 00	166 66
Miscellaneous......	950 00	950 00	316 66
For transportation of indigent lunatics from the State Asylum to their homes.....	2,000 00	2,000 00	666 66

BLIND ASYLUM.

Salary of Superintendent..........	$2,000 00	$2,000 00	$666 66
Salary of principal teacher......	720 00	720 00	240 00
Salary of assistant teacher........	500 00	500 00	166 66
Salary of second assistant teacher	420 00	420 00	140 00
Salary of third assistant teacher	240 00	240 00	80 00
Salary of music teacher...........	600 00	600 00	200 00
Salary of matron....................	480 00	480 00	160 00
Groceries, provisions, and miscellaneous.................	12,200 00	12,200 00	4,100 00
Oculist	900 00	900 00	300 00
Cook and assistant..................	360 00	360 00	120 00
Seamstress...............	300 00	300 00	100 00
Washer and ironer and assistants	360 00	360 00	120 00
To purchase one piano, two sewing machines, books, and prepare for telegraphing.....	1,000 00	....	....

DEAF AND DUMB ASYLUM.

Salary of Superintendent........	$2,000 00	$2,000 00	$666 66
Salary of principal teacher.......	1,200 00	1,200 00	400 00
Salary of second teacher..........	800 00	800 00	266 66
Salary of third teacher............	480 00	480 00	160 00
Salary of fourth teacher...........	420 00	420 00	140 00
Salary of instructor in printing and expert employed by Printing Board.................	1,000 00	1,000 00	333 33
Salary of matron....................	480 00	480 00	160 00
Salary of assistant matron, or seamstress......................	360 00	360 00	120 00
Salary of gardener..................	360 00	360 00	120 00
Salary of driver and laborer.....	240 00	240 00	80 00
Salary of washer and ironer.....	240 00	240 00	80 00
Salary of assistant washer and ironer.......................	216 00	216 00	72 00
Salary of two cooks.................	456 00	456 00	152 00
Groceries, provisions and miscellaneous......................	9,420 00	9,420 00	3,140 00

	Years ending August 31, 1877.	1878.	December 31. 1878.
New building and improvements	$1,000 00	$8,000 00	....
For printing material	500 00	....	....

PUBLIC FREE SCHOOLS.

The entire available school fund, annually derived from all sources, including the poll tax and one-fourth of the general revenue, is hereby set aside annually for the support of the public free schools of this State for the years 1877, 1878, and a proportionate part thereof to the 31st day of December, 1878.

PENITENTIARY.

For conveying prisoners	$30,000 00	$30,000 00	$10,000 00
For building eastern branch Penitentiary	40,000 00	120,000 00	....

QUARANTINE.

For pay of health officers under the quarantine laws on the Gulf coast of Texas	$12,000 00	$12,000 00	$4,000 00

PENSIONS.

For payment of old pensions	$1,800 00	$1,800 00	$600 00
For payment of pensions under present laws	20,000 00	20,000 00	6,666 66

ADJUTANT-GENERAL'S OFFICE.

Salary of Adjutant-General	$2,500 00	$2,500 00	$833 33
Salary of Chief Clerk	1,800 00	1,800 00	600 00
Salary of Clerk	1,200 00	1,200 00	400 00
Stationery, postage and telegraphing	450 00	450 00	150 00
Wood and porter hire	350 00	350 00	116 66
Contingent expenses for repairing arms, and removing arms and ammunition	300 00	300 00	100 00
Storage on arms	600 00	600 00	200 00
Protection of the frontier	150,000 00	150,000 00	50,000 00

ATTORNEY-GENERAL'S OFFICE.

Salary of Attorney-General	$2,000 00	$2,000 00	$666 66
Salary and traveling expenses of Assistant Attorney-General	3,000 00	3,000 00	1,000 00
Salary of Clerks	3,000 00	3,000 00	1,000 00
Stationery	150 00	150 00	50 00
Postage	150 00	150 00	50 00
Wood and lights	100 00	100 00	33 33
Fees in felony cases	1,000 00	1,000 00	333 33
Contingent expenses	300 00	300 00	100 00

JUDICIARY.

Salaries of three Judges Supreme Court	$10,650 00	$10,650 00	$3,550 00
Sa.y of Sheriffs' attendance	1,000 00	1,000 00	333 33

	Years ending August 31,		December 31,
	1877.	1878.	1878.
Books and stationery, Supreme Court............................	$800 00	$800 00	$266 66
Postage and contingent expenses	800 00	800 00	266 66
Porter hire............................	480 00	480 00	160 00
Costs to be paid Sheriffs' clerks an(d) Attorneys in District and County Courts............	50,000 00	50,000 00	16,666 66
Publishing Supreme Court Reports............................	5,000 00	5,000 00	1,666 66
Fees of committing Magistrates, Sheriffs and Constables in committing courts............	35,000 00	35,000 00	11,666 66
Publishing Court of Appeals Reports............................	5,000 00	5,000 00	1,666 66
Librarians of Supreme Court and Court of Appeals..............	900 00	900 00	300 00
Fuel and lights for Supreme Court............................	250 00	250 00	83 33
Fuel and lights for Court of Appeals...........................	250 00	250 00	83 33
For repairing Supreme Court building, etc......................	750 00	....	....
Salaries for three Appellate Judges...........................	10,650 00	10,650 00	3,500 00
Pay of Sheriffs' attendance on Court of Appeals..............	1,000 00	1,000 00	3,333 33
Clerks' fees in criminal cases, Court of Appeals..............	2,000 00	2,000 00	666 66
Books and stationery and furniture, Court of Appeals.....	1,500 00	500 00	300 00
Porter hire, Court of Appeals...	480 00	480 00	160 00
Salaries of twenty-seven District Judges............................	67,500 00	67,500 00	22,500 00
Salary of Judge of Criminal District Court of Galveston and Harris counties................	3,500 00	3,500 00	1,000 00
Salaries of District Attorney in First, Twelfth, Seventeenth, Twentieth, Twenty-third, and Twenty-sixth Judicial Districts............................	3,000 00	3,000 00	1,000 00
Salaries of District Attorney of the Criminal District Court for the counties of Galveston and Harris..................	500 00	500 00	166 66
For salaries of five Commissioners to digest the laws of the State, or so much thereof as may be necessary.............	12,500 00	12,500 00	....

INTEREST.

For the annual interest on debt	$390,000 00	$390,000 00	$130,000 00

SINKING FUND.

	Years ending August 31, 1877.	1873.	December 31, 1878.
For the annual sinking fund on debt..............................	$100,000 00	$100,000 00	$33,333 33

PUBLIC BUILDINGS AND GROUNDS.

Salary of Superintendent.........	$1,200 00	$1,200 00	$400 00
Plants and trees.....................	200 00	200 00	66 66
Binding books of State Library	300 00	150 00	50 00
For labor..............................	500 00	500 00	166 66
For providing the State Capitol buildings and Capitol grounds with water, water works fixtures, etc., for the year 1877........................	3,600 00	....	....

DEPARTMENT OF INSURANCE, STATISTICS AND HISTORY.

Salary of Commissioner...........	$2,000 00	$2,000 00	$666 66
Salary of Clerk......................	1,200 00	1,200 00	400 00
Postage, printing, wood and lights...............................	500 00	500 00	166 66

SEC. 2.   That this act shall take effect and be in force from and after its passage.

SEC. 3.   That the near approach of the close of the session and the accumulation of important bills, create an imperative public necessity for the suspension of the rules in order that this bill may be immediately passed.

NOTE.—The above bill was not approved by the Governor, nor was the same returned to the house in which it originated with his objections thereto, but was filed by the Governor in the office of Secretary of State on the 21st day of August, 1876, at 11 o'clock and 10 minutes, A. M., being before the Legislature adjourned, and becomes a law without the approval of the Governor.

A. W. DEBERRY, *Secretary of State.*

CHAPTER CXLVIII.—*An Act to be entitled "An Act to prevent the forgery of titles to lands."*

SECTION 1.   *Be it enacted by the Legislature of the State of Texas,* That in any county in this State wherein the land records or records of titles to land have been or may hereafter be burned or otherwise destroyed, it shall not be lawful for the Clerk of the County Court to permit any person who files a deed for record to remove said deed from the office of said Clerk for the period of twelve months after the same is filed for record ; *provided,* this act shall not apply to deeds executed, or purporting to be executed, subsequent to the destruction of said land records.

SEC. 2.   Any Clerk violating the provisions of this act shall be deemed guilty of a misdemeanor, and upon conviction therefor, before any court of competent jurisdiction, shall be punished by a fine of not less than one hundred nor more than one thousand dollars ; and in addition thereto may, in the discretion of the jury, be imprisoned in the county jail for any period of time not to exceed one year.

SEC. 3.   Whereas, there are many persons engaged in forging land titles in different counties in the State in which court-houses have been burned, and thereby many citizens may lose their land through such forgeries, a public necessity and emergency exists for immediate legislation to prevent such evils; therefore, it is hereby enacted that this act take effect and be in force from and after its passage.

Approved August 21, 1876.

Takes effect from its passage.

CHAPTER CXLIX.—*An Act to authorize the levy and collection of a special tax in Blanco, Smith, Tarrant, Erath, Denton, Parker, Lampasas, Camp, Sabine, Cameron, Brown, Delta, Nacogdoches, Rockwall, Limestone, Gregg, Franklin, Madison, Lee, Navarro and Angelina counties for the years 1876, 1877 and 1878, to erect a court-house and jail in each, and such other counties as may find it necessary for the construction of court-houses and jails.*

SECTION 1. *Be it enacted by the Legislature of the State of Texas,* That the County Commissioners' Courts of Blanco, Smith, Tarrant, Erath, Denton, Parker, Lampasas, Camp, Sabine, Cameron, Brown, Delta, Nacogdoches, Rockwall, Limestone, Gregg, Franklin, Madison, Lee, Navarro and Angelina counties, and such other counties where it may become necessary to construct court-houses and jails, be and they are hereby authorized and empowered to levy and collect an annual *ad valorem* tax of fifty cents on the one hundred dollars worth of property in said counties for the years 1876, 1877 and 1878, to raise a fund to erect a court-house and jail in each of said counties.

SEC. 2. That an imperative public necessity and emergency exist for the erection of said buildings in said counties, and the immediate passage of this act; therefore, this act shall take effect and be in force from and after its passage.

Approved August 21, 1876.

Takes effect ninety days after adjournment.

CHAPTER CL.—*An Act to encourage irrigation and navigation.*

SECTION 1. *Be it enacted by the Legislature of the State of Texas,* That any person, firm, corporation or company who shall construct a canal or ditch for navigation or irrigation, in accordance with the provisions of this act, shall receive from the State a grant of land as herein provided.

SEC. 2. For canals or ditches of the first class, eight sections of land to the mile; for canals or ditches of the second class, six sections to the mile; for canals or ditches of the third class, four sections to the mile; for canals or ditches of the fourth class, two sections to the mile; *provided,* canals for navigation having a width of forty (40) feet and a permanent depth of water of four feet shall receive sixteen (16) sections of land to the mile.

SEC. 3. Canals and ditches shall be classified as follows: A canal or ditch carrying a stream of water of a uniform width of thirty feet and uniform depth of five feet shall be deemed of the first class. A canal or ditch carrying a stream of water of a uniform width of fifteen feet and of a uniform depth of four feet shall be deemed of the second class. A canal or ditch carrying a stream of water of a uniform width of nine feet and of a uniform depth of three feet shall be deemed of the third class. A canal or ditch not complying with the requirements of a third class canal or ditch, but carrying a stream of water of a uniform width of not less than six feet, and of a uniform depth of not less than two and a half feet, shall be deemed of the fourth class.   All canals or ditches of whatever class, must be at least two miles long and have a permanent and continuous stream of water flowing therein at a rate sufficiently fast for all practical purposes.

SEC. 4.   It shall be the duty of the Governor to appoint an Inspector of Canals and Ditches, who shall perform the duties herein assigned to him and shall receive therefor a compensation at the rate of twenty-five dollars per mile for every canal or ditch inspected by him, to be paid in advance by the person, firm, corporation or company requiring his services ; and the Inspector shall not be permitted to receive a contingent remuneration, or one in any way dependent on the issuance or sale of the certificates granted under this act.

SEC. 5.   Whenever any person, firm, corporation or company shall have constructed in the manner required by this act, a section of two miles or more of any canal or ditch, and the water is actually flowing in the same and ready for use, report shall be made to the Governor, setting out the facts, verified by affidavit, and applying for examination of the work, whereupon the Governor shall direct the Inspector of Canals and Ditches to examine and classify the same, and make a report under oath, showing the class to which the canal or ditch belongs, the dimensions of the same, the amount of water flowing therein, the length of the work completed and in good order, and the location thereof; and if the Governor shall be satisfied that the work has been done in compliance with this act, and that the person, firm or corporation intend in good faith to carry out the provisions of this act, and that the said person, firm or corporation have the ability and do intend to keep said canal or ditch in good repair and efficiency for navigation or irrigation for the period of ten years after it is fully completed, he shall certify the same to the Commissioner of the General Land Office.

SEC. 6.   Upon the presentation of the certificate of the Governor as provided for in the preceding section, it shall be the duty of the Commissioner of the General Land Office to issue to the person, firm or corporation or company entitled to the same, the number of land certificates for sections of six hundred and forty acres each to which the said person, firm or corporation or company may be entitled under the provisions of the second section of this act ; *provided*, that in no case shall any certificates be issued by the Commissioner of the General Land Office until the person, firm, company or corporation whose canal or ditch shall have been certified as provided in the preceding section, shall execute and file with the Commissioner of the General Land Office a bond with two or more solvent sureties, whose solvency shall appear from the Assessor's rolls in the office of the Comptroller, in a sum equal to one hundred and twenty-five dollars for each certificate for the canal or ditch, payable to the Governor of the State of Texas and his successors in office, conditioned that the said person, firm, company or corporation shall keep and maintain said canal or ditch in good and efficient repair for navigation or irrigation, as the case may be, for the full period of ten years from the time of filing the bond, and the Commissioner of the General Land Office shall furnish the form of the bond required in this section.

SEC. 7.   The certificates issued under this act shall be issued and located subject to and under the same conditions as those issued to railroads under the laws of this State.

SEC. 8.   All corporations for irrigation or navigation, are hereby granted the right of way, not to exceed one hundred feet in width, over all public, university, school and asylum lands, with use of necessary rocks, gravel and timber for construction purposes, and may obtain the right of way over private lands by contract, or the damages for any private property appropriated by such corporation shall be assessed and paid for as is provided for in cases of railroads.

SEC. 9. The Legislature shall, at such times as it may deem proper, establish the rates of freight and passage over any canal for navigation, and fix the rates of water supply for towns and cities; *provided*, that until such rates are established by law, said companies may charge such tolls for freights and vessels through canals, and such rates for water supply as may be reasonable and proper.

SEC. 10. Any such canal company shall have the free use of the water of the rivers and streams of this State; but in no case shall any company flow lands to the detriment of owners without their consent, or on due payment to the party aggrieved.

SEC. 11. Said companies, corporations, firms or persons, shall have the right to cross all roads and highways necessary in the construction of their work, and shall, at such crossings, construct and maintain necessary bridges for the accommodation of the public.

SEC. 12. The State shall not be liable under this act for any deficiency in the public domain.

SEC. 13. Whenever any canal or ditch for irrigation shall be constructed under the provisions of this act, all persons owning lands adjacent to and irrigable from said canal or ditch, shall have the right to use the water of said canal or ditch under such regulations as may be prescribed by law.

SEC. 14. Any canal or ditch which shall be constructed where there are already sufficient canals or ditches for the purposes of irrigation or navigation, shall not be entitled to the land grant herein provided for; and no certificate shall be issued for any canal or ditch until the same has been carried to a point at which the water can be used for irrigation or navigation.

SEC. 15. "An act to encourage the construction of canals and ditches for navigation and irrigation," approved March 10, 1875, shall be and is hereby repealed.

SEC. 16. Whereas, there is an imperative public necessity existing for a change in the law upon the subject of irrigation and navigation, and for the operation of the provisions of this act, thus creating an emergency; therefore, that this act take effect and be in force from and after its passage.

Approved August 21, 1876.

Takes effect ninety days after adjournment.

––––––

CHAPTER CLI.—*An Act to enforce the collection of delinquent taxes on lands assessed since January, 1870.*

SECTION 1. *Be it enacted by the Legislature of the State of Texas,* That the Comptroller of Public Accounts be and he is hereby required to prepare and forward to the County Commissioners' Court of the several counties of this State, within six months from the passage of this act, a full and complete abstract of the yearly delinquent list of taxes upon lands in their respective counties, assessed since the first day of January, 1870, showing upon what lands such taxes are due, the year the same was assessed, the amount due the State for each year, and the amount due the county for each year; and he shall describe each tract in the same manner as it is described on the tax rolls by the party assessing the same, and shall also state by and for whom rendered, and shall certify officially to the facts set forth in said list.

SEC. 2. Upon receipt of said list, the County Commissioners' Court shall carefully examine the same, and see that the taxes, both general and special, due said county, are accurately stated, and correct any inaccuracies or omissions that may have been made therein, and shall attach to the same a certificate that it is correct so far as it relates to the county taxes, and shall thereupon deliver the same to the Collector of Taxes for such county, who shall at once post a copy of said delinquent list at the court-house door and at least two other public places in the county, in different Justice's precincts, requiring the owners of said land to come forward and pay said taxes.

SEC. 3. All lands and town lots rendered in one county and situated in another county shall be made out by the Comptroller on a separate list and forward to the Commissioners' Court of the county where such lands are situated, and if any of such lands are situated in any unorganized county, then the Comptroller shall forward a list of such lands to the Commissioners' Court of the county to which such unorganized county is attached for judicial purposes.

SEC. 4. At the expiration of sixty days after posting said notices, if said taxes, or any part of them, are unpaid, or satisfactory evidence furnish(ed) the Collector of Taxes that the taxes have been paid, the Collector of Taxes shall, by virtue of his roll, seize, levy upon and sell so much property belonging to the person, firm, company or corporation, whether residents or non-residents, against whom the taxes were assessed, and due and unpaid, as may be sufficient to pay his, her or their taxes and penalties due, together with all costs accruing thereon; *provided, however*, that if such person, firm, company or corporation, his, her or their agent or attorney, shall point out to the Collector of Taxes sufficient property belonging to the party assessed in said county to pay said taxes before the expiration of the sixty days, as above provided, then the Collector of Taxes shall levy upon and sell the property so pointed out; and in case the property seized and levied on is personal property, the Collector shall proceed to take into his possession so much thereof as will pay the taxes assessed and due, together with all penalties due and costs accruing thereon.

SEC. 5. Every Collector of Taxes for personal property shall give notice of the time and place of the sale of the property so levied on at least ten days previous to the day of sale, by advertisement in writing, to be posted up, one at the court-house door of his county, and one in two other public places in the county; and such sale shall take place at the court-house door of the county in which the property is situated, by public auction; and if the property so levied upon prove to be insufficient to satisfy the taxes and penalties due and costs accruing thereon, the Collector shall seize and levy upon and sell so much other taxable property belonging to the person, firm, company or corporation as will be sufficient to satisfy such tax, penalties and costs, in the manner prescribed in the preceding part of this section; *provided*, should the property sold bring more than the taxes, penalties and costs, the remainder shall be paid to the owner by the Collector, or deposited by him in the County Treasurer's office, subject to the order of the party or parties owning said property.

SEC. 6. If the taxes upon any land or town lots in this State are not paid before the expiration of the sixty days, provided for in section four of this act, the Collector of Taxes shall seize, levy upon and sell such land or town lots, whether belonging to residents or non-residents, for the payment of all taxes and penalties due thereon, together with all costs which have or may accrue thereon; and he shall advertise the same for sale in some newspaper published in the county for three successive weeks, if there be one, and if there be no newspaper in the county, then by posting said advertisement for thirty days at the court-house door, and three other public places in the county where the land or lots are situated; giving in said advertisement such description as is given to the same on the certified statements furnished him by the Commissioners' Court, as furnished the court by the Comptroller of Public Accounts; giving the name of the owner, if known, and if unknown, say "unknown," together with time, place and terms of said sale; said sale to be for cash, to the highest bidder at public outcry, at the court-house door; which sales shall be between legal hours, on the first Tuesday of the month; *provided*, if the sale of all the lands and town lots advertised is not made in one day, the sale shall be continued from day to day. The Collector of Taxes shall make proclamation at the close of each day, of the continuance of the sale the following day, and as far as practicable, all the lands and town lots seized shall be advertised in one notice; *provided*, that the owner of such lands or his agent, shall, upon the payment of all delinquent taxes due upon said land since January 1st, A. D. 1873, prior to the day upon which said land is advertised to be sold, he shall receive a full and complete acquittance from all delinquent taxes due upon such land.

SEC. 7. The Collector of Taxes, in making sales for taxes due upon real estate, shall sell at auction at the time and place appointed so much of said real estate as may be necessary to pay the taxes and penalties due, and all costs accruing thereon; and shall offer said real estate to the bidder who will pay the taxes and penalties due, and costs of sale and execution of deed for the least amount of said real estate; which bidder shall be considered the highest bidder. Should a less amount of said real estate than the whole tract or parcel of said real estate levied upon be sold for the taxes and penalties due, and all costs of sale and execution of deed, the Collector shall, in making his deed to purchaser, begin at some corner of said tract or parcel of land, or town lot, and designate the same in a square as near as practicable.

SEC. 8. The Collector of Taxes shall execute and deliver to the purchaser, upon the payment of the amount for which the estate was sold, and costs and penalties, a deed for the real estate sold; which deed shall vest a good and absolute fee in said land or lots to the purchaser, if not redeemed in two years as herein provided for; which deed shall state the cause of sale, the amount sold, the price for which the real estate was sold, the name of the person, firm, company or corporation against whom the taxes were assessed, provided the name is known, and if unknown, say "unknown;" and when real estate has been sold, he shall convey subject to the right of redemption provided for in the following section, all the right and interest which the former owner had therein at the time when the assessment was made or when the sale was made.

SEC. 9. The owner of real estate sold for the payment of taxes, or

17 GL

his heirs or assigns, or legal representative, may, within two years from the date of sale, redeem the estate sold by paying or tendering to the purchaser, his heirs or legal representative, double the amount of money paid for the land or lots, together with all the subsequent taxes that the purchaser has paid on the same from the day of purchase to the day of redemption. The Collector of Taxes shall give in said deed such description of the real estate as is given on the certified roll or list as shall be furnished him as is required by the provisions of this act, and such other description as may be necessary to the better identification of the same.

SEC. 10.   The provisions of this act in reference to the seizure and sale of real and personal property, for taxes, penalties and costs due thereon, shall apply as well to Collectors of Taxes for towns and cities, as for Collectors of Taxes for counties, and they shall be governed in selling real and personal property by the same rules and regulations in all respects as to time, place, manner and terms, and making deeds, as are provided for Collectors of Taxes for counties.

SEC. 11.   Should the Collecter of Taxes for any city or town fail to make sale of any real estate for want of a purchaser, he shall bid the same off to the city or town for the taxes, and penalties and costs thereon, and make due return thereof to the City Council or Board of Mayor and Aldermen, and said Collector shall on final settlement of his accounts with the municipal authorities of such city or town, be entitled to a credit for the amount of the taxes due the city or town for the amount for which the land or lots were bid off to the city or town; *provided*, that the rolls of dilinquent tax-payers in any city or town when duly certified to by the Recorder or Clerk of said city or town, and placed in the hands of said Tax Collectors, shall be authority to said Tax Collectors to seize and sell the property, as provided in this act.

SEC. 12.   Should the Collector of Taxes fail to make sale of any real estate for want of a purchaser, he shall bid the same off to the State for the taxes and penalties due and all costs accruing thereon, and make due return thereof, under such forms and directions as the Comptroller may furnish and direct, and he shall on final settlement of his accounts with the Commissioners' Court and the Comptroller of Public Accounts, be entitled to a credit for the amount of taxes due the State and county respectively, for which the land or lots were bid off to the State.

SEC. 13.   The Collector of Taxes shall make duplicate lists of all real estate sold for taxes, and file one copy in the County Clerk's office for record, and forward a certified copy to the Comptroller of Public Accounts.

SEC. 14.   All lands and town lots sold to the State, or to city or town, shall be subject to redemption in the manner and under the same regulations as land sold to individuals, and in case of Collectors of Taxes for cities or towns, said Collector shall make duplicate lists of all real estate sold by him for taxes and file one copy thereof with the Clerk or Recorder of said city or town.

SEC. 15.   When lands upon which there are back taxes due were assessed at the Comptroller's office upon the basis for value of an average of the value of all lands in the county, it shall be lawful for the party paying such back taxes, to pay at the rate of the assessed value for the year 1876.

SEC. 16.   No delinquent tax-payer shall have the right to plead in any court or in any manner rely upon any statute of limitation by way of defense against the payment of any taxes due from him or her, either to the State or to any city or county.

SEC. 17. That all laws and parts of laws in conflict with the provisions of this act, are hereby repealed.

SEC. 18. That an imperative public necessity exists for the passage of this act immediately, there being no efficient law for the collection of delinquent taxes.

Approved August 19, 1876.

Takes effect ninety days after adjournment.

CHAPTER CLII.—*An Act regulating the duties of Tax Collectors in reference to the seizure and sale of property of delinquent tax-payers, and to define the further duties, powers, qualifications and liabilities of Collectors of Taxes, and to regulate their compensation.*

SECTION 1. *Be it enacted by the Legislature of the State of Texas,* That there shall be elected by the qualified electors of each county within this State (except such as are provided for, or excepted in the Constitution), at the same time and under the same law regulating the election of State and County officers, a Collector of Taxes, who shall hold his office for two years, and until his successor is elected and qualified; and should the office of Collector of Taxes, from any cause, become vacant before the expiration of said term, it shall be the duty of the Commissioners' Court in the county in which such vacancy shall occur, to appoint a Collector of Taxes, who shall be qualified in the same manner and subject to a like bond as the Collector of Taxes elected, and the Collector of Taxes so appointed shall hold his office for and during the unexpired term of his predecessor, and until his successor shall have been qualified; and the Collector of Taxes so appointed shall have all the rights and perform all the duties required by law of the Collector of Taxes elected.

SEC. 2. In each county in this State, where the Sheriff performs the duties of Collector of Taxes, he shall have and exercise all the rights, powers and privileges, and perform all the duties of Collectors of Taxes elected, as are granted by the provisions of this act; and shall also give a like bond as is required by this act of Collectors of Taxes elected, and shall be subject to all duties, restrictions and requirements imposed by the provisions of this act upon Collectors of Taxes elected.

SEC. 3. That every Collector of Taxes, within twenty days after he shall have received notice of his election or appointment, and before entering upon the duties of his office, shall give a bond, based upon unencumbered real estate of the sureties, subject to execution, payable to the Governor and his successors in office, in a sum which shall be equal to the whole amount of the State tax of the county, as shown by the last preceding assessment, with at least three good and sufficient sureties, to be approved by the Commissioners' Court of his county, which shall be further subject to the approval of the Comptroller, and shall take and subscribe the oath prescribed by the Constitution, which, together with said bond, shall be recorded in the office of the Clerk of the County Court of said county, and be forwarded by the County Judge of the county to the Comptroller, to be deposited in his office; the condition of said bond shall be deemed to extend to the faithful performance of the duties of his office as Collector of Taxes for and during the full term for which he was elected or appointed, and shall not become void upon the first recovery, but suit may be maintained thereon until the whole amount thereof be recovered; such Collector of Taxes may be required to furnish a new bond and additional other sureties, whenever, in the opinion of the Commissioners' Court or Comptroller of Public Accounts, it may be advisable. Should any Collector of Taxes fail to give a new bond and additional security when required, he shall be suspended and dismissed from office by the Commissioners' Court of his county; *provided*, that nothing herein contained shall be so construed as to require the Collectors of Taxes who were elected in February last, and who have given satisfactory bonds, to give additional bonds, unless, in the opinion of the Commissioners' Court, or of the Comptroller of Public Accounts, said bonds are insufficient.

SEC. 4.   That Collectors of Taxes shall give a like bond, with like conditions, to the County Judge of their respective counties, and their successors in office, in a sum not less than the whole amount of the county tax of the county, as shown by the last preceding assessment, with at least three good and sufficient sureties, to be approved by the Commissioners' Court of his county, which bond shall be recorded and deposited in the office of the Clerk of the County Court. A new bond and additional security may be required, and the Collector of Taxes may be removed from office in the manner prescribed in the third section of this act.

SEC. 5.   When the Collector of Taxes of any county shall have recieved the assessment rolls or books showing the amount of taxes due on said rolls or books, said rolls or books shall be full and sufficient authority for the County Collector of Taxes to receive and collect the taxes therein levied.

SEC. 6.   The Collector of Taxes shall be the receiver and collector of all taxes assessed upon the tax list in his county, whether assessed for the State or county, school, poor-house, or other purpose, and he shall proceed to collect the same according to law, and place the same, when collected, to the proper fund, and pay the same over to the proper authorities, as hereinafter provided.

SEC. 7.   The Collector of Taxes shall begin the collection of the taxes of their respective counties annually, on the first days of October, or so soon thereafter as he may be able to obtain the proper assessment rolls, books or data upon which to proceed with the business; and he shall post up notices, not less than three, at public places, in each voting or magistrate's precinct in his county, at least twenty days previous to the day said tax-payers are required to meet him for the purpose of paying their taxes, stating in said notice the times and places the same are required to be paid; and it shall be the duty of said Collector or his deputy to attend at such times and places for the purposes aforesaid, and shall remain at each place at least two days; *provided*, that if the Collector shall from any cause fail to meet the tax-payers at the time and place as provided for in the first notice, he shall, in like manner, give a second notice.

SEC. 8.   The Collector of Taxes shall keep his office at the county seat of his county, and it shall be the duty of every person who has failed to attend and to pay his taxes at the times and places in his precinct, named by the Collector, as provided in the preceding section, to call at the office of the Collector and pay the same between the first day of July, and the last day of February of each year.

SEC. 9.   Each Collector of Taxes may appoint one or more deputies to assist him in the collection of taxes, and may take such bond and security from the person so appointed as he deems necessary for his indemnity, and the Collectors, in all cases, shall be liable and accountable for his proceedings and misconduct in office.

SEC. 10. The Collector of Taxes, or his deputy, whenever any tax is paid, shall give to the person paying the same a receipt therefor, specifying the amount of State *ad valorem* tax, the amount of State poll tax, the amount of county *ad valorem* tax, the amount of county poll tax, and the year or years for which such tax was levied; said receipt shall also show the number of acres of land in each separate tract, number, abstract and name of original grantee; the said receipt shall have a duplicate stub showing the name of the person, the date, the amount of each separate tax and the date of payment. The Collector of Taxes shall provide himself with a seal, on which shall be inscribed a star with five points, surrounded by the words, "Collector of Taxes ——— County," the blank to be filled with the name of the county, and shall impress said seal to each receipt given by him for taxes collected on real estate, and said receipt having the seal attached shall be admissable to record in the county in which the property is situated, in same manner as deeds duly authenticated, and when so recorded, shall be full and complete notice to all persons of the payment of said tax.

SEC. 11. The Collector of Taxes shall make a report, under oath, to the Comptroller of all taxes collected by him for the State, every three months. The first report shall include the months of October, November, December; the second shall include the months of January, February, March; the third shall include the months of April, May and June; the fourth report shall include the months of July, August and September of each year; and he shall also make a like report to the Commissioners' Court of all taxes collected for the county.

SEC. 12. The Collector of Taxes shall file his reports, together with the tax receipt stubs, in the office of the County Clerk of his county, for examination. The Clerk shall have three days (Sundays excepted) for the examination of the same. The reports and stubs must agree in every particular, as regards dates, names and amounts. The Clerk shall, after the examination, certify to the reports as to their correctness or incorrectness, as the case may be, and, if incorrect, state where the incorrectness appears in said reports; he shall then forward the report prepared for the Comptroller to that officer, and shall file the tax receipt stubs in his office for reference and safe keeping.

SEC. 13. The Collector of Taxes shall make out, on and after the first day of June of each year, triplicate lists of delinquent or insolvent taxpayers, the caption of which shall be, the "List of Delinquent or Insolvent Tax-payers." In this list he shall give the name of the person, firm, company or corporation from whom the taxes are due, together with the amount of the State and county taxes due, in separate columns, and he shall post one copy of these delinquent or insolvent lists at the court-house door, and one copy at two other public places in his county. And the Collector of Taxes, upon the certificate of the Commissioners' Court that the persons appearing on the insolvent or delinquent list have no property out of which to make the taxes assessed against them, or that they have moved out of the county, and that no property can be found in the county belonging to such persons out of which to make the taxes due, shall be entitled to a credit on his final settlement of his accounts for the amounts due by the persons, firms, companies or corporations, certified to by the Commissioners' Court, as above provided for; *provided*, he shall use all necessary diligence to collect the amounts due on the insolvent list, after it is allowed, and report and pay over to the proper officers all amounts collected on the same.

Sec. 14.   If any person, firm, company or corporation shall fail or refuse to pay the taxes imposed upon him or them, or upon his, her or their property, by law, until the first day of March next succeeding the return of the assessment roll of the county to the Comptroller, the Collector of Taxes shall, by virtue of his tax roll, seize and levy upon and sell so much property belonging to such person, firm, company or corporation, whether residents or non-residents, as may be sufficient to pay his, her or their taxes and penalties due, together with all costs accruing thereon; *provided, however*, that if such person, firm, company or corporation, his, her, or their agent or attorney, shall point out to the Collector of Taxes sufficient property belonging to the party assessed, in said county, to pay said taxes before the first day of March, of each year, then the Collector shall levy upon and sell the property so pointed out; and in case the property seized and levied on is personal property, the Collector shall proceed to take into his possession so much thereof as will pay the taxes assessed and due, together with all penalties due and costs accruing thereon.

Sec. 15.   Every Collector of Taxes for personal property shall give notice of the time and place of the sale of the property so levied on, at least ten days previous to the day of sale, by advertisement in writing, to be posted up, one at the court-house door of his county, and in two other public places in the county; and such sale shall take place at the court-house door of the county in which the assessment is made, by public auction; and if the property so levied upon prove to be insufficient to satisfy the taxes and penalties due, and costs accruing thereon, the Collector shall levy upon and sell so much other taxable property belonging to such person, firm, corporation or company, as will be sufficient to satisfy such tax, penalties and costs in the manner prescribed in the preceding part of this section; *provided*, should the property sold bring more than the taxes, penalties and costs, the remainder shall be paid to the former owner, by the Collector, or deposited by him in the County Treasurer's office, subject to the order of the party or parties owning said property.

Sec. 16.   If the taxes upon any land or town lots in this State are not paid on or before the first day of March of each year, after the return of the tax rolls of the county to the Comptroller of Public Accounts, the Collector of Taxes shall seize such land, and sell the same, or so much thereof as may be necessary, whether belonging to residents or non-residents, for the payment of all taxes and penalties due thereon, together with all costs which have or may accrue thereon, and he shall advertise the same for sale in some newspaper published in the county, for three successive weeks, if there be one, and if there be no newspaper in the county, then by posting said advertisement for thirty days at the court-house door and three other public places in the county where the land or lots are situated; giving, in said advertisement, such description as is given to the same on the tax rolls in his hands; giving the name of the owner, if known, and if unknown, say, "unknown," together with time, place and terms of said sale; said sale to be for cash to the highest bidder, at public outcry at the court-house door; which sales shall be between legal hours, on the first Tuesday of the month ; *provided*, if the sale of all the lands and town lots advertised is not made in one day, the sale shall be continued from day to day. The Collector of Taxes shall make proclamation at the close of each day of the continuance of the sale the following day ; and, as far as practicable, all the lands and town lots seized shall be advertised in one notice ; *provided further*, that nothing in this act shall be so construed as to subject real estate set apart or used as a homestead to forced sale for taxes other than the taxes due on said homestead.

SEC. 17. The Collector of Taxes, in making sales for taxes due upon real estate, shall sell at auction, at the time and place appointed, so much of said real estate as may be necessary to pay the taxes and penalties due, and all costs accruing thereon ; and shall offer said real estate to the bidder who will pay the taxes and penalties due, and costs of sale and execution of deed, for the least amount of said real estate, who shall be deemed the highest bidder. Should a less amount of said real estate than the whole tract or parcel of said real estate levied upon be sold for the taxes and penalties due, and all costs of sale and execution of deed, the Collector shall, in making his deed to purchaser, begin at some corner of said tract or parcel of land, or town lot, and designate the same in a square as near as practicable.

SEC. 18. The Collector of Taxes shall execute and deliver to the purchaser, upon the payment of the amount for which the estate was sold and costs and penalties, a deed for the real estate sold, which deed shall vest a good and absolute fee in said land to the purchaser, if not redeemed in two years, as herein provided, which deed shall state the cause of sale, the amount sold, the price for which the real estate was sold, the name of the person, firm, company or corporation on whom the demand for the taxes was made ; *provided* the name is known ; and if unknown say, "unknown," and when real estate has been sold he shall convey, subject to the right of redemption provided for in the following section, all the right and interest which the former owner had therein at the time when the assessment was made ; and when the Collector of Taxes shall have made sale of any real estate under this act, it shall be his duty to make return of said sale to the Commissioners' Court, stating in said return the land sold, the name of the owner, if known, and if unknown, state the fact, the time of the sale, the amount for which said sale was made, together with the name of the purchaser, which return shall be entered of record on the minute books of said court.

SEC. 19. The owner of real estate sold for the payment of taxes, or his heirs or assigns, or legal representatives, may, within two years from the date of sale, redeem the estate sold, by paying or tendering to the purchaser, his heirs or legal representatives, double the amount of money paid for the land, together with all subsequent taxes that the purchaser has paid on the same from the day of purchase to the day of redemption. The Collector of Taxes shall give in said deed such description of the land as is given on the tax rolls in his hands, and such other description as may be necessary to the better identification of the same.

SEC. 20. The provisions of this act in reference to the seizure and sale of real and personal property, for taxes, penalties and costs due thereon, shall apply as well to Collectors of Taxes for town and cities as for Collectors of Taxes for counties, and they shall be governed in selling real and personal property by the same rules and regulations in all respects as to time, place, manner and terms, and making deeds, as are provided for Collectors of Taxes for counties.

SEC. 21.　Should the Collector of Taxes fail to make sale of any real estate for want of a purchaser, he shall bid the same off to the State for taxes and penalties due and costs accruing thereon, and make due return thereof, under such forms and directions as the Comptroller may furnish and direct, and he shall, on final settlement of his accounts with the Commissioner's Court and the Comptroller of Public Accounts, be entitled to a credit for the amount of taxes due the State and county for which the land or lots were bid off to the State for.

SEC. 22.　The Collector of Taxes shall, whenever he may receive as much as five thousand dollars ($5,000) or more belonging to the State, pay the same over to the State Treasurer in the manner as may be directed by the Comptroller of Public Accounts, reserving only his commissions on the same.

SEC. 23.　The Collector of Taxes shall, whenever he may receive as much as five hundred dollars ($500) or more belonging to his county, pay the same over to the County Treasurer of his county, reserving only his commissions on the same.

SEC. 24.　The Collector of Taxes shall collect all occupation taxes due the State and county, and he shall make a quarterly report of the same, and one exact copy thereof, which shall state the amounts collected, from whom collected, and for what purpose, and for what time the said taxes were paid. The original shall be filed with the Clerk of the County Court, to be kept in his office for the inspection of the public. The County Clerk shall certify to the correctness of the copy, and that the original has been filed in his office; and the County Clerk shall forward, without delay, to the Comptroller of Public Accounts the copy so certified to, for which the County Clerk shall be entitled to one dollar and fifty cents, to be paid by the Collector of Taxes.

SEC. 25.　For every neglect, failure or refusal to comply with Section 24 of this act, the Collector of Taxes shall forfeit his commissions on the amount of occupation taxes collected by him during each quarter for which he neglects, fails or refuses to comply with Section 24 of this act; should any Collector of Taxes so neglect, refuse or fail to comply with the provisions of Section 24 of this act for two consecutive quarters, the Commissioners' Court, upon a complaint made to them by the Comptroller of Public Accounts, shall remove the said Collector of Taxes from office, unless said Collector of Taxes can render a satisfactory excuse for such neglect, refusal or failure, and he shall also be subject to prosecution on his official bond.

SEC. 26.　The quarterly reports provided for in Section 24 of this act shall be as follows: The first report shall include the months of July, August and September, and shall be made out and reported as required above, on the first Monday in October of each year. The second report shall include the months of October, November and December, and shall be made out and reported on the first Monday in January of each year. The third report shall include the months of January, February and March, and shall be made out and reported on the first Monday in April of each year. The fourth report shall include the months of April, May and June of each year, and shall be made out and reported on the first Monday in July in each and every year.

SEC. 27.　The Collector of Taxes shall also make out and forward to the Comptroller of Public Accounts a statement of all the occupation taxes collected by him during the year, which said annual report shall be made out and forwarded to the Comptroller of Public Accounts on the first Monday in July of each year, and shall show from whom collected, when collected, the amount collected, and on what occupation collected, and for what time collected; and such other facts as the Comptroller may require. And for each failure, refusal or neglect to comply with the provisions of this section, the Comptroller shall deduct one hundred dollars from the commissions of the Collector of Taxes, so failing, refusing or neglecting to comply with the provisions of this section for each month he so fails, refuses or neglects to comply with the provisions of this section, and the Commissioners' Court shall upon complaint made to them, by the Comptroller, remove said Collector of Taxes from office, unless he produce satisfactory reasons for such failure.

SEC. 28. All moneys collected from occupations due the State shall be paid over to the State Treasurer by the Collector of Taxes, in the same manner and under the same restrictions and regulations as is required by section twenty-two of this act.

SEC. 29. All moneys collected from occupations due the county shall be paid over to the County Treasurer by the Collector of Taxes in the same manner and under the same restrictions and regulations as is required by section twenty-three of this act.

SEC. 30. The Collector of Taxes shall receive as compensation for his services, five per cent. on all amounts collected by him for the State, and three per cent. on all amounts collected by him for the county; *provided*, that in counties owing a subsidy to railroads, the Collector shall receive only one per cent. for collecting such railroad tax. And in cases where property is levied on and sold for taxes, he shall receive the same compensation as allowed by law to Sheriffs or Constables for making a levy and sale in similar cases. And he shall be allowed ten cents per mile, once a year, each way for visiting the Capital and making final settlement of his accounts with the Comptroller; the distance to be computed by the Comptroller from the county seat as the mileage of the members of the Legislature is computed.

SEC. 31. There being no law now in force clearly defining the duties and powers of Collectors of Taxes, it is hereby declared that there is an existing imperative public necessity and emergency for the immediate passage of this act, that the Collectors of Taxes may at once enter upon the discharge of their official duties; therefore, this act take effect and be in force, from and after its passage.

SEC. 32. All laws and parts of laws in conflict with the provisions of this act are hereby repealed.

Approved August 21, 1876.

Takes effect from its passage.

CHAPTER CLIII.—*An Act to define the duties, powers, qualifications and liabilities of Assessors of Taxes, and to regulate their compensation.*

SECTION 1. *Be it enacted by the Legislature of the State of Texas*, That there shall be elected by the qualified electors of each county within this State, at the same time and under the same law regulating the elections of State and county officers, an Assessor of Taxes, who shall hold his office for two years, and until his successor is elected and qualified; and should the office of Assessor of Taxes from any cause become vacant before the expiration of said term, it shall be the duty of the District Judge of the county in which such vacancy shall occur, to appoint an Assessor of Taxes, who shall be qualified in the same manner, and subject to a like bond as the Assessor elected; and the Assessor so appointed shall hold his office for and during the unexpired term of his predecessor, and until his successor shall have been qualified; and the Assessor of Taxes, so appointed, shall have all the rights and perform all the duties required by law of the Assessor elected.

Sec. 2.   That every Assessor of Taxes, within twenty days after he shall have received notice of his election or appointment, and before entering upon the duties of his office, shall execute a bond, payable to the Governor and his successors in office, in a sum which shall be equal to one-fourth the amount of the State tax of the county, as shown by the last preceding assessment, with at least three good and sufficient sureties, to be approved by the Commissioners' Court of his county, conditioned that he faithfully discharge all the duties of said office; *provided*, said bond shall not exceed ten thousand dollars ($10,000); and shall take and subscribe the oath prescribed by the Constitution; which oath, together with said bond, shall be recorded in the office of the Clerk of the County Court of said county, and be forwarded by the County Judge of the county to the Comptroller to be deposited in his office; said bond shall be deemed to extend to the faithful performance of the duties of his office as Assessor of Taxes for and during the full term for which he was elected or appointed, and shall not become void upon the first recovery; but suit may be maintained thereon until the whole amount thereof be recovered; such Assessor of Taxes may be required to furnish a new bond, and other additional sureties, whenever, in the opinion of the Commissioners' Court, it may be advisable.   Should any Assessor of Taxes fail to give a new bond and additional security when required, he shall be suspended and dismissed from office by the Commissioners' Court of his county; *provided*, that nothing herein contained shall be so construed as to require the Assessors of Taxes, who were elected in February last, and who have given satisfactory bonds, to give additional bond, unless, in the opinion of the Commissioners' Court, said bonds are insufficient.

Sec. 3.   The Assessor of Taxes shall give a like bond, with like conditions, to the County Judge of their respective counties, and their successors in office, in a sum not less than one-fourth of the amount of the county tax of the county, as shown by the last preceding assessment, with at least three good and sufficient sureties, to be approved by the Commissioners' Court of his county; *provided*, said bond shall not exceed five thousand dollars, ($5,000), which bond shall be recorded and deposited in the County Clerk's office of the county.   A new bond and additional security may be required, and the Assessor of Taxes may be removed from office in the manner prescribed in the second section of this act.

Sec. 4.   That the Assessors of Taxes in this State are hereby authorized and empowered to administer all oaths necessary to obtain a full, complete and correct assessment of all the taxable property situated in their respective counties.

Sec. 5.   The Assessor of Taxes shall also require each person rendering a list of taxable property to him for taxation, under the assessment laws of this State, to subscribe to the following oath, or affirmation, which shall be written or printed at the bottom of each inventory, to-wit: " I, ——— (filling the blank with the name of the person subscribing), do solemnly swear, or affirm, that the above inventory rendered by me contains a full, true and complete list of all taxable property owned or held by me in my own name (or for others, as the case may be, naming the person or firm for whom he rendered the list) in this county, and all personal property in this State, subject to taxation by the laws of this State, on the first day of January, A. D. 18— (filling the blank with the year), and that I have true answers made to all questions propounded to me touching the same, so help me God." The owner, or agent, who is required under the laws of this State to render any property for taxation, may render the same in the county where the same is situated by listing the same and making oath thereto, as required in this act, before any officer authorized to administer oaths in this State, or any officer out of this State that is authorized by law to take acknowledgments of instruments for record in this State, and may forward the same to the Assessor of the county by mail, or otherwise, and the Assessor shall enter the said property on his tax rolls. If the Assessor is satisfied with the valuation as rendered in said list, he will so enter the same. If he is not satisfied with the valuation, he shall refer the same to the Board of Equalization of the county for their action, and shall immediately notify by mail, or otherwise, the person from whom he received said list, that he has referred said valuation to the Board of Equalization; *provided*, said Assessor shall not be required to notify said party unless said list is accompanied by a fee of twenty-five cents.

SEC. 6. That the Assessor of Taxes. for every failure or neglect to administer the oath or affirmation prescribed in section five of this act to each person rendering a list of taxable property to him, unless the person refuses to qualify, shall forfeit fifty dollars, to be deducted out of his commissions, upon full and satisfactory information furnished the County Judge; and for each and every failure or neglect to attest the oath subscribed to, as provided in section five of this act, shall forfeit the sum of fifty dollars, upon satisfactory information furnished the County Judge. The forfeitures imposed by this section shall be deducted from the Assessor's commissions on the assessment for county taxes.

SEC. 7. Each Assessor of Taxes may appoint one or more deputies to assist him in the assessment of taxes, and may require such bond and security from the person so appointed as he deems necessary for his indemnity, and the Assessor of Taxes shall, in all cases, be liable and accountable for the proceedings and misconduct of his deputies.

SEC. 8. The deputies appointed in accordance with the provisions of section seven of this act shall do and perform all the duties imposed and required by the provisions of this act, of Assessors of Taxes; and all acts of such deputies, done in conformity with law, shall be as binding and valid as if done by the Assessor of Taxes in person.

SEC. 9. That the Assessor of Taxes shall, between the first day of January and and the first day of June of each year, proceed to take a list of taxable real and personal property in his county, and assess the value thereof in the manner following, to-wit: By calling upon the person, or by calling at the office, place of business, or the residence of the person, and listing the property required by this act, in his name, and shall require the person to make a statement under oath, as prescribed in section five of this act, of such property in the form prescribed in this act; *provided*, if any property is listed or assessed on or after the first day of June, the same shall be as legal and binding as if assessed before that time ; but nothing herein contained shall be so construed as to relieve Assessors of Taxes from prosecutions on their official bonds for failing or neglecting to have the assessment completed by the first day of June of each year ; *and provided further*, that should the Assessor of Taxes or his deputies fail to administer the oath, or the person rendering fail to subscribe to the list, or should the Assessor of Taxes or his deputy fail to attest the same, as required by this act, the assessment thus made shall be as valid and hold as good as if every requirement of this act had been fully complied with.

SEC. 10.   If any person who is required by this act to list property shall be sick or absent when the Assessor calls for a list of his property, the Assessor shall leave at the office, or usual place of residence or business of such person, a written or printed notice, requiring such person to meet him and render a list of his property, at such time and place as the Assessor of Taxes may designate in said notice.   The Assessor of Taxes shall carefully note in a book the date of leaving such notice.

SEC. 11.   In every case where any person whose duty it is to list any property for taxation has refused or neglected to list the same when called on for that purpose by the Assessor of Taxes, or has refused to subscribe to the oath in regard to the truth of his statement of property, or any part thereof, when required by the Assessor of Taxes, the Assessor shall carefully note in a book the name of such person, who refused to list or to swear, and in every case where any person required to list property for taxation has been absent, or unable from sickness to list the same, the Assessor of Taxes shall carefully note in a book such fact, together with the name of such person.

SEC. 12.   In all cases of failure to obtain a statement of real and personal property, from any cause, it shall be the duty of the Assessor of Taxes to ascertain the amount and value of such property, and assess the same as he believes to be the true and full value thereof, and such assessment shall be as valid and binding as if such property had been rendered by the proper owner thereof.

SEC. 13.   The manner and form for assessing property rendered for taxation in this State shall be substantially as follows, to-wit: *First*— The name of the owner. *Second*—Abstract number. *Third*—Number of the survey. *Fourth*—The name of the original grantee. *Fifth*—The number of acres. *Sixth*—The value of the land. *Seventh*—The number of the lot or lots. *Eighth*—The number of the block. *Ninth*—The value of town lots. *Tenth*—The name of the city or town. *Eleventh*—Number of miles of railroad in the county. *Twelfth*—Value of railroads and appurtenances, including the proportionate amount of rolling stock to the county. *Thirteenth*—Number of miles of telegraph in the county. *Fourteenth*—Value of telegraph and appurtenances in the county. *Fifteenth*—Number and amount of land certificates and value thereof. *Sixteenth*—Number of horses and mules and value thereof. *Seventeenth*—Number of cattle and value thereof. *Eighteenth*—Number of jacks and jennets and value thereof. *Nineteenth*—Number of sheep and value thereof. *Twentieth*—Number of goats and value thereof. *Twenty-first*—Number of hogs and value thereof. *Twenty-second*—Number of carriages, buggies or wagons of whatsoever kind and value thereof. *Twenty-third*—Number of sewing machines and knitting machines and the value thereof. *Twenty-fourth*—Number of watches and clocks and value thereof. *Twenty-fifth*—Number of organs, melodeons, piano forte, and all other musical instruments whatsoever kind and value thereof.

Twenty-sixth—The value of household and kitchen furniture, over and above the amount of two hundred and fifty dollars. *Twenty-seventh*—Office furniture and value thereof. *Twenty-eighth*—The value of gold and silver plate. *Twenty-ninth*—The value of diamonds and jewelry. *Thirtieth*—Every annuity or royalty, the description and value thereof. *Thirty-first*—Number of steamboats, sailing vessels, wharf-boats, barge or other water craft and the value thereof. *Thirty-second*—The value of goods and merchandise of every description, which such person is required to list, as a merchant in hand on the first day of January of each year. *Thirty-third*—The value of materials and manufactured articles, which such person is required to list as a manufacturer. *Thirty-fourth*—The value of manufacturer's tools, implements and machinery, other than boilers and engines, which shall be listed as such. *Thirty-fifth*—Number of steam engines, including boilers and the value thereof. *Thirty-sixth*—The amount of moneys (except legal tender notes of the United States Treasury) of bank, banker, broker or stock-jobber. *Thirty-seventh*—The amount of solvent credits of bank, banker, broker or stock-jobber, and any other person. *Thirty-eighth*—The amount of moneys (except legal tender notes of the United States Treasury) other than of bank, banker, broker or stock-jobber. *Thirty-ninth*—The amounts of credits, other than of bank, banker, broker or stock-jobber. *Fortieth*—The amount and value of bonds and stocks (other than United States bonds). *Forty-first*—The amount and value of shares of capital stock companies and associations not incorporated by the laws of this State. *Forty-second*—The value of property of companies and corporations, other than property hereinbefore enumerated. *Forty-third*—The value of stock and furniture of saloons, hotels and eating houses. *Forty-fourth*—The value of every billiard, pigeon-hole, bagatelle, or other similar tables, together with the number thereof. *Forty-fifth*—Every franchise, the description and value thereof. *Forty-sixth*—The value of all other property not enumerated above; *provided*, that any departure from this form by the Assessor shall not invalidate the assessment thus made.

SEC. 14. If the Assessor of Taxes discover any real property in his county, subject to taxation, which has not been listed to him, he shall list and assess such property in the manner following, to-wit: *First*—The name of the owner; if unknown, say "unknown." *Second*—Abstract number. *Third*—Number of the survey. *Fourth*—Name of the original grantee. *Fifth*—Number of acres. *Sixth*—The true and full value thereof. *Seventh*—The number of lot or lots. *Eighth*—The number of the block. *Ninth*—The true and full value thereof. *Tenth*—The name of the city or town; and give such other description of the lot or lots, or parcels of land, as may be necessary to better describe the same and such assessment shall be as valid as if rendered by the owner thereof.

SEC. 15. If the Assessor of Taxes shall discover in his county, any real property which has not been assessed or rendered for taxation, for any year since 1870, he shall list and assess the same, for each and every year thus omitted, in the manner as prescribed in section fourteen of this act, and such assessment shall be as valid and binding as though it had been rendered by the owner thereof; *provided*, that no real property shall be assessed by the Assessor, under this section, unless he has ascertained by the certificate of the Comptroller of Public Accounts, the fact that the records of his office do not show that the property has been rendered or assessed, for the year in which he assessed it.

SEC. 16. The Assessors of Taxes, in the execution of their duties, shall use the forms and follow the instructions which shall from time to time be prescribed by the Comptroller of the State and furnished to them by the County Judge in pursuance of law.

SEC. 17. In case the person listing property makes oath, and the assessing officer is satisfied that it is correctly valued, he shall list the same, accordingly; but if the Assessor is satisfied that the value is too low, he shall list the same at such value as he, as a sworn officer, deems just; and if the person listing makes oath that the assessment is excessive, the value shall be decided by the Board of Equalization, whose valuation shall be final; *provided,* nothing herein contained shall prohibit the Board of Equalization from exercising the right to equalize all assessments made, in accordance with the law governing the Board of Equalization.

SEC. 18. The Assessor of Taxes shall furnish the Board of Equalization, on the first Monday in June of each year, or as soon thereafter as practicable, a certified list of names of all persons who either refuse to swear or to qualify, or to sign the oath or affirmation, as prescribed in this act; also, a list of the names of those persons who refused to render a list of taxable property, as required by this act. And should any person so failing or refusing to take the oath prescribed, or to render a list of their property, or to subscribe to the oath, as required by the provisions of this act, fail to give satisfactory reasons for such failure or refusal to the Board of Equalization, within one month from the date of the filing of said list by the Assessor, as required by this section, the Board of Equalization shall return a list of all persons who have failed to give satisfactory reasons for such failure or refusal to render, qualify or subscribe to the oath or affirmation, as the case may be, to the Assessor of Taxes, who shall present the said list to the grand jury of his county next empanneled after the Board of Equalization has furnished him with the list above required. Each and every Assessor of Taxes who shall fail or refuse to comply with the provisions of this section, shall be guilty of a misdemeanor and subject to indictment, and upon conviction thereof, shall be fined in any sum not less than fifty nor more than two hundred dollars.

SEC. 19. As soon as the Board of Equalization shall have examined, corrected and approved the Assessor's list, the Assessor of Taxes shall prepare and make out a roll or book, as may be required by the Comptroller, from the list so corrected and approved, and three exact copies of the same; the original to be furnished the Collector of Taxes, the second to the Comptroller of Public Accounts, and the third to be filed in the County Clerk's office for the inspection of the public. He shall also prepare a roll or book and two exact copies thereof, to be distributed: The first one to the Collector of Taxes, the second one to the Comptroller, the third one to be filed in the County Clerk's office, of all the real and personal property that from any cause had been neglected or failed to have been listed to him.

SEC. 20. The Assessor of Taxes shall submit all the lists of property rendered to him prior to the first Monday in June, to the Board of Equalization of his county, on the first Monday in June, or as soon thereafter as practicable, for their inspection, approval, correction, or equalization; and after the Board of Equalization shall have returned the corrected and approved lists of taxable property, the Assessor of Taxes shall proceed to assess all the unrendered property of his county, as provided for in this act, and shall proceed to make out and prepare his rolls or books of all the real and personal property listed to him, in the form and manner prescribed by the Comptroller of the State.

Sec. 21. The Assessor of Taxes shall, after his list of unrendered real and personal property shall have been examined, corrected and approved by the Board of Equalization, as provided by law, prepare and make out his rolls or books of all unrendered real and personal property listed by him, in the manner and form prescribed by the Comptroller of the State.

Sec. 22. The Assessor of Taxes shall add up and note the aggregate of each column on his roll or book, and he shall also make in each book or roll, under proper headings, a tabular statement showing the footings of the several columns upon each page; and he shall add up and set down under the respective h(e)adings, the totals of the several colum(n)s.

Sec. 23. The Assessor of Taxes shall on or before the first day of August of each year for which the assessment is made, return his rolls or assessment books of the taxable property rendered to him or listed by him for that year, after they have been made in accordance with the provisions of this act, to the County Board of Equalization, verified by his affidavit substantially in the following form:

State of Texas, ⎱ ss.
——————County. ⎰

I, (name the Assessor) Assessor of (name the county) county, do solemnly swear that the rolls (or books) to which this is attached, contain a correct and full list of all the real and personal property subject to taxation in ——— (fill the blank with the name of the county) county, so far as I have been able to ascertain the same, and that the assessed value set down in the proper column, opposite the several kinds and descriptions of property, to the best of my knowledge and belief, and that the footings of the several columns in said books, and the tabular statement returned, is correct, as I verily believe. ——— (fill blank with name of Assessor) Assessor. Sworn to, and subscribed to before me, this——— (day of month) day of ——— (fill blank with the month) 18— (fill blank with the year). ——————— (name of clerk), Clerk of District Court, ——————— (name of county) county.

Sec. 24. The Assessor of Taxes shall, at the same time, deliver to the Board of Equalization, all the lists, statements of all property which shall have been made out or received by him and arranged in alphabetical order, together with the roll withdrawn to aid him in the past assessment. The lists and statements shall be filed in the County Clerk's office, and remain there for the inspection of the public.

Sec. 25. After the Board of Equalization shall have examined the rolls or assessment books and made all corrections, if any be necessary, the Assessor shall send one copy of each to the Comptroller of Public Accounts, one copy of each to the Collector of his county, and he shall file the other copies in the County Clerk's office until the next assessment, when the Assessor shall have the right to withdraw them and use as provided in this act.

Sec. 26. Each Assessor of Taxes within this State shall receive as a compensation for his services for assessing the State tax, five per centum of the amount of the State taxes assessed by him, and shall receive from the county three per centum on the amount of county taxes assessed by him.

SEC. 27. The Comptroller, on receipt of the rolls, shall give the Assessor an order on the Collector of his county for the amount due him by the State, for assessing the State taxes, to be paid out of the first money collected for that year.

SEC. 28. The Commissioners' Court shall issue an order on the County Treasurer of their county to the Assessor, for the amount due him for assessing the county tax of their county, to be paid out of the first money received from the Collector on the rolls of that year.

SEC. 29. Should any Assessor of Taxes fail or neglect to make out and return his rolls or books to the Commissioners' Court, in the time and manner provided for in this act, it shall be competent for the Commissioners' Court to deduct from his compensation such amount as they may deem proper and right for such neglect or failure; and should his rolls or books, when presented for approval to the Commissioners' Court, prove to be imperfect or erroneous, the Court shall have the same corrected or perfected, either by the Assessor or some other person than the Assessor of Taxes. Such person so employed by the Commissioners' Court, shall be entitled to such part of the commissions to which such Assessor is entitled as the Court may allow, and said Court shall so certify to the Comptroller, who shall pay such person in the same manner as the Assessor of Taxes is paid, and the amount so paid shall be deducted by the Comptroller from the commissions of the Assessor of Taxes, whose duty it was to have performed such work.

SEC. 30. It shall be the duty of the Assessor of Taxes to take a careful census of the children in their counties who are within the scholastic age, as prescribed by the laws regulating public schools; which census shall contain the name, sex, age and date of each child's birth, as near as practicable, and the name of the parent or guardian, also the scholastic community or district to which each child belongs. The Assessor shall also prepare two abstracts of said census, showing the number of children, white and colored, male and female, and such other data as may be required on the forms furnished by the Board of Education. The Assessor shall make oath, in writing, on each of said abstracts and said census, that the same are correct, and file the same with the Clerk of the County Court of his county.

SEC. 31. The Assessor of Taxes shall receive for taking, making out and reporting the scholastic inhabitants, as required above, four cents for each child for the first thousand, and two and a half cents for each child over and above the first thousand taken and reported by him, to be paid out of the school fund. The Comptroller, on the receipt of the certified copy of the scholastic inhabitants as required in Section thirty (30) of this act, shall give the Assessor an order on the Collector of his county for the amount due him for taking the scholastic census as required by law, to be paid out of the first money collected on such funds for that year; said order, endorsed by the Assessor to the Collector, shall be accredited to the Collector, on settlement of his accounts with the Comptroller, as so much money paid in.

SEC. 32. All laws and parts of laws in conflict with the provisions of this act are hereby repealed.

SEC. 33. There being no adequate law in force for the assessment of taxes in this State, an imperative public necessity exists for the passage of this act at the present session of the Legislature; it shall therefore take effect and be in force from and after its passage.

Approved August 21, 1876.

Takes effect ninety days after adjournment.

CHAPTER CLIV.—*An Act to repeal "An Act to provide for the registration of births."*

SECTION 1. *Be it enacted by the Legislature of the State of Texas,* That "An Act to provide for the registration of births," approved May 3, 1873, be and the same is hereby repealed.

Approved August 21, 1876.

Takes effect ninety days after adjournment.

CHAPTER CLV.—*An Act to provide for the manner of purchasing fuel for the use of the Legislature, and other departments of the government (except the Judicial Department), by contract.*

SECTION 1. *Be it enacted by the Legislature of the State of Texas,* That the Attorney-General, Treasurer and Secretary of State, be and are hereby constituted a Board of Contractors, authorized and required to contract with any suitable person or persons, firm or firms, who are residents of and doing business in this State, to furnish such fuel as may be required by law or needed by any department of the State Government, except the Judicial Department; *provided,* that the said contract shall be for the term of one year, and until a new contract shall be made and approved.

SEC. 2. That the Secretary of State shall every year, and at such other times as are necessary, advertise for thirty days, in one or more weekly newspapers published in the city of Austin, and having the largest circulation, for sealed proposals for furnishing such fuel, and shall, in said advertisement, state a time and place when and where said proposals shall be received and opened, and contract awarded, not exceeding forty days from the date of the first publication of said advertisement; and he shall, in said advertisement, give such specifications and estimates of the probable amount and quality of fuel that will be required, as may be practicable. The proposals shall be sealed and addressed to the Secretary of State, and shall be endorsed with the statement that they are proposals for fuel, and, when received, shall be filed carefully away by the Secretary of State in his office, and the seals thereof shall not be broken until the day named in the advertisement for awarding the contract, and shall be opened in the presence of the Contracting Board, and such bidders as may desire to be present. The bids shall be examined by the Contracting Board, a careful comparison made, and the contract awarded to the lowest and best responsible bidder, whose bid shall be below such maximum rates as are hereinafter prescribed; *provided,* that each bid shall be accompanied by a guarantee, signed by at least two responsible citizens, guaranteeing that, if the contract be awarded to the said bidder, that he or they will enter into contract, and give a good and sufficient bond to carry out the same.

SEC. 3. That at any time after a contract has been made and entered into with any person or firm as herein provided, the Legislature reserves the right to abrogate said contract if not executed, and to alter or amend by enactment the maximum rates for such fuel. The Board of Contractors shall have power, and is hereby required when the Legis-

18 GL

lature is not in session, to cancel the contract, whenever the party or parties fail to comply with the contract as promptly as the exigencies of the public service demand; and it shall be their duty to let out a new contract in the manner herein provided; *provided, however*, such contract shall not be cancelled without the consent of the Governor and Comptroller thereto.

SEC. 4.   That the Secretary of State shall keep a record of his proceedings and the proceedings of the Board of Contractors; *provided*, that a majority of said Board shall be competent to do business.

SEC. 5.   That no member or officer of any department of the government, shall be in any way interested in said contracts, and all such contracts shall be in writing, and signed by the Board of Contractors, and approved in writing by the Governor, Secretary of State, and Comptroller.

SEC. 6.   That the rate paid for fuel in said contracts shall not exceed six dollars and ten cents per cord for dry cedar, and five dollars and ten cents per cord for dry oak and other kinds of wood except cedar.

SEC. 7.   That an imperative public necessity exists for the suspension of the rules and immediate passage of this act, and there being no law now in force under which the necessary fuel for the public buildings can be obtained, the emergency requires, and it is hereby enacted that this act take effect and be in force from and after its passage.

Approved August 21, 1876.

Takes effect from its passage.

CHAPTER CLVI.—*An Act to provide for the change of venue by the State in criminal cases.*

SECTION 1.   *Be it enacted by the Legislature of the State of Texas*, That whenever, in any case of felony, the District Judge presiding shall be satisfied that a trial alike fair and impartial to the accused and to the State cannot, from any cause, be had in the county in which the case is pending, he may, upon his own motion, order a change of venue to any county in his own, or in an adjoining district, stating in his order the grounds for such change of venue.

SEC. 2.   Whenever the District or County Attorney shall represent in writing to the District Court before which any felony case is pending, that by reason of existing combinations or influences in favor of the accused, or on account of the lawless condition of affairs in the county, a fair and impartial trial as between the accused and the State cannot be safely and speedily had, or whenever he shall represent that the life of the prisoner or of any of the witnesses would be jeoparded by a trial in the county in which the case is pending, the Judge shall hear proof in relation thereto, and if satisfied that such representation is well founded, and that the ends of public justice will be subserved thereby, he shall order a change of venue to any county in his own, or in an adjoining district.

SEC. 3.   In all cases where the venue shall be changed under the provisions of this act, the same orders shall be made and the same proceedings had, and the same duties be performed on the part of the Clerks and Sheriffs, as are required by the code of criminal procedure in cases where a change of venue is made on the application of the accused.

SEC. 4.   That, owing to the existence of combinations of lawless men in certain portions of the State, speedy and impartial trials cannot be had in criminal causes, and as there is not in force any law authorizing a change of venue by the State, therefore, this act go into effect and be in force from and after its passage.

Approved August 21, 1876.

Takes effect from its passage.

CHAPTER CLVII.—*An Act defining what money and property is subject to taxation or exemption, and the mode of listing the same.*

SECTION 1. *Be it enacted by the Legislature of the State of Texas*, That all real and personal property in this State, the property of corporations now existing or may be hereafter created, and the property of all banks or banking companies now existing or may be hereafter created, and of all bankers, except such as is hereinafter expressly exempted, is subject to taxation, and such property, or the value thereof, shall be entered in a list of taxable property for that purpose, in a manner prescribed by this act.

SEC. 2. Real property, for the purpose of taxation, shall be construed to include the land itself, whether laid out in town lots, or otherwise, and all the buildings, structures and improvements, or other fixtures, of whatsoever kind thereon, and all the rights and privileges belonging or in anywise appertaining thereto, and all mines, minerals, quarries and fossils in and under the same.

SEC. 3. Personal property shall, for the purpose of taxation, be construed to include all goods, chattels, moneys, credits and effects, wheresoever they may be in this State ; *provided*, that moneys, credits, bonds, and other evidences of debt, shall be included, whether the same be in or out of this State ; all ships, boats and vessels belonging to inhabitants of this State, if registered in this State, whether at home or abroad, and all capital invested therein ; all moneys at interest, either within or without this State due the person to be taxed, over and above what he pays interest for, and all other debts due such persons over and above their indebtedness ; *provided*, that notes that are taken for land shall not be taxed ; all public stocks and securities ; all stock in turnpikes, railroads, canals and other corporations (except National Banks) out of the State owned by inhabitants of this State ; all personal estate of moneyed corporations, whether the owners thereof reside in or out of this State ; and the income of any annuity, unless the capital of such annuity be taxed within the State ; all shares in any bank organized or that may be organized under the law of the United States ; all improvements made by persons upon lands held by them, the title to which is still vested in the State of Texas, or in any railroad company, or which have been exempted from taxation for the benefit of any railroad company or any other corporations, or any other corporation whose property is not subject to the same mode and rule of taxation as other property ; *provided*, that nothing in this section shall be so construed as to exempt from taxation any improvements on lands granted to any railroad company or other corporation, and exempted from taxation for a term of years.

SEC. 4. The term money or moneys, wherever used in this act shall, besides money or moneys, include every deposit which any person owning the same, or holding in trust, and residing in this State, is entitled to withdraw in money on demand. The term "credits," whenever used in this act or any other act regulating the assessment or collection of taxes, shall be held to mean and include every claim and

demand for money or other valuable thing, and every annuity or sum
of money receivable at stated periods, due or to become due; and all
claims and demands secured by deed or mortgage, due or to become
due. The terms "tract," or lot, and piece or parcel of real property, and
piece and parcel of land, whenever used in this act or any act regulating
the assessment and collection of taxes, shall each be held to mean
any quantity of land in possession of, owned by, or recorded as
the property of the same claimant, person, company or corporation. Every word importing the singular number only, may extend to and embrace the plural; and every word importing the
plural number, may be applied and limited to the singular number; and every word importing the masculine gender only, may
be extended and applied to females as well as males. Whenever the
word " oath " is used in this act or any other act regulating the assessment and collection of taxes, it shall be held to mean oath or affirmation; and the word swear, in this act or any other act regulating the
assessment and collection of taxes, may be held to mean " affirm." The
words town or district, whenever used in this act or any other act regulating the assessment and collection of taxes, shall be construed to
mean village, city, ward or precinct, as the case may be. The term
" true and full value," whenever used in this act or any other act regulating the assessment and collection of taxes, shall be held to mean the
fair market value in cash at the place where the property to which the
term is applied, shall be at the time of assessment, being the price
which could be obtained therefor at private sale, and not at force or
auction sale. The term person, whenever used in this act or any other
act regulating the assessment and collection of taxes, shall be construed
to include firm, company or corporation.

SEC. 5. All property described in this section to the extent herein limited, shall be exempt from taxation; that is to say : *First*—Public school-
houses and houses used exclusively for public worship, the books and
furniture therein, and the grounds attached to such buildings necessary
for the proper occupancy, use and enjoyment of the same, and not leased
or otherwise used with a view to profit; all public colleges, public acade-
mies; all buildings connected with the same; and all lands connected with
public institutions of learning; and all endowment funds of institutions of
learning not used with a view to profit; and all buildings used exclusively,
and owned by persons or associations of persons for school purposes.
This provision shall not extend to leasehold estates of real property held
under the authority of any college or university of learning in this
State. *Second*—All lands used exclusively for grave yards or grounds
for burying the dead, except such as are held by any person, company
or corporation with a view to profit, or for the purpose of speculation
in the sale thereof. *Third*—All property, whether real or personal, belonging exclusively to this State or the United States. *Fourth*—All
buildings belonging to counties, used for holding courts, for jails, for
county officers, with the land belonging to and on which such buildings
are erected. *Fifth*—All lands, houses or other buildings belonging to
any county, precinct or town used exclusively for the support or accommodation of the poor. *Sixth*—All buildings belonging to institutions
of purely public charity, together with the lands belonging to and occupied by such institutions, not leased or otherwise used with a view to
profit; and all moneys and credits appropriated solely to sustaining
. . . . to such institutions. *Seventh*—All fire engines

and other implements owned by towns and cities used for the extinguishment of fires, with the buildings used exclusively for the safe keeping thereof. *Eighth*—All market houses, public squares or other public grounds, town or precinct houses or halls used exclusively for public purposes; and all works, machinery or fixtures belonging to any town, and used for conveying water to such town. *Ninth*—All public libraries and personal property belonging to the same. *Tenth*—Household and kitchen furniture, not exceeding, at their true and full value, an amount of two hundred and fifty dollars to each family, in which may be included one sewing machine.

SEC. 6. All property shall be listed for taxation between January 1, and June 1, of each year, when required by the Assessor, with reference to the quantity held or owned on the first day of January, in the year for which the property is required to be listed or rendered. Any property (real or personal) purchased or acquired on the first day of January shall be listed by or for the person purchasing or acquiring it.

SEC. 7. All property shall be listed or rendered in the manner following: *First*—Every person of full age and sound mind, being a resident of this State, shall list all of his real estate, moneys, credits, bonds or stock of joint stock or other companies (when the property of such company is not assessed in this State), moneys loaned or invested, annuities, franchises, royalties and all other real and personal property. *Second*—He shall also list all lands or other real estate, all moneys and other personal property invested, loaned or otherwise controlled by him as the agent or attorney, or on account of any other person, company or corporation, whatsoever, and all moneys deposited subject to his order, check or draft, and credits due from or owing by any person or persons, body corporate or politic. *Third*—The property of a minor child shall be listed by his guardian or by the person having such property in charge. *Fourth*—The property of a wife, by her husband, if of sound mind; if not, by herself. *Fifth*—The property of an idiot or lunatic, by the person having charge of such property. *Sixth*—The property of a person for whose benefit it is held in trust by the trustee of the estate of a deceased person, by the executor or administrator. *Seventh*—The property of corporations whose assets are in the hands of receivers, by such receivers. *Eighth*—The property of a body politic or corporate, by the President, or proper agent or officer thereof. *Ninth*—The property of a firm or company, by a partner or agent thereof. *Tenth*—The property of manufacturers and others, in the hands of an agent, by such agent, in the name of his principal, as real, personal and merchandise.

SEC. 8. All property, real and personal, except such as is required in this act to be listed and assessed otherwise, shall be listed and assessed in the county where it is situated.

SEC. 9. The stock of nurseries, growing or otherwise, in the hands of nurserymen, shall be listed and assessed as merchandise.

SEC. 10. All persons, companies and corporations in this State, owning steamboats, sailing vessels, wharf boats and other water crafts, shall be required to list the same for assessment and taxation in the county in which the same may be enrolled, registered or licensed; or kept, when not enrolled, registered or licensed.

SEC. 11. All railroad, telegraph, plank road and turnpike companies shall list all of their real and personal property, giving the number of miles of road-bed and line in the county where such road-bed and line is situated, at the full and true value, except when such company may own personal property or real estate in an unorganized county or district; then they shall list such property to the Comptroller of the State.

SEC. 12.   Persons required to list property on behalf of others shall list it in the same manner in which they are required to list their own, but they shall list it separately from their own, specifying in each case the name of the person, estate, company or corporation to whom it belongs.

SEC. 13.   Each person required by this act to list property shall make and sign a statement verified by his oath as required by law, of all property, both real and personal, in his possession or under his control. and which by the provisions of this act he is required to list for taxation, either as owner or holder thereof, or as guardian, parent, husband. trustee, executor, administrator, receiver, accounting officer, partner, agent or factor; *provided*, that no person shall be required to list or render a greater portion of his credits than he believes will be received, or can be collected, or to. include in his statement as a part of his personal property which is required to list any share or portion of the capital stock or property of any company or corporation, which he is, of which is required to list or return its capital and property for taxation in this State.

SEC. 14.   Such statements shall truly and distinctly set forth : *First*— The name of the owner. *Second*—The abstract number. *Third*—The number of the survey. *Fourth*—The name of the original grantee. *Fifth*— The number of acres. *Sixth*—The value of the land. *Seventh*—The number of the lot or lots. *Eighth*—The number of the block. *Ninth*—The value of the town lots. *Tenth*—The name of the city or town. *Eleventh*—The number of miles of railroad in the county. *Twelfth*—Value of railroads and appurtenances, including the proportionate amount of rolling stock to the county. *Thirteenth*—Number of miles of telegraph in the county. *Fourteenth*—Value of telegraph and appurtenances in the county. *Fifteenth*—Number and amount of land certificates, and value thereof. *Sixteenth*—Number of horses and mules, and the value thereof. *Seventeenth*—Number of cattle, and value thereof. *Eighteenth*—Number of jacks and jennets, and value thereof. *Nineteenth*—Number of sheep, and value thereof. *Twentieth*—Number of goats, and value thereof. *Twenty-first*—Number of hogs, and value thereof. *Twenty-second*—Number of carriages, buggies, or wagons, of whatsoever kind, and value thereof. *Twenty-third*—Number of sewing machines and knitting machines, and value thereof. *Twenty-fourth*—Number of clocks and watches, and value thereof. *Twenty-fifth*—Number of organs, melodeons, piano fortes, and all other musical instruments of whatsoever kind, and value thereof. *Twenty-sixth*—The value of household and kitchen furniture over and above the amount of two hundred and fifty dollars. *Twenty-seventh*—Office furniture, and the value thereof. *Twenty-eighth*—The value of gold and silver plate. *Twenty-ninth*—The value of diamonds and jewelry. *Thirtieth*—Every annuity or royalty, the description and value thereof. *Thirty-first*—Number of steamboats, sailing vessels, wharf boats, barge or other water craft, and the value thereof. *Thirty-second*—The value of goods, wares and merchandise of every description, which such person is required to list as a merchant (in hand on the first day of January of each year). *Thirty-third*—Value of materials and manufactured articles which such person is required to list as a manufacturer. *Thirty-fourth*— Value of manufacturer's tools, implements, and machinery (other than boilers and engines, which shall be listed as such). *Thirty-fifth*—Number of steam engines, including boilers, and the value thereof. *Thirty-sixth*—Amount of moneys of bank, banker, broker or stock jobber. *Thirty-seventh*—Amount of credits of bank, banker, broker or stock jobber. *Thirty-eighth*—Amount of moneys other than of bank, banker, broker or stock jobber. *Thirty-ninth*—Amount of credits other than of bank, banker, broker or stock jobber. *Fortieth*—Amount and value of bonds and stocks (other than United States bonds). *Forty-first*—Amount and value of shares of capital stock companies and associations not incorporated by the laws of this State. *Forty-second*—Value of all property of companies and corporations other than property hereinbefore enumerated. *Forty-third*—Value of stock and furniture of saloons, hotels and eating houses. *Forty-fourth*—Value of every billiard, pigeon-hole, bagatelle, or other similar tables, together with the number thereof. *Forty-fifth*—Every franchise, the description and value thereof. *Forty-sixth*—Value of all other property not enumerated above.

Sec. 15. Persons listing or rendering real estate shall make a statement, duly signed and under oath, which shall truly and distinctly set forth: *First*—The name of the owner, abstract number, number of survey, the name of the original grantee, the number of acres, and the true and full value thereof. *Second*—The number of the lot and block, and the true and full value thereof, together with the name of the town or city. *Third*—When the name of the original grantee or abstract number, or number of survey is unknown (say unknown); and give such description so that land or lot can be identified, and the true and full value thereof can be determined.

Sec. 16. Every bank, whether of issue or deposit, banker, broker, dealer in exchange or stock jobber, shall at the time fixed by this act for listing personal property, make out and furnish the Assessor of Taxes a sworn statement, showing: *First*—The amount of money on hand or in transit. *Second*—The amount of funds in the hands of other bankers, brokers or others subject to drafts. *Third*—The amount of checks or other cash items; the amount thereof not being included in either of the preceeding items. *Fourth*—The amount of bills receivable, discounted or purchased and other credits due or to become due, including accounts receivable, interest accrued but not due, and interest due and unpaid. *Fifth*—The amount of bonds and stocks of every kind, and shares of capital stock, of joint stock or other companies or corporations, held as an investment or in any way representing assets. *Sixth*—All property appertaining to said business other than real estate (which real estate shall be listed and assessed as other real estate is listed and assessed under this act). *Seventh*—The amount of all deposits made with them by other parties. *Eighth*—The amount of all accounts payable, other than current deposit accounts. *Ninth*—The amount of bonds or other securities exempt by law from taxation, and the amount of shares of stock of any company or corporation which is required to list its capital for taxation, specifying the amount and kind of each, the same being included in the preceeding fifth item. The aggregate amount of the first, second and third shall be listed as money; the amount of the sixth item shall be listed the same as other similar personal property is listed under this act. The aggregate amount of the seventh and eighth items shall be deducted from the aggregate amount of the first, second, third and fourth items of said statement, and the amount of the remainder, if any, shall be listed as credits.

The aggregate amount of the ninth item shall be deducted from the aggregate amount of the fifth item of such statement, and the remainder shall be listed as bonds or stocks.

Sec. 17.   No person, company or corporation shall be entitled to any deduction on account of any bond, note or obligation of any kind, given to any mutual insurance company, nor on account of any unpaid subscription to any religious, literary, scientific or charitable institution or society, nor on account of any subscription to, or installment payable on the capital stock of any company, whether incorporated or unincorporated.

Sec. 18.   It shall be the duty of every railroad corporation in this State to deliver a sworn statement on or before the first day of June in each year, to the Assessor of each county and corporated town into which any part of their road shall run, or in which they own or are in possession of real estate, a classified list of all real estate owned or in the possession of said company in said county or town, specifying: *First*—The whole number of acres of land owned, possessed or appropriated for their use, with a valuation affixed to the same, deducting such portions, if any, as are already devoted to public use and purposes.   *Second*—The whole length of their superstructure, and value thereof, and construing "superstructure" to mean the ties, chairs, rails, spikes, frogs and switches, whether such superstructure be laid on land or on artificial foundation.   *Third*—The buildings, machinery and tools therein belonging to the company or in their possession, describing them by location, with the estimated value.

Sec. 19.   It shall be the duty of every railroad corporation in this State to deliver a sworn statement on or before the first day of June in each year, to the Assessor of each county and incorporated town into which any part of their road shall run, setting forth the true and full value of the rolling stock of such railroad; and the same shall be rendered and listed for taxes to the Assessor of Taxes of the county and incorporated town through which such railroad runs, and shall be proportioned to the county or incorporated town as the number of miles of such railroad in the county or incorporated town is to the entire number of miles of the railroad.

Sec. 20.   All property of private corporations, except in cases where some other provision is made by law, shall be assessed in the name of the corporation; and, in collecting the taxes on the same, all the personal property of such corporation shall be liable to be seized whenever the same may be found in the county, and sold in the same manner as the property of individuals may be sold for taxes.

Sec. 21.   All real property in this State, subject to taxation under this act, shall be assessed to the owners thereof in the manner provided in this act; *provided*, that no assessment of real property shall be considered illegal by reason of the same not being listed or assessed in the name of the owner or owners thereof.   All statements and lists made under this act by corporations, that are required to be sworn to, shall be verified by the affidavit and signature of the Secretary of said corporation; and, if they have no Secretary, the officer who discharges the duties of Secretary of said corporation.

Sec. 22.   The taxes, together with all interests, costs of suit, etc. (if there shall be any necessary), for the collection of the same, shall be a lien on real property, until the same shall have been paid.   It is also provided that should the Assessor fail to assess any real estate for any one or more years, the lien shall be good for every year that he should fail to assess for, and he may, in listing property for taxes any year thereafter, assess all the back taxes due thereon, according to the provisions of this act.

SEC. 23.   Property held under a lease for a term of three or more years, or a contract for the purchase thereof, belonging to this State, or any religious, scientific or benevolent society or institution, whether corporated or unincorporated, or to any railroad company or other corporation, whose property is not taxed in the same manner as other property, and school or other State lands, shall be considered, for all purposes of taxation, as the property of the persons so holding the same.

SEC. 24.   *First*—Each separate parcel of real property shall be valued at its true and full value in money, excluding the value of crops growing thereon.   *Second*—In determining the true and full value of real and personal property, the Assessor shall not adopt a lower or different standard of value, because the same is to serve as a basis of taxation; nor shall he adopt as a criterion of value the price for which said property would sell at auction, or at a forced sale, or in the aggregate with all the property in his county; but he shall value each tract or lot by itself, and at such sum or price as he believes the same to be fairly worth in money at the time such assessment is made.   *Third*—In valuing any real property on which there is a coal or other mine, or stone or other quarry, or springs possessing medicinal properties, the same shall be valued at such a price as such property, including a mine or quarry, or spring, would sell at a fair, voluntary sale for cash.   *Fourth*—Taxable leasehold estates shall be valued at such a price as they would bring at fair, voluntary sale for cash.   *Fifth*—Personal property of every description shall be valued at its true and full value thereof in money.   *Sixth*—Money, whether in possession or on deposit, or in the hands of any member of the family, or any other person or persons whatsoever, shall be entered in the statement at the full amount thereof.   *Seventh*—Every credit for a sum certain, payable either in money or property of any kind, shall be valued at the full value of the same so payable, if for a specific article, or for a specific number or quantity of property of any kind, which shall be valued at the current price of such property at the place where payable.   Annuities, or moneys payable at stated periods, shall be valued at the price that the person listing the same believes them to be worth in money.   Pensions granted under the act of the present session of the Legislature to the surviving soldiers and volunteers of the Texas Revolution, and the surviving signers of the Declaration of Texas Independence, and the surviving widows of such soldiers, signers and volunteers, shall not be taxed.

Approved August 21, 1876.

Takes effect ninety days after adjournment.

CHAPTER CLVIII.—*An Act to authorize the Comptroller of Public Accounts to issue duplicate warrants, and duplicates or copies of certificates, or other evidences of indebtedness, approved by the Auditorial Board of the State.*

SECTION 1.   *Be it enacted by the Legislature of the State of Texas,* That the Comptroller of Public Accounts, when satisfied that any original warrant drawn by the Comptroller of Public Accounts upon the State Treasurer has been lost, or when any certificate or other evidence of indebtedness, approved by the Auditorial Board of the State, has been lost, be and he is hereby authorized to issue a duplicate warrant in lieu of the original warrant; or a duplicate or a copy of such certificate, or other evidence of indebtedness, in lieu of such original; and upon the applicant filing with the Comptroller his affidavit that he is the true owner of such instrument, and that the same is in fact lost or destroyed, and shall also file with the Comptroller his bond in double the amount of the claim, with two or more good and sufficient sureties, payable to the Governor of the State, to be approved by the Comptroller, and conditioned that the applicant will hold the State harmless and return to the Comptroller, upon demand being made therefor, said duplicates or copies, or the amount of money named therein, together with all costs that may accrue against the State, on collecting the same.

SEC. 2.   That if, after the issuance of said duplicates or copies, the Comptroller should ascertain that the same was improperly issued, or that the applicant or party to whom the same was issued was not the owner thereof, he shall at once demand the return of said duplicate or copy, if unpaid, or the amount paid out by the State, if so paid; and upon the failure of the party to return the same, or the amount of money called for, suit shall be instituted upon said bond in the court having jurisdiction of the amount in controversy in the city of Austin, Travis county, Texas.

SEC. 3.   Whereas, there are many persons in this State who have lost original warrants issued by the Comptroller of Public Accounts upon the State Treasurer, and there is no law in force authorizing the Comptroller to issue a duplicate warrant for the same, and such persons are thereby deprived of the money due upon said warrants, thus creating an imperative public necessity and an emergency for the immediate passage of this act; therefore, it shall take effect and be in force from and after its passage.

Approved August 21, 1876.

Takes effect ninety days after adjournment.

CHAPTER CLIX.—*An Act to transfer suits and unfinished business pending in courts of Justices of the Peace at the time of adoption of the Constitution of 1875, for the State of Texas, to the courts of Justices of the Peace of the precincts in which said suits should be tried.*

SECTION 1.   *Be it enacted by the Legislature of the State of Texas,* That all suits and unfinished business pending in courts of Justices of the Peace in the State of Texas where, under the Constitution of 1875, the precincts have been changed, shall be transferred to the courts of Justice of the Peace of the precinct wherein the parties defendants to said causes shall reside at the time of the passage of this act, for the final disposition of said causes, and said Justices of the Peace, to whom said business shall be transferred, shall issue all such process as may be necessary to bring such parties into court for the disposition of said causes; and said Justices of the Peace, to whom said business is so transferred, shall issue all such process as is necessary to enforce such judgments as have heretofore been rendered and duly transferred to said Justices' courts.

SEC. 2.   As much unfinished business yet remains upon the dockets of the different Justices of the Peace of Texas, which, owing to the changes caused by the adoption of the Constitution of the State of

Texas of 1876, and many hardships and inconveniences will result unless speedy relief is had, there exists a great emergency and a necessity that this act take effect and be in force immediately upon its passage, and it is so enacted.

Approved August 21, 1876.

Takes effect from its passage.

CHAPTER CLX.—*An Act to regulate the respective duties of District and County Attorneys.*

SECTION 1. *Be it enacted by the Legislature of the State of Texas,* That the powers and duties of District Attorneys, including the Attorney for the Criminal District Court of the counties of Galveston and Harris, shall be the same as is now or may hereafter be prescribed by law, subject, however, to the following restrictions.

SEC. 2. That in counties where there is a County Attorney, it shall be his duty to attend the terms of the County and inferior Courts of his county, and to represent the State in all criminal cases under examination or prosecution in said county, and also to attend the terms of the District Court, and to represent the State in all cases in said court, during the absence of the District Attorney, and to aid the District Attorney when so requested. And when representing the State in the District Court, during the absence of the District Attorney, he shall be entitled to and receive the fees allowed by law to the said District Attorney, and when he shall, at the request of the District Attorney, aid him in examinations or trial of any case, he shall receive one-half of the fee or fees, and the District Attorney shall have and receive the other half of the fee allowed by law in such cases.

SEC. 3. That all laws and parts of laws in conflict with this act be and the same are hereby repealed.

SEC. 4. That there being no sufficient law upon the subject herein named, an imperative public necessity exists for the immediate passage of this act, it shall therefore take effect and be in force from and after its passage.

Approved August 21, 1876.

Takes effect from its passage.

CHAPTER CLXI.—*An Act to authorize the State Board of Education to collect and invest the interest due on the bonds belonging to the Agricultural and Mechanical College in six per cent. State bonds.*

SECTION 1. *Be it enacted by the Legislature of the State of Texas,* That the State Board of Education is hereby authorized to collect the interest that will be due at the end of the present fiscal year on the bonds belonging to the Agricultural and Mechanical College of Texas, and invest the same in six per cent. State bonds, except twelve thousand dollars ($12,000).

SEC. 2. It shall be the duty of the State Board of Education to collect the semi-annual interest on the bonds contemplated in this act, as the same may become due, as well as the interest that may become due on the bonds already belonging to the Agricultural and Mechanical College fund, and place the same in the Treasury of the State to the credit of said College fund.

SEC. 3. Whereas, it is important for the prompt collection and investment of the interest due on the said bonds, creates an emergency; this act shall go into effect from its passage.

Approved August 21, 1876.

Takes effect ninety days after adjournment.

CHAPTER CLXII.—*An Act to regulate the compensation of jurors in certain cases.*

SECTION 1.   *Be it enacted by the Legislature of the State of Texas,* That whenever a special *venire facias* may be ordered for the trial of any cause, as is provided for in Articles 548 and 549 of the code of criminal procedure, only those persons who are accepted and actually sworn as jurors to try the cause shall be entitled to compensation as jurors.

SEC. 2.   The laws on this subject being imperfect and the present session of this Legislature rapidly drawing to a close, an emergency and public necessity exists for the immediate passage of this act; therefore this act shall take effect and be in force from and after its passage.

Approved August 21, 1876.

Takes effect ninety days after adjournment.

CHAPTER CLXIII.—*An Act supplemental to an act entitled "An Act making appropriations for the deficiencies for the present year, beginning September 1, 1875, and ending August 31, 1876, and previous years."*

SECTION 1.   *Be it enacted by the Legislature of the State of Texas,* That the sum of two hundred and thirty-seven dollars be and the same is hereby appropriated out of any money in the Treasury not otherwise appropriated, to pay John D. Elliott for public printing during the **year** 1876.

SEC. 2.   As this session of the Legislature is drawing to a close, an emergency and public necessity exist for the passage of this act at the present; it shall therefore take effect and be in force from and after its passage.

NOTE.—The above bill was neither approved or disapproved by the Governor, but was filed in the office of Secretary of State on the 23d day of August, 1876, at 10 o'clock A. M., being after the adjournment of the Legislature, and will become a law without his approval, and will take effect ninety days after the adjournment of the Legislature.

A. W. DEBERRY, *Secretary of State.*

CHAPTER CLXIV.—*An Act to fix and regulate the fees of all the officers of the State of Texas, and the several counties thereof.*

SECTION 1.   *Be it enacted by the Legislature of the State of Texas,* That the various officers hereinafter named shall demand and receive the fees herein designated for the services indicated, and that the same shall be due and payable in the lawful currency of the United States.

SEC. 2.   The Attorney-General shall receive the following fees: In every conviction of offenses against the penal laws in cases of misdemeanor, when the judgment is affirmed or when the appeal is dismissed, ten dollars; in cases of forfeitures and fines taken to the Court of Appeals, ten per cent. on the amount collected under final judgment of Court of Appeals; for each affirmance of judgment or dismissal in a felony case, twenty dollars; for each case of *habeas corpus* heard before the Court of Appeals, twenty-five dollars; for each affirmance of

judgment in cases to which the State may be a party involving pecu-
niary liabilities to the State, ten per cent. on the amount involved, if
under one thousand dollars, and five per cent. for all above that sum,
to be paid out of the money when collected; for all cases involving
the forfeiture of charters, heard on appeal before the Supreme Court or
Court of Appeals, twenty-five dollars; *provided*, the whole amount of fees
shall not exceed two thousand dollars per annum.

SEC. 3. The Assistant Attorney-General shall receive as mileage and
traveling expenses one thousand dollars per annum.

SEC. 4. The Clerks of the Supreme Court, shall receive the following
fees: For entering the appearance of either party in person or by attorney, to be charged but once, fifty cents; for docketing each cause, to
be charged but once, fifty cents; for filing the record in each cause,
fifty cents; for entering each rule or motion, twenty-five cents; for
entering the order of the court upon any rule or motion, or for entering
any interlocutory judgment, fifty cents; for administering an oath or
affirmation without a certificate, fifteen cents; for administering an oath
or affirmation and giving a certificate thereof with seal, twenty-five
cents; for entering each continuance, twenty-five cents; for entering
every final judgment or decree, one dollar; for each writ issued, one
dollar; for making out and transmitting the mandate and judgment
of the Supreme Court to any inferior court, one dollar and fifty cents;
for making copies of any papers or records in his office, including certificate and seal, when applied for by any person, for each hundred words,
fifteen cents; for recording the opinions of the Judges, for each hundred
words, twenty cents; for taxing the bill of costs in each case, with
copy thereof, fifty cents; for every service not herein provided for,
such fees as may be allowed by the Supreme Court, not to exceed the
fees herein allowed for services requiring a like amount of labor. There
shall be allowed to said Clerk reasonable office rent, stationery and furniture for his office, to be paid on the approval and order of the Supreme Court, out of the appropriation for the contingent expenses of
said court.

SEC. 5. The Clerk of the Court of Appeals shall receive the following fees: In every appeal by the defendant in case of misdemeanor,
when judgment is affirmed, ten dollars, to be paid by defendant; in
civil cases, the same fees as are allowed to Clerks of the Supreme Court
for like services; the Clerk of the Court of Appeals, in every case of
felony upon which an appeal is taken, ten dollars, to be paid by the
State.

SEC. 6. County Judges shall receive the following fees: For each
civil cause finally disposed of before him, by trial or otherwise, three
dollars; probating a will, two dollars; for granting letters testamentary
of administration or of guardianship, fifty cents; for each order of sale,
fifty cents; for each approval and confirmation of sale, fifty cents; for
each decree of partition and distribution, two dollars; for each decree
approving or setting aside the report of commissioners of partition and
distribution, two dollars; for each decree refusing order of sale or confirmation of sale, fifty cents; for each decree removing an executor, administrator or guardian, one dollar, to be paid by the executor, administrator or guardian; for each fiat or certificate granted by him, fifty
cents; for each continuance, ten cents; for each order made by him,
except otherwise provided for, fifty cents; they shall be allowed a commission of one-half of one per cent. upon the actual cash receipts of

each executor, administrator or guardian, upon the approval of his exhibits and the final settlement of his accounts, but no more than one such commission shall be charged on any amount received by any executor, administrator or guardian; for every case of lunacy disposed of by him, three dollars, to be paid by the county; for each hearing, deter(m)ining and rendering a final order on each motion submitted to him, ten cents; for every case of misdemeanor or *habeas corpus* finally disposed of by him, five dollars, to be paid by the defendant, if convicted; for presiding over the County Commissioners' Court, ordering elections and making returns, and transacting all other county business not otherwise provided for, such sum as shall be allowed by the County Commissioners' Court. There shall be allowed to the County Judge such books, stationery and office furniture as may be necessary for him in the discharge of the duties of his office, and the same shall be paid for out of the county treasury on the order of the County Commissioners' Court.

Sec. 7. The County Attorneys shall be entitled to the following fees and no others, to-wit: For every conviction under the laws against gaming, where no appeal is taken, or when on appeal the judgment is affirmed, fifteen dollars, to be paid by the defendant as other costs; in all other cases of misdemeanor where the defendant is convicted and no appeal is taken, or when upon appeal the judgment is affirmed, ten dollars, to be paid by defendant as other costs; for all convictions of a capital felony, when the defendant fails to appeal, or escapes after appeal is taken, before final judgment of the Appellate Court, or when upon appeal the judgment is affirmed, and in all cases of felonious homicide, above and including the grade of manslaughter, fifty dollars; and in all other convictions of felony, when the defendant fails to appeal, or escapes after appeal is taken, before final judgment of the Appellate Court, or when upon appeal the judgment is affirmed, thirty dollars, to be paid by the State; on all fines, forfeitures, or money collected for the State or county, recovered by him, the County Attorney shall be entitled to ten per cent. of the amount so collected; for services rendered in the examining courts in every felony case, where the party is finally convicted, and no appeal is taken, or where upon appeal the judgment is affirmed, ten dollars; for representing the State in each case of *habeas corpus* where the defendant is charged with a felony, twenty dollars, to be paid by the State; *provided*, that only one fee shall be paid in each case of *habeas corpus*, without regard to the number of defendants. District Attorneys shall be allowed the same fees and commissions as are herein allowed to County Attorneys for all services by them performed. The District Attorney shall also receive a salary of five hundred dollars per annum, to be paid by the State.

Sec. 8. Clerks of the District Court shall receive the following fees: For each writ or citation, seventy-five cents; for docketing each cause, to be charged but once, twenty cents; for filing each paper in a cause, fifteen cents; for each appearance, to be charged but once, fifteen cents; for entering each continuance, twenty cents; for docketing each motion or rule, fifteen cents; for entering each final order, decree or judgment upon a motion or rule, one dollar; for swearing each witness, ten cents; for administering each oath or affirmation without certificate, fifteen cents; for administering each oath or affirmation, and authenticating the same with the impress of the seal of his office, fifty cents; for each subpœna, twenty-five cents; for each additional name inserted in each subpœna, fifteen cents; for writing and taking a bond in every case where a bond is required (except bond for costs), one dollar and fifty cents; for swearing and empanneling a jury, thirty-five cents; for receiving and recording the verdict in each case tried by a jury, thirty-five cents; for assessing the damages in each case not tried by a jury, fifty cents; for each commission to take deposition, seventy-five cents; for taking depositions, each hundred words, fifteen cents; for swearing witness, with certificate and seal, fifty cents; for each *scire facias*, including copy thereof, one dollar; for entering each interlocutory judgment, seventy-five cents; for entering each final judgment, seventy-five cents; for entering each decree, exceeding two hundred words, each one hundred words, fifteen cents; for taxing the bill of costs, in each case, with copy thereof, twenty-five cents; for each execution, seventy-five cents; for each order of sale, or *venditioni exponas*, seventy-five cents; for each writ of possession or restitution, seventy-five cents; for entering and recording the return of each writ of execution, etc., seventy-five cents; for copies of petition, interrogatories, cross-interrogatories, and of all records or j   their offices, with certificate and seal, each one hundred word   nts; for transcript in any case, when appeal or writ of error is   ificate and seal, each one hundred words, twenty cents   to any fact or facts contained in the records of his of   seal, seventy-five cents; for entering each order   eventy-five cents; for taking the acknowledg   d, power of attorney, or other instrument   certificate and seal, fifty cents;   arried woman to any such doc   tting the records and   ty or Justice cour,   the Clerk shall f   , or for app tainin, ment, certifi recognizant, original writ in a criminal cause, mitting the mandate or judgment of the District Court, upon an appeal from the County Court, one dollar. There shall be allowed to said Clerk such books, stationery, and office furniture as may be necessary for his office, to be paid on the order of the County Court, out of the County Treasury, and a suitable office shall also be provided by the County Court at the expense of the county. For filing a record in a cause appealed to the District Court, fifty cents. That the District Clerk shall receive, in addition to the fees herein allowed, such sum as may be allowed by the Commissioners' Court, not to exceed three hundred dollars, for the care and preservation of the records of his office, keeping of the necessary indexes, and other labor of a like class, to be paid by the county.

SEC. 9. Clerks of the County Courts shall receive the following fees:

CLERKS' COSTS IN PROBATE MATTERS.

For filing each paper in relation to estates of decedents or wards, ten cents; for issuing notices, including copies for posting or publication, twenty-five cents; for docketing each application, complaint, petition or

proceeding, to be charged but once, ten cents ; for each writ or citation, in—
cluding copy thereof, fifty cents ; for each copy of an application, complaint or petition, that is required to accompany a writ or citation, with certificate and seal, for each one hundred words, ten cents ; for making and
attesting letters testamentary or of administration or guardianship, fifty
cents ; for entering each judgment in relation to estates of decedents or
wards, fifty cents, and ten cents per hundred words for all in excess of
two hundred words ; for recording all papers required to be recorded by
them in relation to estates of decedents or wards, for each one hundred
words, not otherwise provided for, ten cents ; for administering oath to
an executor, administrator or guardian, ten cents ; for administering
oath or affirmation in all other cases, and giving certificate with seal
when necessary, twenty-five cents ; for each writ or citation, including
copy thereof, fifty cents ; for docketing each cause, to be charged but
once, ten cents ; for filing each paper in a cause, ten cents ; for each
appearance, to be charged but once, ten cents ; for entering each continuance, ten cents ; for docketing each motion or rule
entering each final order, decree or judgment, une
except for costs, not otherwise provided for.
for each one hundred words in excess
swearing each witness, ten cents
affirnation, without certificate
or affir ation, with cert
poena, twenty-five cer
poena, ten cents
where a bond
ing and
cents

ty-five cents, for each writ or
entering and recording the return of each, interrogatories, cross interroga-
etc., fifty cents ; for copies of petition, interrogatories, cross interrogatories and of all records or papers in their offices, with certificate and
seal, each one hundred words, where not otherwise provided for, fifteen
cents ; for transcript in any case where appeal or writ of error is taken,
with certificate and seal, each one hundred words, fifteen cents ; for
each certficate to any fact or facts contained in the records of his office,
with certificate and seal, where not otherwise provided for, fifty cents :
for entering each order, not otherwise provided for, ten cents ; for each
acknowledgement, fifty cents ; for each acknowledgement of husband
and wife, one dollar and fifty cents ; for each declaration of citizenship,
one dollar ; for each letter of citizenship, with decree, two dollars and
fifty cents ; for recording each mark and brand, twenty-five cents ; for
issuing each marriage license, one dollar, and recording the same, fifty
cents. It shall be the duty of the County Judge, at each term of the
court, to enquire into and examine the amount of labor actually and

necessarily performed by the Clerk, in the care and preservation of the records of his office, in the making and keeping of the necessary indexes thereto, and other labor of a like class, and to allow said Clerk a reasonable compensation therefor, not to exceed the fees therein allowed for services requiring a like amount of labor, to be paid out of the County Treasury, upon the sworn account of said Clerk, approved by the County Judge, not to exceed one hundred dollars per annum. There shall be allowed to said Clerk of the County Court, such books, stationery and office furniture as may be necessary for his office, to be paid on the order of the Commissioners' Court, out of the County Treasury, and a suitable office shall also be provided by the Commissioners' Court at the expense of the county. All clerks and their deputies are hereby prohibited from charging any fees or commissions for writing deeds, mortgages, bills of sale, or any other conveyance for any person, unless they pay a tax as conveyancers. There shall be allowed for the use of the County Clerk such books and stationery as are necessary for his office, to be paid for out of the County Treasury; *provided*, the Clerk shall receive no pay for motions or judgments for costs, or for approving bond for costs, and that judgments containing several orders shall not be considered as more than one judgment for which charges may be made. For making out and transmitting the mandate or judgment of the County Court, upon an appeal from the Justice's Court, one dollar; for all *ex-officio* services in relation to roads, bridges and ferries, issuing jury script, and all other public services not otherwise provided for, such sum as may be allowed by the Commissioners' Court, not to exceed one hundred dollars per annum.

SEC. 10. Fees of County and District Clerks in criminal cases: For issuing each *capias* or other original writ, seventy-five cents; for entering each appearance, fifteen cents; for docketing cause to be charged but once, twenty-five cents; for swearing and empanneling a jury, and receiving and recording the verdict, fifty cents; for swearing each witness, ten cents; for issuing each subpœna, twenty-five cents; for additional names, fifteen cents each; for issuing each attachment, fifty cents; for entering each order not otherwise provided for, fifty cents; for entering judgment, fifty cents; for filing each paper, ten cents; for entering each continuance, twenty-five cents; for entering each motion or rule, ten cents; for entering each recognizance, fifty cents; for entering each judgment *nisi*, fifty cents; for entering each indictment or informaation, ten cents; for each commitment, one dollar; for each transcript on appeal, for each one hundred words, ten cents; for each copy of indictment or information, for each hundred words, ten cents; for felony cases tried in the District Court or County Court, to be paid by the State, ten dollars.

SEC. 11. Sheriffs shall receive the following fees: For serving each original writ or citation in a civil suit, and a copy of petition, one dollar and fifty cents; for executing each warrant of arrest or *capias*, or making arrest without warrant, one dollar; for each mile he may be compelled to travel in executing criminal process or summoning or attaching witness, five cents; for traveling in the service of any process, not otherwise provided for, the sum of five cents for each mile going and returning, computing the distance from the place of service to the place of return; if two or more persons are mentioned in the writ, he shall charge for the distance actually and necessarily traveled in the service of the same; these fees in cases of felony to be paid by the

19 GL

State, where the defendant is brought to trial; for summoning each witness in the County or District Court, fifty cents; in cases of felony to be paid by the State, where the defendant is brought to trial; for summoning a jury in a felony case, to be paid by the State where the defendant is brought to trial, two dollars; for serving each *scire facias*, one dollar; for levying and returning each writ of attachment or sequestration, two dollars and fifty cents; for serving each citation and writ of garnishment, one dollar; for each cause tried in the District or County Court, a jury fee shall be taxed for the Sheriff, fifty cents; for taking and approving each bond, and returning the same to the proper court when necessary, one dollar; for serving any writ, not otherwise provided, one dollar; for each commitment or release, one dollar; for levying each execution, one dollar and fifty cents; for returning each execution, seventy-five cents; for executing and returning each writ of possession and restitution, three dollars; for posting the advertisements for sales under execution, or any order of sale, one dollar; for endorsing the forfeiture of any bond required to be endorsed by him, fifty cents; for executing a deed to each purchaser of real estate under an execution, or an order of sale, two dollars; for executing a bill of sale to each purchaser of personal property, under an execution or an order of sale, when demanded by the purchaser, one dollar; for making money on an execution or an order of sale, when the same is made by a sale, for the first hundred dollars, four per. cent.; for the second hundred dollars, three per cent.; for all sums over two hundred dollars, two per cent.; when the money is made without a sale, one-half of said rate shall be allowed; for executing each death-warrant, fifty dollars, to be paid by the State; for removing a prisoner, for each mile, going and returning, including guards and all other expenses, when traveling by railroads, fifteen cents; traveling otherwise, twenty-five cents; in cases of felony, to be paid by the State when the defendant is brought to trial; for attending a prisoner on *habeas corpus*, for each day, two dollars, and mileage as above when moving him out of the county; for taking care of property levied on by a writ of execution, sequestration or attachment, all reasonable and necessary expenses, to be taxed and allowed by the court to which such writ is returnable; for conveying a witness attached by him to any court out of his county, his actual, necessary expenses by the nearest practicable public conveyance, the amount to be stated by him under oath, and approved by the Judge of the court issuing the attachment; for summoning jurors in the District Court and County Court, serving all election notices, notices upon overseers of roads, attending the District and County Courts, and doing all other public business, not otherwise provided for, such sum as may be allowed by the Commissioners' Court, not to exceed two hundred dollars per annum, to be paid out of the County Treasury; and for every day the Sheriff or his deputies shall attend the District and County Courts, he shall receive two dollars a day, to be paid by the county for each day that the Sheriff, by himself or a deputy, shall attend said courts; for keeping and feeding from one to four prisoners, he shall be paid not exceeding forty-five cents per day for each prisoner; but whenever the number of prisoners in jail shall be more than four, then the pay for feeding prisoners shall not exceed forty cents each per day; this shall be inclusive of all fees or allowances to Sheriffs for the support, maintenance, keeping and feeding prisoners; for guards necessarily employed in the safe keeping of prisoners, one dollar and fifty cents per day for every guard so employed by the Sheriff; and there shall not be anything allowed for the board of such guards, nor shall any allowance be made for jailor or turnkey.

Sec. 12. Justices of the Peace shall receive the following fees: For each citation or writ in civil suits, fifty cents; for each warrant in criminal cases, seventy-five cents; for taking each recognizance in a criminal case, fifty cents; for taking each bond not otherwise provided for, fifty cents; for each subpœna for one witness, twenty-five cents; for every additional name inserted in a subpœna, ten cents; for docketing each cause, ten cents; for each continuance, twenty cents; for swearing each witness in court, ten cents; for administering an oath or affirmation without a certificate, ten cents; for administering an oath or affirmation with a certificate thereof, twenty-five cents; for administering the oath, taking bond, and issuing a writ of attachment or sequestration, one dollar and fifty cents; for causing a jury to be summoned, swearing them, and receiving and recording their verdict, in each cause tried by a jury before them, fifty cents; for each order in a cause, twenty-five cents; for each final judgment, fifty cents. For each application to set aside a judgment by default or of non-suit, or for a new trial, with the final order or judgment of the Justice thereon, fifty cents; for taking the acknowledgment for a stray, in each cause, fifty cents; for taking each appeal bond, twenty-five cents; for each commission to take deposition of one or more witnesses, fifty cents; for copy of interrogatories, or cross interrogatories, for each hundred words, ten cents; for making out and certifying a transcript of the entries on his docket, and filing the same with the original papers of the cause in the District Court, in each case of appeal or *certiorari*, one dollar and fifty cents; for each execution, sixty cents; for each writ of possession or restitution, seventy-five cents; for receiving and recording the return on each execution, writ of possession or restitution, thirty cents, if a levy is returned; ten cents, if not; for each search-warrant, thirty cents; for each commitment, fifty cents; for taxing costs, including copy thereof, in each cause, ten cents; for every certificate not otherwise provided for, twenty-five cents; for making copies of any papers or records in his office, including certificate, for any person applying for the same, for each hundred words, ten cents; for taking down the testimony of witnesses, swearing them, taking the voluntary statement of persons accused, certifying and returning the same to the proper court, in examinations for offenses, for each hundred words, if collected from the defendant, twenty cents; for summoning a jury, and all other business connected with an inquest upon a dead body, including certifying and returning the same to the proper court, five dollars, to be paid out of the County Treasury.

Sec. 13. Constables shall receive the following fees: For serving each writ or citation in civil suit, seventy cents; for serving each warrant in a criminal cause, one dollar; for serving each notice for the taking of depositions and copy of interrogatories, seventy cents; for executing a search warrant, one dollar; for levying and returning each writ of attachment or sequestration, one dollar and fifty cents; for summoning each witness, fifty cents; for committing a person to jail, seventy-five cents; for taking each bond, one dollar; for levying each execution, seventy cents; for executing writ of possession or restitution, one dollar; For returning each execution, writ of possession or restitution, forty cents; for summoning a jury in a Justices' Court, one dollar; for summoning a jury to hold an inquest before a Coroner, to be paid by the county, two dollars and fifty cents; for advertising sale under execution on any order of sale, seventy cents; for making title to purchaser of real estate under execution or any order of sale, two dollars; for making title to purchaser of personal property under execution or order of sale, when demanded by the purchaser, fifty cents; for making money under execution or or order of sale, when a sale is made, four per centum on the amount; when money is made without a sale, two per cent. on the amount; for conveying a prisoner to jail, including guard and other expenses, twenty-five cents a mile in going and returning; if by railroads, fifteen cents; for taking care of property levied on by a writ of execution, sequestration or attachment, all reasonable and necessary expenses, to be taxed and allowed by the court to which such writ is returnable. For all services done by Constables in business connected with the County and District Courts, they shall only receive the same fees as are allowed Sheriffs. For each mile actually and necessarily traveled in executing criminal process or making arrest without warrant and summoning witnesses in criminal cases, five cents going and returning, computing the distance from the place of service to the place of return. If two or more persons are mentioned in the writ, he shall charge for the distance actually traveled in the service of the same.

SEC. 14. Each Commissioner shall receive three dollars per day, for each day he is engaged sitting as a member of term of the County Commissioners' Court; *provided*, no per diem shall be paid said Commissioners for more than one special term per month.

SEC. 15. County Treasurers shall receive the following fees: The County Treasurer shall receive not more than two and one half per cent. on all sums received by him; and not more than two and a half per cent. on all sums paid out by him; but shall receive not more than one per cent. for receiving and paying out monies belonging to the school fund. The commissions of the County Treasurer shall be fixed by the County Commissioners' Court, within the limits prescribed in this act; *provided*, that the County Treasurer shall receive no commissions for receiving money from his predecessor or for paying over money to his successor in office; *provided, further*, that the compensation allowed to any County Treasurer shall not exceed three thousand dollars per annum, in any county of this State.

SEC. 16. District and County Surveyors shall receive the following fees: For inspection and recording of the field notes and plat of a survey for any tract of land over one-third of a league, three dollars; for one-third of a league, two dollars; for any quantity of land less than one third of a league, one dollar; for each examination of papers and records in his office, at the request of any person wishing to examine them, twenty-five cents; for copies of all field notes and plats, or any other papers or records in his office, for each hundred words, including certificate, twenty cents; for surveying any tract of land, for each English lineal mile actually run, including all expenses of making the survey and returning the plat and field notes of survey, three dollars a mile.

SEC. 17. Inspectors of Hides and Animals for each county or district shall receive the following fees: For each hide of neat cattle and animal inspected, ten cents each for the first one hundred so inspected for any one person at one time; and for the next one hundred so inspected, eight cents each; and for any number of two hundred so inspected, three cents each; for each horse, mule or cattle imported from Mexico, five cents; and for each hide of neat cattle imported from Mexico, and inspected, five cents, to include hides of cattle and not those of sheep or goats; and such other fees as may be designated by law relating to the inspection of hides and animals.

SEC. 18. Notaries Public shall receive the following fees: For protesting a bill or note for non-acceptance or non-payment, registering and seal, two dollars and fifty cents; and for each notice thereof, fifty cents; for protest in all other cases, twenty cents for each hundred words, and fifty cents for certificate and seal; for taking the acknowledgments or proof of any deed or any other instrument of writing, for registration, with certificate and seal, fifty cents; for administering an oath or affirmation, with certificate and seal, twenty-five cents; for taking the acknowledgment of a married woman to a deed, or any other instrument of writing, authorized to be executed by her, with certificate and seal, one dollar; for all certificates not otherwise provided for, with seal, fifty cents; for all notarial acts not otherwise provided for, fifty cents; for copies of all records and memorandums in their offices, with certificate and seal, fifty cents, if less than two hundred words, and fifteen cents for each hundred words in excess of two hundred words.

SEC. 19. The several officers and persons authorized to perform any of the services named in this section, shall be entitled to the fees herein allowed for such services, namely: For taking the acknowledgment or proof of any deed, or any other instrument of writing, for registration, with certificate and seal, fifty cents; for taking the acknowledgment of a married woman to a deed, or any other instrument of writing authorized to be executed by her, with certificate and seal, one dollar; for taking the deposition of a witness, in answer to interrogatories or cross-interrogatories under a commission, for each hundred words, fifteen cents; for swearing the witness to such answers, making certificates thereof, with seal, and all other business connected with taking such depositions, fifty cents; for recording any instrument required by law to be recorded, not otherwise provided for, fifteen cents for each hundred words, including the certificate and seal.

SEC. 20. The fees hereinbefore mentioned pertaining to suits or actions in court, shall be taxed and allowed in the bill of costs against the party cast in each suit or action wherein any such services shall be rendered; but no copy not required by law shall be allowed in the bill of costs, and if any party or his attorney shall take out copies of his own pleadings, or of papers filed by him in any cause, no charge for such copies shall be allowed in the bill of costs.

SEC. 21. No Clerk of the Court or Justice of the Peace shall be allowed to charge any practicing attorney of this State any fee for the examination of any papers or records in his office.

SEC. 22. Every Clerk of a Court, County Judge, Sheriff, Justice of the Peace and Constable in this State shall keep a fee book, and shall enter therein all fees charged for services rendered; which book shall at all times be subject to the inspection of any person wishing to see the account of fees therein charged.

SEC. 23. None of the fees hereinbefore mentioned shall be payable by any person whatsoever, until there be produced, or ready to be produced, unto the person owing or chargeable with the same, a bill or account in writing containing the particulars of such fees, signed by the Clerk or officer to whom such fee shall be due, or by whom the same is charged.

SEC. 24.　In all cases where any person shall be presented or indicted by the grand jury, and shall be discharged from such presentment or indictment, neither the Clerks nor the Sheriffs shall charge fees for the same, but if the party or parties so presented or indicted shall be convicted, the Clerk or Sheriff shall charge him, her or them, with all the fees accruing thereon. And in all cases where parties are convicted of felonies, judgment shall be rendered against said parties for all costs accruing in such cases, and execution shall issue thereon, in the name of the State.

SEC. 25.　If any of the officers herein named shall demand and receive any other or higher fees than are prescribed in this act, for any services herein mentioned, he shall be liable to the party aggrieved for fourfold the fees so unlawfully demanded and received, to be recovered in any court of competent jurisdiction ; and it is hereby made the duty of the Sheriff, Clerks of the District and County Courts, and Notaries Public of the several counties of this State, to keep posted up, at all times, in a conspicuous place in their respective offices, a complete list of the fees herein allowed to be charged by them respectively.

SEC. 26.　It shall be lawful for any Justice of the Peace, or Clerk of the Supreme, District or County Court, within this State, when any suits are determined in their respective courts, and the fees are not paid by the party from whom they are due, to make out executions for the same, directed to any lawful officer of the county where the party resides, and it shall be lawful for the Clerks of the County Courts to make out executions in like manner for the fees that may become due the officers of said courts, directed to any lawful officer of the proper county ; and the officers to whom any of such executions shall be directed shall levy and proceed with the same as in other cases ; *provided*, that a bill of costs shall in all cases accompany such execution ; *and provided, further*, that this section shall not apply to costs due by administrators, guardians or executors.

SEC. 27.　In all cases where a citation or other process is required to be served by publication in a newspaper, the officer whose duty it may be to make such service, shall be furnished with the printer's fee for such publication before he shall be required to have such service made.

SEC. 28.　It shall be lawful for the Clerk of any court, or Justice of the Peace to require security for costs, before issuing any process in any suit about to be commenced, unless the party applying for such process, his agent or attorney, shall make oath that the party so applying is unable to give such security.

SEC. 29.　That all laws and parts of laws in conflict with the provisions of this act, for prescribing other and different fees to any of the officers herein named, are hereby repealed.

SEC. 30.　That for all services performed since the seventeenth day of April, 1876, by any of the officers herein named, they shall receive the same fees as are herein provided ; *provided, however*, that this section shall not prevent the officer from charging the rates heretofore allowed by law, for any service performed by him before the passage of this act.

SEC. 31.　The fact that there is no law in force fully defining the fees of County Clerks and County Judges, and other officers, creates an emergency that, and it is hereby declared that, this act shall be in force and effect from and after its passage.

Approved August 23, 1876.

Takes effect ninety days after adjournment.

CHAPTER CLXV.—*An Act to encourage stock-raising and for the protection of stock-raisers.*

SECTION 1. *Be it enacted by the Legislature of the State of Texas,* That each organized county of this State shall be created an inspection district for the inspection of hides and animals; and that an Inspector of Hides and Animals shall be elected by the qualified voters of each county; and that, in case of a vacancy, the Sheriff of the county shall be *ex-officio* Inspector until an Inspector shall be appointed by the County Commissioners' Court, which power of appointment of an Inspector, in case of a vacancy in the office, is hereby vested in said court.

SEC. 2. Every Inspector so appointed shall hold his office for the term of two years; and in case of a vacancy in the office of Inspector of any district, the County Court of such district shall immediately order an appointment therein, and the Inspector so appointed shall hold his office for the unexpired portion of the term for which his predecessor was appointed.

SEC. 3. Every person appointed to the office of Inspector of Hides and Animals, before entering upon the duties of his office, shall enter into a bond, with two or more good and sufficient securities, to be approved by the County Commissioners' Court of the county constituting his district; which bond shall be in a sum to be fixed by said County Commissioners' Court, which sum shall be not less than one thousand dollars nor more than ten thousand dollars, payable to the County Judge, conditioned that he shall well and truly perform the duties of his office in accordance with the provisions of this act; and he shall also take and subscribe the oath of office prescribed by the Constitution, which shall be endorsed on or attached to said bond, together with the certificate of the officer administering the oath, which bond and oath shall be deposited and recorded in the office of the Clerk of the County Court of the county. The bond herein provided for shall not be void for want of form, or on the first recovery; but may be sued on from time to time, in the name or names of any person or persons injured by a breach thereof, until the whole penalty shall have been recovered.

SEC. 4. Every Inspector shall have power to appoint as many deputies as shall be necessary to perform the duties imposed on them by this act, and such deputies shall have the same power and authority to perform the duties of their office as their principal; and the Inspector shall require bond and security of their deputies for the faithful performance of their duties; and the said deputies shall, before entering upon their duties, take and subscribe the oath prescribed by the Constitution, which, together with the certificate of the officer administering the same, shall be endorsed upon the bonds; and he shall receive a certificate of his appointment as deputy, signed by the Inspector, which shall be recorded in the office of the County Clerk.

SEC. 5. The appointment of each deputy shall be in writing, with the seal of the Inspector thereon, and shall with their bonds and oaths of office be recorded by the Clerk of the County Court of the county constituting their district, and the Inspector shall be responsible to any persons injured thereby, for the official acts of each of their deputies, and they shall have the same remedies against their deputies and their securities as any person can have against the Inspectors and their securities.

SEC. 6.   The County Commissioners' Court shall furnish to each Inspector the necessary seals of office, having upon them the words, "Inspector of Hides and Animals, ——— County, Texas," the blank to be filled with the name of the proper county, which seals shall be of the design selected by the Governor, and now in use by Inspectors of Hides and Animals in this State.   Each Inspector and Deputy Inspector shall certify all his official acts with the seal herein provided for, and shall deliver his seal of office, and all books, papers or records relating to his office, to his successor.

SEC. 7.   It shall be the duty of the Inspector, in person or by deputy, to faithfully examine and inspect all hides or animals known or reported to him as sold, or as leaving or going out of the county, for sale or shipment, and all animals driven or sold in his district for slaughter, packeries or butcheries; and the Inspector shall keep a record, in a well bound book, in which he shall record a true and correct statement of the number, ages, marks and brands of all animals inspected by him, and the number, mark and brand of all hides inspected by him, and whether the same are dry or geeen, and the name or names of the vendor or vendors, and of the purchaser or purchasers thereof; and he shall return a certified copy of all entries made in such record, during each month, to the Clerk of the County Court of the county, on the last day of each month, which report shall be filed among the records of the County Court.   The book of records herein provided for shall at all times be open for the inspection of any person interested therein; provided, this act shall not be so construed as to include sheep, goats, swine or hides of either, nor to involve the re-inspection of salted hides in packeries or other slaughter houses, taken from animals previously inspected and returned, as provided in this section.

SEC. 8.   No Inspector shall grant any certificate of inspection of any unbranded hides or animals; or of hides or animals upon which the marks or brands cannot be ascertained, and shall prevent the same from being taken or shipped out of the county, unless the same be identified by proof or by exhibiting a bill of sale duly signed by the owner of such animal and acknowledged before some officer authorized to authenticate instruments for records in this State.

SEC. 9.   Every Inspector shall have power to, and may seize and sequestrate all unmarked or unbranded calves or yearlings; and all calves or yearlings freshly marked or branded, and on which the fresh marks or brands are unhealed, which are about to be slaughtered, or driven, or shipped out of the county, unless such animals are accompanied by the mothers thereof, or are identified by the presentation of a bill of sale from the person proved to be the owner thereof, signed by him or his legally authorized agent, and acknowledged before some officer authorized to authenticate instruments for record in this State.

SEC. 10.   Every Inspector shall have power to, and may seize and sequestrate all unbranded animals or hides, and animals or hides upon which the mark or brand cannot be ascertained, which are about to be taken or shipped out of the county, or which animals are about to be slaughtered, unless such animals or hides are identified as provided in section nine of this act; and the Inspector shall have power to sell the same at public auction to the highest bidder, after having given ten days' notice of such sale and no owner for such animals or hides being found. The Inspector shall be entitled to retain one-fourth of the net proceeds of such sale, after deducting therefrom all expenses connected therewith, and he shall immediately pay the remaining three-fourths thereof into the County Treasury, and all sums so paid in shall be placed to the credit of the general fund of such county.

SEC. 11. Every person who shall buy or drive any animal or animals for sale or shipment, out of any county in this State, or who shall buy or drive any animal or animals for slaughter, shall, at the time of purchasing and before driving the same, procure a bill of sale from the owner or owners thereof, or from his or their legally authorized agent, which bill of sale shall be in writing, properly signed and acknowledged before some officer authorized to authenticate instruments for record in this State. Such bill of sale shall distinctly enumerate the number, kind and age of animals sold, together with all the marks and brands discernible on said animals; said animals shall, before leaving the county in which they have been gathered, be inspected by the Inspector of such county or his deputy.

SEC. 12. Every person who shall purchase any hides of cattle, shall at the time of purchasing the same, obtain from the owner thereof, or from his legally authorized agent, a bill of sale in writing, certified to by the Inspector or by any officer authorized to take acknowledgments, which bill of sale shall recite in full the marks and brands of each hide, the weight thereof and whether the same is dry or green.

SEC. 13. Whenever an Inspector shall have inspected any animal or animals, as herein provided, he shall on the presentation of a bill of sale or power of attorney, from the owner or owners of such animal or animals, or his or their agent duly authorized in writing, which bill of sale, power of attorney or authority of agent shall be in writing, duly signed and acknowledged by the person executing the same, before some officer authorized to authenticate instruments for record in this State, and on payment to said Inspector of the fees hereinafter provided for, deliver to the purchaser of the animals mentioned in such bill of sale or power of attorney, or his agent, a certificate, setting forth that he has carefully examined and inspected such animal or animals, and that said purchaser has, in all respects complied with the provisions of this act, which certificate shall not be complete until the same and bill of sale herein provided for shall be recorded in the office of the Clerk of the County Court of the county, and be certified to, and by said Clerk under his hand and seal. Such certificate shall be then delivered to the purchaser or purchasers, and shall protect him or them from the payment of inspection fees in any other district in the State for the animals therein described, except the county from which the same may be exported.

SEC. 14. Any person or persons driving cattle in his or their own mark and brand shall be entitled to the certificate of inspection hereinbefore provided for, on payment of the fees to the Inspector hereinafter provided for, and on presentation to the Inspector of the certificate of the Clerk of the County Court of the county where such mark and brand is recorded, to the effect that the mark and brand named therein is duly recorded in his office as the mark and brand of the person so driving such cattle.

SEC. 15. Any person or persons who shall drive any cattle to market beyond the limits of this State, shall, before removing such cattle from the county where the same are gathered, place upon each and every animal so to be driven a large and plain road brand, composed of any device he may choose; which brand shall be branded on the left side of the back, behind the shoulder; and every person or persons using or causing to be used any road brand, shall place the same on record as in the case of other brands, in the county from which the animals upon which said brand is to be placed are to be driven, and before their removal from such county.

SEC. 16.   Any person intending to drive or ship any animal or animals to the Republic of Mexico, may ship the same from any point on the coast of Texas, or may drive or ship them across the Rio Grande river at any point where a custom-house of the United States is located ; and shall not drive or ship such animal or animals across the Rio Grande at any other point or points ; and he shall cause all such animals to be inspected by the Inspector of the district in which the point of shipment or place at which they are to be driven across said river is situated; such inspection shall be made before shipment from the State or passage across said river of said animals.

SEC. 17.   Every Inspector inspecting animals, as required by Section 16 of this act, shall be governed in such inspection by the provisions of this act defining the duties of Inspectors in ordinary cases, and shall be entitled to charge and collect, for the services prescribed by said Section 16, the sum of ten cents for each animal inspected by him ; which sum shall be paid by the person or persons for whom the inspection be made.

SEC. 18.   Whenever a drove of cattle may be passing through any county, it shall be the duty of the Inspector, if called upon so to do by any person, to stop and inspect said drove without any unnecessary detention of the same ; and he shall exercise the same powers and perform the same duties in the inspection of said cattle as are prescribed in Sections 7, 9 and 10 of this act ; *provided*, that if any cattle be found in said drove not included in the certificate of the Inspector of the county in which the drove may have been gathered, the fees of the Inspector shall be paid out of the proceeds of the sale of said cattle ; but if no cattle shall be found in said drove, except those covered by the Inspector's certificate, then the Inspector's fee shall be paid by the person at whose instance and request said drove may be inspected.

SEC. 19.   That the hides of all cattle, including all ages and sexes of said animals, which shall be imported into this State, from the United States of Mexico, shall be inspected by the Inspector of Hides and Animals of any county or district into which the same may be introduced or imported, for which service said Inspector shall receive the sum of five cents for each hide so inspected; and should the importer of said hides fail or refuse to pay the inspection fees, as above provided for, the Inspector is hereby authorized to retain possession of said hides, and to sell a sufficient number of said hides, after public notice of three days, to the highest and best bidder, to pay said inspection fees, and all necessary expenses incurred in connection therewith. That horses and mules imported from Mexico into this State, shall be inspected in accordance with the provisions of the preceding section, and with like authority to retain and sell as therein provided, and for each horse or mule, so inspected, the Inspector shall receive ten cents. That should an Inspector of Hides and Animals find among hides imported from Mexico, any hide or hides, which from the brand or from other evidence, to-wit: Brands blurred, blotched or defaced by the use of chemicals or by other agents or means, or brands recently made, he has reasons to believe that said hide or hides have been stolen from the lawful owner, it shall be his duty to separate said hide or hides from the others undergoing inspection, and to notify any person he believes to be interested therein to come forward and institute suit for the recovery of the same; and should no person appear to claim said hide or hides, the Inspector shall within twenty-four hours make oath before the County Judge of the county, or before a Justice of the Peace of the county, that he has reason to believe that said hides have been stolen; whereupon the said County Judge or Justice of the Peace shall take possession of said hide or hides, and shall issue a citation, directing the importer or party claiming the same to appear before him at his office within a time specified, not to exceed twenty-four hours, to show that said hide or hides have been legally acquired by him or them. And should said importer or claimant make proof that he is the lawful owner of said hide or hides, by showing a bill of sale from the owner of the same, or his legally authorized agent, and by showing a complete chain of transfer or title from the original owner of the brand to himself, or his firm, as the case may be, the County Judge or Justice of the Peace shall direct that the same be delivered to said importer or claimant, upon his paying the inspection fees. That should the said importer or claimant of said hide or hides, fail to establish his claim as the lawful owner of the same, or to any number of said hides so seized, it shall be the duty of the County Judge or the Justice of the Peace to direct that said hide or hides shall be sold at public auction by the Inspector of Hides and Animals or his deputy, after a notice of ten days, published in a newspaper, should there be one published in said county; or by notice in writing, posted at the court-house and two or more other places in said county, and the said hide or hides shall be sold to the highest and best bidder. That the Inspector of Hides and Animals shall retain twenty-five per centum of the purchase money, after having deducted and having paid all necessary expenses incurred by reason of said sale, and he shall deposit the remainder of said purchase money with the County Treasurer and take his receipt therefor; and said County Treasurer shall place one-half of said sum of money to the credit of the school fund, and the other to the credit of the jury fund of said county. That should any person appear, either by himself, his agent or attorney, and claim any hide or hides imported from Mexico, at any time before said hide or hides shall have been sold as above directed, and should said claim be established before the County Judge or a Justice of the Peace of said county, the said hide or hides shall be delivered to the said claimant, and all costs accruing therein shall be paid by the importer; *provided*, that at any time before proceedings shall have been commenced as above directed, the importer may be permitted to pay the lawful owner, his agent or attorney, for any hide or hides imported by him from Mexico, and presented in any county of this State for inspection.

SEC. 20. Any person or persons, having marks and brands recorded in the office of the Clerk of the County Court may file with the Inspector a list of his recorded marks and brands, certified by the said Clerk under his seal, to which certified list shall be attached the names of any person or persons whom the owner of said stock may wish to authorize to gather, drive, or otherwise handle his stock; and the filing of said list with the Inspector shall be deemed sufficient authority to the person or persons named in such list to gather, drive, or otherwise handle any animals of the marks and brands therein described.

SEC. 21. In all cases where the counter-branding of any cattle shall be deemed necessary or expedient, the person so counter-branding shall counter-brand the existing brand of the animal, by which the owner thereof is then known, or by which it is then claimed and owned, by branding below the said brand its *fac-simile*, that is, similar letters, characters, or numbers, as the case may be; and he shall also place on said animal the brand of the then owner thereof; but no person shall change or alter the ear marks of any animal, but in counter-branding, shall leave the ears bearing the same mark or marks as before counter-branding.

SEC. 22. No person owning and claiming stock shall, in originally marking and branding animals, make use of more than one mark and brand; *provided*, that any person may own and possess animals in many marks and brands, the same having been by him acquired by purchase, and bills of sale in writing, properly acknowledged from the previous owner or owners, or his or their legally constituted agent, shall be sufficient evidence of such purchase; but the increase of such animals, or of any animals counter-branded by such person from other stocks of cattle owned by him, and all animals so counter-branded, shall be branded or counter-branded by one and the same brand; and when marked by such person, shall be marked in one and the same mark.

SEC. 23. The Clerk of the County Court in each county shall transcribe the list of all recorded marks and brands in his county, and revise the same. Such revised list shall be written in a well bound book, kept for that purpose only, and shall be arranged as follows, viz: All brands of the letter class shall be placed in alphabetical order, following which shall be the numeral, character and device brands, in the order of the date of their registration. Opposite each brand shall be stated the marks corresponding to said brand, the name of the owner of the brand, his place of residence; if the same be sold, the name of the person to whom sold and his residence, the date of registration of the brands and marks, or particulars relating thereto. Before each brand shall be placed its number, commencing at one for the first brand on the revised list; and the name of the owner of each brand shall be indexed, reference being had in such index to the list number of the brand or brands of such owner; and all new marks and brands placed on record shall be immediately recorded and indexed in said book, which shall at all times be open to the inspection of all persons; *provided*, that the provisions of this section shall apply only to counties in which the work of transcribing the records has not already been done in accordance with law.

SEC. 24. In all cases where application for registration of any mark or brand shall be made, the Clerk of the County Court shall receive and record the same, unless an examination of the recorded list of marks and brands shows that a similar mark and brand is already upon record in such county, in which event he shall refuse to register or give any certificate for the same; *provided*, that if such applicant shall have previously had such mark and brand recorded in some other county, and shall have a certificate from the Clerk of the county in which said brand had been recorded, and if said certificate shall state that said brand and mark had been recorded in said county at some time anterior to the time of the registration of the similar mark and brand in the county in which the said applicant may desire to have his brand recorded, then said brand and mark shall be recorded, and the Clerk shall, on the record, make a minute setting forth said facts.

SEC. 25. Every Inspector, or Deputy Inspector, provided for in this act, shall be entitled to receive for each hide or animal inspected, ten cents; but if more than fifty hides or animals are inspected in the same lot, then ten cents apiece for the first fifty, and three cents each for all above that number.

SEC. 26. Each Clerk of the County Court shall be allowed to collect the sum of fifteen cents for each hundred words in recording and certifying to every bill of sale provided for in this act; and the sum of seventy-five cents for recording each mark and brand and certificate thereof, and such compensation for revising the list of registered marks and brands of cattle stocks in his county as the County Commissioners' Court may allow.

SEC. 27. Whenever, in this act, the word, "Inspector" is used, it shall be taken and deemed to be "the Inspector of Hides and Animals;" and the words, "Deputy Inspector of Hides and Animals," and the words, "county, district or inspection district," shall be held to include each organized county in this State, together with any unorganized county that may be attached for judicial purposes to any such county.

SEC. 28. All marks and brands of cattle shall be recorded in the county or counties in which they usually range; *provided*, that when cattle are gathered near the county line, the bills of sale of the same shall be recorded in both counties; and when any stock of cattle is sold, the fact shall be noted on the record opposite or near the record of its mark and brand, giving the name of the vendor and vendee, and date of sale, and this shall be done as often as there may be a sale. It is made the duty of the Inspector to procure certified copies of the marks and brands of his county for himself and his deputies, and monthly to have added thereto the marks and brands that may be recorded.

SEC. 29. It is made the duty of the Inspector and his deputies carefully and personally to inspect and examine each animal separately, so as to see and know himself the marks and brands, ages, sexes and number of cattle inspected, and shall not trust to the statement of any person, and shall also carefully examine the bills of sale and lists of brands and marks for the cattle inspected by him; and if satisfied that the person claiming the cattle inspected has correct bills of sale or chain of transfer, in writing, from the recorded owner, or is the owner himself, in whole or part, of the mark and brand of each animal in his drove or herd, which should be inspected, and that he has none other in his said inspected herd, or under his control, to be carried with it, he will then, and not until then, make out a certificate, which he shall first enter in his record, under his hand and seal, containing the number of cattle in each mark and brand, with their respective ages and sexes thus inspected, and that they appear to be the property of the person for whom they were inspected, naming him or her as appears by bills of sale from the recorded owner of the said marks and brands, on the cattle inspected by him, or the owner of the brand and mark, himself or herself, and that he has none other in his herd or under his control that should be inspected; and that he intends to drive or ship them, naming the place in the State, for sale or slaughter; or if out of the State, he shall then name the place on the border of the State; and should any owner or owners designate a point on the border of the State, where there are no settlements or organized counties, such owner or owners shall have his herd inspected in the last organized county through which he drives. And when he reaches the said place of destination in this State, before he shall sell, or slaughter or ship any of said cattle, he shall have them inspected there; and it is made the duty of that Inspector or deputy to carefully inspect all the cattle belonging to the herd in the manner prescribed for the first inspection, and compare the certificate of the first Inspector with the cattle, and if it appear that he has none in his herd or under his control but those mentioned or described in the Inspector's certificate, he will so certify in duplicate, and under his hand and seal, giving the date of the first certificate, by whom made, in what county, and the number of cattle found by him in each mark and brand, with ages and sexes. One of these certificates the Inspector will immediately remit by mail, postage paid, to the first Inspector, and the party will desposit the other with him, in two months from the date of the original inspection, both to be kept by him in his office; and the Inspector, at the point of destination, shall carefully examine and know, if possible, whether he has cattle under his control other than those originally inspected, and if he has, then he will take charge of the same and sell them as if under execution; or if not voluntarily delivered to him, then he may sue for and sequest them without giving bond and security; and by order of the Justice of the Peace, County Judge or District Judge of the court where the suit may be instituted, on application of said Inspector or his successors, the cattle shall be sold in like manner, and the proceeds of sale, less one-fourth retained by him for compensation and costs of suit, shall be deposited with the County Treasurer for the owner of the cattle sold, for one year; if not called for at the end of that time, the proceeds shall vest in the county. He will also file with the Treasurer a statement of the number in each mark and brand sold, and the amount each sold for. If the owner of the inspected herd should desire to sell, slaughter or ship the cattle, or any of them, at any other place than the destination named in the certificate of inspection, he may do so by first having his herd inspected and certificate to be compared by the Inspector with the original certificate, made and returned in the manner prescribed at the point of destination, as far as applicable; and the duty of such Inspector shall be the same as those prescribed for Inspectors at places of destination. Any Inspector or deputy who shall wilfully fail, refuse or neglect to comply with the provisions of this section shall, on conviction, be punished by imprisonment in the penitentiary for not less than two nor more than five years, or by fine not exceeding one thousand dollars, in the discretion of the jury, and shall be removed from office by the court having jurisdiction of the offense.

SEC. 30. Every Inspector shall have authority to authenticate bills of sale of animals, and give certificates of acknowledgment of the same under his hand and seal, and shall be allowed to collect fifty cents for every acknowledgment so taken.

SEC. 31. Every Inspector who shall give any certificate of inspection, without first having made the inspection in accordance with the seventh section of this act; or shall fraudulently issue a certificate of inspection of any hides or animals, shall be deemed guilty of a misdemeanor, and, upon conviction, shall be fined in any sum not less than fifty dollars, nor more than five hundred dollars; and in addition thereto, shall be removed from his office by a decree of the court trying the same.

SEC. 32. Any person who shall counter-brand any cattle without the consent of the owner or his agent, shall be deemed guilty of a misdemeanor, and, on conviction, shall be fined in any sum not less than ten nor more than fifty dollars for each animal so counter-branded.

SEC. 33.   Any person who shall alter the mark of any animal, shall be deemed guilty of a misdemeanor, and, on conviction, shall be fined in any sum not less than ten nor more than fifty dollars for each animal whose mark is so altered; *provided*, this section shall not be construed so as to include sheep, hogs or goats, whereby it is here provided that any person or persons hereafter buying or selling the same may change or alter the marks of the same; *provided*, such change be made in the presence of two adult persons, and by stating in the bill of sale what the original mark was before the change or alteration and what it is after the change or alteration; and as often as the said stock is sold all the original change in the marks shall be stated in the bill of sale, with the names of the witnesses thereto, which bill of sale shall be legally authenticated.

SEC. 34.   Any person who shall drive any cattle across the Rio Grande river into Mexico, at any other point than where a United States custom-house is established, or place of inspection by United States custom-house officers, or without first having the same inspected in accordance with the sixteenth section of this act, shall be deemed guilty of a felony, and, upon conviction, shall be confined in the penitentiary not less than two nor more than five years.

SEC. 35.   Any person who shall ship from any part of this State any hides of cattle imported from Mexico, without first having procured a certificate of importation and inspection, as provided in section eighteen of this act, shall be deemed guilty of a misdemeanor, and, upon conviction, shall be fined in any sum not less than one dollar nor more than five dollars, for each hide not so inspected.

SEC. 36.   Any person who shall sell any hides of cattle without the same having been inspected, shall be deemed guilty of a misdemeanor, and, on conviction, shall be fined in any sum not less than one dollar nor more than five dollars for each hide so sold.

SEC. 37.   Any person who shall drive any cattle out of any county, with the intention of driving the same beyond the limits of the State, to a market without first having road branded the same, in accordance with the fifteenth section of this act, shall be deemed guilty of a misdemeanor, and on conviction shall be fined in any sum not less than twenty dollars nor more than one hundred dollars for each animal so driven.

SEC. 38.   Any person who shall drive any cattle or horses out of any county without the written authority of the owner thereof, duly authenticated as the law requires, and without first having the same duly inspected, shall be deemed guilty of a misdemeanor, and on conviction shall be fined in any sum not less than twenty dollars nor more than one hundred dollars per head for each animal so driven.

SEC. 39.   Any person who shall purchase any animals or hides of cattle without obtaining a bill of sale from the owner or his agent, as required by sections eleven and twelve of this act, shall be deemed guilty of a misdemeanor, and on conviction shall be fined in any sum not less than twenty dollars nor more than one hundred dollars for each animal or hide so purchased.

SEC. 40.   Any person who shall as the agent of another sell any cattle without first having obtained a power of attorney duly authenticated, shall be deemed guilty of a misdemeanor, and on conviction shall be fined not less than fifty dollars nor more than five hundred dollars.

SEC. 41.   Any person who shall in originally branding and marking cattle, use more than one mark or brand, shall be deemed guilty of a misdemeanor, and on conviction shall be fined in any sum not less than twenty-five nor more than one hundred dollars for each animal so branded or marked; and any person or persons who shall brand or mark any animal, except in a pen, shall be deemed guilty of a misdemeanor, and on conviction shall be fined in any sum not less than ten nor more than fifty dollars for each animal so branded or marked.

SEC. 42.   Any person who shall brand or mark any cattle without first having recorded his mark or brand shall be deemed guilty of a misdemeanor, and on conviction shall be find in any sum not less than twenty-five nor more than one hundred dollars for each animal so branded or marked.

SEC. 43.   No Clerk shall record any brand, unless the person having the same recorded shall designate the part of the animal upon which the same is to be placed, as required by section — of this act, and any Clerk violating this section, shall be deemed guilty of a misdemeanor, and on conviction thereof by a court of competent jurisdiction, shall be fined not less than ten nor more than fifty dollars.

SEC. 44.   When the Inspector has seized any hides or animals as provided for in sections nine and ten, he shall report the fact to some Judge of the District or County Court or Justice of the Peace, and and it shall be the duty of said Judge or Justice to issue or cause to be issued, a citation addressed: "To all whom it may concern," setting forth a seizure of said property, with a description of the same, commanding them to appear at a day named in said citation to show cause why the said property should not be forfeited to the county wherein the same was seized, and sold for the benefit of said county; said citation shall be directed to the Sheriff or other officer of said county, who shall cause certified copies of the same to be posted in three public places in said county for a period of ten days before the day mentioned in said citation.   Upon the proof of the posting of said citation, as herein required, it shall be the duty of the Judge or Justice of the Peace issuing said citation, to proceed to condemn the property mentioned in said citation, unless satisfactory proof should be made of the ownership of said property, or other sufficient cause be shown why the same should not be condemned; and he shall order the same to be sold by the Inspector at public auction to the highest bidder.   The Inspector shall be entitled to retain one-fourth of the net proceeds of such sale, after deducting therefrom all expenses connected therewith, and he shall immediately pay the remaining three-fourths thereof into the County Treasury; and all sums so paid in shall be placed to the credit of the general fund of such county.

SEC. 45.   It shall be unlawful for any agent of any railroad, steamship or shipping company of any kind, to receive for shipment any cattle, unless they have been duly inspected under the provisions of this act; and it shall be the duty of such agent to examine the list of marks and brands before he receives them for shipment, and should any cattle be in the herd not inspected as provided in this act, such agent shall not receive such animal or animals for shipment.   Should any agent or agents violate the provisions of this act, he shall be guilty of a misdemeanor, and on conviction shall be fined not less than twenty-five nor more than one thousand dollars for each animal so shipped.

SEC. 46.   That the counties of Grimes, Madison, Walker, Trinity, Dallas, Ellis, Hopkins, Franklin, Titus Red River, Grayson, Cooke, Rockwall, Hunt, Rains, Wood, Van Zandt, Kaufman, Limestone, Freestone, Navarro, Anderson, Henderson, Cherokee, Fannin, Lamar, Delta, Rusk. Panola, Shelby, Brazos, Leon, Robertson, San Jacinto, Polk, Tyler, Jasper, Newton, Hardin, Nacogdoches, Houston, Angelina, Sabine, San Augustine, Smith, Upshur, Gregg, Camp, Denton, Collin, Bowie, Cass, Marion, Morris, Hill, Johnson, Fayette, Austin, Washington, Burleson, Bastrop and Harrison, are hereby exempted from the operation of this act, and the provisions of the same shall in no wise relate or apply to the aforesaid counties; *provided*, that in those counties bordering on the lines of the State, the Governor shall appoint an Inspector whose duty it shall be to inspect, under the provisions of this act, all stock about to be driven or shipped out of the State; or in any other county exempt from the operations of this act, where there is a depot or place for the shipment of cattle; *provided*, that such cattle shall not be subjected to inspection on board any railroad train unless the same has been placed on board of such train for the purpose of evading the provisions of this act.

SEC. 47. That in counties exempted from the operations of this act, there shall be no elections held for the election of Inspector of Hides and Animals; and, in case there should be now a point or points in any of said counties for the shipping of cattle beyond the limits of the State, or should any point or points be hereafter designated in any of said counties for shipping cattle from the State, it is hereby made the duty of the Governor to appoint an Inspector of Hides and Animals to inspect any and all cattle intended for exportation from the State; and said Inspector shall be governed by the provisions of this act in performance of said duties; but he shall not inspect animals not intended for exportation beyond the limits of the State; that it shall be the duty of the Judge of the County Court of each county from which cattle are now shipped, or may hereafter be shipped from this State, to notify the Governor of the fact without unnecessary delay; that any County Judge of any county exempt from the operations of this act, who shall fail to give the notification above mentioned within thirty days from the date of shipment of cattle from his county, shall be deemed guilty of a misdemeanor, and for each omission shall be fined in a sum of money not less than one hundred dollars nor more than five hundred dollars upon conviction before a court of competent jurisdiction; and any person, firm or corporation, who shall export by rail, steam or shipboard from the State, or who shall drive from the State any cattle, without having the same inspected in the county, on the coast or border from which the same may be exported, shall be fined not less than one hundred nor more than one thousand dollars.

SEC. 48. That all laws and parts of laws in conflict with the provisions of this act are hereby repealed.

SEC. 49. There being grave doubts as to the constitutionality of the present stock law, an imperative public necessity and emergency exists, that this act take effect and be in force from and after its passage, and it is so enacted.

Approved August 23, 1876.

Takes effect from its passage.

CHAPTER CLXVI.—*An Act regulating elections.*

SECTION 1. *Be it enacted by the Legislature of the State of Texas,* That the election precincts of the counties of this State, as now established, shall constitute election precincts; but the Commissioners' Court of each county may change the same at any regular or called term prior to December 31, 1876; and thereafter, at their first regular term in each year, if they deem it necessary, may divide their respective Justices' precincts into as many election precincts as they shall deem expedient, which shall all be numbered. No election precinct shall be formed out of any two or more Justices' precincts, and they shall designate one place in each of such election precincts, at which elections shall be held; and they shall at the same time, and at their first regular or called term in each year, select and appoint from among the residents of each election precinct some suitable person to be the presiding officer of such precincts; but each Justice's precinct shall contain at least one election precinct; *provided,* that in any incorporated city of this State, each ward of said city shall constitute an election precinct, and the Commissioners' Courts of the counties in which said cities are situated shall, as above provided, select and appoint some competent person from among the residents of such precinct, a presiding officer thereof, and that such presiding officer shall have all the powers and authority, and shall discharge all the duties of other presiding officers of election; and said Commissioners' Courts shall, as above provided, designate at least one place in each of said precincts, at which elections shall be held.

SEC. 2. The County Judges of the several counties, and in case of vacancy in that office, or any inability, failure or refusal of the County Judge to act, then any two of the County Commissioners of the county shall order all elections for county and precinct officers in their respective counties.

SEC. 3. The Governor shall, by proclamation, order all elections for State and district officers, members of Congress, members of the Legislature, and all other elections required to be ordered by him by the Constitution or laws of the State.

SEC. 4. When any election is ordered, at least twenty days' notice of the election shall be given by notice posted up at the place or places designated for holding the election in each election precinct, specifying the time and place or places at which such election is to be held, and the officer or officers to be chosen; and it is hereby made the duty of the County Judge of each county to have posted, as required in this act, all election notices.

SEC. 5. In all cases of vacancy in any civil office of the county, district, or State, by death, resignation, or otherwise, which by law is filled by election of the people, the officer or officers authorized by this act to order elections shall immediately make such order for an election, fixing the day, not exceeding thirty days off, to fill the unexpired time made vacant, and cause like notice to be given, and issue writs as prescribed for regulating elections.

SEC. 6. Forms for notices, writs and returns of elections, shall be furnished by the Secretary of State to the County Judge of each county.

SEC. 7. It shall be the duty of the County Judge of each county, or, in case of vacancy in his office, or any inability of the County Judge to act, then any three of the County Commissioners, to order all elections for county and precinct officers, and to issue writs of election, in which writs shall be stated particularly the officer or officers to be chosen, and the day of election, and a copy of the form of election returns, furnished by the Secretary of State, shall accompany such writs.

SEC. 8. The presiding officer of each election precinct, shall, on or before the day of election, select two judges and two clerks, from the different political parties, if demanded, so far as practicable, and there be present a sufficient number of the party making the demand, and willing to serve, who, together with the presiding officer, shall be the managers of election; and the presiding officer shall administer to each of them an oath that they will each well and truly conduct the election, without partiality or prejudice, and agreeably to law, according to the best of their skill and understanding; and one of the judges of the election shall, before opening the polls, administer to the presiding officer an oath that he will faithfully and impartially discharge the duties of presiding officer of election, to the best of his skill and understanding.

SEC. 9. In case the presiding officer should fail to attend on the day of election, or refuse or fail to act, or in case no manager has been appointed, it shall be lawful for the electors present at the precinct voting place on that day to appoint, from among the electors of the precinct, a presiding officer to act as such at that election; and the person so appointed shall be authorized to act as presiding officer as fully as the presiding officer hereinbefore provided for could do, if such presiding officer was present and acting; and in making their return of the election they shall certify that the presiding officer was appointed from the electors present at the precinct voting place on that day, because the regular presiding officer failed to attend, or refused to act, as the case may be.

SEC. 10. That all presiding officers, judges and clerks of elections, are hereby authorized to administer all oaths necessary or proper in the discharge of their duties as such, and to administer all oaths connected in any way with the holding of elections.

SEC. 11. Electors in all cases shall be privileged from arrest during their attendance at elections, and in going to and returning from the same, except in cases of treason, felony, or breach of the peace.

SEC. 12. That all the elections in this State shall be held for one day only at each election, and the polls shall be open on that day from eight o'clock A. M. to six o'clock P. M.

SEC. 13. The following classes of persons shall not be allowed to vote in this State, to-wit: *First*—Persons under twenty-one years of age. *Second*—Idiots and lunatics. *Third*—All paupers supported by any county. *Fourth*—All persons convicted of any felony. *Fifth*—All soldiers, marines and seamen employed in the service of the army or navy of the United States.

SEC. 14. Every male person, subject to none of the foregoing disqualifications, who shall have attained the age of twenty-one years, and who shall be a citizen of the United States, and who shall have resided in this State one year next preceding an election, and the last six months within the district or county in which he offers to vote, shall be deemed a qualified elector; and every male person of foreign birth, subject to none of the foregoing disqualifications, who, at any time before an election, shall have declared his intention to become a citizen of the United States, in accordance with the federal naturalization laws, and shall have resided in this State one year next preceding such election, and the last

six months in the county in which he offers to vote, shall also be deemed
a qualified elector; and all electors shall vote in the election precinct of
their residence; *provided*, that electors living in any unorganized county
may vote at any election precinct in the county to which such county
is attached for judicial purposes. The residence of a married man, if
not separated from his wife, shall be where his family resides; and that
of a single man where he boards and sleeps; and should any single man
board in one ward or precinct, and sleep in another, then his residence
shall be in the ward or precinct in which he sleeps, and he shall not
vote in any other precinct or ward. And it shall be the duty of the
judge of election, when requested by any bystander, to swear any person offering to vote, as to his residence, and to have placed in writing
opposite his name, the word "sworn;" and any person voting at any
other place than that of his residence shall be guilty of a misdemeanor,
and upon conviction thereof, shall be fined not exceeding one thousand
dollars, or imprisoned in the county jail not to exceed six months, at
the discretion of the jury.

SEC. 15. All qualified electors of the State, as herein described, who
shall have resided for six months immediately preceding an election
within the limits of any city or corporate town, shall have the right to
vote for Mayor and all other elective officers; but in all elections to determine expenditure of money or assumption of debt, only those shall
be qualified to vote who pay taxes on property in said city or incorporated town.

SEC. 16. That each of the clerks shall write and number the name of
each voter at the time of voting; and one of the judges, in every case,
at the time of receiving the ticket or ballot, shall write upon it the voter's
number, corresponding with the number on the clerk's list; and no manager or other officer of election shall unfold or examine the vote received,
nor shall they examine the indorsement on the tickets, by comparing it
with the clerk's list of voters when the votes are counted out, nor shall
they examine, or permit to be examined by any other person, the tickets, subsequent to their being received into the ballot-box, except as
hereinafter provided; and any presiding officer, judge or clerk of election, who shall violate any of the provisions of this section, upon conviction thereof shall be deemed guilty of a felony, and shall be punished
by imprisonment in the penitentiary not less than one nor more than
two years. No ticket, not numbered as provided in this act, shall be
counted or noticed in counting out the votes, nor shall either of two or
more tickets folded together. That immediately after the counting of
the votes by the managers of election, the presiding officer thereof shall
place all the tickets or ballots voted into a wooden or metal box, of sufficient size to contain them, and to securely fasten the same with nails,
screws or locks; and he shall, within five days after the election, deliver
said box to the County Clerk, whose duty it shall be to keep the same
securely, and, in the event of any contest growing out of the election
within one year thereafter, he shall deliver said box to any competent
officer having a writ or subpoena therefor from any tribunal or authority authorized to issue such process; and in the event that no contest
grows out of said election within one year after the election, then the
said Clerk shall destroy the said tickets or ballots by burning the same.
The violation of any of the provisions of this section shall be deemed a
misdemeanor, and any person convicted thereof shall be punished by
fine not less than fifty nor more than five hundred dollars, and by im-

prisonment in the county jail not to exceed six months. Any presiding officer, judge, or clerk of an election, who shall divulge how any person shall have voted at any election, from an inspection of the tickets, unless in a judicial investigation, shall be deemed guilty of a misdemeanor, and on conviction shall be fined in any sum not less than fifty nor more than five hundred dollars.

SEC. 17. Immediately after closing the polls, the managers of election shall proceed to count the votes in the presence of two voters of their county, of good repute, and also of different politics, if convenient to get, and shall continue such count, without interruption, until all the ballots voted at such election are counted, and make out a return, signed by the managers, which shall be sealed up and delivered to the County Judge of the county (or, in case of his absence, to the Clerk of the County Court, who shall file the same in his office and deliver the said return to the County Judge on the day appointed to open and compare the polls), by the presiding officer or one of the managers of the election, a duplicate of which return shall be kept by the presiding officer of the election.

SEC. 18. The election returns shall not be opened by the officer to whom they are returned before return day, which shall be ten days after the election, Sundays excluded; at the expiration of that time he shall open them and estimate the result, recording the state of the polls of each precinct, in a book to be kept by him for that purpose; and, after making such estimate, he shall deliver to the candidate or candidates for whom the greatest number of votes have been polled for county and precinct officers, a certificate of election, naming therein the office to which he has been elected, the number of votes polled for him, and the day on which the election was held, and shall sign the same and cause the seal of the County Court to be thereon impressed, and shall also, at the same time, make an estimate of the votes polled for members of the Legislature, and shall, if his county constitute a senatorial or representative district, give a like certificate of election to the person or persons receiving the highest number of votes for Representatives or Senators, and transmit a duplicate of the same to the Secretary of State.

SEC. 19. In all elections of Comptroller of Public Accounts, Treasurer of the State, Commissioner of the General Land Office, Attorney-General, Judges of the Supreme, Appellate and District Courts, and District Attorneys, and for Representatives in the Congress of the United States, the County Judge or other officer to whom the returns in each county are made, shall, on the tenth day after the election, and not before, make out duplicate returns, one of which shall be transmitted by such officer to the seat of government, directed to the Secretary of State, and endorsed, " Election returns of ——— county, for ———;" the other shall be deposited in the office of the District Clerk; and on the fortieth day after the election, and not before, the Secretary of State, in the presence of the Governor and Attorney-General, or in case of vacancy or inability of either of those officers to act, then any two of said officers, shall open and count the returns. And the Governor shall immediately make out, sign and deliver a certificate of election, with the seal of the State thereto affixed, to the person or persons who shall have received the highest number of votes for each or any of said offices. The County Judges of the several counties of the State shall promptly make duplicate returns of the election for Governor and Lieutenant-Governor, carefully sealed up; one of which shall be transmitted to the seat of government, and directed to the Speaker of the House of Representatives, endorsed, "Election returns of ——— county, for ———;" and the other shall be deposited in the office of the Clerk of the County Court. The transmitted returns, directed to the care of the Secretary of State, shall be taken charge of by him, and preserved in his office, the package and seal thereon to remain unbroken until the organization of the next Legislature, when he shall, on the first day thereof, deliver the said returns to the Speaker of the House of Representatives.

SEC. 20.   That the Judges of the election, while in the discharge of their duties, shall have the power of a District Judge to preserve order and keep the peace. They may appoint special Constables to act during the election, and they, or either of them, may issue writs of arrest for felony or breach of the peace, to the Sheriff or Constable, who shall forthwith execute such writ, and may commit the party arrested to jail during the election, if so ordered by the judge of the election ; but he shall first be permitted to vote, if entitled to do so; and as soon as practicable, after the close of the polls, he shall be taken before the proper magistrate for examination, as law directs in such cases.

SEC. 21.   That during the entire day of any election in this State for municipal, county, district, or State officers, it shall be unlawful for any bar-room, saloon, or other place, house, or establishment where vinous, malt, spirituous, or intoxicating liquors are sold, to be open, but the same shall be closed by any Sheriff or Constable of the county, or by any Constable whose special appointment is provided for by this act, on the order of the judges of election; and it shall be unlawful for any person or persons, or firm, to sell, barter or give away any vinous, spirituous, malt or intoxicating liquor within the limits of the county within which such election is being held, during the day thereof. And any person violating any provision of this section shall, for each offense, be guilty of a misdemeanor and subject to indictment, and may be fined in any sum not less than one hundred dollars nor more than five hundred dollars for each offense ; *provided*, nothing herein contained shall prevent the sale of liquor at any drug store, or establishment where drugs are sold for medical purposes, on the prescription of a practicing physician, nor to the sale of liquor by regular wholesale merchants to be shipped or sent out of the county ; *and provided, further*, that nothing herein contained shall prevent stores from being opened for the sale of other goods, wares, and merchandise.

SEC. 22.   That the Governor shall commission all officers except members of Congress, members of the Legislature, the Governor and municipal officers.

SEC. 23.   That in all city or town elections, where not otherwise provided for by the charter of said city or town, the Mayor thereof, or in the event he fails or refuses to act, then any two of the Aldermen, shall order elections, give notices, appoint presiding officers, who shall hold the election and make returns to the Mayor, under the same regulations and with like effect as in county elections, so far as applicable.

SEC. 24.   That in all elections hereafter, if there should be any [an] equal number of votes given to two or more persons for the same office, and no one elected thereto, the election of such officer shall again be returned to the people, and an election be ordered, notices given, and another election [held] in the same manner as the general election.

SEC. 25.   That any persons who shall vote, or attempt to vote, more than once at the same election, shall be deemed guilty of a felony, and on conviction shall be confined in the penitentiary not less than two nor more than five years.   Any person who shall disturb any election by exciting [inciting] or encouraging a tumult or mob, or shall cause any disturbances in the vicinity of any poll or voting place; or any person who shall wilfully aid, or abet, or advise any one not legally qualified in voting or attempting to vote at any election; or any person or persons who shall, by force or intimidation, obstruct, or attempt to obstruct, or influence any voter, in his free exercise of the election [elective] franchise; or any person who may carry any gun, pistol, bowie knife, or other dangerous weapon, concealed, or unconcealed, on any day of election, during the hours the polls are open, within the distance of one-half mile of any poll or place of voting, shall be deemed guilty of an offense, and on conviction thereof shall, for every such violation, be fined not less than one hundred nor more than five hundred dollars, and may, in addition thereto, be imprisoned in the county jail, not exceeding one month.

Sec. 26.   That the County Judges of the several counties shall discharge the duties of returning officers, as required by law for senatorial and representative districts.   When an election shall have been held for members of the Legislature, in a district composed of more counties than one, the County Judge or other officer to whom the returns in each county are made, who are not authorized to give certificates of election to such persons aforesaid, shall make out and send complete returns of such election, after examining and recording the same, to the returning officer of said district, which returns shall be sealed up, and the name of the officer forwarding them shall be written across the seal, and the package marked on the outside, "Election returns," which package may be sent by mail.   The returning officer to whom the returns are so forwarded, or in case of his inability, absence, refusal, or failure to act, the County Clerk, or his deputy, shall, upon the thirtieth day after the election (Sunday excluded), open and count said returns in the presence of at least one of each political party; and, after recording the same, shall give a certificate of election to the person or persons receiving the highest number of votes for Senator or Representative in that district; *provided*, that if all the election returns from the district shall have been received by the returning officer of the district before the said thirtieth day, then the said returning officer may count said returns and issue the certificate herein provided for.

Sec. 27.   That in every year in which an election shall be held for President or Vice-President of the United States, such election shall be held on the first Tuesday next after the first Monday in November, and in accordance with an act of Congress of the United States, approved January 23, 1845, entitled: "An Act to establish a uniform time for holding elections for electors of President and Vice-President in all the States of the Union;" and such elections shall be held and conducted, and returns made thereof, as in the manner and form provided by law for the general election.

Sec. 28.   That the provisions of this act shall apply to the elections of all officers, or for any other purposes, where not otherwise provided by law.

Sec. 29.   That those that may hereafter receive certificates of election to the Senate and House of Representatives of the Legislature of this State; and those Senators whose terms of office shall not have terminated, and none other, shall be competent to organize the said Senate and House of Representatives.

SEC. 30. That the. act entitled, "An Act to provide for the mode and manner of conducting elections, making returns, and for the protection and purity of the ballot-box," approved August 15, 1870, and "an act to regulate elections," approved March 31, 1873, and all other laws and parts of laws in conflict with the provisions of this act, be, and the same are hereby repealed.

SEC. 31. In view of the fact that elections will soon be held throughout the State, and there being no adequate law in force to regulate the same, an imperative public necessity and emergency exists for the immediate passage of this act, and it is therefore enacted that this act be in force and effect from and after its passage.

Approved August 23, 1876.

Takes effect from its passage.

CHAPTER CLXVII.—*An Act to provide for the judicial forfeiture of charters, and prescribing the duties of the Attorney-General in relation thereto.*

SECTION 1. *Be it enacted by the Legislature of the State of Texas,* That it shall be the duty of the Attorney-General, unless otherwise expressly directed by law, whenever sufficient cause exists therefor, to seek a judicial forfeiture of the charters of private corporations; and he shall at once take steps to seek such forfeiture in all cases where satisfactory evidence is laid before him that any corporation receiving State aid has by the non-performance of its charter conditions or the violations of its charter, or by any act, or omission, mis-user' or non-user, forfeited its charter.

SEC. 2. All suits and proceedings, under the provisions of this act, shall be commenced and prosecuted in the District Court of Travis county.

SEC. 3. That the sum of one thousand dollars be, and the same is hereby appropriated, out of any moneys in the State Treasury, not otherwise appropriated, for the purpose of paying such costs and expenses as it may become necessary to pay in prosecution of suits under this act, and the Comptroller shall, upon accounts approved by the Attorney-General, draw his warrants on the Treasurer therefor.

SEC. 4. That owing to the near approach of the close of the session, and in order to carry out the provisions of Section 22, Article 4 of the Constitution, there exists an imperative public necessity and an emergency for the suspension of the rules, and the immediate passage of this act; and it is therefore enacted that this act go into effect, and be in force from and after its passage.

Approved August 21, 1876.

Takes effect ninety days after adjournment.

JOINT RESOLUTIONS.

No. 1.—*Joint Resolution granting leave of absence to Judge Gustave Cook.*

WHEREAS, the Hon. Gustave Cook, Judge of the Criminal Court of Galveston and Harris counties, is dangerously ill from the effects of un-healed wounds received in battle during the late war; and whereas, his physicians advise him that a change of climate and treatment is neces-sary to save his life; therefore,

Be it resolved by the Legislature of the State of Texas, That the Hon. Gustave Cook be and is hereby granted leave of absence from the State for the period of ninety days, at any time between the first day of June and the first day of October, 1876.

Resolved, further, that it is a matter of imperative public necessity that the life of one of the Judges of the State be saved if possible, and that the condition of the said Gustave Cook is an emergency requiring im-mediate action, and that this joint resolution take effect from and after its passage.

Approved May 25, 1876.

Takes effect from its passage.

No. 2.—*Joint Resolution providing for the printing and distribution of such general laws as take effect from and after their passage, passed at this session of the Fifteenth Legislature.*

SECTION 1. *Be it resolved by the Legislature of the State of Texas,* That the Printing Committees of the two Houses of the Fifteenth Legisla-ture are authorized and required to have printed two thousand copies of each general law, duly authenticated by Secretary of State, that takes effect from and after its passage, passed at this session of the Legisla-ture, immediately upon its becoming a law. Two hundred copies of each shall be delivered to the Secretary of the Senate for the use of the Senators; six hundred copies to the Clerk of the House for the use of the members of the House of Representatives; and the residue to the Secretary of State for immediate distribution among the different offi-cers of the State.

SEC. 2. The necessity for a general knowledge for the laws by the people of Texas causes an emergency, and it is hereby enacted that this joint resolution shall take effect from and after its passage.

Approved June 1, 1876.

Takes effect from its passage.

No. 3.—*Joint Resolution validating the election for County Treasurers, County Surveyors and Inspectors of Hides and Animals, held on the fifteenth day of February, eighteen hundred and seventy-six.*

SECTION 1. *Be it resolved by the Legislature of the State of Texas,* That the election of County Treasurers, Surveyors and Inspectors of Hides and Animals of the various counties of the State of Texas at the recent election, to-wit: on the third Tuesday, the fifteenth day of February, eighteen hundred and seventy-six, be and is hereby ratified and made valid ; *provided,* that where the officer has already qualified and given bond as required by this joint resolution, the same shall be deemed sufficient, and that until otherwise provided by law, said County Treasurers, Surveyors and Inspectors of Hides and Animals be required to take the oath of office as required by the present Constitution of the State of Texas, and give bond as required by existing laws, and that their compensation be the same as under existing laws, until otherwise provided by law.

SEC. 2. That all official acts of said County Treasurers, County Surveyors and Inspectors of Hides and Animals, elected at the election held on the fifteenth day of February, eighteen hundred and seventy-six, are hereby declared to be valid, and of full force and effect.

SEC. 3. That the confusion arising from misinterpretation of the rights and powers of said County Treasurers, County Surveyors and Inspectors of Hides and Animals elected at said February election, creates an emergency that this joint resolution go into effect at once, therefore this joint resolution take effect and be in force from and after its passage.

Approved June 12, 1876.

Takes effect from its passage.

———

No. 4.—*Joint Resolution to provide for the survey, condemnation and sale of certain property belonging to the State of Texas.*

WHEREAS, Much damaged property, embracing broken furniture and other articles useless to the State, has accumulated about the public buildings and grounds; and, whereas, said property occupies room and space needed for other purposes; therefore,

SECTION 1. *Be it resolved by the Legislature of the State of Texas,* That a Board of Survey, consisting of one Senator, to be designated by the President of the Senate, and one Representative, to be designated by the Speaker of the House, and the Adjutant-General of the State, be appointed, whose duty it shall be to examine, condemn, and inventory any and all property belonging to the State, about the public buildings and grounds, which they may deem of no further use to the State.

SEC. 2. *Be it further resolved,* That it shall be the duty of said Board of Survey when said property shall have been so condem(n)ed, and inventory thereof made, to contract with some auctioneer or commission merchant of the City of Austin to sell the same at the best price to be procured therefor.

SEC. 3. *Resolved further,* That when such sale has been made, a full itemized report of such sale shall be made by said auctioneer, and the proceeds of said sale less the commissions allowed, shall be delivered to said Board of Survey, and the money so received shall be by said Board deposited in the Treasury of the State, and placed to the credit of the general revenue.

SEC. 4. *Resolved further*, That as delay will further reduce the value of the property herein referred to, a public necessity exists and an emergency requires, that this resolution take effect and be in force from and after its passage.

Approved June 21, 1876.

Takes effect from its passage.

No. 5.—*Joint Resolution instructing our Senators and requesting our Representatives in Congress to ask protection for the frontier, and compensation for past expenditures by the State in that behalf.*

SECTION 1. *Be it resolved by the Legislature of the State of Texas*, That the Federal Government owes to Texas protection of her exposed frontier, by virtue of her rights, as a member of the Union, to an equal participation in the benefits and blessings which its Constitution guarantees to all the States, among which is defense against invasion; and the Republic of Texas, upon her accession to the Union, having ceded to the United States all public edifices, fortifications, barracks, ports and harbors, navy and navy-yards, docks, magazines, arms, armaments and all other property and means pertaining to the public defense; the faith of the United States thereby became solemnly pledged to extend to the frontiers of the said Republic of Texas the most ample protection, without which, as a condition precedent, Texas would have had no sufficient inducement to surrender her independent political position.

· SEC. 2. That our Senators in the Congress of the United States are hereby instructed, and our Representatives are hereby requested, to present to Congress now assembled, these resolutions of the Legislature of the State of Texas, and to urge upon that body the enactment of such laws as will secure to our frontiers ample military protection against Indians and Mexican freebooters, the military forces of the United States on our borders being too weak, under the most effective command to afford such protection, and the State of Texas being compelled in defense of the property and lives of her citizens to maintain in the field a considerable military force at her own expense.

SEC. 3. That our said Senators be instructed and our Representatives requested to present and urge before Congress the passage of a bill reimbursing the State of Texas for the large appropriations of money which from time to time have necessarily been made by her Legislature, because of the failure of the Federal Government to provide sufficient protection to our frontiers.

SEC. 4. That the Governor of the State be requested to transmit to our Senators and Representatives in Congress, a copy of these resolutions, together with an itemized statement of all expenditures made by the State in the protection of her frontiers.

SEC. 5. The fact that Congress will adjourn at an early day, and the necessity for prompt action requires that this joint resolution take effect and it is hereby declared, that it do take effect from and after its passage.

Approved July 6, 1876.

Takes effect from its passage.

No. 6.—*Joint Resolution instructing our Senators, and requesting our Representatives in Congress to secure, if possible, the permanent establishment of a line of steam vessels to carry the United States mail once a week between the city [of] Galveston and Brazos Santiago.*

SECTION 1. *Be it resolved by the Legislature of the State of Texas,* That our Senators in Congress are hereby instructed, and our Representatives are requested to, procure, if possible, the passage of an act by the Congress of the United States, authorizing and requiring the Postmaster-General to contract, on proper terms, with some suitable and responsible parties for the term of ten years for the carrying of the United States mail, by steamer, direct from the city of Galveston to Brazos Santiago once a week each way, touching at Aransas.

SEC. 2. That the Governor be and is hereby requested to transmit a copy of this joint resolution to his Excellency, the President of the United States, Postmaster-General, and to each of our Senators and Representatives in Congress.

SEC. 3. In view of the fact that Congress will adjourn at an early day, and the necessity for prompt action creates an emergency that this joint resolution pass at once; it is therefore enacted that it be in force from and after its passage.

Approved July 11, 1876.

Takes effect from its passage.

No. 7.—*Joint Resolution.*

WHEREAS, Immigration is rapidly filling the western portion of our State, and the present mail facilities are wholly inadequate to the want of communities; and, whereas, the important route from Fort Concho to El Paso is the only direct communication connecting the military stations protecting our frontier, and is the only route making direct connection with the more populous provinces of the Republic of Mexico; and, whereas, service on said route was formerly three times each way per week, and instead of increasing with the increasing demands was reduced to only two trips per week, when there ought to be at least three trips per week mail service from the capitol of our State to the western end of this important line; therefore,

SECTION 1. *Be it resolved by the Senate and House of Representatives of the State of Texas,* That we do hereby memorialize the Postmaster-General to immediately increase the present mail service upon the important route from Fort Concho to El Paso, and we do hereby instruct our United States Senators and request our Representatives in Congress to use all honorable means to have the mail service made not less than three times a week upon said route; *be it further resolved.* that the official copies hereof, properly attested, shall be forwarded to the Postmaster-General and to each of our United States Senators and Representatives.

SEC. 2. The facts set forth in the preamble hereof, and the prospect of an early adjournment of Congress causes such an emergency as requires immediate action in this matter, and it is hereby enacted that this joint resolution take effect and be in force from and after its passage.

Approved July 19, 1876.

Takes effect ninety days after adjournment.

No. 8.—*Joint Resolution.*

WHEREAS, General G. A. Custer has endeared himself to the people of the frontier of Texas and elsewhere, by his bold and dashing operations against the Indians; and, whereas, the news of his late sudden death, while in discharge of his dangerous duties is received; therefore,

SECTION 1. *Be it resolved by the Legislature of the State of Texas,* That we tender our sincere condolence to the family of the deceased, and to the people of our suffering frontier, and that the Governor be requested to forward a copy of this joint resolution to our Senators and Members of Congress, with the request that the same be spread upon the journals of Congress; and a copy of the same be forwarded to the family of the deceased.

Approved July 28, 1876.

Takes effect ninety days after adjournment.

No. 9.—*Joint Resolution.*

WHEREAS, The Constitution inhibits this State from expending money in the interest of immigration, and whereas an impression prevails that the people of this State are indifferent or opposed to immigration from the older States of the Union, and from foreign nations, and whereas the Texas Land and Immigration Company of St. Louis, a corporation organized under the general statutes of the State of Missouri, composed of men of known integrity of character, business reputation, possessing ample means, have undertaken to carry on a free communication with the other States of the Union, and with foreign countries, furnishing information of the great resources of the State of Texas, her climate, soil, minerals, and advantages presented for the investment of capital in manufactures, and other advantages to the immigrant; therefore,

SECTION 1. *Be it resolved by the Legislature of the State of Texas,* That the people of Texas extend a cordial invitation to the good and industrious immigrant to come and make his home among us, and that we will extend to him a hearty welcome, and that the State officers are authorized and requested to furnish the agents and officers of said company such official documents at their disposal as will aid the said company in the work of securing immigration to this State; *provided,* the same be done without any cost to the State.

Approved August 28, 1876.

Takes effect ninety days after adjournment.

No. 10.—*Joint Resolution.*

WHEREAS, W. T. Neale, a citizen of the town of Hearne, in Robertson county, Texas, was nominated and confirmed a Notary Public, in and for said county, on the first day of February, 1875, and duly qualified as such, but the Clerk of the District Court of said county failed to attach the oath to the bond; and whereas, great damage and loss may arise from the acts of said Notary to numerous parties, if the same be not legalized; therefore,

SECTION 1. *Be it resolved by the Legislature of the State of Texas,* That all and every act of the said W. T. Neale, as such Notary Public, be and the same are hereby declared legal, with all the force and effect, as if done under full warrant and authority.

Approved August 10, 1876.

Takes effect ninety days after adjournment.

No. 11.—*Joint Resolution.*

Be it resolved by the Legislature of the State of Texas, That the trustees of the Methodist Episcopal Church, South, in the city of Austin, be and they are hereby authorized to take charge of and control for the use of said church a certain tract or lot of land belonging to the Capitol Grounds, lying adjoining and north of said church and south of Mesquite street, in the city of Austin, until the State, through her proper officers, may demand the same; whereupon the said trustees shall cease to have control of the same, and shall deliver said property peacefully and without delay, to such officer as may demand the same for the use of the State.

Approved August 16, 1876.

Takes effect ninety days after adjournment.

No. 12.—*Joint Resolution.*

Whereas, By a joint resolution of the Congress of the United States approved July 3, 1876, the Secretary of War is authorized to issue to the Territories and the States bordering thereon, such arms as he may deem necessary for their protection, not to exceed one thousand to said States, each, etc.; and, whereas, the Governor of each State receiving its quota of said arms is required to give good and sufficient bond for the return of said arms or payment for the same at such times as the Secretary of War may designate, and their being no authority vested in the Governor of the State of Texas to make such bond; therefore,

Section 1. *Be it resolved by the Legislature of the State of Texas,* That the Governor of this State be, and is hereby authorized and empowered to give or make such bond, in the name and behalf of the State, as is required to secure to this State the quota of arms to which it may be entitled by virtue of said joint resolution of the Congress of the United States, approved July 3, 1876.

Sec. 2. As the session of the Legislature is drawing rapidly to a close, and it being necessary that this resolution be of effect immediately, creates an emergency as is contemplated by the Constitution, and it is therefore enacted that this resolution be of force and effect from and after its passage.

Approved August 21, 1876.

Takes effect from its passage.

No. 13.—*Joint Resolution providing for the leasing of three hundred feet square in the block or lot of land, in the city of Austin, lying north of the State Capitol, and known on the map of said city, now on file in the General Land Office, as College Hill.*

Section 1. *Be it resolved by the Senate and House of Representatives of the State of Texas,* That the Governor, Comptroller and the Treasurer of the State be and are hereby authorized to lease, for a period not exceeding twenty years, to the City Water Company of Austin, three hundred feet square of ground in the block or lot of land known as College Hill; beginning two hundred feet from the corner of San Marcos and Orange streets, running east three hundred feet; thence south three hundred feet; thence west three hundred feet; thence north three hundred feet to Orange street; to be used for the purpose of erecting a reservoir thereon.

SEC. 2. In consideration of such lease, the said City Water Company shall bind itself to keep any reservoir to be erected by it in good repair, and to furnish water for all State, school or college buildings which may be erected on said block; also, for the Capitol, Land Office, Supreme Court and Comptroller's buildings, Governor's mansion and the Capitol grounds, free of charge; *provided*, that if said company shall fail, neglect or refuse to comply with the terms of this resolution, then they shall forfeit all right to the privileges and land granted them in this resolution. No contract shall be made under this resolution which will, in the opinion of the Governor, permit a structure to be erected that would impair or injure the value of the forty acres for university purposes.

SEC. 3. There being a public necessity that an abundance of water should be constantly kept in and about the public buildings, for extinguishing fire and for other purposes; therefore, an emergency exists that this resolution go into effect from and after its passage, and it is so enacted.

Approved August 21, 1876.

Takes effect from its passage.

No. 14.—*Joint Resolution authorizing a sale or lease of and cession of jurisdiction over certain lands to the United States for the erection of a fort, arsenal, barracks, military station and camp.*

SECTION 1. *Be it resolved by the Legislature of the State of Texas,* That the Governor, in conformity to the provisions of "An Act for ceding to the United States jurisdiction of certain lands in this State for public purposes," approved December 19, 1849, and "An Act supplemental thereto," approved February 13, 1852, be, and he is hereby authorized and empowered to sell or lease to the United States, and cede the jurisdiction over such reasonable quantity of land in the vicinity of Fort Elliott, in the northwestern portion of Texas, as may be required by the United States, for the purpose of erecting forts, arsenals, barracks military stations and camps, and for other needful military purposes, the Legislature of the State hereby giving its approval to said sale or lease.

SEC. 2. If the land so sold or leased shall belong or pertain to the public school fund, the proceeds arising therefrom shall be placed to the credit of said fund.

SEC. 3. Whereas, a necessity exists for the better protection of the frontier, which protection will be afforded by the immediate sale or lease of said lands for the purposes before mentioned, thus creating an emergency; therefore, resolved that this resolution take effect from [its passage.

Approved August 21, 1876.

Takes effect from its passage.

No. 15.—*Joint Resolution to authorize the Governor to make such endorsement on registered U. S. bonds as may be necessary to sell or transfer them.*

Resolved by the Legislature of the State of Texas, That the Governor, or such other person as may be required by law, be and is hereby authorized to make such endorsement on all the registered United States bonds now held for the benefit of the permanent school fund, as may be necessary to sell and transfer them; and, whereas, interest to accrue to the school fund will be materially enhanced by the early conversion of said United States bonds into the six per cent. interest bearing bonds of this State; and, whereas, as the necessities of meeting promptly the maturing liabilities of the State may render the negotiation of these bonds desirable at an earlier period than ninety days from and after the adjournment of this Legislature; therefore, be it further resolved that an emergency exists and that this joint resolution take effect and be in force from and after its passage.

Approved August 21, 1876.

Takes effect from its passage.

DEPARTMENT OF STATE, }
AUSTIN, TEXAS, OCTOBER 28, 1876. }

I, A. W. DeBerry, Secretary of State of the State of Texas, do hereby certify that I have compared the foregoing laws and joint resolutions of the Fifteenth Legislature with the originals now on file in the Department of State, and that they are true copies of such originals. I further certify, that the session of the Fifteenth Legislature of the State of Texas commenced at the city of Austin on Tuesday, the eighteenth day of April, A. D. eighteen hundred and seventy-six, and adjourned on the twenty-first day of August, A. D. eighteen hundred and seventy-six.

In testimony whereof, I have hereto signed my name, and affixed the seal of State, at the city of Austin, this the day and date above written.

{ SEAL }

A. W. DeBERRY,
Secretary of State.

Index to General Laws.

A

B

E

F.

H

I

K

L

INDEX.

R

S

T

U

V

W

Y